THE CATHOLIC CHURCH, DISSENT AND NATIONALITY IN SOVIET LITHUANIA

V. STANLEY VARDYS

EAST EUROPEAN QUARTERLY, BOULDER
DISTRIBUTED BY COLUMBIA UNIVERSITY PRESS
NEW YORK

1978

EAST EUROPEAN MONOGRAPHS, NO. XLIII

V. Stanley Vardys is Professor of Political Science at
The University of Oklahoma, Norman, Oklahoma

Copyright © 1978 by East European Quarterly
Library of Congress Card Catalogue Number 78-050546
ISBN 0-914710-36-2

Printed in the United States of America

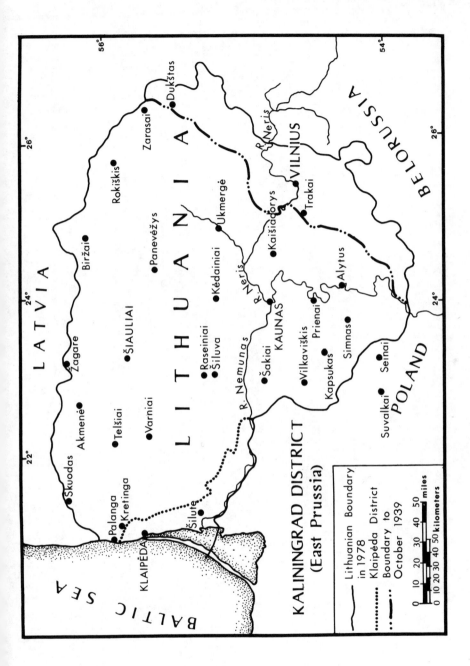

LITHUANIA IN 1978

To my family,

Nijolė

and

Ina,
Elizabeth Rasa,
Rūta,
Vytautas,
Linas

Contents

Introduction

Originally, I intended to write a study of the current struggle for religious rights in Lithuania. However, as soon as I immersed myself in the reading of the literature of Lithuanian Catholic dissent — the main source of information — it became clear that to be fully understood, Catholic efforts of winning full rights of citizenship need to be examined in a deeper and broader context. Such an approach is required because, on the one hand, Lithuania's Catholic struggle remains very closely intertwined with national dissent, and on the other, it constitutes a considerable part of the general Soviet civil rights movement that in recent years has sprouted in Russia and the border republics. Thus, while focusing attention on the goals, scope and social dynamics of Lithuanian Catholic dissent, I examined it in the perspective of Lithuania's modern development which especially since the middle of the XIX century has been distinguished by a nearly symbiotic relationship between Catholicism and nationality. This closeness frequently made the defense of religious rights identical or co-terminal with the promotion of nationalist aspirations and yes, even of political sovereignty. In order to explain this complex relationship and for a better understanding of Catholic dissident aspirations — it is easy and tempting to oversimplify the convergence of Catholicism and nationalism — I examined Catholic dissent goals and philosophies against the backdrop of church-state conflict in the Tsarist empire and also analyzed the by no means always cooperative church-state relations in the Lithuanian state between the two world wars.

It appeared, furthermore, indispensable to discuss the Lithuanian Catholic relationship to the Soviet civil rights movement. The Lithuanian sharing in the latter's democratic philosophy not only found for the Catholics common cause especially with the non-religious or other-religious Soviet dissidents, but in a sense secularized the Lithuanian religious dissent by transforming purely religious group concerns into universal principles of rights applicable to all. In this way, the Lithuanians added strength to the forces which seek inner renewal and progressive democratic change in the Soviet Union. This rather articulate democratic disposition, furthermore, reveals an ability in a mature way to reconcile the religious and secular elements of modern society and also attests to a high level of civic culture among Lithuanian Catholic dissidents.

I considered it, moreover, imperative to analyze the dissent movement and its struggle for religious rights within the broader context of the legal and socio-ideological environment of the Soviet Union. Hence the discussion of constitutional and legal Soviet principles, and of Communist party policies as they apply to religion. Pursuing the connection between law and policy, it also became critically important to dissect the enormous though frequently overlooked and minimized Soviet involvement in atheist activities. Atheism represents the officially promoted institutionalized Soviet surrogate for religion. In this volume, the examination of Soviet legal conflict is supplemented by an appendix that contains translations of the most recent constitutional and legal provisions controlling religion in the Soviet Union. Since the examined period covers the time span governed mainly by the Stalin Constitution of 1936 and by the law on religious associations of 1929, as amended, translations of these documents are reproduced together with the provisions of the new Constitution of 1977 and the new version of the law on religious associations adopted by the Lithuanian SSR in 1976. The Soviet Union formally adopted the new Constitution on October 7, 1977, but this change, it should be pointed out, necessitated only minor revisions of the already completed manuscript of this book.

The asymmetric and prejudicial Soviet allocation of freedom of communications to religious activities on the one hand and to promotion of atheism on the other is unique for modern politics. The Soviets practice a formula of a reversed separation of church and state which is found to be too radical even in a number of Communist countries, not to speak about Western democracies. In several Communist ruled lands, freedom of religion recently has gained ground while in the Soviet Union, generally, the new Constitution and legislation has revealed that no such improvement was contemplated. While this fact has demonstrated Moscow's determination to keep the churches and the believers as second class citizens, the Kremlin has nevertheless indicated a possibility of future betterment of the actual conditions of the Catholic church in Lithuania. The Kremlin and the Vatican indeed are engaged in a dialogue that covers, there is no doubt, the affairs of the Lithuanian Catholic church as well. Lithuanian dissenters have perceived this dialogue to have a life or death importance for the future of Catholicism in Lithuania and generally in the Soviet Union. I have therefore closely examined Lithuanian Catholic views on this matter and added their own long statement in the Appendix though I have refrained — primarily to avoid speculation caused by the lack of information — from attempting to pierce through the shroud of mystery that surrounds the Vatican's motivations and goals in negotiations with Moscow.

My chronological coverage of events ends in December of 1977, when the volume was completed for the press. Thus, I could no longer make use of information contained in numerous dissent literature which reached the West afterwards. It needs to be stressed, however, that while the KGB has succeeded in somewhat containing the outpour of serious underground literature in Russia, the authorities failed doing so in Lithuania where arrests and harassment neither stopped the publication of the established *Chronicle of the Catholic Church of Lithuania* (published since March of 1972) nor prevented the appearance of a number of other underground publications.

Some words need further to be said about the use of sources and references most of which were either Lithuanian or Russian of both dissident and official origins. All translations of the quoted texts are mine, with some exceptions that occur in the appendix. For the Russian texts I used transliteration that is recommended by the Library of Congress. Lithuanian names and titles, however, are not transliterated. Their much preferable citation in original form should present no problem for the reader since the Lithuanians use Latin print. The use of documentation and references is explained in the section on bibliography. I would like to point out, nevertheless, that I used two methods for the citation of Russian and Lithuanian periodicals. In the references which are listed only at the end of the text, I kept original titles of articles published in Russian periodicals. For better or for worse, I produced, however, only English translations of similar Lithuanian language articles, thus at least in this instance following a practice recently adopted for foreign source citation by some leading publications.

Finally, I would like to express appreciation to scholars who read the manuscript and to many persons in the United States and in Europe who helped me with research. I am indebted to Professor Dietrich A. Loeber of the University of Kiel, Germany, a specialist on Soviet law, for his reading of Chapter VII which examines Soviet laws on religion and for his valuable commentary. I am also thankful to Mr. Vytautas Vaitiekūnas of New York for his suggestions that similarly helped to improve Chapters II and III. Bishop Dr. Vincentas Brizgys, Auxiliary of the Archdiocese of Kaunas, now in Chicago, provided for my use the yet unpublished protocols of the conferences of Lithuania's bishops as well as a number of other archival documents. Rev. Rapolas Krasauskas of Lithuanian Religious Information in Rome supplied critical documentary and statistical data. Rev. Pranas Garšva, editor of the Lithuanian Catholic daily *Draugas* in Chicago, and Rev. Dr. Viktoras Rimšelis aided with documentation and shared their vast knowledge of the Lithuanian situation. Msgr. Dr. Jonas Aviža of Munich, Germany, Rev. Vytautas Bagdanavičius, MIC, Mr. Česlovas Grincevičius, Mr. Petras Indreika, Rev. Kazimieras Kuzminskas of Chicago, and Rev. Dr. Pranas Gaida, editor of the Lithuanian Catholic daily *Tėviškės žiburiai* in Toronto, Canada, secured some not readily available texts. Mr. Bronius Kviklys of Chicago graciously permitted the use of his rich private collection on Lithuanian politics and culture. Rev. Stasys Yla initiated me in the use of the library treasures of *Alka,* a museum originally established by Msgr. Francis Juras in Putnam, Connecticut. Local Marian Fathers opened their priceless Lithuanian newspaper collection at odd hours and Sisters of Immaculate Conception, also of Putnam, helped with duplication of research materials. *Arkhiv samizdata* in Munich, Germany, supplied me with requested documentation. Mr. Adolf Sprudzs, international law librarian at the University of Chicago Law Library, secured some documents. Librarians at the Interlibrary Loan Division of the Bizzell Library at the University of Oklahoma tirelessly searched for many locally unavailable titles. Oleks Rudenko, Ph.D. candidate in the Department of History, helped as part time research assistant during the winter of 1975/76. The burden of typing a manuscript studded with numerous foreign names and diacritic marks was valiantly borne by Ms. Geri Rowden and Ms. Betty Anderson, secretaries in my own Department of Political Science. Support from Lithuanian Religious Aid, Inc. bought summer time and research travel to complete the project; its Executive Director, Rev. C. Pugevičius, furthermore, translated the Catholic dissident report on the situation of religion in the Soviet Union (see Appendix B). Professor Catherine V. Ewing of Phillips University translated the Constitution of the Lithuanian SSR (see pertinent articles in Appendix A). The Lithuanian Foundation, Inc., subsidized the preparation of the map of Lithuania; it was drawn by Mrs. Mary Goodman of Norman, Oklahoma. Finally, the Russian Research Center of Harvard University made it possible for me as its visiting associate to start an investigation of linkages between Moscow's policies on religion and on nationalities.

Needless to say, all opinions and interpretations found in this book are mine, and so is the responsibility for any possible errors of fact.

Norman, Oklahoma   V. Stanley Vardys
March 30, 1978

Catholicism and Nationality: The Lithuanian Perspective

The Catholic church is the oldest national institution of Lithuanian society. Its development, naturally enough, has been much intertwined with the changing fate of the Lithuanian people. As a result, the Lithuanians have been frequently identified as a "Catholic" nation in the tradition of Poland or Ireland.[1] Lithuanian Catholicism, however, is neither as old as the Irish nor as ethnocentrically oriented as the Polish. While the church is the oldest social institution of Lithuania, it represents the youngest branch of Latin Christianity in Europe. Attempts to conquer and baptize Lithuania that were made by the Teutonic Knights in the early XIII century were defeated by the stronger Lithuanian forces. The country became Christian only at the turn of the XIV-XV centuries, 1387–1413. Thus, the medieval Lithuanian state founded by Mindaugas (Mindovg) in 1231–36 preceded the establishment of the Catholic church by more than a century. It is known of course that already Mindaugas had accepted Christianity through the Teutonic Bishop of Riga and was crowned King under the authority of Pope Innocent IV in 1251, but he was soon assassinated and his nobles reverted to pagan worship. This initial rejection of Christianity so late in the Middle Ages had for Lithuania fateful consequences. It prolonged the isolation of the country from medieval Europe and delayed the development of its native cultural and legal institutions. Furthermore, it eventually prevented the rise of an independent Lithuanian church, free of foreign influences, and thus for centuries stunted the growth of articulated Catholicism in the Lithuanian idiom. While under Mindaugas the Lithuanians had a chance of developing an independent church organization, the finally established Lithuanian dioceses were subordinated to the Polish church province of Gniezno.[2] This occurred because the Lithuanian Grand Duke Jogaila (in Poland known as Jagiełło) who baptized most of Lithuania did so in conjunction with his election as King Wladyslaw II of Poland. Jagiełło further paid for the Polish crown by the formation of a personal union with Poland which brought Polish influence into the country and Polish clergymen to run the early church hierarchy. Efforts by Jagiełło's cousin Grand Duke Vytautas (Vitovt in Russian, Vitold in Polish and Latin) to diplomatically dissolve this union and gain for Lithuania the immediacy of communications with Western Europe were thwarted by Polish efforts that Jagiełło, reportedly, was willing but unable to help to overcome. In 1413, after regaining Samogitia (Polish, *Żmudź*, Lithuanian *Žemaitija*) from the Teutonic Order that the two cousins had practically destroyed in the battle of Tannenberg (1410), Vytautas brought Christianity to this traditionally most stubborn part of Lithuania. He, however, failed to crown himself king though the Pope and Roman Emperor Sigismund had agreed to his elevation and ambition.

Early Polish Influence

As a consequence of Vytautas' failure to separate himself from Poland, the two dioceses, the Vilnius (Wilno in Polish, otherwise Vilna), established in 1387, and the Samogitian or Medininkai (Medniki), founded in 1417, fell under heavy Polish influence. They were ruled, especially the Vilnius See, mostly by bishops of Polish nationality who helped substantially to Polonize not only the church organization but also the Lithuanian nobility and the urban population.

For this reason, the Lithuanian church suffered from a prolonged crisis of national ethnic identity that was resolved only in our century. While the believers were Lithuanian, their clergymen were mostly Polish or Polonized Lithuanians. For centuries, furthermore, access to priesthood was almost hermetically closed to the youth of peasant background.[3] The clergy — especially the hierarchy — consisted of the nobility, some real, some nominal, who did not pay much attention to the development of either the language or the culture of the ordinary people. It is paradoxical to consider that the first Lithuanian book, a catechism with some psalms, was not published by Catholics in Lithuania but by Lutherans in Prussia (1547). This was followed by the publication of Sunday gospels (1579), parts of the Bible and ultimately the entire New Testament (1701). Furthermore, the newly opened university in Königsberg trained Protestant pastors for ministry in the native language among the Lithuanian speaking population that inhabited the largest part of the region.[4] Only this activity, combined with a vigorous reformation movement that almost succeeded in the XVI century, galvanized Catholic response which benefited the Lithuanian speaking population in the Grand Duchy of

Lithuania. The counter-reformation was spearheaded by the Jesuits in Vilnius, supported by Bishop Radziwill (in Lithuanian, Radvila, 1579–91) who established a theological seminary to train Lithuanian priests. In 1569, the newly arrived Jesuits founded a college that nine years later became an academy, at present celebrated as the oldest university in the Soviet Union. Beginning with 1585, the Jesuits began publishing catechisms and religious books. One of the earliest religious works (1585), the *Postilla* of Canon Daukša of the Vilnius diocese, was prefaced by a praise of the native Lithuanian language — alas written in Polish! — admonishing the nobility that only barbarians throw away their native tongue. Daily liturgical gospels in Lithuanian were printed in 1637, but the entire New Testament, translated by the Samogitian Bishop Arnulf Giedraitis (Giedrojć, 1802–1838), appeared only in 1806. The reformation movement in Samogitia was contained largely by Bishop Merkelis Giedraitis (Giedroyć, 1576–1609), who promoted the use of Lithuanian in word and in print.

It was, however, only in the XIX century that the native Lithuanians of ordinary peasant background began to fill the clerical ranks. This change occurred under the Russian rule when the nobility, discouraged by Tsarist depredation of church property and the reduction of social status of the clergy, largely forsook careers in church hierarchy. The new priests better identified with the needs of the villagers. This transformation, however, was very gradual. Prior to mid-XIX century, the bishops' houses, the theological seminaries and the better parishes were dominated — as was the case with the nobility — by assimilated Poles, many of them fervent Polish patriots.

This Polish consciousness and orientation was the fruit of the centuries old Polish efforts of nation building in Central Eastern Europe. In the XIX century it looked as if Poland had succeeded in ethnically absorbing the Lithuanians and very large portions of the Belorussians and the Ukrainians. These appearances, as we now know, were misleading. With the collapse of the Polish-Lithuanian Commonwealth in 1795, it was bound, sooner or later, to dissolve the ethnically mixed society that Poland's rulers had consolidated with the help of the nobility and the Church. The Lithuanian state was submerged into a Polish dominated federation in 1569. Assimilation of the Lithuanian nobility took longer, but in time produced a novel — later to be in various versions imitated by others — concept of imperial nationality. This was the formula of "Polish by nationality, Lithuanian by origin" *(Gente Lituanus, natione Polonus)* to which the great

Polish classic Adam Mickiewicz gave a poetic expression in the epic *Pan Tadeusz* (1836).[5] After World War I this Polish idea of imperial nationality was promoted by Josef Piłsudski, the founder of the modern Polish state, who exemplified it in his life and even in his death. A native of a Lithuanian estate, he willed his body to be buried in Kraków but his heart in Vilnius. Piłsudski tried to reestablish Poland within its historical boundaries; he ultimately failed because the phenomenon of imperial nationality, needed as the underpinning for such a Polish state, was already dead.

It was however still a very viable social and cultural reality in 1795 when, as a result of the third partition of Poland, Lithuania was annexed by Russia's Catherine II. In our context, Russian policies toward the Catholic church in Lithuania in the XIX century are important — not for ascertaining how the Tsars dealt with Polish domination in Lithuania, though this is very much intermeshed with Russian actions — but for illuminating the traditional pattern of church administration and policies that the Tsars bequeathed to their XX century successors in the Kremlin.

Church Policies of Tsarist Russia

While dependent on the idiosyncrasies and whims of individual Tsars, Tsarist policies generally were inspired by two long sustained and widely shared Russian perceptions of Catholicism. On the one hand, this Latin religion was regarded as a heretical competitor to Russian Orthodoxy; on the other, its Roman connections impugned its loyalty to the Russian state. The Russian population was considered off limits for *Latinstvo;* this separation was enforced to the point of forbidding Catholic bishops to consult or work together on common moral problems, as the case of XIX century alcoholism in Russia. The treatment that Tsar Nicholas I meted out to Peter Chaadayev[6] accurately reflected the belief that a Russian who favored Roman Catholicism literally must be out of his mind. Furthermore, Catholicism was a foreign religion in more than one way. Unacceptable ideologically, it was foreign because it was subordinate to the Pope and thus served as a channel for spreading foreign influence in the Russian empire, and finally, Catholicism was identified as a tool of Polish nationalism within Russian borders.

These views were not only revealed in theoretical discussions of the times but were also reflected in the policies of the Tsars. In 1772, immediately after she acquired large numbers of Catholic subjects in Belorussia, Catherine II forbade the clergy's direct communication with Rome. A generation later, after the annexation of Lithuania in 1795, both Catholic bishops and monasteries were ordered to cut relations with the Pope. The Tsarina had respect for Jesuit sponsored education and paradoxically — though consistently with the general Russian policy — she disregarded the Pope's decree of 1773 disbanding the Jesuit order, thus making the Jesuits free in autocratic Russia when they were hunted down in the enlightened Western Europe. But the Jesuits were banished later, in 1820, after they successfully began to compete with Russian Orthodoxy for converts to Catholicism.

Furthermore, Catherine paid no attention to canon law that had protected the Church in the Polish-Lithuanian state. Thus, she freely took over church properties, as if these were spoils of war, and abolished public privileges that the hierarchs had enjoyed in the Polish councils of state. In addition, Catherine arbitrarily carved up diocesan boundaries and in 1773 established a Belorussian diocese with the seat in Mogilev without as much as consulting the Pope. Her son Paul I formally detached the Vilnius and Samogitian dioceses from Polish jurisdiction and subordinated them to the Russian church province that he founded in 1798 with a metropolitan See in the same Belorussian town of Mogilёv. The Pope again had no choice but to accept this arrangement. However, unlike his mother, Paul attempted to normalize relations with Rome, granted a short-lived freedom of religious propaganda to the Jesuits, and allowed the new Metropolitan Bishop Bohusz Siestrzencewicz to largely run church affairs through a department that was established in the Ministry of Justice. Governmental supervision and administration of these affairs, so new to the Catholics of former Poland, would continue during the Tsarist rule and would be reintroduced, in the form of the Council on Religious Affairs, by the Communists. Alexander I, the "liberal" Tsar, created a collegiate council for the administration of the Catholic church in St. Petersburg and subordinate diocesan consistories in the provinces. The latter were run by government-appointed secretaries who had the right to veto decisions considered contrary to the government's policy. This structure of administration survived until World War I. In 1847, Nicholas I — in a good mood after marrying off his daughter to a Bavarian duke — concluded a concordat with Rome, but this document did not eliminate sometimes very prolonged conflicts over appointments and a variety of pastoral activities because, by this agreement, Rome allowed the Tsar to interfere with aspects of church administration.[7] Nicholas and all of his successors regarded the bishops to be his — not the Pope's[8] — appointees and expected them to function not only as religious leaders but also as officials of the Tsarist regime. In an audience that the Tsar gave to the newly consecrated Samogitian Bishop Motiejus Valančius (Wolonczewski, 1801–1875) in 1850, Nicholas complained that the people of the Samogitian diocese, which in those days covered most of the ethnic Lithuanian territory, kept secret contacts with Prussia. When Valančius conceded that the matter produced moral problems because, caught by Tsarist officials, people lied to avoid punishment, the Tsar remarked that this constituted a minor difficulty. "Of greater concern to me is that the spirit of foreign countries would not penetrate into my state; I therefore request of you that by your influence you stop these trips to Prussia by my subjects."[9]

In further conversation Nicholas revealed that he was especially worried over the situation in Lithuania because "that land has sinned against us in 1831."[10] This was a reference to the first Polish insurrection against the Russian rule that, from Warsaw where the Tsar's brother Constantine let it develop by benevolent though inept handling of Polish complaints, had spread to Lithuania where it was supported by student circles of Vilnius university and by the nobility of the land. This insurrection was rather quickly suppressed, the university of Vilnius closed down, but the Church had to bear the further consequences of Nicholas' reaction. It was singled out for repressive treatment because its monasteries and clergy were considered "the nests of Latin propaganda and the source of insurrection."

The same charge would be repeated by the Tsarist government a generation later, after the insurrection of 1863.[11] The Tsar therefore concentrated on closing monasteries — only six of them were left in Lithuania at the time of World War I — and on abolishing schools — again mostly monastery institutions — that used Polish as the language of instruction. To further cut the really strong Roman and Polish influences, Tsar Nicholas in 1839 forced the merger of most of the Uniate (Ruthenian, Ukrainian) Eastern rite church with the Russian Orthodox in Moscow. Thus bleeding Ukrainian Catholicism, the Tsar dealt a blow to Catholic influence in the Lithuanian metropolis of Vilnius as well; in this city the Uniates maintained one of their strongest religious centers.[12] Similarly inspired, in 1842, was the transfer of the Latin rite Vilnius' higher theological academy to the vicinity of the Tsar's watchful eye in St. Petersburg.

The government, furthermore, initiated in Lithuania a number of other restrictive measures, some of which were poorly enforced though they formally survived for half a century or more. Among these was the censorship of preaching in church except from approved books that was decreed in 1832. Seven years later, the clergy were forbidden to baptize children of mixed Catholic-Orthodox families and also to hear confessions of people in other parishes but their own. Difficulties were made in the building of new and repairing of old churches. Construction of roadside crosses was forbidden in 1845. Finally, in 1841–42, the Tsar confiscated all church lands and as compensation introduced salaries for the clergy and the bishops. This step obviously was intended to strongly enhance the regime's control over church policies and clerical attitudes. In 1842, Pope Gregory XVI widely publicized these repressive measures, in this manner hoping to effect their repeal, but Nicholas did not relent, and in 1847, Rome accepted a concordat based on the status quo, including the government's right to confirm appointments made by the bishops. In 1852, St. Petersburg decreed that an appointment of professors in the theological seminary which was left in the bishop's jurisdiction needed an approval of the Ministry of the Interior. Appointment of a parish pastor had to be approved by the governor of the *guberniia* in which the appointment was made. These matters, however, did not cause great disagreements until the next Polish insurrection in 1863 which virtually destroyed any validity this document had. Though an international agreement, the concordat had never been promulgated by St. Petersburg and had never been considered as part of Russian law.[13] Its text was never published for public knowledge either.

The Revolt of 1863 and its Consequences

The insurrection of 1863 in Lithuania was much more widespread than the rebellion of the earlier generation. However, it was not a national Lithuanian revolt, but as previously, a Polish attempt to reestablish the Polish Rzeczpospolita. It relied on the consciousness of the imperial Polish nationality that was still alive among the nobility, the gentry, the clergy, and portions of the urban population. The peasants, however, just then emancipated by Alexander II, could not easily identify with Polish nationalist objectives and their participation in the revolt was therefore limited. The Polish *Rzada* (Council) solicited the badly needed peasant aid by promises of free land grants (the Tsarist reform required payment) and exhortations of the need to defend the Catholic faith against the forced imposition of Orthodoxy by "the dirty *maskolus* (a derogatory name for Russian nationality) who has been cursed by the Holy Father."[14] Support that the clergy-

men gave to the insurrection was conspicuous, but in a sense, provoked by the Tsar's repressive decrees of the previous decades. The
small but rising Lithuanian intelligentsia and the Samogitian Bishop
Valančius were caught in confusion. Russian response to this insurrection was this time stronger than in the day of Nicholas I. By then,
Russian autocracy had reached the zenith of power, had articulated
the ideology of "autocracy, nationality, and Orthodoxy" and thus was
set to deal with "the Polish question *(Pol'skoe delo)*" in a very radical
manner. Alexander II sent to Lithuania General Mikhail Nikolaevich
Muravёv (1796–1866), the Minister of Tsarist Properties.[15] As a young
man, the general had been marginally involved with the Decembrists
but survived the Tsar's wrath and became a loyal helper of the Tsarist
regime. Already in 1831, as a participant in the suppression of the first
insurrection, Muravёv had advocated a radical course of action, and
now he had a chance to put down the new rebellion in conformity with
his own prescription.

Muravёv pacified the country in two years, but his ruthlessness cost
so many lives and so much suffering — sometimes his troops would
burn down entire villages with people in them[16] — that he earned the
name of "Hangman." According to official reports, in 1863–64, he
executed 128 people, a majority of whom (83) were put to death in the
ethnic Lithuanian *guberniias,* Kaunas (Kovno) and Vilnius (Wilno).[17]
In the six Lithuanian and Belorussian *guberniias,* furthermore, he
internally banished or put under police supervision 9,229 people.
Another 12,483 were punished more severely, namely, by deportation
into the depths of Russia and Siberia. Among the executed, in the
entire region, there were seven clergymen. The number of deported
clergymen reached 159. Additionally, 135 were exiled or otherwise
residentially restricted within the Northwestern territory. Of these
variously punished priests, 106, in other words, one third, belonged to
the Samogitian diocese.[18] While the largest majority of the executed
and otherwise penalized population consisted of the estate owners, the
gentry, and the peasants, the relative number of punished priests was
conspicuously high. The number of killed, exiled, and imprisoned
clergymen of the Samogitian diocese constituted one sixth of the total
diocesan clergy (out of 654). Many of these pastors were punished just
on the basis of denunciation; the crime of others consisted of merely
reading, under the gun of the insurrectionists, their manifests in
church. A number, relying on official assurances that priests and
physicians would not be punished, served as chaplains. Still others had
given food to the rebels. Some had actually borne arms and com-

manded troops.[19] The scope and severity of punishment showed Muravëv's aim. Convinced as he was that the Church was the mainspring of the rebellion and the headquarters of Polish nationalism, he sought to use the opportunity to decimate clerical ranks and to instill fear in the survivors.

The perception of the clergy's political role held by Russian officials in Lithuania was succinctly articulated by a post-rebellion governor of Kaunas who defended many restrictive measures subsequently imposed on the clergy. Duke Mikhail Obolenski (1821–86), a former Russian diplomat appointed to the governorship most likely because of his experience in the Catholic capitals of Vienna and Munich, suggested to his superior, General Alexander Potopov Lvovich (1818–1896) in Vilnius, that "the Catholic clergy always did injury to our fatherland."[20] The government therefore should not consent to any concessions that might strengthen the clerical "corporation." Obolenski of course considered this "corporation" to be Polish.

However, while Polish nationalists and supporters of imperial Polish nationality still had many activists and sympathizers among the clergy, the identification of Lithuania's Catholic priests with Polish nationalism was no longer so unequivocally possible. Rev. Antanas Mackevičius, a Samogitian leader of the revolt, considered that "very many of them [clergymen] are fanatics who hate everything Polish and the gentry; they are ready to sacrifice everything for Lithuania."[21] He further explained that he supported the rebellion which he knew was Polish not for Poland's sake but to "elevate the people so they would become self-conscious and able to say for themselves whether they want to be united with Poland or with Russia. This right already exists in Europe." The leader, characterized as a man of "strange piety,"[22] however, was ahead of his time. While the Lithuanian intelligentsia, secular and clerical, already had found its spokesmen during the first half of the century, the idea of self-determination had not yet become part of its beliefs. Bishop Motiejus Valančius, the man who more than anyone nursed Lithuanian nationality in the XIX century,[23] did not consider a "separate" existence from Russia politically possible.[24] Generally, the insurrection found the tiny Lithuanian intelligentsia confused and painfully aware of the hopelessness of their country's situation. Bishop Valančius did not approve of the rebellion though his early pronouncements were sufficiently ambiguous to encourage support. Pressured by both the insurrectionists and the Russian officials to come out clearly in their favor, he attempted to evade the issue of taking sides by simply calling for prayers and penance.[25]

However, the government would not allow him to adopt this nonpolitical stand. Tsarist authorities needed a positive declaration for the government and consequently, Muravëv revised the text of Valančius' pastoral letter to the people that the Bishop had agreed to issue at the governor's request; it called on the rebels to put down their arms. The letter contained many Russian inserts, including an admonition that the rebel hope for help from abroad was "unwise" and that "our land constitutes an inalienable whole with Russia under the benevolent rule of the Illustrious Tsar, our Benefactor."[26] The pain Valančius suffered writing this letter can be seen from the gentleness of addressing his people as "my dearest children" and the sad warning that "if you will not subside, you will all perish." Nevertheless, he had the letter read in the churches, and with it forever incurred the disdain of the pro-Polish nobility. At the same time he did not win the officialdom's favor either. The letter made it clear he did not support the rebellion; however, the Russians now desired much more than the expression of the Bishop's loyalty to the Tsar. Valančius, like many of his priests and the intelligentsia, was caught in a crossfire between the Poles and the Russians with no apparent easy or quick way out of the predicament.

The bishop had apparently chosen to cooperate with the government in an expectation that the government will "cease suppressing those who attached themselves to the rebels" and also will allow the return of imprisoned and deported clergymen. However, the authorities had other plans. Russian officials refused to recognize in Valančius a different Catholic voice and a spokesman not beholden to Polish nationalism. Muravëv further failed to acknowledge that the loyal Bishop Valančius and the disloyal pastor Mackevičius represented a new element in the Church that barely existed in 1831 but that now constituted a part of the budding new intelligentsia in the land. It was still under strong Polish influence, but already conscious of its Lithuanian identity and the divergence of Polish and Lithuanian political goals. This disregard of the Lithuanian element in the conflict, so characteristic of the views of the Tsar's administration in Lithuania, was not, apparently, shared by all policy makers in St. Petersburg. Russian Academician Alexander Gilferding [Hilferding] (1831–72), a linguist and an official in the Ministry of Education, would have based the Tsar's solution of the "Polish question" on the promotion of the Lithuanian language in schools and in print — though in Cyrillic alphabet — for the purpose of educating an independent Lithuanian intelligentsia friendly to the Russians.[27] The Tsar, advised by Muravëv, rejected this interpretation of triangular conflict in Lithuania. For his officialdom as well as for influential Slavophile intellectuals like Iurii Samarin, the problem was strictly Polish; Lithuania did not exist as a separate entity.[28] The Samogitian and Lithuanian masses, the argument ran, should not be encouraged to develop their own identity — these people were considered very "backward, stubborn and fanatical"[29] anyway — but should be wrestled away from the Poles by instilling in them Russian consciousness and by replacing the Polish language with the Russian.

The Tsarist Program of Nation Building

The Tsar's administrators in Lithuania therefore were not satisfied with mere pacification of the region but initiated double-edged assimilation policies designed, on the one hand, to sweep away Polish political and cultural influences and, on the other, to Russianize the land. Muravëv proceeded in the economic field where he showed himself more liberal than his superiors in St. Petersburg.[30] As a consequence, the Tsar's land reform of 1861 in Lithuania was executed with greater dispatch than in the Russian provinces. Furthermore, St. Petersburg approved additional land distributions to unattached, landless peasants. This was done in order to reduce peasant dependence on local estate owners who were considered to be both Polish and revolutionary. The additional land, like the acreage for emancipated serfs, was to be taken away from the estates. In Lithuania therefore the estates surrendered more land to the Tsarist reforms than in other parts of the Empire. Consequently, the percentage of peasant land owners in Lithuania became higher than in Russia or the Baltic provinces of Courland, Livland and Estonia. This anti-revolutionary and anti-Polish policy benefited the peasants, most of whom were Lithuanian.

But the cultural and political offensive that Muravëv began against Polish domination produced for these peasants different results: for the first time since Lithuania's annexation by Russia it brought on a direct ethnic Lithuanian-Russian clash.

Since the public practice of Catholic religion and customs was identified with Polish nationalism, the brunt of the Russian attack, as after the 1831 insurrection, again had to be borne by the Church. But this time, as already suggested, the situation was different. The convergence between Polish loyalties and the Catholic faith had been eased by the rising Lithuanian self-consciousness. Under Bishop Valančius, Lithuanian commitment was already divided between Poland and Russia. Better to say, Valančius had decided that for the welfare of the Church he should keep out of politics, and at the moment the only way to extricate the Church from involvement was to come out on the Russian side. Actually, as events would soon prove, his loyalties lay solely with his Church and his "children," the Lithuanian people. The Bishop was concerned with the preservation of the Catholic faith among the masses which the end of rebellion and peace with the Russians was thought to facilitate, but Valančius considered this preservation possible only in the native Lithuanian, not Russian or Polish, idiom.[31]

The Russian administration discounted this view. In their eyes, the Church was still Polish and therefore to attack the Church meant to struggle against Polish nationalism. In reality, however, by constraining the Church, Tsarist officials were bound to suppress Lithuanian religious expression and even nationality. Most likely, they did not consider it important because they had consistently underrated the political strength of the Lithuanian element in the region.

The futility of such policy was quickly, in 1868, understood by the new governor of the Kaunas *guberniia,* the already mentioned Duke Obolenski. He warned the governor-general of Vilnius not to hope "that even in a distant future it will be possible to expect a rappochement of the Lithuanian population with the nationality and church that dominates in Russia." But Obolenski himself very severely and strictly enforced the new repressive policies because he saw in Catholicism a danger to the Russian state. The source of this danger, as he understood it, was the Catholic faith and Lithuanian origin of the people and their "enormous" and "fanatical" piety.[32]

The ultimate aim of the newly instituted post-rebellion policies, therefore, aside from their immediate purpose of destroying Polish influence, was the Russianization of the Lithuanian population. Since in the Russian view the Lithuanians had been Polonized through the Polonization of Catholicism, the Tsar's officials now proposed to Russianize them by Russianizing the Catholic church. To achieve this goal, the authorities issued a number of decrees. One of these, adopted in 1864, ordered all teaching of religion in public schools to be conducted in the Russian language. Another forbade the use of Polish or Lithuanian as languages of instruction in any school. Furthermore, with the help of some cooperating Church hierarchs, the administrator of Vilnius, Peter Żylinski, and Metropolitan of Mogilëv Bishop Josef Staniewski, Tsarist authorities ordered incorporation of the Russian language into the ritual of Catholic church services.[33] A liturgical book prepared by the government replaced the Polish texts with the Russian. The Lithuanian language again was overlooked. Use of Russian, in addition, became mandatory in all services held for students. Finally, on September 6, 1865, Muravëv's successor General K. Kaufman, who later conquered Central Asia for the Tsar, proposed, and Interior Minister Petr Valuev (1814–1890) a week later decreed the most crucial and, as it later appeared, the most counterproductive measure, namely, the prohibition of Lithuanian printing in "Latin-Polish" characters.[34] Instead, the authorities now spent considerable budgetary allocations for the promotion of Lithuanian texts in the Russian cyrillic alphabet.[35] A former Catholic priest was appointed censor of religious books; plans were made for the production of prayerbooks, gospels, catechism, biblical stories in the new way. Later the authorities began printing secular Lithuanian texts as well, in an obvious attempt to forestall the development of general "Polish" Lithuanian literature.

These decrees did not exhaust the list of prohibitions. Further orders limited the exercise of Catholic rites and customs. On July 8, 1864, Muravëv outlawed construction of crosses outside of the church yards, thus reviving the sanction of 1845. Grounds for this limitation were found in the alleged purpose of their construction. The cross builders, the general claimed, sought to make with it "political-religious Polish propaganda."[36] A good year later, Muravëv's successor Kaufman forbade church processions outside of church buildings in the cities and outside of church yards in the villages. In the past, Kaufman said, during these processions the people were instigated by the clergy to sing "revolutionary" hymns. "No religion protected by our government," the general continued, "is as stubborn as the Roman Catholic," and he was determined to break that stubbornness.

On April 18, 1865, Muravëv further outlawed parish associations that sought to promote abstinence from alcohol. In the 1850s, Bishop Valančius had extremely successfully organized an anti-liquor movement that so much reduced alcohol consumption in the diocese as to cause complaints to the government by distillery owners, tavern keepers and the state treasury. The movement was sustained by religious societies specifically established for the purpose, but in 1858, as a result of lobbying by affected economic interests, buttressed by allegations of political anti-government activity, the government declared them illegal. Muravëv reconfirmed this prohibition, adding such stiff fines for violation that it became risky even to preach against alcohol from the pulpit.[37] Generally, the government did not tolerate any religious associations whatsoever.

Especially repressive were the government's policies concerning the clergymen. The administrators now very strictly enforced the old requirement that not only pastors but also their assistants be appointed with the approval of the governor's office. This limitation very much reduced the Bishop's appointing powers and made it possible for the Tsarist officials to promote and reward clergymen who not only fully executed all political and religious ordinances but who also disobeyed their bishops. Preaching, furthermore, was not merely censored, as in previous days, but the government strictly enforced the requirement to preach from a specially prepared textbook. In addition, clergymen were denied visitation rights within the parish without the permission of the local police chief. Similarly, they could not participate in religious festivities of neighboring parishes without the authorization from higher civil authorities. Thus constraining the mobility and work of the clergymen, the Tsarist officials — unbelievably — hoped to destroy and severely reduce the effectiveness and even the size of the clerical corps. In November of 1866, Bishop Valančius, who fruitlessly objected to all of these prohibitions, further protested to the Governor General in Vilnius the latter's refusal to confirm the appointments of 28 young priests the Bishop had ordained in 1865.[38] In addition, he politely but firmly demanded that the governor lift the embargo on the admission of new theology students to the seminary that was first imposed in 1863 and that threatened to leave the seminary completely empty. His diocese, the Bishop insisted, faced an enormous shortage of priests caused by deaths, previous arrests and deportations as well as by the current prohibition of appointment and education. Governor Obolenski, however, who handled the Bishop's petition, made his own calculations of how many clergymen the Bishop needed and refused, at first, to admit any new seminarians.[39]

Finally, the Tsarist officials decided to reduce the number of actively working churches and monasteries. This was done by requiring permission for even the smallest repairs, refusing to license new church construction and finally by shutting them down altogether. In a number of localities in Western Lithuania people organized themselves to defend their churches. This resistance led to bloodshed. Especially tragic and violent was the defense of the church in Kražiai (Krože, in the literature of the period) in 1893. For weeks, even against the order of the bishop who ultimately succumbed to government pressure after exhausting all possible appeals — Paliulionis ruled the diocese by then — the parishioners seized the church and held it for weeks, without allowing the pastor to remove the Eucharist. When Governor Kauman arrived from Kaunas with a detail of 20–40 policemen and gendarmes to take over the building, he was himself seized. The defenders demanded that he cancel the order of closure. But knowing of the impending coming of a large company of Cossacks, Kaufman played for time and fooled the peasants. The Cossacks arrived at six o'clock and, as the London *Times* described it, bloodshed followed as soon as they entered the church:[40]

> The church ornaments were thrown out of the building in the heap and the dead bodies of the victims were tumbled into a lime pit. The people fled in all directions, but their flight was arrested by the Cossacks, who used the knout freely. Several fugitives were drowned in attempting to escape across the river Krozanta, which was but slightly frozen over. The bulk of them were driven into the town, where they were subjected to summary judgment at the hands of the Governor. All the delinquents were flogged with the knout, a doctor being present to see how many strokes could be borne in each case. Two sick women, who also received their share, died during the night without being allowed to see a priest of their own faith. All this went on the whole day, and only ceased in order that the Cossacks themselves might rest. The latter were afterwards allowed to plunder the town. . . .

The number of arrested — and later tried — approximated one hundred. The number killed was set at sixty-nine, but no one but the government really knew. The trial of the alleged offenders of the governmental decree of closure in October of 1894 attracted international attention and brought to Vilnius distinguished Russian lawyers to defend the accused "who filled eight benches" in the courtroom. Among them was "a totally blind old man, and all the women and girls who were outraged by the drunken Cossacks."[41]

The Emergence of Articulated Lithuanian Nationality

It took the Tsarist authorities a generation of time to realize that such policies, as Duke Obolenski had predicted, would not help the population's expected rapprochement with the "dominant nationality and religion in Russia." After the insurrection of 1863, Russian influence in Lithuania grew many-fold, but it was successfully promoted by economic measures, colonization, by the Russianization of the bureaucracy and educational institutions, and even by government-sponsored missionary activities of the Russian Orthodoxy, not by the repressive decrees adopted against the Catholic church. As a result, these decrees were either revoked or shelved. Thus, from 1870, new students were again admitted to the seminary of Varniai. The year of 1876 marked the end of the ridiculous struggle against the crosses. In 1897, the prohibition was lifted against the construction of new churches, and in the same year students were freed from compulsory attendance of Orthodox church on days of Tsarist festivities. In 1904 came the long sought-for freedom for Lithuanian publication in Latin characters. In the next year the authorities eased restrictions on clerical appointments, and finally, the Tsarist proclamation of freedom of conscience that followed the revolution of 1905 made it possible for many Catholics who had, under pressure, converted to Russian Orthodoxy to return to their native Church.

The consequences of this frontal assault on the Church, however, could not be erased as easily as the decrees themselves. The anti-Catholic policies had borne fruit, indeed, but this fruit was bitter for the Tsar: instead of strengthening Russian influence among the masses of the piously religious Lithuanians, the attempts to Russianize the Church helped to undermine it. Especially damaging proved to be the prohibition of Lithuanian press in Latin letters. The key figure who completely frustrated this policy of assimilating the population by Russianizing Catholic communications was Bishop Valančius. Rev. Antanas Mackevičius, the hanged Lithuanian rebel leader of 1863, had regarded the bishop as a good priest but a man of weak character,[42] but Valančius was a political realist, not a pliable pro-Russian opportunist. He saw the military hopelessness of the insurrection and therefore could be persuaded to come out against it. However, as soon as it became clear to him that the government would seek to replace the Polish influence with the Russian, he resisted it and — transferred by the authorities from the provincial Varniai to the gubernatorial city of Kaunas to live under strict supervision — continued to pay fines rather than obey government edicts, always in danger of deportation. Valančius opposed the introduction of the Russian language into church rituals and regarded the prohibition of Lithuanian press as an attack on the Church's basic function of teaching. He therefore not only protested government policies — sometimes organizing these protests as petitions of the faithful — but also organized against them in the underground.

Thus, as soon as permission for publication in Latin characters was denied, Valančius negotiated the printing of prayerbooks and other religious literature in the German-ruled East Prussia, the territory that Nicholas I had requested Valančius to seal off for his people. These

books, in time augmented by secular writings of the Bishop himself —
he is a classic of the XIX century Lithuanian literature — and supplemented by various other publications, were smuggled into Russian
Lithuania and secretly sold throughout the land. In addition, forced to
teach children in Russian, Valančius encouraged secret schools on
farms, in family circles, where children learned prayers and catechism
in native Lithuanian. Both of these activities usually were punished by
deportation to Siberia, but this did not deter the bishop who encouraged his clergymen to write, to publish and to teach in Lithuanian.
It is estimated that approximately one thousand people were repressed
by the Tsarist government during the forty years of prohibition, but
for the Lithuanians the gains far outreached the sacrifices. The real
accomplishment of secret printing and education in a country where
publicly operated schools were few and far between came to light in
1897, during the first Imperial census that showed the literacy of the
Kaunas *guberniia* higher than that of Moscow (54% for Kaunas, 49%
for Moscow).[43] This enormous clandestine educational engagement,
furthermore, while derided by the Russians as producing half-literates
because the teaching was focused on religious texts,[44] helped to
develop a readership for the journals of national awakening that followed in 1883 (*Aušra* [The Dawn]) and 1887 (*Varpas* [The Bell]) and
were organized no longer by the clergy but by the secular intelligentsia.

It became clear that the Tsar's efforts of Russianization had backfired. Religious education that was organized by Valančius and his
followers inspired and sustained not only Catholic beliefs but also
Lithuanian nationality. Inadvertently, Tsarist policies produced not
Russian loyalties but an articulated Lithuanian identity as distinguished from the Polish. The success of Valančius and many other
clergymen after him refuted the basic Russian policy assumption that
Catholicism was a strictly nationalist, in this case, an essentially
Polish, religion. Valančius' program nursed both Catholicism and
Lithuanian ethnicity. Pressed by the Tsar, these two forces, the first
sharply visible, the second latent, intertwined into the phenomenon of
the "Catholic Lithuanian nation." This convergence of nationality and
Catholicism though infrequently flickering in earlier centuries, really
occurred only in the second half of the nineteenth. Convergence with
Lithuanian nationalism, in a manner somewhat similar to the Polish,
would come only after World War I.

Finally, these clandestine activities also had far reaching social
consequences for the Church itself. In the main, they encouraged a
close communication between the peasant and his pastor, and ulti-

mately, put a brake on the Polonization of the clergy. A contrary process began, aided by the influx into the priesthood of young men from emancipated peasant families and, furthermore, spurred by the need to offer a Catholic alternative to programs of social and national movements that at the end of the 1880s and in the 1890s produced ideological and political differentiation of Lithuanian society. In 1900, the underground Catholic publication *Tėvynės sargas* (The Guardian of the Fatherland), printed in East Prussia, estimated that of the 650 priests of the Samogitian diocese a group of 315 supported the Lithuanian national movement. These were young people, not above 40 years of age. A group of 145, consisting of older clergymen, between 60 and 90, represented the "old epoch" while the remaining forty priests, between the ages of 40 and 60, were neutral. This reflected a great change of clerical attitudes and promised a complete transformation in the near future.[45]

All factions of Lithuanian society acknowledged the importance of Catholicism for Lithuanian nationality. The church defense in Kražiai aided not only the religious spirit, but also boosted the movement of national awakening. However, the secular Lithuanian intelligentsia strongly criticized the pro-Polish orientation of still many pastors and hierarchs. Clergymen themselves showed great concern with the behavior of their Polish or Polonized colleagues. In 1912, a large group of priests of the Vilnius diocese, driven to exasperation by the Polish nationalism of their bishop, directly petitioned Pope Pius X to interfere for the protection of the rights of the Lithuanian language and Lithuanian clergy.[46]

This Polish preponderance showed a further failure of Russia's anti-Polish policies. Two generations after these policies were initiated, Polish influence in the region appeared to be only dented, not destroyed. It would be overcome, as it shortly was, through the emergence of a clear Lithuanian identity of the Church itself. This occurred during the administration of the last Samogitian Bishop, Pranciškus Karevičius (1861–1945), appointed in 1914. Under his leadership there ended the crisis of the Lithuanian church's ethnic identity that had plagued the institution through several centuries.

The Church and the National State: Independent Lithuania, 1918–40

The tenure of Bishop Karevičius coincided with World War I and with the subsequent emergence of Lithuania as an independent nation. The new bishop was well suited for the times. In the epoch dominated by the idea of national self-determination, he supported the goal of Lithuanian statehood and even travelled to Berlin to speak to Chancellor Georg von Hertling, General Erich Ludendorff and others to promote the Lithuanian claims.[1] Furthermore, he restored the Lithuanian language in formal church communications while his colleague Msgr. Jonas Mačiulis-Maironis (1862–1932) made Lithuanian the language of instruction at the Kaunas theological seminary. Mačiulis-Maironis, it may be added, for a quarter of a century had dominated the Lithuanian literary scene as the classic poet of national awakening. Many of his lyrics became patriotic songs and church hymns, still very popular in our times. In Vilnius, on the recommendation of Eugenio Pacelli, the Vatican's envoy in Berlin, the Pope, in 1918, appointed a Lithuanian, Rev. Jurgis Matulevičius-Matulaitis (1871–1927), as bishop of the oldest Lithuanian See.[2] This rather unusual selection provoked much discontent among the local Poles. Matulevičius, though distinguished for his pastoral activities in Poland, was a patriotic Lithuanian who supported goals of independence. However, he did not upset tradition the way the outspoken Karevičius did in Kaunas, but merely added, where appropriate and in a secondary role, the use of Lithuanian and Belorussian that were as widely spoken in his diocese as was Polish.

The Church in Political Life

As a result of these adjustments, the Church in Lithuania not only smoothly survived the transition from Russian to Lithuanian rule but also was able actively to participate in the newly created democratic system of the land. Bishop Karevičius, furthermore, strongly promoted the Church's social involvement beyond the church walls and parish boundaries. This public engagement gave the Lithuanian church an activist social character that it did not lose until the Soviet occupation in 1940. At the same time, however, such activism inevitably embroiled the Church in politics.

Originally, clerical involvement in public life had little to do with political participation. Because of a desperate shortage of secular intelligentsia, Lithuanian clergymen traditionally had to bear not only their own pastoral but also many other burdens. These clerical obligations became heavier after the Tsar, in 1894, forbade employment of secular Lithuanian Catholics in Lithuanian territory. Paradoxically, this discriminatory legislation had a beneficial effect on the clergy. The priesthood now attracted nationally-conscious talented youth who did not want a career somewhere in Russia after achieving education. The priesthood guaranteed employment in the homeland. This expectation boosted the quality of the clerical ranks that abounded with talent.

Clerical participation in journalistic, educational, economic and eventually political activities therefore was a national consequence of social changes and of discriminatory Tsarist policies. Clergymen were very active in the massive Vilnius conference of 1905 that demanded — the first nationality to do so in the Russian empire — domestic autonomy for Lithuania. In 1918, of the twenty signers of the declaration of Lithuanian independence five were clergymen. The membership of the Constituent Assembly, elected in 1920, included 11 clerics out of the total of 150 assemblymen.[3] Clergymen were, furthermore, elected to the democratic parliaments of the 1920s and played an important part in both the parliament and the government. For example, Rev. Justinas Staugaitis (1866–1943), the future Bishop of Telšiai, was president of one of the parliaments and vice-president of others; the execution of the radical land reform of 1922 is inextricably connected with the name of Rev. M. Krupavičius (1885–1970), who co-authored the legislation and implemented it as Minister of Agriculture. In 1926, the future Archbishop of Vilnius, Mečislovas Reinys (1884–1953), served as Minister of Foreign Affairs and, ironically, negotiated a non-aggression pact with the Soviet Union. In the early twenties it was not unusual to find a parish pastor running a consumers' cooperative, working as a school principal or managing a local political campaign for the parliament.

Furthermore, an ideological differentiation of Lithuanian society encouraged very active social and political participation by Catholic laymen. Lithuanian political and cultural life was organized on an ideological *(Weltanschauung)* basis. This ensured fierce ideological competition in which the word "Catholic" gained a special meaning. It began to signify a group or position that supported the "Catholic" approach to problem solutions and of course that sought to strengthen and maintain the Church. Catholic organizations, too, became differentiated; each age and social segment in practice had its own group. Among them, the Federation "Ateitis," established in 1911, developed into the strongest intellectual movement, combining high school pupils, university students and the alumni who published journals and newspapers and played an important role in the nation's educational and humanistic endeavors.

Politically, the Church was supported by the "Catholic" parties, namely the Christian Democrats, established in 1896, and their partners: the Farmers' Alliance and the Federation of Labor.[4] The first group covered largely the professions and business, while the two others existed for the benefit of the rural and urban population. The coalition of the three groups, in arrangements somewhat similar to the German CDU/CSU, won majorities to the Constituent Assembly and the 1st Diet. This Diet drafted the new nation's basic documents. Thus, from its very beginnings, the Church had influence on the development of Lithuanian statehood because the Christian Democratic Bloc decided the shape of Lithuania's Weimar-type system of government. The Bloc, supported by Jewish minority representatives, adopted the Constitution of 1922 as well.[5]

The Church, thus, became a factor in the struggle for power and in legislative politics. This struggle enticed participation by a considerable number of clergymen and ultimately led the bishops to devise rules for their involvement. In a meeting under Bishop Karevičius that convened three months before the viciously fought electoral campaign of May, 1926, they adopted a revealing statement that not only set the rules but also explained the Church's attitude toward politics.[6] Although defensive in their formulations, the bishops nevertheless declared that "politics touches upon the affairs of religion and the Church" and that there is a need for the defense of "the rights of Catholicism and the Church" in the Diet. Since clergymen are citizens and since the Church has rights to be defended, it is not only permissible but in some cases even obligatory for priests to participate in politics. It is therefore "desirable," the bishops said, that clergymen run for the parliament though not more than one from a diocese need be elected. However, the bishops warned, the priests should not hold membership in political parties nor should they accept positions that would subordinate them to party discipline. Clergymen belong to the jurisdiction of the bishops and are subject to the discipline of the Church. Even their participation in elections must be approved in writing by their bishops. This philosophy, however, was not universally accepted, but criticized, especially by politicians who were Catholics but not Christian Democrats.[7] Active clerical leadership in the political arena, it must be added, created grave problems and not only hurt the Church's reputation, but also lost religious loyalties. In addition, it helped Leftist or other partisan groups that did not carry the "Catholic" label. The bishops understood the message that the electorate delivered in 1926 by defeating Christian Democrats, and in their May 14–17 meeting, made two pertinent suggestions on further political work by the clergy and the laity. First, "it is more suitable," they said, "for a priest to be active in pastoral Catholic work rather than as a member of a political party," and second, "political parties should not carry the 'Catholic' name in their title."[8]

The Constitutional Position of the Church

It is not surprising therefore that when the Christian Democrats had parliamentary majority, the final text of the Constitution of 1922 failed to include limitations on the Church that the Social Democrats and the Populists (an alliance of agrarian pro-Socialists) sought to incorporate in it. The lack of consensus on this matter had very unfavorable consequences for the future of the Lithuanian democracy; it is not too much to say that it contributed to the democracy's downfall. On the other hand, the Constitution did not elevate the Church above the rest of the nation as the Irish constitution did in its Article 44. The rights granted to the Catholic church were equally guaranteed to other religious denominations. All "religious organizations," as Art. 84 stated it, were given equal rights to self-government, the right freely to preach, teach, perform religious services, keep schools and charitable institutions, establish monasteries, own property. In addition, they were granted rights of legal person. Finally, religious certificates of birth, death or marriage were declared to have legal validity (Art. 83–87). The state itself kept no records of this kind. The most controversial sections involved religious education and marriage. According to the Constitution (Art. 80), "religious education [was] obligatory with the exception of schools established for children whose parents do not belong to any religious organization." Each religious denomination was left in charge of religious teaching that the state pledged to finance. Similarly, the Constitution allowed state support for private denominational schools. Leftist parties and "Leftist" (frequently, merely meaning "secular") groups objected to the obligatory character of religious education and protested the absence of civil marriage and divorce. The Constitution of 1938 that was promulgated by the authoritarian regime of President Antanas Smetona did not change these provisions, though it no longer guaranteed financial support for private schools and generally stressed the state's authority to limit the enumerated rights.[9]

While the Constitution thus did not confer upon the Catholic church any exclusive rights, the Church's sheer size, in comparison with the others, guaranteed it a dominant position; 85 percent of the Lithuanian population were Catholics. The Socialists, Populists and later Nationalists fought this commanding and sometimes overbearing position of the Church in the political arena and in various other forums. Among its ideological opponents who crossed the party lines, it is important to mention the Alliance of Freethinkers, led by Dr. Jonas Šliūpas (1861–1944), that conducted atheist propaganda, promoted secularization of public life and attempted to tear down the Church's influence, especially in education. The Freethinkers further opposed Church-controlled marriage laws and the concordat with the Vatican that in 1927 recognized the newly-established Lithuanian church province.[10]

The Establishment of the Church Province

The church province of Lithuania was founded in 1926, thus making the Lithuanian church independent of foreign supervision for the first time in its history. Its creation therefore should have been an occasion for jubilation as it signified a historical milestone. But while the occasion produced festivities to the accompaniment of ringing church bells when it was announced on Easter day, 1926, the establishment of the church province was marred by political difficulties and dissatisfactions. These were caused essentially by Lithuanian nationalist attitudes and policies that the Church, however prestigious at the time, was helpless to control.

As a result of very active Catholic involvement in the nation's social life, it was not surprising to find that Catholic groups in general and many churchmen in particular felt strongly about issues that caused the Lithuanian conflict with Poland. By seizing the capital city of Vilnius shortly after concluding an armistice on October 7, 1920, Warsaw became extremely unpopular and no government in Kaunas that counselled a calm approach to Lithuanian-Polish relations could survive in office.

The affairs of the church, unfortunately, were intertwined with the territorial conflict between the two nations. Boundaries that emerged after World War I had effectively destroyed the viability of old diocesan divisions, and the capture of Vilnius by General Żeligowski further aggravated the partition.[11] In Lithuania, only the Samogitian diocese remained intact. Pieces of other dioceses (Vilnius and Sejny), with at least one bishop exiled by Poland to Lithuania, now loosely adjoined the Samogitian diocese that was administered from Kaunas. It was, then, necessary to establish a new church organization capable of operating within the frontiers of the recently arisen national states. The main obstacle to reform was the unresolved territorial conflict with Poland. In 1923, the Lithuanians were scandalized by the decision of the Ambassadors' conference to recognize Vilnius to Poland. Two years later, on February 10, 1925, the Vatican added insult to this perceived injury by concluding a concordat with Warsaw which similarly acknowledged Polish sovereignty over the Vilnius region. Another consequence of this concordat was a compelled resignation of Bishop Matulevičius; Poland had earlier sought to remove him in favor of a bishop of Polish nationality. Even though the Vatican attempted to soothe Lithuanian sensitivities by elevating the Vilnius See to an archbishopric, with the Pinsk and Lomźa dioceses subordinated to it, the Lithuanians failed to perceive this gesture as a sufficient recognition of their claim to the territory. They expected from the Pope a clear support of Lithuanian objectives of regaining Vilnius. As a result, a storm of protests exploded in the country. Demonstrations were staged against the papal envoy, Msgr. A. Cechini, the negotiator of a concordat with the Lithuanian government, and voices of disapproval reached so high a pitch that the government, though in the hands of Christian Democrats, broke off negotiations with the Vatican, protested the Polish concordat and asked Cechini to leave the country.[12]

Discussions for reorganizing the Lithuanian church province never resumed, but the Pope, the former Achilles Ratti, a wise leader from the point of view of the Vatican, on December 7, 1925, appointed Matulevičius, now a titular archbishop, as his representative to Lithuania for organizing the church province and normalizing relations with the government. The new archbishop, though a highly respected man of pristine personal integrity, was criticized for resigning from the Vilnius See under pressure[13] and, though in Lithuania he found sympathy among the clergy and the Catholics, he was denied official support by the Christian Democratic government. However, on February 15, 1926, together with Lithuania's bishops, he already had a plan for the church province that was submitted to Rome.[14] Matulèvičius further worked on this draft at the Vatican and by the end of March prepared the final, somewhat revised, text that he considered "a document without political or national colors, but in my estimate, the best from the point of view of the Church."[15]

The final draft provided the province with five dioceses: the archdiocese of Kaunas (with 680,000 Catholics), the diocese of Telšiai (with 378,000), Panevėžys (378,000), Vilkaviškis (320,000), and Kaišiadorys (with 220,000). Kaunas served as the seat of the province with the Metropolitan Archbishop in charge. The small prelature of Klaipėda-Memel, consisting of a formerly German territory, was attached to Telšiai. The first three dioceses covered the territory of the old Samogitian diocese, thus abolishing its historical name, while the other two were rump territories of the dioceses of Vilnius and Seinai (Sejny). The Lithuanians wanted to keep their historical names, but the Vatican refused, for it would provoke conflict with Poland. The Lithuanians similarly objected to the designation of the province as simply a Kaunas province but insisted on naming it for Lithuania. A compromise formulation established a province "consisting of territories now within the boundaries of the Lithuanian Republic."

The plan, finally, provided for a new hierarchy. Bishop Karevičius of the Samogitian diocese was asked to resign. It will never be known whether his confrontation with Achilles Ratti, who had lectured Karevičius about the latter's nationalism but for whom Karevičius produced documents proving that the Vatican envoy appeased Polish nationalism, had anything to do with the bishop's removal.[16] He was elevated to titular archbishop and joined Archbishop Matulevičius' Marian Congregation. The departure of this outspoken, courageous and controversial hierarch was deeply mourned in Lithuania. Karevičius was replaced by the scholarly and withdrawn translator of the Bible, Juozapas Skvireckas (1873–1959), his Auxiliary. The dioceses of Vilkaviškis and Kaišiadorys received senior bishops whose previous dioceses were now under Polish rule. Bishop Antanas Karosas (1856–1947), already 72 years old, was reluctantly approved for Vilkaviškis. He had been exiled by Poland from his home diocese of Seinai (Sejny). The Vatican had encouraged him to resign from administration altogether, but the hierarch stubbornly insisted on an appointment in the reorganized church organization. The Pope then gave him as an Auxiliary (co-adiutor) the Rev. Mečislovas Reinys (1884–1953), a friend of Archbishop Matulevičius, who possibly, more than anyone else, had helped the archbishop to draft the plan for the church province. Canon Juozapas Kukta (1873–1942), a former assistant of Bishop Matulevičius in Vilnius whom Polish authorities had arrested and banished to Lithuania, was chosen Bishop of the Kaišiadorys diocese. This new administrative territory formerly had belonged to the Vilnius See. Panevėžys was given to Kazimieras Paltarokas (1875–1958), a learned theologian and social philosopher who later had to bear the brunt of Stalin's attacks on the Church. Justinas Staugaitis, a signer of the declaration of 1918 restoring Lithuanian independence and a parliamentary leader, was appointed to reign in the new diocese of Telšiai, the ethnic Samogitian part of the old Samogitian diocese.

Because of strong nationalistic opposition that combined with considerable anti-Church feelings, Archbishop Matulevičius urged Cardinal De Gasparri to approve of the plan without delay while the Christian Democrats were still in power. However, the Vatican took time to iron out diplomatic difficulties concerning the Klaipėda-Memel region and thus the arrangements were not completed until Easter of 1926. On April 4th, finally, the Pope issued the "constitution" for the Lithuanian province entitled *Lituanorum gente*. Pius XI stressed that he expected the new arrangements to be "very useful not only for the Catholic affairs but also for the prosperity of the Republic."[17]

While favorably received by the Church leadership and many Catholics, the papal message and the new arrangement was announced at a rather inopportune time, namely, just before a new parliamentary election. Christian Democratic leaders doubted the wisdom of the immediate proclamation of the document, especially that it was prepared without official government participation. Indeed, it became an issue in the elections, though it was not clear how much it hurt the Christian Democrats who ran scared because of various bread and butter issues and charges of corruption. The bishops, including the newly appointed hierarchs, attempted to help by issuing a pastoral letter in which they charged that "the enemies of the Church are forcing their way into the parliament so that later they can enchain the Church with the help of laws more severe than those that existed under the Russian rule."[18] The Catholic parties lost anyway.

In this perspective, it is not surprising that the new government coalition of Populists and Social Democrats refused to accept the papal reform and to recognize the legality of the Church province. They showed it by declining to honor various baptismal or marriage certificates issued on the stationery of the new diocesan chancellories.

The Minister of Education, furthermore, rejected transfers and new appointments of school chaplains and religion teachers that the new bishops made during the summer.[19] Finally, some Leftist deputies, with only slightly veiled government support, introduced legislation designed to withdraw financial support for religious education and for administering records of vital statistics on grounds that the state had no formal knowledge of papal reorganization and had not agreed on it. The bishops became alarmed that the new government "started a struggle against the Catholic church."[20]

This Leftist threat, if it ever was real, never materialized. The government of Populist Premier Mykolas Sleževičius (1882–1939), while publicly interested in clipping the Church's wings, at the same time privately showed signs of desire to normalize relations with the Vatican.[21] It did not proceed, however, because of unresolved disagreements in the ruling coalition, and very quickly lost the chance of acting altogether because on December 17th, 1926, it was overthrown by a military coup. The officers brought to power a well known former temporary president of the Republic (1919–1920) and professor of classics, Antanas Smetona (1874–1944), a conservative Nationalist leader. Together with another very talented classicist, Augustinas Voldemaras (1883–1942), and their tiny Nationalist Alliance, Smetona now organized the support of the Right against the Leftist parties, and having temporarily secured it, sought to outflank the Christian Democrats in order to seize complete power. Therefore immediately after severing relations with those elements of the Christian Democratic leadership that had supported the coup, the two professors, almost without checking, rushed to accept the long delayed concordat with the Vatican. The document, to which Voldemaras affixed his signature in the Vatican on September 27th, 1927, was practically identical with the draft that the Christian Democratic government had rejected in 1924–25.[22]

Relations with the Vatican

The concordat that was concluded by Lithuania's authoritarian rulers essentially confirmed the Church's existing position. Some say that it gave the Church more control over education than the previous laws because it eliminated exceptions from religious instruction that were possible in the democratic days.[23] The agreement further promised financial aid for the support of theological seminaries and salaries for the clergy. It also guaranteed freedom of the Catholic Action organizations. Lithuanian bishops were not altogether happy with certain provisions, especially those that concerned the oath the bishops were supposed to take to the state. They similarly disliked provisions that dealt with the appointments of clerics and the affairs of theological seminaries.[24] They had no choice, however, but to accept it and hope that their disappointment would be compensated by obtaining state funds for the establishment of new diocesan seminaries and various other capital construction that the newly established dioceses needed and that the government promised.

No sooner, however, than the ink dried on the document, the bishops saw many of these prospects destroyed. Financial aid was available though not in expected amounts. All Lithuanian governments had financially supported all religious denominations, and the government of President Smetona was no exception. The Catholics usually received a lion's share of annual tax support which for religious groups in 1938 amounted to Lt 1,691,718 (ca $286,000). Of this amount, the Church received Lt 1,376,778 (ca $243,000).[25]

Smetona continued to pay salaries, but the bishops soon discovered many violations of the concordat. Thus, in 1930, Smetona outlawed high school student groups that constituted a part of the "Ateitis" Federation. He also put pressure on the Theological-Philosophical Faculty at the University of Kaunas that was protected by the concordat. This Faculty constituted a Catholic college which offered degrees not only in Catholic theology and philosophy but also in education, history, literature and linguistics, and a number of other disciplines. There began, in the words of Polish historian Piotr Łossowski, a Lithuanian *Kulturkampf.*[26]

The President's moves against the Catholic church were politically inspired. He considered the Church a part of the Christian Democratic establishment and did not distinguish between pastoral activities of the Church and partisan activities of Catholic parties. By prohibiting the youth organization and by limiting the work of the Catholic college, he apparently hoped to choke off the growth of Christian Democratic influence among the young and throughout the land. The bishops protested and moved youth activities to the underground. They also complained to the government and to the Vatican, though their voices usually were softened by Archbishop Skvireckas whom some people found "wanting in the determination of clearer and firmer policies."[27] Smetona's supporters even considered the archbishop "their man."[28] The minutes of the bishops' conferences of the period betray an extreme anxiousness and concern with the worsened relations between church and state. The bishops recorded withdrawal of government aid to private schools, conflict over payment of clerical salaries (the government wanted to make individual payments to the clergy instead of lump sum payments to the bishops), occasional arrests of priests and intellectuals, outlawing of Catholic cooperatives and banks, the closing down of political parties, censorship of the newspapers. To counter Smetona's plans of "cutting down to size" the Catholic college at the University, the bishops ordered a feasibility study of the establishment of a Catholic university. In August of 1932, the founding of the school was celebrated by a solemn Mass, but the Minister of Education refused to license it. Thus, the bishops' plan could not be implemented. Smetona's government nevertheless began temporarily restraining itself from further encroachment on the activities of the Catholic college. The bishops, on the other hand, further satisfied themselves by encouraging the work of the newly founded Catholic Academy of Sciences.

Relations, however, steadily worsened. In 1931, the government expelled the Papal Nunzio Msgr. Riccardo Bartaloni and nearly severed diplomatic relations with the Vatican because of the latter's support of the bishops' struggle for the freedom of Catholic Action groups. In October of that year the bishops prepared an official denunciation of Smetona's dictatorship, formulated in a pastoral letter that began with the words "In our land the Church has a record of great suffering."[29] However, the accommodating Archbishop Skvireckas prevailed and the letter was not published.

Only after Smetona's rule began to shake and World War II engulfed the continent did the Vatican and Lithuania make peace. For Smetona, the crucial event was the ultimatum by Poland that, in March of 1938, demanded resumption of diplomatic relations. This ultimatum was not only meekly accepted but it also exposed the weakness of Smetona's domestic power base. The new Prime Minister, Rev. Vladas Mironas (1880–1953), now sought to regain Catholic support for the regime. He worked hard to win the approval of his secularized Nationalist colleagues for the normalization of relations with the Vatican. The regime's original reason for the *Kulturkampf* had been a fear of Catholic competition for power; its efforts now were motivated by the need of political support from the Church and the Catholic population. The Nationalists again attempted to outflank the Catholic politicians. On May 8, 1938, the Prime Minister declared:

> The government is determined to end the disastrous conflict with the Church. The Church is not restricted in church activities, however, the government is concerned that these activities would not serve to

attract partisan elements so that the government's relations with the Church would not strengthen some political party. It is necessary to ensure that partisan elements would not interfere with church affairs and that the Church would perform solely its direct duties; this performance can be very useful. The government has pursued this road for understanding, but obstacles arose. Today, however, in different conditions, the government considers that it is not necessary to delay the regulation of church-state relations; the question must be solved now. It is necessary to clarify the issue, one way or another.[30]

The progress, however, was slow. The main disagreement centered on the issue of freedom for the "Ateitis" groups in secondary schools. An additional impetus for negotiations was needed. It came in March of 1939, when the loss of Klaipéda-Memel to Hitler's Anschluss further weakened Smetona's control and required the creation of a government of "national unity" with Christian Democratic and Populist participation. As a result, in three months a draft agreement was approved by the government and on October 11th, Lithuania's Minister, for the first time since 1931, replaced a chargé d'affaires in the Vatican.

The Vatican, it must be said, was generally slow, but usually more prepared to settle the differences than the Lithuanian bishops who sought a real solution of the difficulties they had to cope with. In the fall of 1939, the matter became urgent for all. In a Europe dominated by the Hitler-Stalin axis, Lithuania's neutrality offered poor protection while the Vatican suddenly discovered a strong interest in strengthening Lithuania's position. This occurred after Germany and the Soviet Union jointly destroyed Poland and effectively suppressed the Polish church, until then the stronghold of East European Catholicism. Now Pope Pius XII, who knew Lithuanian affairs since his diplomatic service in World War I, looked toward the small country as the sole remaining free Catholic land between the Nazi and Communist giants. It was therefore not a mere flattery on his part at a reception of the new Lithuanian Minister to refer to Lithuania as "the northernmost outpost of Catholicism in Europe."[31] The Lithuanians, on the other hand, not without reason, saw in the papal expression not only a recognition of the importance of the Lithuanian church but also his concern with the future of the Lithuanian state.[32]

The Lithuanian accreditation of a Minister to the Papal Court opened the doors for further rapprochement. Though the Vatican took its time, four months later, on February 11th, the Pope appointed a Nunzio. Msgr. Luigi Centoz presented himself to President Smetona still some weeks later, on April 30th.[33] He was received very warmly and reciprocated, in later interviews, with compliments to the "great people" of Lithuania, wishing its Church recognition in the appointment of a Lithuanian Cardinal.[34] The new rapport allowed the solution of a number of mutually important problems. The Lithuanian government, for example, ceased demanding the removal of Archbishop Romuald Jałbrzykowski of Vilnius (1876–1955), but in return — though not without public demands — Jałbrzykowski allowed Lithuanian language services in more than one Vilnius church as the case had been until then.[35] Furthermore, it delayed the promulgation of new marriage laws that would allow civil marriage.[36] The Vatican, too, strengthened the aging hierarchy by appointing new auxiliaries for Archbishop Skvireckas and Bishop Staugaitis. On April 3, Rev. Vincentas Brizgys (b. 1903), a theology professor, was selected for the Kaunas diocese while the rector of the local theological seminary, Vincentas Borisevičius (1887–1946), on March 10th, was consecrated in Telšiai.

The Church and Society

As events would soon demonstrate, the Lithuanian state organization, that on the one hand fought and on the other protected the Church, was very fragile while the Church was vigorous and strong. Conflict with the government had not hurt it. On the contrary, its credibility and influence increased precisely because of its willingness to take a stand against dictatorial policies.

The measurement of the strength the Church in Lithuania had achieved at the outbreak of World War II is elusive, but it can be attempted in terms of numbers and the endurance of its moral impact on the people's behavior. Statistically, the number of priests had grown from 957 in the early twenties to 1279 in the spring of 1939, before the incorporation of Vilnius into Lithuanian territory.[37] The number of theology students, however, since the 1920s did not keep pace, and rose only slightly, from 263 in 1927 to 283 in 1939 (with Vilnius territory, that is, in current Lithuanian boundaries, their number in 1940 was 435). The levelling off of seminary enrollment provided one of the crucial reasons for the bishops' insistence on freedom for the high school "Ateitis" group. It supplied almost ninety percent of the candidates for the priesthood. Together with the priests of the reestablished monastic orders, and including the regained Vilnius territory, the total number of clergymen stood at 1451. This statistical ledger may be completed by adding 14 monastic orders, six for men, eight for women, that kept 27 monasteries with 434 monks and 76 convents with 629 nuns. They were mostly engaged in education and charitable work. Under the Tsars, they were illegal, though at least one, the Marian Fathers, had survived in the underground.

The number of Catholics between 1920 and 1939 increased from 1,717,000 to 1,898,000. At the end of 1939, this number was augmented by approximately 250,000 ethnically mixed — Polish, Lithuanian, Belorussian — Catholics of the Vilnius region. Characteristically for the Lithuanian church, its people were systematically and well organized to attract various age groups and occupations. The rural youth group *Pavasaris* (Spring), for example, had a membership of 90,000. The clandestine "Ateitis" group enlisted every fifth high school student. University students and school teachers had their own organizations and publications. Catholic-oriented newspapers and journals, generally, had the largest circulation among their peers.

To a large degree, this growth was a product of an episcopal policy of promoting the education of secular Catholic leadership. Under Archbishop Skvireckas, clergymen were generally discouraged from partisan political activities — Smetona's regime of course had curtailed political participation altogether — and the clergy directed its energies toward the solution of cultural and social problems. As a result, in the late 1930s, the secular Catholic intelligentsia took over the intellectual and political leadership of the Catholic community, frequently straining relations with some of the hierarchs, though not, interestingly enough, with the younger clergy. For the most part, both these clergymen and the secular intellectuals were educated after Lithuania became independent and thus were inclined to seek inspiration in West European Catholicism and culture. Partly as a result of this new orientation and the turning back on Russia, Eastern-rite Catholicism and the idea of preparing for eventual missionary work in Russia — though much promoted by the Vatican — did not attract noticeable attention in Lithuania.

Furthermore, while led by a generally conservative hierarchy — the possible exception is Bishop Paltarokas — the Church nevertheless was vibrant with ideas of reform and renovation, nursed by senior theology and philosophy professors in Kaunas, usually on wave lengths with the trend of Catholic development in Western Europe. There existed, in addition, a proclivity toward social reform among a stratum of older church leaders that was inherited from the revolutionary period of 1917–18. Thus, for example, a number of Catholic intellectuals defied the bishops by proposing the introduction of the option of civil marriage.[38] Still others advocated the distribution of church lands for charitable or cultural purposes, arguing that the reform would free the pastor-farmer for the pursuits of his real vocation. Both of these issues were very sensitive. They provoked heated arguments which indicated that the Church had problems in adjusting its pastoral philosophy from a purely rural to a modernizing society. The Church's landed property, it should be said, was not large. Churches and monasteries ploughed or otherwise utilized (for church yards, rectory grounds, orphanages, etc.) about 20,000 hectares (44,000 acres) of land which constituted only 1.5 percent of total arable land of the country.[39] However, this ownership was conspicuous. Most of the church farms were well managed and some pastors were suspected of spending more time in the fields than in the church. Yet these farms — while their usefulness was argued on grounds that without them it would be difficult to support the priests — were becoming social and political millstones for the institution.[40]

Furthermore, Catholic intellectuals and the clergy broke out of the earlier self-imposed "Catholic" ghetto. Vigorous communication, fostered by publications like *Naujoji Romuva* (The New Romuva), *Židinys* (The Hearth), or *XX Amžius* (XX Century), reached intellectuals of other than "Catholic" convictions and successfully involved them in cooperative ventures.[41] A political alliance between the Christian Democrats and the Populists — so important in the earlier political history of independent Lithuania — further helped to build bridges to ideologically different segments of society.

This growing weight of church organizations, their involvement and the vigor of the new secular and clerical leadership kept the Church close to the average Lithuanian concerns and projected a socially progressive image. Closely communicating with the masses, the Church was bound to have more influence on its people's behavior. This influence, unfortunately, is considerably more difficult to measure than the statistical scope of the Church's activities. One helpful empirical index is provided by statistics on family stability and divorce. The Church, as is well known, adamantly stood and remains committed to the insolubility of marriage. Soviet data show that after the introduction of civil marriage and legalization of divorce in 1940, Lithuania's divorce rate for a generation remained extremely low. In 1950, the rate of registered divorces for the entire population, not just the Catholics, was a negligible 0.2 per thousand of population.[42] In the rural areas, inhabited almost exclusively by Lithuanian Catholics, it was zero. The rate began climbing after the post-Stalinist legislation allowed easier separation, and in 1960 it reached 0.3 in the villages. By

1970, the village rate was 0.9, while in the cities it ran up to a rather high 3.5.

Another measuring index, useful in the appraisal of the Church's influence on behavior, is attendance of classes of religious education. Figures are not available on this matter, but the estimated attendance of these classes in churches after religion teaching was eliminated from schools was almost perfect in 1940/41 and then again in 1944/46. It dropped only slightly at a later time, but soon religion classes were outlawed altogether. Religion teaching for pre-Communion children remains very popular in the 1970s, and according to statistics of the *Chronicle of the Catholic Church of Lithuania,* attendance remains extremely high. (See Ch. XIV).

Finally, in a broader spectrum of life, the Church helped, on the whole, to contain Smetona's nationalistic regime from swerving to extremism and to Fascism. It must be said, however, that the Church itself, especially its younger intelligentsia and clergy, were not free of nationalistic sentiments. Ethnic pride in the establishment of an independent state and frustration caused by the losses to the Poles had dominated Christian Democratic politics in the 1920s and made it quite impossible for the Church and the government calmly to discuss questions of such importance as the creation of the first Lithuanian church province. Later this ethnic pride led to demands, for example, that the German leadership of the Jesuits be changed to Lithuanian or at least put in the hands of other West Europeans not interested in promoting German influence.[43] In itself, this demand was reasonable but its public and impolite discussion and altogether the raising of the issue was new and signified that for the Catholics it was no longer just the Catholic religion that mattered — as was the case primarily in the epoch of Bishop Valančius — but that both religion *and* nationality, as a prominent Catholic priest put it, "constituted the two strong pillars of our life, the two powerful initiators and promoters of our cultural activity and progress."[44] However, if Professor Kemėšis (1879–1954) sought to establish a symbiotic relationship between the two forces in the concept of their mutual service to God, at the same time he scolded Catholics, especially the clergymen, for poorly participating in non-partisan patriotic organizations, as for example, the Alliance for the Liberation of Vilnius. While a liberal Catholic editor complained that the Lithuanians did not develop "any healthy or necessary" national-ism, not to speak about its unhealthy "zoological" variety,[45] Kemėšis urged "very serious concern" with such education. At the end of the same decade of the 1930s, some Catholic theorists already proposed the identification of state and nationality. A young, but already prominent Catholic philosopher, Antanas Maceina, urged the necessity "of our times to identify the borders of the state with the boundaries of nationality."[46] This view, of course, was not tolerant of ethnic minorities which in Lithuania constituted about 20 percent in 1939. For them, this identification would leave no other alternative but either to assimilate with the Lithuanians or to lose the rights of citizenship.

Maceina himself later retreated from this stand and on the whole, the younger intelligentsia subscribed to the principle enunciated by the last President of Kaunas University, Professor Stasys Šalkauskis (1886–1941), the dominant Catholic intellectual of the 1930s. According to him,

> . . . the nationalist striving to achieve an exclusivist (isolationist) national individualism poorly serves the nation; it actually weakens national individuality because this individuality is prevented from developing on a world-wide scale. When a nation, together with religion, adopts the Catholic *Weltanschauung*, there occurs a process of assimilation that helps a nation to gain universally significant ideas while it provides for the Catholic ideology an opportunity of national idiomatic communication. The individuality of a nation is enriched and matures as a result of acquiring universally significant contents.[47]

The distinction that such leaders as Šalkauskis impressed on their peers in practical life was the difference between patriotism and chauvinism. Patriotic feelings were healthy, chauvinism was perverted.

Concern for the legally-guaranteed independence of the Church from the state led its leaders to advocate limited government and to oppose Smetona's authoritarian rule. Even symbolically, the state — though it was a national Lithuanian state — was not accepted as the Church's co-equal. For example, churches did not fly national flags except on the most festive national occasions; flags of partisan Nationalist organizations were not allowed into churches altogether. Such organizations, similarly, were denied the services of Catholic chaplains, though such were very much desired. In strictly pastoral terms, this probably was a questionable practice; in broader national terms, such gestures — sometimes violently debated in newspapers — defied the absolute supremacy of state power and of its official Nationalist ideology. The Church's effectiveness in this process of the taming of the Nationalist regime was frequently spoiled by the complacency and disagreement of some of the older bishops, tired of forever fighting "the Tsar." Paradoxically, the Church itself thrived because of the protection of this national state. Indeed, Catholicism flourished and the Church developed as never before in any period of Lithuanian history.

III

The Collapse of the Lithuanian State

Lithuanian independence, however, was short-lived. After an interlude of only twenty-two years (1918–40), Lithuania's statehood was snuffed out by the combination of the same Russo-Germanic powers that had destroyed the Polish-Lithuanian Commonwealth a century and a half ago. In June of 1940, Lithuania again was annexed and absorbed by the rulers of Russia.

The drama started unfolding a full year earlier, on August 23rd, in Moscow where, in the late evening hours, German Foreign Minister Joachim von Ribbentrop and Soviet Chairman of the Council of Commissars Viacheslav Molotov sealed an alliance between Stalin and Hitler by signing a non-aggression pact between Germany and the Soviet Union. A secret appendix to this agreement provided for the fourth partition of Poland between the Russians and the Germans, for a vague division of the Balkans and, as the Lithuanian government was informed by both parties on October 4th and 5th, a "delimitation of German and Soviet spheres of influence" in the Baltic region.[1] Lithuania's northern neighbors, Latvia and Estonia, were assigned to the Soviets while Lithuania itself was left to Hitler.[2] Thus was initiated the partition of Europe, to be completed after World War II.

Attacked by the perfidious ally less than two years later, Stalin was at pains in explaining to his people that despite Hitler's aggression of June 22nd, 1941, the pact had not been a mistake. "We secured our country," he said in a radio address on July 3rd, 1941, "peace for a year and a half and the opportunity of preparing its forces to repulse fascist Germany."[3] Actually, Stalin could have protected the Soviet Union against the Nazis by a pact with Great Britain and France which then sought to contain further German expansion by an alliance with the Soviet Union. But as a price for Soviet partnership, the British hesitated giving the Communist dictator a free hand in Poland and the Baltic States without the consent of the affected nations, and Stalin therefore signed with the Nazis who did. In fact, the clever Georgian had baited both the British and the Germans, respectively, on April 16th and 17th of that spring, and had even handed to the British

Ambassador in Moscow a draft treaty for consideration while conducting talks about "normalization of relations with Germany" through his Ambassador and trade officials in Berlin.[4] Soviet negotiations with the British were public. With the Nazis, however, the contacts were secret. In the spring, the British sent a delegation to Moscow. The Nazis, on the other hand, like the undecided predator, played uninterested in Soviet overtures. "We must now sit tight," German State Secretary Ernst von Weizsäcker on May 21th telegraphed German Ambassador Friedrich Werner von Schulenberg in Moscow, "and wait to see whether the Russians will speak more openly."[5] The Germans still hoped to destroy Poland, as they did Czechoslovakia, peacefully, and with British and French acquiescence. They were not yet ready to seek Soviet aid. However, Neville Chamberlain could not be talked into another Munich. Poland, therefore, would have to be subdued and crushed by military means, and for an armed campaign the Germans needed summer weather. Therefore in the late summer of 1939, on August 14th, Hitler dashed for an agreement with Moscow.[6] German diplomats now noted, however, that the Soviets — though making no progress in their negotiations with the British — suggested a slow and gradual approach. Stalin apparently wanted to ascertain himself that his pact with Hitler would produce an irrevocable German breach with Great Britain. This would occur, Stalin judged, only if Hitler militarily invaded Poland. On August 21st, after a flurry of diplomatic exchanges in which the Germans heatedly urged immediate action, Stalin became convinced that the Germans were in such an extraordinary hurry for precisely this reason and agreed to Hitler's personal proposal that the Führer's Foreign Minister come to Moscow to conclude the treaty.[7] Joachim von Ribbentrop arrived in the morning of August 23rd, and in the evening signed the agreement. In the cocktail party that followed, Stalin drank to Hitler's health.

The first victim of the Nazi-Soviet non-aggression pact was Poland. It was destroyed by Hitler's war machine in less than two weeks and divided between the two partners who at first entertained an idea of a rump Polish state as a buffer between themselves. However, on September 25th, Stalin proposed that its establishment "might create friction between the allies" and that it would be better if Germany exchanged Lithuania for the Polish province of Lublin.[8] The Germans agreed, and, on September 28th, Lithuania was transferred to the Soviet zone of influence.[9] A minor problem of territorial adjustment in the Lithuanian border region of Suvalkai (Suwalki) that was supposed to fall under German jurisdiction was later resolved, again at Soviet suggestion, by compensating Germany for its loss in cash or in materials. After protracted negotiations, on January 10th, 1940, the Soviets agreed to pay the Nazis a sum of $7,500,000 gold dollars.[10]

The Russian Return to the Baltic Region

Within weeks after the fall of Poland the Soviets proceeded to cash in the chips they had won in the Baltic region. Since the time for immediate and outright occupation was inopportune, the Kremlin sought only a partial takeover to ensure that the Baltic States would not escape future Soviet annexation. Starting with Estonia, the Soviets now demanded conclusion of mutual-assistance pacts that would allow the Soviet Union to keep Red Army bases on the Baltic soil. The governments in Kaunas, Riga, and Tallinn were caught by surprise.[11] Furthermore, upon inquiry with the Germans and the Western Allies, they found no encouragement for resisting Soviet demands. The only Baltic country that refused to submit was Finland. But Finland was helped by its geography, its better preparation for defense, and its more resolute leadership.

The Lithuanians signed the mutual-assistance pact on October 10th. Article IV of the treaty provided for the stationing of Soviet troops on Lithuanian territory though their number was determined in a separate, and typically for the Soviets, secret agreement. At first, 20,000 troops were allowed.[12] On the other hand, Article VII stipulated that the treaty will "not affect, in any way, the sovereign rights of the contracting parties, in particular their state organization, economic and social system, military measures, and the principles of non-intervention in internal affairs generally."[13] The Lithuanians, understandably, placed great value on this provision. In their view, it protected their independence, despite the fact that Soviet garrisons would be equal in size to the entire Lithuanian army. Unlike the Estonians and the Latvians, however, the Lithuanians were served the bitter pill sugar coated. While forcing on the country his garrisons, Stalin returned to Lithuania the city of Vilnius (Yiddish, Vilna; Polish, Wilno; German, Wilna) with a portion of its district that had been seized and held by Poland since 1920.[14]

Lithuania's claims to Vilnius were mutually recognized by both the Soviets and the Nazis in the secret supplement of August 23rd. At first, the Germans attempted to entice the Lithuanians into taking the city by an attack on Poland. However, Lithuania declared neutrality and later very politely pushed aside German suggestions of a military alliance that would put Lithuania under German protection.[15] It was then that the little country was traded to Stalin from whom now the Lithuanians had to take Vilnius together with the Soviet Trojan horse. Stalin was unhappy that the Lithuanians did not sign the agreement on October 9th, the anniversary of Polish seizure of the city in 1920, but the Soviets earned their propagandistic reward anyway because the Lithuanians were grateful for the gift of their historic capital and at least for a moment were distracted from the contemplation of the grim future that the presence of Soviet bases portended.

At first, life in Lithuania and the other Baltic States seemed to continue without changes. While Western journalists began referring to the three republics as Soviet protectorates,[16] the Soviets barely interfered in their domestic affairs. In foreign relations, Baltic options after Poland's collapse became extremely limited and the presence of Soviet garrisons did not make that much difference, at any rate, not in the winter months of 1939. Thus, while there was concern about the future after the introduction of Soviet troops, a rare Baltic leader or intellectual realized that their nations already lived on borrowed time.

This situation, however, continued only into the late spring of 1940. By then the Soviets had completed their Finnish campaign and thus were free for other adventures. The Germans, in the meantime, on May 10th, invaded Belgium and were about to vanquish France. Stalin feared German victories. They were *Blitz* performances of conspicuous efficiency. Just before the Germans entered Paris, the Soviet Ambassador in Sweden, Madame Kollontai, had confided to the Belgian Minister that "the German danger was far greater than had been believed" and that all European nations should band together against "German imperialism."[17] It is not known whether she expressed Stalin's sentiments, but the dictator moved once and for all to settle the Baltic question. Available documents contain no proof that the Kremlin acted, as the Soviets claimed in later years, in fear of Hitler's design on the Baltic countries. In the spring of 1940, the Soviets had at least 70,000 troops with armor and air force stationed in Estonia, Latvia, and Lithuania. In 1939–40, the German Führer had ordered the repatriation of the Baltic Germans, thus giving Stalin a clear signal that Germany was withdrawing from the Baltic region.[18] It was possible, of course, that victorious Germany might renege on the agreement for the Soviets to occupy the Baltic States, but this would lead to an armed conflict, and it is well known that Stalin did not expect a war with Germany. It is more likely that the basic reason for the Soviet desire completely to occupy the Baltic countries was Stalin's belief that the Baltic region was traditionally Russian, that it had only temporarily escaped Russian rule, and that the agreement with Hitler made its immediate recovery possible. As he showed time and again in his later relations with the Western powers, the Kremlin's master was very cautious, but always alert to the exploitation of favorable situations for carrying the Soviet flag into areas where at the moment it was safe to do so.

Stalin's Games in Lithuania

Stalin started action in Lithuania, the state adjacent to the German border. After unsuccessful negotiations in Moscow that had lasted for two weeks, on June 14th, the day Paris surrendered to Hitler, the Lithuanians were handed an ultimatum that accused the Lithuanian government of kidnapping Soviet soldiers and conspiring against the Soviet Union in a military alliance with Latvia and Estonia. Moscow demanded immediate admission of an unlimited number of Soviet troops, "sufficient to guarantee the possibility of realizing the Soviet-Lithuanian mutual-assistance treaty and to prevent provocative actions against the Soviet garrison."[19] A divided Lithuanian cabinet agreed, with President Smetona, his Defense and Education ministers and the State Comptroller dissenting, and on June 15th, as specified, Soviet divisions began crossing the border. In the meantime, armored troops from bases in Lithuania rushed to the capital city and other strategic locations to prevent organized Lithuanian resistance. Thus Stalin had his *Blitz*.

At that time, Europeans had not yet learned that Soviet occupation involved changes of larger proportions than just the formation of a pro-Soviet government and the drafting of policies friendlier to the Kremlin. It is clear from the discussions in the last meeting of the independent Lithuania's Council of Ministers that many political leaders still had hopes of preserving a semblance of Lithuanian statehood, not to speak of the essentials of the social system. For at least two or three weeks this view was shared by segments of Lithuanian society. This illusion made it easier for the Soviets to destroy independent statehood without provoking open resistance.[20] Five months later, the Lithuanian Communist Party's secretary, Antanas Sniečkus (1903-1974), suggested that open opposition was prevented not only by this political disorientation but also by the suddenness of events and the disbelief that in only seven weeks Lithuania could find itself completely absorbed by the Soviet Union.[21] Soviet historians and politicians refer to this period as a peaceful Socialist revolution, a transition from capitalism to socialism, led by the Lithuanian Communist party.[22] The summer indeed was relatively quiet, if arrests and police persecution are discounted, but at the most, the period can be termed a synthetic revolution, led not by the clandestine Communist party which at that time had barely between 1,350 and 1,700 members,[23] but by the Kremlin through its plenipotentiary, Vladimir G. Dekanozov, the Deputy Commissar of Foreign Affairs. He was sent to Kaunas to direct "the revolution," better to say, to manage the process of incorporation of Lithuania into the Soviet state.

Dekanozov's immediate objective was a smooth seizure of the state apparatus and the staging of elections to a new Diet. This Diet was expected to petition the Kremlin for Lithuania's admission to the Soviet Union. In this manner a legal formula would be produced that would justify the Kremlin's occupation and absorption of Lithuania.

Since the ideas of incorporation and sovietization were alien and even scary to most of the Lithuanian population, including its non-Communist Left, the Kremlin did not advertise them. The newly-legalized Communist party did not list these objectives among its immediate political goals either.[24] These ideas, furthermore, were conspicuously absent from the platform of the Union of the Working People of Lithuania that sponsored the single list of candidates for election to the puppet "people's Diet."[25] Thus the elections did not serve as a referendum on the question of joining the Soviet Union, though they were organized exactly for that purpose.

Lithuania's President Antanas Smetona correctly foresaw that the Soviets would use him for giving the cloak of legality to their actions[26] and left the country for Germany, from where, within a year, through Switzerland and Brazil, he reached the United States. However, before departing, Smetona signed an authorization for the Prime Minister, Antanas Merkys (1887–1955), to act in his absence. This was a legal constitutional act.[27] Merkys, however, obliged Dekanozov by stretching this constitutional provision and signing the appointment of a "people's government," chaired by a pro-Soviet journalist Justas Paleckis (b. 1899). Merkys did not have a constitutional right to do so. The fact that Paleckis was not known as a party member suited the situation. The people's cabinet included two prominent men, a former Prime Minister, the politically independent Ernestas Galvanauskas (1882–1967), and the well-known and liked Lithuanian writer, Vincas Krėvė-Mickevičius (1882–1954), who had a Leftist reputation. At the beginning, the cabinet did not include formally known Communists, though the situation changed within days. Similarly, Justas Paleckis, within hours, assumed the position of acting president because Merkys was forced to resign. Smetona's authorization of course was not valid for Paleckis, but this was a small detail from the Soviet point of view. Merkys was removed from the scene altogether: Paleckis signed papers consenting to his deportation to the Soviet Union.[28]

As noted earlier, until the Kremlin's plans became better visible, the "people's government" enjoyed some non-Communist support. President Smetona had run an authoritarian regime that many disliked, and therefore individual Social Democrats, Populists and even Christian Democrats did not see an irretrievable loss in the collapse of Smetona's Nationalist rule.[29] On the contrary, some intellectuals, for example, Vincas Krėvė-Mickevičius, the new Deputy Prime Minister and Foreign Minister, even hoped for opportunities of making new democratic beginnings. Such expectations, of course, were totally unfounded. Within a week it became clear to the non-Communist members of the government that they functioned but as a window dressing for the Kremlin's pro-consul Dekanozov. This discovery so perturbed Krėvė-Mickevičius that he flew to Moscow to denounce Molotov's deputy. Your man, Dekanozov, Krėvė-Mickevičius complained to the Soviet Foreign Minister, interfered in Lithuania's domestic politics.[30] On June 30th, Molotov explained to the well-intentioned, but naive writer that the Kremlin's emissary acted as told, that small nations would disappear, that the future of the world belonged to Communism and that Lithuania would be incorporated into the Soviet Union.[31] After hearing this, Krėvė-Mickevičius sought to resign. His Communist colleagues, however, would not let him because they still needed the use of his prestige with the Lithuanian intelligentsia. Finally, he was given a leave of absence for health reasons but his name was kept on the roster of ministers. Krėvė's colleague, Ernestas Galvanauskas, also resigned, and moreover, fled the country. Krėvė left only in 1944.

The elections to the people's Diet were set for July 14th, just eight days after the promulgation of the new electoral law. Actually, the balloting continued for two days, the 14th and the 15th. The Kremlin, it appeared, had designated July 14th–15th for elections in Estonia and Latvia, and the Lithuanians had to comply. A twofold preparation was made for this event in Lithuania. On the one hand, the Communists neutralized possible opposition; on the other, they passed control of the electoral process to the Communist party.

Thus, the Soviets immediately secured the direction of the administrative apparatus and the army, eliminated non-Communist public organizations, and purged the most conspicuous anti-Communist leaders and administrators. The purge began on June 18th. It was conducted by the Lithuanian Communist Party's first secretary, Antanas Sniečkus, just released from prison and appointed director of the Security Department in the Ministry of the Interior. There he worked with the help of NKVD experts from Moscow and collaborated with the new Minister of the Interior, Mečys Gedvilas (b. 1901), an experienced undercover Communist and Russian sympathizer who now fronted for the party secretary. On June 19th, they suppressed the ruling Nationalist party; on June 27th, closed down all organizations that had been licensed by Smetona's government — among them many non-political associations and Catholic societies — and on July 1st, dissolved the Nationalist Diet *(seimas)*. The Communist party was legalized on June 25th, and after the outlawing of other organizations became the sole legal political force in the country.[32] On the night of July 11th–12th, that is, just two days before the elections, Sniečkus' agency arrested some 2,000 national and community leaders to prevent the possibility of organized opposition to the electoral masquerade.[33] Potential voters were further intimidated by the announcement that passports would be stamped at the polling places.

On July 6th, the people's government finally overcame Krėvė's opposition and passed the election law to set in motion the electoral organization. As in the Soviet Union, candidates were to be nominated in mass meetings to be sponsored by electoral commissions. This provision of the law (Part III, Art. 20) and the interpretation by the Supreme Electoral Commission that only newly licensed organizations had the right to nominate candidates[34] actually put the entire nominating process in the hands of the Communist party; however, the party did not run candidates under its own label. Instead, it organized a coalition of the Union of the Working People of Lithuania, a bogus alliance consisting of the Communist party, the Bureau of the Trade Unions, the Society of Freethinkers — a miniscule group — and the Tenants' Association that in independent Lithuania had acted as a Communist front in the republic's larger cities. This Union offered a single list of candidates that consisted only of Communists and fellow travellers.

Elections took place as scheduled, without major interference or disturbance, and in cities, though not in small towns and villages, attracted long lines of voters; many came to get a stamp on their passports. The reported results showed that 99.51% of all eligible voters actually cast ballots, and of those 99.16% voted for the single list of candidates of the Union of the Working People of Lithuania.[35] The percentages were unrealistic; the ballot boxes were stuffed. Moscow's purpose nevertheless was achieved.

The Diet met the next Sunday, July 21st, and in its three-day session, proclaimed what already had been a reality since June 15th, namely, the existence of Soviet power; Lithuania was declared a Soviet Socialist Republic.[36] In the next breath, the Diet asked the Supreme Soviet of the Soviet Union for admission to the Soviet federation.[37] A delegation was chosen to go to Moscow to bring back to Lithuania, as newspapers then heralded, "the sun of Stalin's constitution."[38] On August 3rd, the Supreme Soviet, on Belorussian motion, approved the Diet's petition and thus completed the string of formalities that certified Lithuania's "legal" annexation by the Soviet Union.[39] In the West, the vote of the Diet on July 21st, as well as the processes by which it was organized, were well understood. The *New York Times* editorially commented that the Baltic elections of July 14th–15th were "a travesty of democracy" that excelled "any of Hitler's notorious plebiscites in Germany."[40] The English government was "saddened" by the demise of Baltic independence,[41] while in Washington the Department of State, even before the final act was played in Moscow's Supreme Soviet, charged that Lithuanian, Latvian, and Estonian independence was "deliberately annihilated" by "devious processes."[42] President Roosevelt refused to recognize the legality of Lithuania's incorporation into the Soviet Union. This non-recognition policy has been continued by all subsequent administrations in Washington, by the Vatican, by Canada and several other nations.

The Catholics and the Commissars: The First Experiences

Nothing showed better the linkage between religious and national freedoms than the collapse of Lithuania as an independent nation. The country's sovietization not only radically changed its political and social structure, but also essentially altered the relationship between the church and the state.

It is important to stress a frequently overlooked fact, namely, that the Kremlin considered the containment of the Catholic church only very slightly less important than the seizure of the state apparatus or the control of the armed forces. The new rulers, therefore, proceeded to act within ten days after their installation in power. The government took its cue from the Communist party, which in its very first statement on June 25th demanded the separation of church and state. "Our goal is to put into practice the real freedom of conscience," the Party declared. "Let the believers believe, but the nonbelievers should not be forced to study religion, marry in church, be baptized, or pay for the support of the church."[1] This did not sound like a program of persecution but rather secularization which had been needlessly delayed in Catholic Lithuania against considerable opposition, and the Party therefore could expect support for this policy. Indeed, the exact Communist attitude toward the Catholic church — though it later emerged as very hostile — could not be determined at the time. After the rise of Nazism in Germany, the Kremlin no longer regarded Catholicism as its number one enemy.[2] Contacts were sought with Catholic intellectuals and politicals through "popular front" policies designed to stem the Fascist tide.[3] Communists began infiltrating Catholic organizations. Yet in the summer of 1940, the Kremlin formed an alliance with Hitler, the high priest of Fascism, and in Lithuania the Communists no longer competed for influence but were in complete command. Would "popular front" attitudes still color their relations with the Catholic church in the first Roman Catholic country the

Kremlin had absorbed? Or would the Communists seek outright to destroy the Church as they had done in the Soviet Union?

Soviet Secularization of Society

At the time, Soviet behavior was not easily predictable. The Vatican, familiar with Soviet enmity of religion from the experiences of Uniate and Latin Catholics in the recently occupied Western Poland, had no illusions about the proposed secularization and took no chances. On the very day, June 25th, Papal Nunzio Luigi Centoz cabled to the Vatican for the same special faculties that earlier the Pope had conferred on the bishops in the Russian-annexed Poland.[4] Cardinal Maglione immediately consented to the request.

The use of these emergency powers, however, was not immediately necessary. The measures of "secularization," though numerous and quick, were not violent,[5] were not designed to drive the church underground, but to exclude it from society. The separation of church from school and public institutions, declared the same day the Communist party called for action, was followed by a Cabinet decision on June 26th to abrogate the concordat with the Vatican. The Holy See, it seems, was not immediately informed. The Nunzio was asked to the Foreign Ministry only on July 3rd, and the Lithuanian Minister in the Vatican handed the note of abrogation to the Secretary of State, Cardinal Maglione, only on July 5th. Nunzio Centoz was told that the ties between church and state in Lithuania were not "normal" and that the concordat represented an obstacle to the establishment of "suitable" relations. Pijus Glovackas, the new secretary general in the Ministry, counseled the Nunzio and the Lithuanian hierarchy to "understand the new situation" and "to adjust to it."[6] Centoz himself was immediately deprived of an apartment and of office facilities and was given until August 25th to leave the country.

By the time the Vatican was officially notified of the severance of relations, the pro-Communist Lithuanian government had already innundated the country with decrees designed not merely to cut the Church's ties with the state, but also to curtail the rights of religion altogether. The list of these measures shows how deeply the Catholic faith had penetrated Lithuania's public life and how intimately the Church had influenced the work of state institutions. Thus, on June 27th, the Ministry of Education struck religious instruction from the school curriculum and dismissed school chaplains. At the same time, the Ministry outlawed prayers and religious symbols in all school buildings. On June 28th, the Ministry of Defense curtailed the jurisdiction of military chaplains and on July 2nd, fired them. On July 1st, the same Ministry banished the traditional military evening ceremonies that had a partly religious character. Furthermore, on the same day the government stopped paying salaries and pensions to clergymen. The numerous private schools and nurseries that in Lithuania were sponsored mostly by Catholic religious orders and by Jewish organizations were formally taken over on August 24th. The School of Catholic Theology and Philosophy at the University of Kaunas was "suspended" on July 16th, a day after the elections to the people's Diet. Its faculty was fired on August 19th, and had difficulty finding new positions. Nuns who sought employment in public nurseries were sincerely advised "to get married first."[7] Generally, however, a number of priests and nuns were rehired for school work to teach secular subjects. This was one of the very few instances of the temporary *modus vivendi* that was tacitly established between the new authorities and the Church.

This list of anti-religious measures cannot be completed without noting several other important decrees. While religious organizations were outlawed on June 27th, religiously-oriented publications were kept under new management for the seven weeks of the "peaceful revolution" to promote the elections to the Diet. Better to say, they were continued to disorient the Catholic readers. On July 19th, the government issued an edict that prohibited any publication not licensed by the Ministry of the Interior and not previously screened by censorship.[8] This spelled out the death of all Catholic publications, with the exception of the daily *XX Amžius* (The Twentieth Century) that, under a new editorship since July 8th, folded only on August 1st. Furthermore, on August 15th, the government promulgated a law of civil marriage that not only instituted civil registration but also abolished the legality of the religious ceremony. Divorce was also legalized, though at the same time the Communist party declared itself an "enemy of loose family morals."[9] On the same day, the Ministry of Justice took over the registration of births, deaths and weddings. Half a year later, all these records were transferred to the Central State Archives, and documents issued by the churches after January 1st, 1941, were declared invalid.[10] Abolition of religious holidays followed on October 11th.

Secularization of marriage and the work calendar was complemented by discriminatory social and economic legislation. The new regime, it soon appeared, had ready made prescriptions for dealing with the Church, but delayed administering medicine for fear of provoking or losing the acquiescence of the Catholic masses. For example, already, on July 2nd, the Director of the Land Reform Office publicly announced that the government would confiscate all parish and monastery lands.[11] However, within hours, another government controlled paper denounced this intention as well as other proposed confiscations as "an invented and provocative information."[12] The director was fired. This reaction apparently stemmed from the fear by actual decision makers that such premature revelation of the future social order would alienate the Catholic Lithuanian population, most of which — about 75 percent — lived on farms. This would make it more difficult to play the game of "democratic" elections. When the land reform ultimately was adopted, however, it showed that on the whole, the announcement of July 2nd was correct. In the case of church properties, the director had been absolutely precise.

All landholdings were nationalized on July 22nd.[13] The Diet left up to thirty hectares (66 acres) for "perpetual use" to those farmers who owned and worked it. The remaining land was collected into a state fund and distributed to the landless or kept for governmental purposes. The reason for this questionable distribution — a radical land reform had been executed in Lithuania in 1923 — was not economic but strictly political. In this way, the Soviets attempted to buy adherents among the landless and the poorer village groups. They also sought to ruin the average farmsteader, the mainstay of Lithuanian village society, in preparation for future collectivization of agriculture. Finally, this kind of distribution — taking some acres of land from one neighbor and donating them to another — was designed to promote social divisiveness, the so-called "class struggle" in the village.

According to a law of August 5th, the 66-acre allowance did not apply to religious institutions.[14] The government confiscated all the land held by monasteries and convents. The parishes were allowed to keep only one-tenth of the regular norm, namely 6.6 acres. Since these acres had to include church and parish premises, the parish pastor was left no arable land to speak of. Expropriated church possessions constituted only 3.2 percent of the newly formed land fund, but it represented over 90 percent of the total owned by all church institutions.[15] Nationalization of housing that was ordered on October 31st hit the Church in a similar fashion, so that actually all church housing was taken over. In addition, priests who were allowed to rent the parish houses that the Church had previously owned were required to pay higher rents than the other citizens.

Passage of such laws indicated that a mere separation of church and state was not the final objective of the Communist regime. The goal and the scope of the early Soviet secularization was further revealed by the Communist treatment of the clergy. At first, when the Kremlin still paid attention to public opinion, the Communists generally left the clergy alone. The press extolled the achievements of the Soviet Union, especially of its nationality policies, but refrained from discussing religion or interpreting Soviet religious legislation. Occasional outbursts that occurred against the clergy had no material consequences as yet.[16]

On July 7th, the new Minister of Education, Antanas Venclova, a Leftist writer, ridiculed the prediction that the Soviets would suppress religion and the clergy: "People said that the churches will be closed and the priests knifed, but we see that this is not true."[17] This, however, changed with Lithuania's formal incorporation into the Soviet Union. On August 28th, *Darbo Lietuva* (Labor Lithuania), the official government newspaper, accused the clergy of conducting "anti-people agitation" and warned that "the smell of the Middle Ages" will not be tolerated in Socialist Lithuania. The Church shall not regain its previous position, the newspaper said, and "the clergy must, in good faith, show an understanding for the essential requirements of the new life."[18] On October 2nd, Deputy Commissar of Internal Affairs Gladkov — a mysterious secret police officer from Moscow whose origins, including his first name, never became known — issued an order "to take the clergy into formal accounting."[19] In concrete terms, Gladkov wanted to recruit informers and through them to create dissension among the clergy and also between the clergy and the Catholic population. Secret police began intensively recruiting clergymen, students, and church servants, though at that time, their efforts apparently yielded negligible results. Three months later, on January 21st, 1941, Commissar of Internal Affairs A. Guzevičius issued another instruction. This one requested secret police agencies to take complete inventory of all churches, clergy, and all religious organizations, defunct or yet in existence. The order applied to all denominations. The commissar, furthermore, demanded information about internal conflict, difficulties and needs of individual clergymen. He finally sought more detailed background data about the already-recruited clerical and secular informers. Guzevičius acted on orders from Moscow that already was preparing "a plan of available means that operative agencies could use concerning the believers in the newly established Soviet republics."[20]

Such actions indicated the government's presumption that the churches were endemically hostile to the regime. This attitude was confirmed by a secret order of October 27th that was issued to district agencies of the NKVD: Guzevičius' Deputy B. Baranauskas ordered police readiness for the All Souls evening of November 2nd, the traditional Lithuanian commemoration of the dead. The need for the alert was justified by the speculation — unfounded as it was — that "the clergy doubtlessly will endeavor to use the occasion for agitation, for anti-Soviet outbursts, for distribution of counterrevolutionary leaflets, etc."[21] On November 28th, Commissar Guzevičius, in still another classified order, demanded action against "Nationalist anti-revolutionary elements," but especially the clergy, who were again expected to use the forthcoming Christmas celebrations for "hostile" anti-Soviet propaganda.[22]

Active police supervision of the clergy, it should be added, generally began only after Lithuania's formal incorporation into the Soviet Union. During the twelve months of Communist rule, some 150 priests, that is, about 10 percent of Lithuania's clergy, were interrogated by the secret police, pressured into spying on their colleagues and parishioners or intimidated to refrain from privately teaching religion.[23] Of these clergy, the NKVD successfully recruited three informers. Twenty-four priests were arrested and imprisoned until the beginning of the German-Soviet war; eighteen came out alive. Fifteen additional priests were killed — some tortured — by the withdrawing Communist activists or the military. Nine were deported to Siberia.[24] Together with the Vilnius diocese, the total number of imprisoned priests was 39, the number killed was 21. In May of 1941, these figures seemed to be atrociously high, but in comparison to mass deportations that began on June 14th–15th, they were a drop in the ocean.

The Search for Peaceful Coexistence

The Communist aim completely to eliminate the Church from societal life emerged even more clearly in the government's response to the Catholic hierarchy's search for peaceful coexistence with the new order. As suggested earlier, the thrust of Communist policies toward religion was predictable, but the goal of hermetically isolating it from society was not known to Lithuanian Catholics, many of whom did not believe it altogether. At the time of Lithuania's occupation, Catholic opinions were divided.[25] Some intellectuals considered that Lithuania would more easily survive a Soviet than a German occupation because the Russians were a less culturally developed and disciplined people. Still others thought that Communism had changed and that the revolutionary terror and anti-religious policies would not be repeated in Lithuania, at least not in the same acid form. The Church, these people argued, should therefore not despair, but adopt new methods of pastoral work. The main Catholic daily, *XX Amžius,* as if anticipating the use of violence by the Soviets, suggested an "ideological disarmament," and if a struggle, then a competition of ideas without the use of force.[26] The article, penned by Stasys Yla, Professor of Theology, who soon had to flee the Soviets and whom the Nazis later sent to the Stutthoff concentration camp, was actually written and published earlier and referred to peaceful competition of ideas under Smetona's regime. Now, however, it fit the situation much better, and was provocatively reprinted on June 24th, just before the imposition of absolute Communist censorship. On that day, there apparently still was a drop of hope left that some kind of peaceful coexistence between Communism and Catholicism would be possible. It seemed that the appreciation or concern the Catholics conspicuously showed for the "working class" and for social reform might establish a common ground with the Communists and might buy Soviet admission of the positive role religion played in public life.[27] Another editorial writer of this Catholic daily sought to discover further mutual interest by criticizing Smetona's authoritarian system and voicing hope that the new pro-Communist government would concentrate primarily on economic and social reform, the kind of progressive change that the younger generation of Catholic intellectuals had been promoting before Lithuania's collapse.[28]

In individual instances, furthermore, Catholic leaders sought direct communication with the dominant Communist personalities. Shortly after Paleckis became acting president, the Rev. Mykolas Krupavičius, a Christian Democratic co-author of the Lithuanian land reform of 1922, attempted contacts with Paleckis, Gedvilas, and the Communist party secretary, Karolis Didžiulis-Grosmanas (1894–1958). In approaching Paleckis, the Christian Democratic leader is said to have wanted to encourage the new president to maintain independence in relations with the Soviets.[29]

But Paleckis and his friends were instruments of the Kremlin, and all these gestures and feelers, even if they did not have self-serving motives, were doomed to failure. After June 25th, it became clear to the discerning minds that there would come a radical and violent change of the social order and ideology that dominated in independent Lithuania. On the next day, *XX Amžius* already strongly implied that "national values" were in great danger. Dr. Ignas Skrupskėlis (1903–

1942), the daily's chief editorial writer, shortly afterwards arrested and deported by the Soviets, urged the new rulers, though they be Communists, to protect national traditions and nationality itself. They should be preserved as much, he said, as the Russians had preserved theirs under Soviet rule. "In the whirl of today's events," Skrupskelis wrote, "we should not forget what is specifically our own. Healthy national self-esteem demands it, the heritage of our fathers demands it; it is a duty to the future of our nation and of our state."[30]

All of these matters were considered by the episcopal conference of July 2nd–3rd, 1940. The bishops spoke cautiously. In the concluding statement, they neither actively endorsed the "people's government" nor acquiesced in the measures of "secularization" that, by then, had already cut the Church from the school and had undermined it financially. However, the bishops did not voice opposition either. They merely "took note" of the basic changes in government. The conference acknowledged the new government's professed aim to serve the interests of the working people and declared that the Catholic church in Lithuania had always been doing the same. The Lithuanian clergy, the bishops said, were of working class origins and understood very well that "material poverty represented one of the main causes of spiritual poverty." On the question of new methods, the bishops expressed the view that it was not "necessary to change the basic direction of the clergy's activities." In this way, the hierarchy rejected the optimistic assumption by some Catholics that Communist views toward religion had changed. Instead, the bishops insisted on strengthening the clerical apostolate and, tongue in cheek, expressed happiness over the fact that now there were "more people [meaning the pro-Communist government] who were pledged to work for the welfare of the workers."[31]

But the Church's wish to be left alone in pastoral work was granted only temporarily and, furthermore, only very sparingly. The people's government did not obstruct the nomination, on July 9th, and consecration, on August 4th, of Msgr. Vincentas Padolskis (1904–1960) as a new auxiliary bishop for the diocese of Vilkaviškis nor the elevation and transfer, again on July 9th, of Auxiliary Bishop Mečislovas Reinys from Vilkaviškis to Vilnius where he would serve with the title of Archbishop under the Polish Ordinary Archbishop Romuald Jałbrzykowski.[32] On the other hand, Soviet authorities rejected Archbishop Skvireckas' request to leave more agricultural land for the parishes and monasteries and to distribute only what was left over 17.6 acres (8 hectares). Skvireckas wanted this remainder to go to civilian church servants and to institutions that helped the indigent and the needy.[33] The authorities similarly disregarded Bishop Brizgys' petition to leave limited acreage to convents on grounds that the nuns had acquired the property by the sweat of their work.[34] But on the other hand, already after Lithuania's formal incorporation into the Soviet Union, the Communists sanctioned the work of the archdiocesan theological seminary in Kaunas.[35] The school freely admitted 180 students. The other seminary that used Polish as a language of instruction was allowed to continue in Vilnius. Yet at the same time the authorities kept the remaining two seminaries (Telšiai and Vilkaviškis) closed by using their facilities for the quartering of Red Army troops. The Council of Commissars at first did not oppose the teaching of religion in the churches either, although Commissar of Education Venclova never answered Bishop Brizgys' request of free school time to students who wanted to learn about religion "on their own initiative."[36] In a manner very reminiscent of the most recent Soviet practice, the Commissar failed to answer other petitions for religious instruction on school time that were submitted to him from various parts of the country.[37] However, personal contacts with Mečys Gedvilas, then the Chairman of the People's Commissars, were regarded by the hierarchs as satisfactory. Orally, Gedvilas permitted the work of the Kaunas theological seminary and also wrote a letter that granted the seminary buildings immunity from sequestration by the government. Similarly, the authorities exchanged Lt 10,000 (old Lithuanian currency) into rubles for the seminary's needs.[38] On September 17th, the same Gedvilas promised to consider the hierarchy's request for the publication of a Catholic bulletin.[39]

In this atmosphere, Rev. Mykolas Krupavičius wrote a memorandum to the authorities in which he explained the Church's old concern with social reform and suggested Catholic willingness to work for social improvements under the Soviet system, provided the government would reciprocate by granting conditions for pastoral work.[40] Contents of this memorandum had been agreed upon by Church dignitaries who attended the consecration of Bishop Padolskis on August 4th. Vatican Nunzio Msgr. Luigi Centoz was also among them. Thus, the memorandum represented an attempt of a dialogue with the Communists. In the perspective of a generation, this proposal was judged as an effort of delaying the Church's persecution by the Kremlin. This objective, of course, may have dominated the thoughts of its authors. In the fall of 1941, however, its immediate objective certainly was more concrete. It must have been written in hope of some accommodation with the authorities.

The government, however, never answered this memorandum. Instead, Krupavičius began receiving visits from a "journalist" in Moscow who started hinting at a need of establishing a "progressive" Catholic church that would center around Bishop Kazimieras Paltarokas, well known for his reformist social views. The Soviets apparently interpreted Krupavičius' statement as exposing a wedge between "conservative" and "progressive" clergy that could be exploited for the splitting up of Lithuanian Catholics.

On the whole, the Lithuanian hierarchy's attitude toward the Communist rulers was conciliatory, though firm and confident. Reports Bishop Brizgys was able to smuggle to the Vatican were very factual. The bishop spoke, furthermore, of surviving courage and a "realistic but not pessimistic" spirit among the clergy.[41] In self-defense against charges of meddling in politics, the hierarchy was not only willing, but also anxious, to stay out of affairs traditionally regarded as secular, though they may have strongly disliked many of these secular policies. For example, the bishops insisted that religion teachers in the widely spread after-school network clearly distinguish between Communism as economic theory, on the one hand, and political ideology on the other. In this way, the hierarchy wanted to eliminate from religion classes any discussion of the radically Socialist economic system the new authorities had introduced, and also to show that they were concerned only with the matters of faith. Their view was that "Communism as an economic system has nothing to do with atheism."[42]

The bishops thus pressed ahead with religious apostolate while avoiding direct confrontation, but most of all, they sought not to provoke the authorities into any rash hostility. For this reason, on January 9th, 1941, Bishop Brizgys, Auxiliary of the Archbishop of Kaunas, asked the Vatican to refrain from commenting on the Lithuanian situation over the newly started Vatican radio broadcasts in the Lithuanian language. Information the radio broadcast, the bishop said, frequently was incorrect.[43] Brizgys sent his request through private channels — the Soviets had cut direct communications with the Vatican and the outside world — and addressed it therefore to the nearest Papal Nunzio, namely, Msgr. Cezare Orsenigo, in Berlin. To stress the importance of this matter, Brizgys repeated the request through Karl Fulst, a German Jesuit who, for many years, had worked in Lithuania and who, in 1941, was able to leave as a repatriating German national. In this message that Fulst related to Orsenigo, Brizgys explained that the Lithuanians appreciated radio information about Catholic life in the world because such information otherwise was not available. "But the broadcasts on conditions in Soviet Lithuania," the bishop said, "that until now were almost always false or distorted, do not help us at all. Most of all, we ask you not to broadcast any anti-Bolshevik propaganda (lectures on Marxism, Leninism, jokes, etc.) . . . Propaganda is absolutely unnecessary because the daily life here is the best anti-Bolshevik propaganda. Such broadcasts merely incite state authorities and, as many sad experiences have shown, hurt the already repressed Church very much."[44]

The Bolsheviks Tighten the Ring

The relative tolerance that the authorities displayed toward the Church until the end of September was not caused by the change in Moscow's long-range plans for the Church, but by the regime's preoccupation with radical economic reforms and with immediate political difficulties in Lithuania.

In four months of Soviet rule, the country's economic situation had worsened to a considerable degree; production went down, shops were empty, wages could not catch up to the prices. Furthermore, political opposition, at first stultified into immobility by the lightning speed of the Soviet onslaught, regained composure. At the same time, the Communists failed to win enough new friends to squelch dissatisfaction. The new land reform, for example, did not produce the expected adherents to the new regime. Again, the promise of administrative reincorporation of an Eastern Lithuanian district that Stalin had refused to transfer to Lithuania on October 10th, 1939, did not soothe deeply hurt nationalist sentiments.[45] Introduction, on December 1st, of free medical care, furthermore, failed to compensate people for shortages in stores and for the rising arbitrariness of the secret police. "We know," party secretary Antanas Sniečkus publicly said on November 6th, that "the class enemy is spreading rumors that the Soviet rule will be destroyed and that the Soviet Union will be sucked into the war. Chauvinism, anti-Semitism, and various gossips are spreading; the priests are trying to scare people into refusing to vote for the anti-Christ, etc."[46] Chairman of the Commissars Mečys Gedvilas frankly discussed the situation during the festivities of the October revolution. He distinguished four reasons for popular discontent: apprehension about the future of Lithuanian national culture and national identity, the fear of religious persecution, rejection and discrimination of the Lithuanian intelligentsia, and economic difficulties that were exemplified especially by the rising prices. "The critics say," Gedvilas told his audience, "that the Bolsheviks will erase God." However, the Commissar insisted, "our constitution guarantees freedom of conscience to every citizen. No one is conspiring to transform good Catholics into atheists."[47]

Although Gedvilas enjoyed a relatively good reputation with the leaders of the Church, his assurances brought little, if any, comfort. First, his speech was widely interpreted as propaganda for the upcoming elections to the Supreme Soviet of the USSR. Second, the belief was forming that he did not have any autonomy in policy making, but merely implemented Moscow's dictates. Therefore, it was assumed that Gedvilas could not contain, even if he wanted, the rising government harassment of the Church that after the opening of schools in September became part of the country's daily life. Such appraisal of the chairman, while it contained the basic truth about Moscow's power, appeared still too optimistic concerning Gedvilas' own disposition. On September 8th, together with the Estonian and Latvian government leaders, Gedvilas was told by Stalin in the Kremlin that they must be "wise" but "firm" with their people.[48] After treating the Balts with a long midnight dinner, richly supplemented with toasts of vodka, Stalin stressed the need of firmness by showing a clenched fist and pausing in the middle of the sentence to give the word "firmness" a special emphasis. From this, Gedvilas and the other Balts knew that the honeymoon with the real or alleged opponents of Soviet power was over. The three republics were considered firmly absorbed and the time for dealing with the possible opposition had arrived. Consequently, after returning home, Gedvilas "wisely" misled church hierarchs about the possibilities of a *modus vivendi* for which the Kremlin had no desire.

In October, almost at the very time Gedvilas was verbally assuring the country that the Soviets opposed neither nationality nor religion, the authorities destroyed thousands of copies of the earlier printed catechism for children. Its distribution had been held up by the incoming Communist authorities. The bishops were especially incensed over this event because the government had promised that a prepayment for the printing and the binding would release the catechism for public use. They felt deceived by the man they had trusted.

Soon afterward, Lithuanian authorities acquired new legal instrumentalities for further limiting the work of all religious denominations. On December 1st, the code of laws of Socialist Lithuania was replaced by the code of the Russian Republic.[49] On questions of religious freedom, the Russian laws were incomparably stricter than anything that was promulgated by the Communists of Lithuania. The clergy began to feel the weight of the new regulations in a very brief time. From January 1st, the Church could not issue any legal document. It was, in other words, formally deprived of the rights of legal person, as the Russian law required. The next jolt came immediately after the Supreme Soviet elections of January 12th.

While on January 11th the new Soviet Ambassador to Berlin, Vladimir Dekanozov, the man who "revolutionized" Lithuania, was personally assuring Nunzio Orsenigo that the situation of the Church in the Baltic republics had remained "unaltered,"[50] Soviet authorities in Kaunas dispersed the theological seminary. Its students were on vacation through election day, but when they returned, they found the seminary building taken over by the Red Army. The written exemption that Gedvilas had signed in September did not help. The authorities intimated that the building was taken over because the students did not return to vote on January 12th; it appeared, however, that the order of sequestration was issued already on January 8th.[51] It was not signed by Gedvilas, but by the bureaucrats of the city administration of Kaunas. Higher authorities professed innocence. Bishops Brizgys and Borisevičius went to see N. G. Pozdniakov, the former Soviet Minister in Lithuania who continued as the central government's proconsul in the republic, but found no encouragement. Pozdniakov angrily criticized the bishops for not arranging the seminarians' vote in the elections and furthermore, told them to stop religious instruction in the churches. In church buildings, the Kremlin's representative said, you should not do anything that you did not do under the old regime. The bishops refused to comply, explaining that the two situations were not comparable. In independent Lithuania, religion classes were offered at schools, and thus there was no need to use the churches for teaching it. Since now the state did not allow religious studies in public buildings, churches had to be used. Pozdniakov considered this a useless circumvention of the legal prohibition of religion teaching. He advised Bishop Brizgys, the younger of the two men, to consider a secular profession because "what was achieved in Russia in twenty years will be accomplished in Lithuania in two or three." He further counselled the bishops gracefully to accept the imminent destruction of the church's apostolate because "neither Hitler, the Pope, nor Roosevelt will be able to wrestle you away from us."[52]

The seminarians found lodgings in private homes, and the academic year continued in makeshift auditoriums in the city. Pozdniakov, however, clearly served notice that both the seminary and religious instruction would have to go.

Religious education became the immediate target. In their July 2nd–3rd, 1940, and August 28th–29th, 1940, meetings, the bishop had stressed the need of continuing it "in any possible way."[53] High schools were assigned unofficial chaplains whose main duty was to organize religious instruction in churches or in private homes. Attendance at such religious classes was extremely high, and since it frustrated the already beginning atheist indoctrination, this educational activity soon incurred Communist wrath. The authorities began to seek ways of destroying it. Thus started the intimidation of the teachers. Individual priests would be invited first by the secret police and then by local government functionaries to sign promises not to give religious instruction.[54] Such action had the appearance of a locally-contrived arbitrariness by some overzealous Communist bureaucrat. As the Lithuanians would understand it years later, it was not. The new Russian law, generally unknown to the population, required suppression. Its enforcement, however, was disguised so there would be no written record of centrally issued instructions. Thirty years later, local authorities would be formally entrusted with the supervision of local churches and clergymen. By 1940, local governments already had such authority in the Soviet Union. It was now tested in Lithuania. However, it created too much opposition and was temporarily abandoned.

In their meeting of April 24th, the bishops found the Church's situation quite different from what it had been at the beginning of the Soviet regime. In this last conference that the bishops held before the temporary interruption of Soviet rule, the hierarchs compiled a list of grievances and, in May, handed it to Pozdniakov and Gedvilas, the Muscovite and the Lithuanian representatives of the Kremlin.[55] Specifically, the bishops charged the government with the violation of three articles of the Soviet Lithuanian constitution. These were Art. 99, 96, and 95 that respectively guaranteed inviolability of person, freedom of conscience, and equality of citizenship. The bishops noted that twenty-four clergymen were imprisoned without anyone knowing the charges against them. Some of these priests, the bishops further said, were simply kidnapped from the street and disappeared into the darkness. This was the fate, for example, of the popular Jesuit Father Jonas Bružikas, who survived the ordeal to tell about his secret incarceration. Arrested Catholic laymen, the bishops continued, were not allowed to keep religious devotionals; similarly, they could not receive the sacraments. The priests were forbidden to visit not only prisons but also hospitals. They could not come even if invited to the death bed to administer the sacrament of extreme unction. Religious literature was banned from these institutions.

The bishops further demanded that the authorities stop the harassment of the clergy, especially the earlier noted pressure to withdraw from teaching religion. At the same time, Church leaders protested efforts by the Ministry of Education to force religiously-minded teachers to preach atheist propaganda in the schools. The bishops' list of complaints also included denial of religious, even of liturgical literature, sequestration of academic and living quarters, and a protest against financial discrimination of the clergy. The priests, the memorandum explained, were charged forty percent higher income tax than the rest of the citizens.

The memorandum ended with nine requests that could be summarized as demanding freedom from administrative arbitrariness, liberty to exercise religious apostolate, and finally, equality with the atheists in all matters, including the use of media of communications. The bishops confidently stressed that their statement represented the views of "an absolute majority of Lithuania's population." For this reason, they expressed hope that their petition would be granted.

The Soviets, however, completely disregarded this memorandum, without hedging or hints of future consideration as they had done in the past. In addition, Bishops Borisevičius and Kukta, who delivered the letter, were told that the seminary in Kaunas would no longer be tolerated and that it would have to close down with the expiration of the academic year, that is, in June.[56] The hierarchy, however, temporarily withheld this information from the students and the population so as not to create panic or destroy hope.

Thus, for the Church, the first year of Soviet rule ended on a very pessimistic note. But it was even worse for the country. Early on June 14th, NKVD troops, aided by local Communist officials, began rounding up marked families; they were packed into railroad freight cars for exile from Lithuania. By the time these troops were rudely interrupted on the morning of June 22nd, they had arrested over 34,000 people and shipped them to labor camps in the Altai region, the Novosibirsk and Karelian districts, Kazakhstan and Komi ASSR.[57] Neither expectant mothers nor the sick nor children were exempted from deportation. The ranks of the deportees included members of politically and socially unreliable groups, from Catholic to Marxist, and certain social classes, mainly the more prosperous farmers, businessmen, and community leaders. Clergymen, generally, were spared. Their turn came in later years.

This deportation was the most massive of the "prophylactic measures," in Chairman Gedvilas' words, that the regime felt necessary to

take against the "enemies of the government."[58] After the war, Gedvilas regretted that these measures were insufficiently radical to
eliminate all possible organizers of the "fifth column." This diehard
Stalinist view, however, was not fully shared by all Lithuanian Communists nor, after the XX party congress, by Moscow itself.[59]

V

The Iron Curtain Descends:
The Years of Stalin

Communist rule was interrupted by Hitler's invasion of the Soviet Union on June 22nd, 1941. As during World War I, for three years, 1941–44, Lithuania was overrun by the German armies and was governed by a Nazi occupation regime.[1] Differently from the earlier generations, however, World War II did not end with the re-emergence of an independent Lithuanian state, but with the perpetuation of the Soviet regime.

The Arrival of the Age of Stalin

The Red Army recaptured Lithuania during the summer and fall of 1944. The troops of the 3rd Belorussian army, commanded by General Ivan Cherniakhovsky, took the burning capital city of Vilnius on July 13th. On August 1st, the fleeing Germans abandoned Kaunas, but their stiff resistance in the coastal region of the Baltic sea postponed the fall of the port city of Klaipėda (Memel) until January 27th, 1945. However, by the end of the month, the entire Lithuanian territory, including the coastal strip that in 1939 had been wrestled away by Hitler, found itself under firm Soviet control.

On July 5th, before returning to Lithuania from Moscow, Soviet Lithuania's Council of Ministers issued a proclamation in which the Lithuanians were asked to greet the Red Army as liberator.[2] Communist functionaries, however, were disappointed in the received response. Despite the Lithuanian dislike and fear of the Nazis, the population turned a cold shoulder to the liberating army and to the Communists.[3] In turn, the Lithuanians were surprised at the initial behavior of Soviet military and civilian authorities. The expected blood bath did not occur. For the most part, the military treated the civilians as friends. Communist politicians, furthermore, eagerly sought new ties to the people, especially to the Lithuanian intelligentsia. They found, however, that the ranks of professionals had thinned because many of them withdrew from the country. More than

60,000 people, among them an unusually high percentage of writers, doctors, teachers, administrators, left Lithuania, primarily for neighboring Germany, the only possible route of escape, in hopes of evading a repeated experience of Soviet occupation.[4] These thousands included people of diverse background, among them, the former Deputy Prime Minister of the pro-Soviet People's government, Vincas Krėvė Mickevičius, the former President of the free Lithuanian Republic, the Populist liberal, Kazys Grinius, and the leader of the Lithuanian "free-thinkers" (atheist) movement, Dr. Jonas Šliūpas. Some population in the front line areas were evacuated by the German order, among them the Archbishop of Kaunas, Juozapas Skvireckas, with his Auxiliary, Msgr. Vincentas Brizgys. The tens of thousands of refugees included still another bishop, Msgr. Vincentas Padolskis of Vilkaviškis, and two hundred and fifty-three Catholic priests or 15 percent of the total number of Lithuania's clergy.[5]

The suspicions with which the victorious Soviets were greeted and the disappointment that Communist functionaries experienced showed how much the Lithuanians had become alienated from the system that claimed them as citizens. The conflict that developed between the two in 1940-41 had grown into a deeply emotional enmity. The population's image of Communism was irreparably soiled by the collective memory of mass murders by the retreating Communists in 1941, and especially by the deportations of the thousands of innocents just a week before the start of the German attack on June 22nd, 1941. Lithuanian Communists, however, regarded these events as an unfortunate affair of an already distant past. As everyone in the Soviet Union in those days, they hoped that the future would improve. Their enthusiasm about the bright tomorrow, however, was considerably dampened that summer and fall of 1944, when possibly for the first time after their retreat to Russia, they learned first hand the extent of the suffering their rule had inflicted and the degree of hatred it had generated among the Lithuanian masses. The future course of action was no longer as clear as it had seemed in exile in Moscow, far away from home where the world was simplistically, but comfortably, divided into the Nazis, on the one hand, and the Communists on the other.[6] Lithuanians at home, they now found, were neither.

Native Communist attitudes, however, influenced only the implementation, not the shaping or direction of governmental decisions. These were made in Moscow. The Kremlin at that time was still very busy fighting the war and the domestic scene was dominated by policies that inspired Lithuanian functionary hopes, namely, compromise and conciliation. Stalin had initiated them for the purpose of uniting the country in the struggle against the Germans.

One of the most successful moves that Stalin made on the domestic scene was his historic reconciliation with the Russian Orthodox church. Soviet treatment of this Church eased almost immediately after the German attack, and in 1943, for the first time since 1917, the Church was allowed to restore its hierarchical organization. In February of 1945, the Church's synod in Moscow established new rules for administrative self-government that disregarded the limitations previously imposed by Soviet decrees. These decrees were not revoked, but the Church was allowed to broaden the scope of its freedom without changes in the law. Patriarch Alexei reciprocated by invoking God's help to Stalin (on this occasion, *Pravda* uniquely spelled "God" with a capital "G"). He also announced a donation of one half million rubles for the defense of the Soviet Union.[7] The established collaboration brought to the Orthodox church additional benefits. After the victorious end of the war, it was given the right of obtaining means of transportation, buying equipment and even the right for the construction of housing.[8] In other words, at least in some situations, the Church was granted the rights of legal person. This represented a reversal of Communist policy since the revolution. Furthermore, it put the Orthodox church in a privileged position in comparison with other religious denominations.

Another policy decision that, during the war, greatly improved the situation of all churches concerned atheist activities. For the duration of hostilities, the Communist party had stopped anti-religious propaganda.[9] This move created a more favorable atmosphere for religion and helped not only the Russian Orthodox church, but also the others. Stalin's generosity spilled over, at least temporarily, to the Catholics and Lutherans in the Baltic countries and in Western Ukraine. Nikita Khrushchev, then the first secretary of the Ukrainian Communist party, even attended the funeral of the extremely popular and respected Metropolitan of the Uniate Catholic Church, Archbishop Andrew Szeptitsky of Lviv (Lvov).[10]

Aided by these policies, the Lithuanian Catholic church continued its work in almost the same manner as it had under the German occupation. In 1944–45, three existing diocesan theological seminaries continued their work.[11] The number of students in these seminaries approximated the figures of the last year of Lithuanian independence. In the same years, men of military age were mobilized into the Red Army, but clergymen, seminarians, and even church servants were exempted from the draft as they had been by the Germans.[12] Parishes sponsored church choirs and the clergy were free to enrich the festive character of liturgical services. There was no interference with family visitations by pastors. While all schools were completely secularized, at least at first, religious classes were permitted in churches.[13] Antireligious propaganda was not renewed until sometime after the end of the war in 1945. The situation worsened toward the end of the year of victory. Among the first signs of the changing climate of tolerance was the rise of anti-clerical propaganda and the imposition of very high taxes on church buildings. For example, in December in 1945, the Archbishop of Vilnius was ordered to pay 45,172.50 rubles (in old currency) for the cathedral; 30,990.97 rubles for St. John's church that served the university community; and 24,835.50 rubles for the church of St. Casimir that, in 1961, was converted into a museum of atheism.[14] The payment of these exorbitant amounts had to be made in less than two months. Archbishop Reinys appealed the assessment, and at least initially, the Ministry of Finance in Moscow modified the rate of taxation. Similarly, the Ministry exempted members of monastic orders from paying bachelor taxes. Monasteries and convents, however, were soon ordered to be disbanded altogether.

Until the end of 1945, on the whole, the clergy exercised religious apostolate with reasonable discretion though the parish priests, and especially the bishops, were faced with a number of problems that ultimately proved to be unsurmountable.

The Problems of the Times

One of the immediate problems was the attitude that the bishops should adopt toward Soviet limitations of religious freedom, especially in the education of youth, their recruitment to Communist organizations, the future of theological training. Should the bishops acquiesce in the controls the regime imposed or should they resist their new confinement? The hierarchs apparently could not develop a united stand on this crucial question. On the initiative of Bishop Teofilis Matulionis (1873–1962), they met in August of 1944, in Ukmergé, an Eastern Lithuanian town, to consider an appeal to the government concerning religious education. A decision was reached to reopen the seminary in Kaunas, to teach religion and catechism in churches, and to persuade the government of the necessity of religious instruction in schools. However, the authorities considered this meeting an illegal conference, and it ended abruptly.[15] Archbishop Reinys was seized and interrogated by the police on his way home, though eventually the hierarch was allowed to return to Vilnius. A memorandum was written to the Chairman of the Council of People's Commissars of the Lithuanian SSR after the meeting, but no answer was received. Nevertheless, the regime did not immediately object to religious classes in churches, though the bishops had to become reconciled to the banishment of religious instruction from schools. The wave of terror, however, that started sometime in 1946, made the teaching in church buildings impossible, and three years later, in 1948, the government completely enforced the ban on such education as unconstitutional.[16]

While there was no disagreement on the furthering of religious instruction, opinions apparently differed on whether the bishops should oppose the government's recruitment of the youth for Communist causes and, generally, whether the bishops and the clergy should actively react to government violations of the traditional religious rights and freedoms. Bishop Matulionis, the oldest of the hierarchs in age and experience, supported a strong and direct policy while the others preferred evasion to outright confrontation. In a letter[17] that Matulionis wrote to the Chairman of the Council of People's Commissars, Mečislovas Gedvilas, the bishop objected to the practice of "those school principals, teachers, and Komsomol organizers who, sometimes by illicit means, attempt to induct Catholic children and the youth into anti-religious organizations that are canonically forbidden by the Church." Just before Easter of 1945, he ordered a public announcement of this opposition in his cathedral and, needless to say, drew Communist ire. To those colleagues and subordinates who cautioned the bishop that such action would not help, Matulionis replied that "it does not matter whether it will or will not help. We simply cannot keep silent. We have to tell the government what contradicts our own rules."

In his letter to Gedvilas, the bishop further objected to interference with religious services by government troops that more thoroughly, than previously the Germans, would surround church buildings and check the documents of the assembled worshippers. Sometimes they would simply come to the church for a smoke, shouting various obscenities. Matulionis similarly protested arbitrary arrests and the disappearance of his priests. Yet, at the same time, he considered that the government's attitude toward the Church was "considerably different and better than in 1940–41," and suggested that a useful dialogue could develop between them. Therefore, without waiting for many signals from the authorities, he presented Chairman Gedvilas, whom he met on June 16th, 1945, at the latter's invitation, with a list of requests prefaced by classically Catholic philosophical considerations about the church and the state. Both are sovereign in their respective fields, Matulionis said, and "the Catholic church usually finds a *modus vivendi* with diverse systems of government if she is not obstructed in performing the mission ordained by Christ; however, the Church will never consent to becoming an instrument of the government." He then stressed the Church's traditional ties with the Lithuanian nation and for the Commissar, defined the Church's historical role, which included the protection of both religious and national values. In Tsarist times, he said, "the Church fought for the Lithuanian book and for its Catholic contents. During the period of independence, it wrestled with the Lithuanian free-thinker movement, with religious indifference and with exaggerated nationalism." The bishop then appealed to the Communist leader "to take the Church as she is, if you want correctly to understand our position, because only then can you properly appraise her salutary role among nations and in mankind. If you try to force her to act against her own nature you will damage her essential spirit and paralyze her beneficial activities."

After this warning, Matulionis enumerated his concerns. The bishop's list was long. It began with the request of direct communications with the Vatican. It further included freedom of religious education in schools after the regular class hours and demands of a "minimum" of religious press, respect for church holidays, freedom to perform marriage ceremonies without prior civil wedding, the easing of discriminatory tax burden, restraint of local authorities from violating the constitutional guarantee of the freedom of conscience. Altogether, it was a very comprehensive and detailed petition, coupled with the assurance that the Church would stay away from politics. This was the field, Matulionis said, that the Church "purposefully avoided." Politics interested the Church only if, and inasmuch as, politicking was "founded on erroneous principles or interfered with the Church's principal work."

The bishop, no doubt, realized that everything he said in the lengthy communication exposed Communist principles concerning the Church as "erroneous," and thus he probably knew that he, too, could be accused of meddling in politics. Matulionis, however, appealed to the Communists' national feelings and seemed to have a glimmer of hope that Gedvilas and his colleagues, being, after all, Lithuanians, would adopt a moderate religious policy because they, too, would be interested in continued Church contribution to the national Lithuanian survival. This hope, if it was real, was not justified, and if for no other reason, then simply because it was not the Lithuanians in Vilnius but the Russians in the Kremlin who were dictating the policies.

Matulionis' letter to the Commissar revealed the Lithuanian hierarchy's and the bishop's own further concerns. He informed Gedvilas that the bishops had collectively asked for the appointment of military chaplains to Lithuanian Red Army units — an unheard-of proposition — but that the government did not respond to this request. He also requested permission to offer religious services to Catholics scattered in prisons and camps of the Soviet Union. "The Church would desire," he said, "that the government gave the clergymen an opportunity to minister to the faithful wherever necessary. This right exists everywhere in the world where there exists freedom for religion."

On another occasion, Matulionis further elaborated the idea of Catholic apostolate in the Soviet Union. The bishop regarded it as a natural extension of Lithuanian pastoral efforts. After all, Lithuanian priests traditionally had been Russia's pastors. Before World War I, 40 percent of all Catholic priests in the Mogilëv archdiocese had been Lithuanian. Matulionis himself had deep roots in Russia and a life-long commitment of service to Russia's Catholics. Active as a priest before the revolution, he stayed in Leningrad after the Bolshevik takeover, but, in 1923, was imprisoned together with Msgr. Jan Cieplak, the Archbishop of Mogilëv. He then was released, but again rearrested, and finally was secretly consecrated a bishop. In 1936, the government of Lithuania freed him and a dozen other priests in exchange for Communists imprisoned in Lithuanian jails, and thus Matulionis was able — however unwillingly — to return to his native land. He was appointed Bishop of Kaišiadorys in 1943. Already during the German occupation, Matulionis had received permission from the Vatican to reestablish Catholic apostolate in German-held areas of Russia,[18] primarily the region of Leningrad, but the Germans refused entry on the grounds that such priests must be of Russian or Belorussian birth.[19] Now Matulionis requested Moscow's permission and even suggested the appointment of a church administrator for Russia. The Kremlin responded with the arrest of the priest whom Matulionis had suggested as a candidate for the position.[20]

Theological education that the government at first tolerated soon added to the burdens of the bishops. In 1946, the government abolished two of the seminaries and on August 13th, 1946, ordered the remaining seminary in Kaunas to cut down its student body from three hundred and eight to one hundred and fifty.[21] This required a painful surgery. In a typical fashion, this order of the Lithuanian Council of Ministers was communicated only orally, and consequently, the hierarchy had no opportunity for a direct written response. The measure was strongly disliked, but each bishop reacted in his own way. We are familiar, unfortunately, only with the response of Archbishop Reinys of Vilnius. On September 23rd, 1946, he wrote a letter to Justas Paleckis, the Chairman of the Presidium of the Supreme Soviet of the Lithuanian SSR, in which he asked that the Council of Ministers revoke the order and allow an uninterrupted theological education. The situation was especially grave for the Vilnius diocese, he said, because its own theological seminary had been ordered closed at an earlier date. To support this petition, the archbishop used arguments that twenty years later would be echoed by Moscow's dissidents as well as by Lithuanian Catholics.[22] Reinys insisted that theological education was a right guaranteed by the constitution of the Lithuanian SSR, by international law, and by the Charter of the United Nations. Article 96 of the Lithuanian constitution, he said, guarantees freedom for the exercise of religious cults; this guarantee logically implies a right to train the "servants of the cult." Second, the Soviet law, Reinys said, guarantees the autonomy of such training. According to judicial literature — he cited a Soviet publication — the government is assumed merely to supervise church compliance with the law, not to interfere in the church's internal affairs. Third, Reinys wrote, since the Military Tribunal in Nuremberg had sentenced Nazi leaders for the closing of church-sponsored schools (he cited *Pravda*, No. 7, 1946), this meant that the Tribunal disapproved of the closures of theological seminaries as well. Finally, as a member of the United Nations, the Soviet Union was obligated to observe the United Nations charter and thus to grant the rights that are listed in that charter (Art. 2, par. 2).

The archbishop's letter, unfortunately, did not help. It merely angered the Communists who were already dissatisfied with him because of the criticisms of Soviet policies he had been publicly voicing in his sermons and because of his refusal fully to cooperate on the proposed amnesty for the anti-Soviet guerillas in Lithuania.

The issue of Lithuanian guerilla activities presented one of the most important and controversial problems of the postwar period. Guerilla organizations sprang up in 1944–45.[23] Hostilities began in the fall of 1944 and continued through 1952, though on a massive scale the war was fought only for four of these eight years, 1944–48. During this period, generally, guerillas controlled the countryside, and neither Soviet functionaries nor known Communist sympathizers felt safe except in the cities and fortified smaller towns. In addition to Lithuanian nationalist guerillas, the remnants of the Polish Home Army (Polska Armja Wojskowa) still functioned in the forests of the Vilnius region and frequently took action not only against the Communists but also against the Lithuanian or pro-Lithuanian officials.[24] The Polish guerillas, however, folded their activities in 1945 as a result of the Soviet-Polish agreement that sponsored the repatriation of the Poles from Lithuania to Poland.[25]

Insurgency wars usually are very cruel and the Lithuanian war was no exception. According to Soviet estimates, it cost at least forty thousand casualties.[26] In all probability, these are conservative figures. In any case, the extent of conflagration was of greater scope than the Algerian war against the French that had required sixteen thousand dead in the battlefields. The Algerian struggle for independence, however, made world news, while the Lithuanian events were shielded from the West by an Iron Curtin that already firmly separated Stalin's empire from the rest of Europe. Therefore the Lithuanian drama was little known at the time.[27]

Parish priests and the hierarchy were too close to the people not to become involved in this armed confrontation. There is little doubt of course that most clergymen sympathized with the guerillas because the latter represented the last hope of Lithuanian independence and Church freedom. In those days, Lithuanians shared the underground's view that World War II was not yet over because there shortly had to occur an armed conflict between the United States and the Soviet Union. Hope for this conflict provided a rationale for the partisan war. However, this belief was far from unanimous. Some important church administrators saw in the guerilla war merely a tragic and futile destruction of the country and its people. In many ways, it seems, the clergy's reaction to the guerilla war was reminiscent of its involvement in the insurrection of 1863. A rare priest participated in actual military operations. The existing record shows only one such priest — Justinas Lelešius, a regional guerilla leader, who died with arms in his hands. There were some others — published Soviet records indicate their number as less than two dozen — who took part as liaison men, suppliers of food and medication or as political organizers. In November of 1945 and July of 1946, two show-trials of thus involved priests were held in Kaunas, Vilnius and the province. Clergymen tried in these courts were charged with violent crimes though after the XX Party Congress, some of these priests were secretly exonerated of such accusations.[28] With small exceptions, the majority of clergymen, however, can be characterized as sympathetic bystanders who, when requested, offered religious services to guerillas though they were by no means sure that the partisan war had either chances of success or was the proper way for reaching the ultimate goals they shared.

It was difficult for the priests to choose any other course of action since an absolute majority of the partisans came from a strongly Catholic farm background and thus expected aid and understanding from their spiritual leaders. The Communist regime, on the other hand, considered that even the administration of the sacraments to the insurrectionists was treasonable. Thus, in many parishes the pastors found themselves caught between the anvil and hammer. Furthermore, since the government could not subdue the underground by the force of arms and since the guerillas refused to accept an amnesty that was offered to them on February 10th, 1945,[29] the Communists decided to enlist the Church's authority for extinguishing the conflagration. As a consequence, the bishops were asked to issue appeals to the underground fighters that endorsed government amnesty and demanded, in the name of the faith, their surrender to the authorities.

The hierarchy, however, could not achieve a consensus on this question. The administrator of the Kaunas archdiocese, Msgr. Stanislovas Jokubauskis — both local bishops had been evacuated to Germany — was the first to compromise and to issue such an appeal. He did so very early, on June 14th, and July 7th, 1945.[30] Three months later Archbishop Reinys issued a pastoral letter reminding his people of God's commandment "Thou shalt not kill."[31] This, however, applied to both antagonistic forces and therefore did not satisfy the Communists. Bishop Teofilis Matulionis flatly refused. In an answer to Gedvilas, the bishop explained that the guerilla movement represented the people's response to the political and social environment created by the government and since "it was not the Church that created conditions for the emergence of armed groups, it can not assume responsibility for the consequences of their liquidation."[32] Matulionis told the Commissar that while the hierarchs understood the government's concern, he personally doubted that the government would keep the "solemn promise of the pardon of punishment" because the government's past behavior did not inspire confidence. "And if the government will keep the promises it made, why," the bishop asked, "is the Church's guarantee needed?" "As a Catholic bishop and a Lithuanian," he continued, "I cannot in conscience personally accept responsibility for the security of the 'amnestied' people who are still hiding in the forests. If they are later punished, even on some different charges, they will reproach me for deceiving them."

Dissatisfied with individual responses, the government tried to induce the hierarchs to sign a collective appeal thus obliging the support of bishops who refused cooperation. For this purpose, the Council of Ministers authorized an episcopal conference in Kaunas. It met on February 21st, 1946. To assure success, the authorities arrested Bishop Vincentas Borisevičius of Telšiai, who was not as outspoken as Matulionis, but equally as adamant in the persistence of his independence. The conference noted the bishop's absence and signed an appeal to the Chairman of the Supreme Soviet, Justas Paleckis, requesting Borisevičius' release. At the same time, the conference chose Archbishop Reinys' draft of a broadly phrased letter, not an appeal that the authorities wanted. The proposal, consequently, was denounced as "provocative" and "anti-Soviet," and the government prematurely dispersed the meeting as useless.[33]

Eventually, however, the government enforced its will on diocesan administrators, but only after all the bishops, with the exception of Paltarokas, were arrested and deported.

The third problem in relation with the Communist government was, in a sense, even more fundamental since it related to the organization and legality of the Church itself. Since 1944, the affairs of the Catholic church were supervised by the Council on Religious Affairs in Moscow that had a representative in the Council of Ministers of the Lithuanian SSR. In Vilnius, at first A. Gailevičius, and then B. Pušinis, served in this position.[34] Both men had previous experience in the secret police. This Council and its representatives demanded that the bishops comply with the law of 1929, which abolished the canonical order of the Church's self-government and provided for the establishment of religious communities in the form of *dvatsatka* (a Russian term literally meaning a group of twenty). These groups of twenty parishioners were to run all religious and financial affairs of the parish under the supervision of local government committees. Such an arrangement, of course, sought to emasculate and eventually destroy the hierarchical structure of the church, eliminate the clergy's leadership in parish affairs, and abolish its control over the administration of the sacraments. A system of such *dvatsatkas* existed in the Soviet Union, though the government's concession to the Orthodox church brought back the role of the priest and the hierarchy. Without Archbishop Reinys' approval, the *dvatsatkas* already had been introduced into that part of Vilnius diocese that remained outside the boundaries of the Lithuanian republic. Now the Kremlin's chief of the Council on Religious Affairs demanded that the bishops themselves decree this reorganization for the Lithuanian territory. Moscow's reasoning was transparent. If the government ordered this organization on its own, the resulting unrest might push church organization underground. In addition, a record of government interference would be left, thus undermining public assurances that the Soviets were not mixing in the internal affairs of the churches. If the bishops instituted the arrangement, all of these dangers would be minimized and, furthermore, the bishops themselves would learn a lesson of obedience to the state.

Thus, this matter was of crucial importance to the state as well as to the Church. As much as the bishops were concerned, they again could not unite on a single response. Each hierarch wrote to the authorities objecting to the scheme, but each one did it differently.[35] For example, Archbishop Reinys considered it in violation of canon law. The government, he wrote to the Council on Religious Affairs in Moscow, is proposing a system that is completely foreign to the structure of the Church and the rights of the bishop. Pope Pius X, he reminded the Council, in 1907, had opposed a French project for the separation of church and state that provided for the creation of similar religious communities. Bishop Matulionis, familiar with the government's proposal from his previous experiences, rejected it categorically. Other church administrators were not so adamantly opposed. Msgr. Stankevičius, the new administrator in Kaunas, counselled its adoption while Bishop Paltarokas of Panevėžys sought to devise a compromise. In 1946, he persuaded the bishops to draft a statute that would incorporate both the government's principles and the essential requirements of canon law. The project became known as "Paltarokas' statute," named after its main author.[36] In this document, the bishops agreed to enlarge the role of parish committees and, as the Council on Religious Affairs desired it, to register these committees with the government as solely responsible for all property and financial affairs of the parish. On the other hand, the bishops included safeguards to prevent the use of these committees against the clergy; these groups, according to the bishops, should be chaired by the pastor, their membership should be confirmed by the bishop, and their members should be publicly and loyally practicing Catholics. Finally, the bishops sought an expressly stated guarantee forbidding interference by this group in the administration of the sacraments, in religious instruction, and generally, in pastoral and liturgical matters.

As could be expected, the Council on Religious Affairs rejected the Paltarokas compromise; it frustrated the Kremlin's purpose of taking church organization out of the hands of the hierarchy and the clergy. The bishops were squeezed further, and the government plan, though with some concessions to the clergy's participation, was finally accepted in 1948.[37] At the same time, on July 8th, the republic's Council of Ministers nationalized all church buildings and all religious objects belonging to them.[38] In conformity with the newly-established rules for church organization, these buildings were turned over to local government authorities for leasing to the newly formed religious communities. Thus, the organization of the Church was brought closer in line with that of the entire Soviet Union.

The Kremlin Strikes the Clergy

This governmental success was not achieved easily. The Communists first had to use violence and to crush resistance to the proposed changes.

Unable to persuade the hierarchy, Moscow decided to break it. The destruction of the "old" church leadership that was not socialized into the Soviet system would have come sooner or later since, in the Soviet view, new policies usually require new cadres for their administration. For Lithuanian Catholics, the first danger signals were flashed from the Ukraine, where, in April of 1945, the government arrested the new Metropolitan of the Uniate church, Joseph Slipyi, together with several of his bishops. The hierarchs were imprisoned. Their church was merged with the Russian Orthodox patriarchy and thus was forced out of existence.

Lithuania's turn came a full year later. In the same month that the Soviets arrested the future Cardinal Slipyi, the Central Committee of the Lithuanian Communist party ordered a move against the Lithuanian Catholic clergy and — though at first indirectly — against the Church. The party, as its historians later explained it, was determined "to liquidate the class foundations of clericalism in the republic and in this way to cut the ties between the bourgeoisie and the Church."[39] The campaign began with selective propaganda in the newspapers and public forums charging that some "reactionary" clergymen slandered the Soviet system and directed clandestine "bourgeois nationalist" organizations. This accusation quickly grew into a wholesale indictment of the entire Church as an opponent of Socialist industrialization, collectivization, and "cultural revolution." The progress of this anti-Church activity was periodically reviewed in Central Committee meetings between 1945–50. New denunciations, added especially in the plenum of July 9th, 1948, further identified the Church as a "helper" of German Fascist occupants, as an "inspirer and organizer" of the nationalist underground, as "an agent of international reaction" in the land. The thrust of the regime's propaganda was summed up in the title of a book, published in 1948, by Juozas Žiugžda, linguist turned propagandist, which read, *Reactionary Catholic Clergy — Eternal Enemy of the Lithuanian Nation.*

These denunciations of the clergy, however, merely camouflaged and rationalized the reasons for the already completed purge of the Lithuanian hierarchy. The anti-Church campaign that began as a verbal war in the spring of 1945 turned to violence at the end of 1946. The first victim among the Church leaders was Msgr. V. Borisevičius, the bishop of Commissar Gedvilas' home town of Telšiai.[40] Ordered to a meeting in the capital city, the bishop was first arrested on December 18th, 1945, but freed on Christmas Eve. The second time, under similar circumstances, he was arrested on February 5th, obviously in connection with the scheduled episcopal conference. This time he was kept in prison despite the pleas of the conference that the bishop suffered from a serious condition of vericose veins and the protest that his arrest occurred in violation of procedures stated in Art. 99 of the constitution of the Lithuanian SSR. Shortly afterward he was tried and sentenced. The government informed his sister that the bishop died on October 12th, 1946; however, it did not make clear whether he was executed, as it was earlier reported in the West, or died in prison somewhere in Lithuania or Russia.[41]

Borisevičius, in charge of the diocese as Ordinary Bishop only since 1943, had been a chaplain in the Tsarist army during World War I and later, rector of the theological seminary in Telšiai. Pro-western in international politics and of Christian Democratic convictions in domestic affairs, Borisevičius was a man of principle who did not avoid confrontation with the Communists. He sought, however, to frustrate the government's demands by stalling for time, in hope of a change in the international situation. The question of the reorganization of the church structure apparently was not the main reason for his imprisonment. The official indictment charged him with supporting the anti-Soviet underground. His articulate anti-Communism was an issue as well. During the German occupation, he had written a pastoral letter against Communism, and there is little doubt that he sympathized with the Lithuanian guerillas. To Soviet interrogators, he confessed helping some members of the guerilla movement to find civilian jobs. He was not involved in any military or intelligence operations. Known as a Nazi opponent, Borisevičius had saved the lives of several Jews who, during his secret trial, reportedly testified on the integrity of his personality.[42] The next victim was Borisevičius' Auxiliary, Msgr. Pranas Ramanauskas.[43] He was arrested in December of the same year, some weeks after Borisevičius' trial. Ramanauskas was not executed but sentenced to exile in Siberia. Thus, within a year, this Western Lithuanian diocese lost both of its bishops. The government's concentration on this administrative region — the homeland of the XIX century anti-Russian Bishop Valančius — was conspicuous but cannot be satisfactorily explained.

In the same year of 1946, Lithuania lost its third bishop, the outspoken Msgr. Teofilis Matulionis, who was arrested on December 18th and received a term of seven years in prison.[44]

Finally, half a year later, on June 12th, 1947, secret police came for Archbishop Reinys.[45] He was charged under the infamous Art. 58 that identified him as an "enemy of the people." Reinys, a former Lithuanian foreign minister, had negotiated the improvement of Lithuanian-Soviet relations in 1926. After serving as Auxiliary to the Bishop of Vilkaviškis, in 1940, he was transferred as Auxiliary Archbishop to Romuald Jałbrzykowski of Vilnius, a post in which Reinys' diplomatic talents were needed and useful. Educated in Western Europe, Reinys was an erudite philosopher who published, among others, a work against Hitler's racist theories and who, during the German occupation, both wrote public denunciations of Communism and helped the Jews from the Nazis.[46] The government continuously harassed him because of these anti-Communist statements, but Reinys survived longer than the other bishops except Paltarokas. He was eliminated, according to samizdat sources, largely because of his strong opposition to the scheme of church reorganization.[47] The archbishop was sentenced to a ten year term that he served mostly in the notorious Vladimir prison from which he did not return. Reinys died there on November 8th, 1953. An English private, Frank Kelly, who spent eight years in Soviet prisons and survived to tell the story, found the archbishop, together with Bishop Matulionis, Rev. Vladas Mironas, the former Prime Minister of Lithuania, and other senior Lithuanian clergymen, in the Vladimir confinement.[48]

Thus, in the middle of 1947, only one bishop, Msgr. Kazimieras Paltarokas, was left. He moved to Vilnius where he assumed Reinys' functions as well. The other dioceses were leaderless. According to canon law, the remaining bishop could not consecrate replacements without the Vatican's approval, and since the situation seemed desperate, Lithuanian churchmen sought to communicate with the Pope. Rev. P. Račiūnas was sent to Moscow to find a way of piercing the Iron Curtain. There he contacted Father Laberge, chaplain to the American Embassy.[49] Despite the permission he had received from Moscow's police to stay with Father Laberge in the latter's apartment, Father Račiūnas was seized as a spy and summarily sentenced to twenty-five years of hard labor. In Lithuania, appointments of new bishops had to wait for Stalin's death and the "thaw."

While striking against the bishops, the Kremlin did not forget the clergy nor the rest of the Church. In 1947, the authorities closed all monasteries and convents, dispersed their members and arrested their superiors.[50] Between 1946 and 1948, furthermore, the government proceeded against the middle levels of church administration, that is, the deans of diocesan districts, and finally, against the more energetic and conspicuous pastors and priests. A total of three hundred fifty-seven clergymen, or one-third of all of Lithuania's priests, were arrested and deported. This of course represents an enormous percentage of the total though it constituted only a tiny part of the estimated 350,000 Lithuanians who were deported in 1945–51.[51] These people, like the exiles of 1941, were scattered mainly in the northern climate zones, all the way from Mordovia to the Far East. Traces of deported clergymen were found in Central Asia, in Mordovian camps, in the Bratsk, Irkutsk and other Siberian and Far Eastern regions. An American Jesuit, Father Walter Ciszek, discovered in Krasnoyarsk that a Lithuanian priest had died there under mysterious circumstances while trying to legalize the already established Catholic parish that consisted mainly of Lithuanian parishioners.[52] Dr. Joseph Scholmer, a pro-Communist German doctor who was sentenced to Vorkuta for alleged espionage activities, attended a Mass secretly said at the camp, deep down in the mines, by a Lithuanian priest (it was Father Račiūnas).[53] Rev. Joseph Hermanowicz, a Marian Father of Belorussian nationality, reported finding Lithuanian priests scattered in many Central Asian and Eastern Siberian corners.[54] Many of these priests actively pursued their vocation by secretly serving congregations and groups of all Catholics: Lithuanians, Poles, and Germans in Central Asian settlements to which they had been deported in 1941.

For the priests who escaped deportation the representative of the Council on Religious Affairs planned to establish an *artel'* (a collective enterprise) to which he would select two hundred of the more energetic clergymen.[55] Fortunately for the Church, this idea of a special labor camp for priests died a bureaucratic death. It showed, however, to what length the authorities considered going in order to crush the Church's organization.

All of these implemented or planned measures were violent, yet in comparative terms, short of the "final solution." Such a solution was taken in the Ukraine where the Uniate church was liquidated by forcing its merger with the Russian Orthodox. Since Lithuanian Catholics belonged to Roman rites, the Lithuanian church could not be so conveniently abolished. Thus, the Kremlin had to seek other ways of domination. The regime therefore attempted to gain complete control over the Lithuanian church by cutting its subordination to Rome. Information about Soviet efforts of organizing a National Lithuanian Catholic Church is incomplete, but at least one source, the Letter to the Pope by the Lithuanian guerillas that their representatives brought to the West in early 1948, placed the beginning of such scheming already in 1944.[56] These efforts were very much intensified in 1949–50, after Pope Pius XII, on July 13th, 1949, issued his famous letter, *Responsa ad dubia de communismo,* that threatened excommunication to Catholics who either belonged to Communist organizations or voted for the Communist party in Italy. This papal clarification of Catholic relations with the Communists incurred Stalin's wrath. In response to the papal decree, G. G. Karpov, the chief of the Council on Religious Affairs in Moscow, demanded that the Catholic clergy sign a public letter denouncing the Pope as a "warmonger" and "a satan of the war spirit."[57] Clergymen were ordered to appear before Representative B. Pušinis in Vilnius or at local government offices to sign the statement. However, very few (19) did. For the priest, this pressure amounted to something worse than physical torment. The pastor of St. Theresa's church in Vilnius, Rev. J. Vaičiūnas, a distinguished old priest, compared the demand for his signature to a request that Representative Pušinis denounce the Communist party and Lenin.[58] It is doubtful that Communist functionaries in Stalin's day appreciated the meaning of Vaičiūnas' objection, though this priest was not imprisoned for refusal as were many others. Collected signatures were to provide a document for the separation of the Lithuanian church from Rome.[59] It has been reported that Moscow had even chosen the Lithuanian "Pope," but that he refused. This was a clergyman sentenced to twenty-five years of labor camps. He was offered the position in return for freedom, the pastorate of St. John's church in Vilnius, and a reward of 100,000 rubles.[60] He rejected it all.

Karpov's and Pušinis' success thus was negligible, and the idea of an independent church was abandoned.

Unable to divide the clergy and to establish a national church, the regime concentrated on appointing reliable church administrators. They were used for Soviet foreign policy purposes. Thus, in 1951, clergymen were mobilized to sign the Stockholm peace appeal, while church administrators had to attend Soviet as well as international conferences directed against the American policy in Korea. Four representatives of the Lithuanian church participated in the fourth conference "in defense of peace" that was held in the Russian city of Zagorsk on May 9th-13th, 1952.[61] These four, three Lithuanians and a Polish prelate, were prominent churchmen led by Bishop Paltarokas. Although generally their speeches, especially those of Paltarokas and Stankevičius, were dignified, they invariably paid homage to Stalin, and Paltarokas denounced "the capitalist states" for the alleged use of bacteriological weapons in Korea. Ironically, the Soviet script writers had the quietest of the four, the Very Rev. Petras Maželis, who then administered the diocese of Telšiai, to say the harshest sentences about the United States. Contribution to such propaganda did not end with participation in conferences. After returning home, the bishops and diocesan administrators had to convene a meeting of the clergy for a further discussion of resolutions they brought back, and the clergymen, in turn, had to preach in church, collect signatures for various petitions, and otherwise promote the propaganda of Soviet peace.

Destalinization and the Church:
Liberalization without Religion

Stalin's death rekindled hope, but also created uncertainty about the future. In politics, this uncertainty was generated mainly by the struggle for power in Moscow's Politbureau which at first feigned unity; the leaders apparently feared that an open discord after the loss of Stalin might unbalance the Soviet system itself. In societal relations, ironically, relaxation was promoted by Lavrenti Beria, the dreaded chief of secret police whose power still rested in this notorious institution. Searching for allies in competition for Stalin's succession, Beria eased police pressures and encouraged non-Russian Communist leaders to seek more autonomy for national cadres as well as for national languages.[1] Beria's moves caused many Russians to lose jobs in national republics, and though such personnel policy was restrained after his arrest and liquidation in the summer of 1953, the republics nevertheless were allowed gradually to reabsorb much of their native cultural tradition that Stalin had forced them to eschew.[2] This spirit of tolerance, so aptly named "the thaw" by Ilya Ehrenburg, like a cleansing tide soon spread over the cultural sphere and even religious life, thus producing immense psychological relief for most societal groups.

The relaxation was due, as it soon appeared, to the Party's temporary loss of direction caused by the shock of Stalin's death. Political confusion nevertheless blunted ideological aggressiveness, and in the religious sphere, produced a softening and even neglect of atheist propaganda. On July 7th, 1954, the Central Committee noted that some party and government workers wrote off the need of atheist propaganda in the new circumstances.[3] On July 24th, 1954, *Pravda* editorially complained that unidentified party, youth and government organizations misinterpreted Art. 124 of the Soviet constitution which guarantees freedom of religious cults and liberty of anti-religious propaganda. These organizations, *Pravda* ironically remarked, "for

some reason understand that freedom of conscience means freedom for propagating only religious views."[4]
Party leaders deplored this development and ordered an intensified and systematically upgraded atheist work.[5] At the same time, they did not lose sight of the problem that in relations with religious denominations they inherited from Stalin, namely, an almost total alienation of those Soviet people who practiced religion. In the last years of Stalin's rule, millions of religious Soviet citizens were classified as incorrigible enemies of the Soviet system. The leadership now sought to reconcile the believers and the clergy. Their estrangement was blamed on the faulty behavior of atheist activists. The Party's Central Committee confirmed its Leninist dedication to a religion-less Soviet society, but suggested a new, more "scientific" approach of persuasion rather than persecution. A better use of media of communications, the Committee suggested, would immensely improve the scope and quality of atheist propaganda. Furthermore, on November 10th of the same year, the Party not only attacked "vulgar mistakes" in atheist work, but also ordered their elimination.[6] Sometimes, the Central Committee wrote, lecturers and speakers "make slanderous outbursts against the clergy and the believers." At other times, the propagandists as well as the press, "without any foundation picture some servants of the cult and the believers as people who do not deserve any political confidence." In a number of districts, the Committee continued, "administrative interference in the activities of religious groups is allowed." Such behavior, the leaders admonished, deviates from the Party's policy and contradicts the Soviet constitution. This was a candid admission of legal violations, alas, not to be nationally acknowledged at any later time.

The Zigzags of Party Policy

This new approach brought change to Lithuania as well. The party improved the condition of the Catholic church in hopes of gaining the confidence of the earlier rejected Lithuanian Catholics. Thus, in 1954–56, atheist propaganda in the press was toned down. Instead there appeared a number of articles that spoke kindly of the believers. Religious faith, one such article conceded in 1956, "does not necessarily make bad collective farmers, bad workers or generally inept citizens of our Socialist country. All of us, surely, are acquainted with religious people who are industrious, conscientious, and capable of performing their duties."[7] The author of another article suggested that "religion is no obstacle to an educated man. Presently [in 1956], religion is so modernized and makes so many allowances that one can not say that it hinders the development of science, engineering or the arts."[8] The author, a university graduate whose academic career later was stymied by the authorities, even praised religious influence and concluded that "a religious fanatic and his anti-religious opposite number are equally stupid."[9] The official press, furthermore, for the first time in years carried some news about the status of the Church in Lithuania. Though possibly targeted for foreign consumption, Soviet radio broadcast the text of the pastoral letter by Bishop Paltarokas that revealed the losses the Church had suffered in Stalin's epoch, 1944–53.[10] In early 1954, Paltarokas said, 688 churches of Lithuania were served by 741 clergymen. The theological seminary in Kaunas had 75 students. This indicated the closure of all chapels, monasteries and convents, but only of 20 churches, and a loss of some 300 priests and about the same number of theology students. The revealed damage was horrendous, but nevertheless Paltarokas' naked data testified that the Church had survived.

In this new climate, the Kremlin allowed a number of other improvements. First, the amnesties of February 27th, 1954, and September 17th, 1955, facilitated the return to Lithuania of several thousand Lithuanians deported in 1945–51. These included 130 priests, that is, slightly less than one-third of those originally banished, among them two bishops, Matulionis and Ramanauskas.[11] The hierarchs, however, were not allowed to resume their duties and were confined to provincial domiciles.

In 1955, furthermore, Moscow allowed a partial replacement of the earlier decimated Lithuanian episcopate. On September 11th, 1955, two appointees of the Vatican, Rev. Julijonas Steponavičius and Canon Petras Maželis, were consecrated bishops respectively for the Vilnius and Telšiai dioceses. Furthermore, for the first time since the war, the bishops were permitted to visit parishes and locally to administer the sacrament of confirmation. In addition, again for the first time, the Kremlin licensed the publication of a prayerbook and a religious calendar. In an interview that appeared in the Italian Communist daily L'Unita on May 23rd, 1956, Msgr. Petras Maželis, one of the newly consecrated bishops, described the Lithuanian religious situation in very optimistic terms. The bishop even announced plans for building a new Catholic church in Klaipeda to serve the swelling population of this rapidly growing harbor city. In the perspective of the Church's experience with the Kremlin, Maželis' announcement sounded extravagant. Yet, the church was already designed and was indeed built. This era of "good feeling" finally created conditions favorable generally for repairs (and even new construction) of church buildings that had been left in decay since prewar days. Many of these concessions were made after Khrushchev's denunciation of Stalin in the Party Congress of 1956. De-Stalinization ushered in broader intellectual and cultural freedoms and greater patience for the politically-deviant views. However, it soon appeared that Khrushchev did not include the churches among the beneficiaries of post-Stalinist liberalization.

The first threatening clouds in Lithuania appeared in 1957. The conflict with the regime was precipitated by Bishop Matulionis, who refused to accept the terms of freedom granted to him. From provincial exile, Matulionis returned to his cathedral to reclaim the position as the Ordinary of Kaišiadorys. On September 25th, 1957, furthermore, he consecrated Rev. Vincentas Sladkevičius as his successor. Matulionis had the Vatican's approval for this consecration, but the government dragged its feet in consenting to the nomination and the old bishop refused to wait any further. Contrary to its acquiescence in 1955, the Kremlin now refused to accept the new bishop, and after some deliberation, in 1958 banished both the young bishop as well as his old sponsor from the diocese. Later the Communists claimed that Pope Pius XII sought to appoint bishops without the government's knowledge from priests "disloyal to the present state system."[12] However, it was not much worried about it in 1955, nor would it be worried again in 1965 in an almost identical situation.

The government's hostility to the church further intensified in the early 1960s. The growing enmity resulted from a change in the national Soviet policy. Now in complete command of the Party and the government bureaucracies, Khrushchev attempted to apply the brakes to the snowballing emancipation of artistic and intellectual life. He also declared war against the Russian Orthodox church and severely tightened controls of all religious activities. Decisions on these matters were made after the XXI Party Congress in 1959. On January 9th, 1960, the Central Committee issued one more call for intensification of atheist propaganda, and three weeks later, party leaders — Kosygin, Suslov, Mikoyan, Brezhnev — lent prestige to such activities by attending the congress of *Znanie,* the national organization mainly responsible for atheist indoctrination of the masses. Shortly afterwards, republic party leaders began demanding that "not a single violation of Soviet legislation by the clergy go unpunished."[13] In Belorussia, the party's first secretary not only deplored the weakness of governmental controls over religious activities but also claimed that in many cases local officials turned into the clergy's assistants.[14]

On February 11th, the government announced another change that underscored the worsening turn in religious policy. The president of the Council for Russian Orthodox Church Affairs, G. G. Karpov, a man who had maintained a *modus vivendi* relationship between the Orthodox church and the government since 1943, was replaced by V. A. Kuroedov, who "transformed this Council from an instrument for the control of the Church into a tool of aggressive suppression."[15] In July of 1961, Kuroedov forced upon the Church a new stiff regulation that took church affairs further out of the clergy's control. This, in effect, withdrew some concessions of 1945 and established the *dvatsatka* as the clergyman's employer and sole agent in the dealings with the government. Under Kuroedov's direction, the government closed down thousands of Orthodox churches, initiated very strict measures against unofficially functioning denominations or religious splinter groups, and with the use of *dvatsatka* groups, stopped children and young people under 18 from participating in church services. Local commissions "on observation of the legislation on cults" were now activated to help local government authorities in the supervision of the clergy.

Although these measures originally were directed against the Orthodox church in Russia, their adoption deeply hurt the Baptists and signaled a harder treatment of the Catholics as well. In August of 1960, the authorities seized the already completed church of Mary, Queen of Peace, in Klaipėda. Its tower was torn down and the building was converted into a concert hall. The following year, the government arrested the builder of the church, Rev. Liudas Povilonis, who was its pastor.[16] His assistant, Rev. Burneikis, and five civilians involved in construction also were imprisoned. In January of 1962, the two priests and the five civilians were brought to trial for stealing state property, black market activities, speculation in foreign currency, abuse of government position, bribery, and charges stemming from alleged violations of the Russian Republic's criminal code as well as a 1958 national law concerning "state crimes." All were found guilty and sentenced to prison terms from three to eight years. A correspondent of the *Chronicle of the Catholic Church of Lithuania* has suggested that the church was seized on orders of Nikita Khrushchev, who was enraged when told about its existence.[17] This explanation is plausible since it reflects his attitude toward Lithuania. In 1961, Khrushchev was similarly upset by the restoration of the medieval castle of Trakai, a prominent monument of Lithuanian history, that was authorized by the Lithuanian Communist party functionaries. However, whether or not Khrushchev had heard about the church, his policy toward religion in 1960 was immensely different from 1954, the year Rev. Povilonis received governmental permission for its construction. The administrators in Moscow who ordered the church's seizure, too, were different from the men who had licensed its building.

At the same time, the authorities kept a very watchful eye over the activities of church administrators and took drastic action in cases of hierarchical noncompliance. Thus, in 1961, the Commissioner for Religious Cults removed from office and the government banished from Vilnius the administrator of the Vilnius archdiocese, Bishop Julijonas Steponavičius. He was exiled to a small North Lithuanian town for allegedly refusing to ordain two seminarians who were approved by government authorities but whom the leadership of the theological seminary suspected as working for the secret police.[18] The bishop himself did not confirm this explanation, but in 1975, in a letter written to the Chairman of the Council of Ministers of the Lithuanian SSR, Steponavičius indicated that he was dismissed without any stated reasons and merely surmised that he was exiled as punishment for disobeying demands made by the Commissioner for Religious Affairs, Justas Rugienis (1909–1978).[19] In 1958, Bishop Steponavičius said, he was directed but refused to issue an order forbidding the priests to teach religion to children, to admit them to religious processions, and to serve as altar boys. He further disregarded the Commissioner's efforts to deny appointments to priests the government disliked and, finally, he objected to the removal of the rector and faculty members of the theological seminary, as well as protested the governmental screening of theology students for ordination. In other words, Steponavičius rejected the government's tutelage and interference in running the affairs of the Church. In 1976, pressed by clergymen in a conference he had convened, the new Commissioner Kazimieras Tumėnas explained that Steponavičius' fault was the observance of only the canon law of the Church while disregarding the orders of the government. "The Soviet state," the Commissioner said, "can not tolerate that the Church behave like a state within a state."[20] On another occasion, the Commissioner declared the bishop "disloyal" to the government.[21] Steponavičius was removed by a decision of the Council of Ministers of the Republic which acted on the Commissioner's recommendation. The fact that the bishop had loyally participated in Soviet "peace" conferences at home and abroad and had tried to keep low the voices of discontent among his flock frequently angered by government harassment was not regarded as sufficient expression of loyalty for holding the position.

After removing the bishop, the Kremlin appointed to the Vilnius seat its own candidate, Rev. Česlovas Krivaitis, who soon became very controversial among Catholics because of his compliant disposition toward the authorities. The seminary, as already noted, did not escape unscathed either. Rev. Alfonsas Lapė, a priest of the old tradition, who directed the seminary, fell into disfavor and was replaced by Dr. Viktoras Butkus, a postwar graduate who received his doctorate in Rome where he studied on a Soviet government scholarship. The number of seminarians certified by authorities for theological studies was reduced from 80 in 1958–59 to 60 in 1959–60, and then to 55 for the next two years, to 45 and finally to 28 in the last year of Khrushchev's rule.[22]

In 1960, the scope of the clergy's activities was further limited.[23] The authorities outlawed the traditional family visitations by pastors during the Christmas season[24] and banned group retreats for the laymen as well as for the clergymen. A permit, moreover, had to be secured from the government to have a priest from a neighboring parish help during religious festivities. Finally, as Bishop Steponavičius noted in his letter, the Commissioner for Religious Cults forbade children to serve as altar boys and to participate in religious processions.

The truth was that already, in 1957, the Kremlin's "liberal" church policy in Lithuania began to freeze after the brief "thaw" of 1954–56. From that time on, the Kremlin frequently dismissed canonically chosen diocesan administrators and forced the diocesan councils to appoint the government's candidates. The change in Communist attitudes was further reflected in the proliferation of atheist publications and new attacks on the clergy that started after 1958.

The Paradox of Hostility and Rapprochement

During the years of Khrushchev's rule two seemingly contradictory policy lines emerged in the Kremlin's treatment of the Lithuanian Catholic church. On the one hand, the regime enormously intensified atheist propaganda[25] and imposed on the clergymen more stringent controls, while on the other, Khrushchev strove for better relations with the Vatican under Popes John XXIII and Paul VI.

One result of this attempted rapprochement was the opening for the Lithuanian churchmen of official channels of communications with

Rome. A mixed clerical and civilian Lithuanian delegation visited Rome and Venice already in 1958, carefully feeling out possibilities for contacts,[26] and early in the 1960s a number of church administrators— but yet no bishop — received permission to attend the Vatican Council II and also to participate in the work of some of its committees.

On the whole, these seemingly divergent, though in reality complementary, policies were continued by Khrushchev's successors after the latter's overthrow in October of 1964. As in the post-Stalin period, however, under the collective leadership of Brezhnev, Kosygin and Podgorny, there immediately followed a period of relaxation, though the new "thaw" lasted only a short time and produced only minor concessions. This new breather helped primarily the Russian Orthodox church, which had suffered most under Khrushchev's regime. Church and monastery closings stopped. Theological seminaries, though cut in size, were left pretty much alone.

In Lithuania, too, the need for moderation was voiced immediately after Khrushchev's demise in October. A month later, A. Barkauskas, the Lithuanian Communist party's secretary for ideological affairs, reminded Lithuania's atheists that the Party's Central Committee on November 9th, 1954, had denounced the use of arbitrary measures against religion. Such behavior, he said, violated both the Party's policy and the Soviet constitution.[27] In May of 1966, new statutes, adopted in Russia as well as in Lithuania and the other republics, forbade dismissal of employees on account of their attitude toward religion.[28]

The new leaders continued their search for "normalized" relations with the Vatican. On November 21st, 1965, while on a visit in Rome, Dr. Juozapas Matulaitis-Labukas was appointed administrator of the Kaunas archdiocese and on December 5th, consecrated bishop. Moscow knew about this matter but, as far as it can be determined, was not formally consulted on Labukas' acceptability, and there were fears that the Soviets would not allow him to return to rule the diocese. These fears, however, were dispelled by the congratulations the Soviet Ambassador in Italy extended to the prelate when he came for the visa to go home. Similarly, in 1966, the regime allowed the publication in Vilnius of a collection of revised Lithuanian liturgical texts for the administration of the sacraments. At the same time, or possibly after these diplomatic preparations, on April 27th, 1966, Foreign Minister Andrei Gromyko paid a visit to Pope Paul VI. Half a year later, on January 30th, 1967, the Pope solemnly received Nikolai Podgorny, a member of the Soviet triumvirate and Chairman of the Supreme Soviet of the USSR.[29]

On the other side of the coin, at the same time that Secretary Barkauskas praised the Party's moderation of an earlier decade, he also urged the use of all means for stopping "the violations of Soviet laws by individual servants of the cult and by church supporters." Furthermore, statutes that were passed in 1966 not only forbade discrimination against the believers at work, but also specified fines and prison sentences for the teaching of religion and for other newly formulated violations of the law.[30] The enrollment quota for the seminary in Kaunas was again cut, to 24 in 1965–66, and kept at 30 afterwards.[31] Exiled bishops were not allowed to return to their sees.

Brezhnev's ascendancy to the dominant position in the Politbureau did not bring about any substantial changes. Episcopal appointments continued.[32] In 1967, Rev. Juozas Pletkus was consecrated bishop and appointed to administer the diocese of Telšiai, while in 1969, the Vatican and the Kremlin agreed on the consecration of Rev. Romualdas Krikščiūnas and Rev. Liudvikas Povilonis, formerly a member of the forbidden Marian Congregation. In 1963, Krikščiūnas had received a doctorate in canon law from the Lateran University in Rome where he studied on a Soviet scholarship. Povilonis was the pastor who had built the church in Klaipėda and in 1962 was given an eight-year prison sentence for his work. Obviously, his sentence had been cut. In 1968, furthermore, two more religious publications appeared in Vilnius: the decrees of the Vatican Council II and the missal. Finally, in 1973, the government released for publication a new Lithuanian translation of the New Testament.[33] The edition appeared in ten thousand copies.

Brezhnev, however, softened neither religious propaganda nor the enforcement of the newly-added stringent regulations of the clergy's activities. This made especially the question of religious instruction of pre-Communion children an explosive issue in relations between the Church and the Kremlin. Moreover, signs appeared that the regime finally decided to force on the bishops the notorious legislation of 1929 that demoted the clergy and put *dvatsatka* in complete control of the priests and of the administration of the sacraments.

The Constitution, the Law and the Church

After the analysis of forces that by their historical interplay have shaped the character of Lithuanian Catholicism during the social and political upheavals of recent generations, it is necessary to take a closer look at the legal and political arrangements that influence the development of the Church and condition its responses to modern Soviet society and government. They not only constitute the legal framework for religious life, but also help to explain the very roots of the conflict that has newly flared up in Lithuania between church and state: this time not a nationalist dictator or revolutionary commissar, but between the parish pastor and the Red bureaucrat of post-Stalinist Russia. These Soviet arrangements, time and again mentioned in our previous discussion of Soviet policies, have been in principle formulated in Art. 124 of the Soviet Constitution of 1936 (Art. 52 of the Constitution of 1977) and cover the two sides of the religious question in Soviet society: first, church rights in the state, and second, competition to religion by what the constitution calls "anti-religious propaganda."[1] The failure carefully to consider the symbiotic relationship between these two principles has frequently misled Westerners into attaching the same meaning to religious freedom in the Soviet Union as it is generally given in advanced industrial democracies. These two sides of the coin represent the subject matter of the current and the subsequent chapters.

The Constitutional Context of Rights of Religion in the Soviet Union

In discussions concerning constitutional provisions for religion — and generally in matters of civil rights — the Soviets use concepts of Western liberalism but pour different wine into traditional sheepskins. In this manner, terms like "freedom of conscience," "separation of church and state," the formula "within the law" project the impression that freedom of religion in the Soviet Union, and especially regulations that govern church behavior, are very similar, and even more liberal than in "any other state."[2] For their own reasons, some Soviet churchmen help to maintain the same illusion. For example, in a 1975 interview arranged by the *Novosti* press agency of Moscow, Bishop Romualdas Krikščiūnas asserted — without formally telling a lie — that his relations with the state were "normal" and that "according to existing laws," he and other clergymen "have an opportunity to perform our duties."[3] In June of 1976, Rev. Viktoras Butkus, the rector of the theological seminary in Kaunas, was similarly reported as saying in Moscow's foreign language press, that is not freely available in the Soviet Union itself, that "there is full freedom of conscience in Soviet Lithuania. It is guaranteed by Art. 96 of the Constitution of the Lithuanian SSR [almost *verbatim,* the equivalent of Art. 124 (Art. 52) of the federal Constitution]. Every citizen is free to worship in any church or in his home, to adorn his own dwelling with crucifixes and holy images, to have prayer books, the Bible and other religious books. Soviet law guarantees rights of believers."[4]

Such splendid statements indicate that in order to avoid misunderstanding, 'the laws that formally govern religion need to be put in the context of systemic Soviet arrangements.

The Soviet Union is organized as a party-oriented society. Institutionally, it is structured in a manner that places all power in the Communist party, yet creates an appearance of dichotomy between the ruler's policy and the law of the land. Paradoxically, the principle of the Party's arbitrary supremacy is formally declared in the Constitution, a state document that traditionally is associated with limitations of absolute power rather than with its legitimization. Art. 126 of the 1936 Constitution (it became Art. 6 in the Constitution of 1977) not only pronounced the Party an association of "the most active and politically conscious citizens," but also designated it as a "vanguard of the working people" and "the leading core of all organizations of the working people, both public and state." No other group, governmental or societal, was entrusted with a similar or auxiliary role. The Constitution, in effect, endowed the party with exclusive leadership over society and specified that this leadership would be exercised by means of "inside" control of societal groups or governmental institutions. The Party's essential role was even more explicitly defined in Art. 6 of the Constitution of 1977, which declared that the Party was "the leading and guiding force of Soviet society and the nucleus of its political system, of all state organizations and public organizations." To control all of these organizations, the Communists both overlap with them and, at the same time, maintain a separate institution.

It may be said that the Communist party is not a product of the Constitution but the other way around, the Constitution and the laws are instruments of the Party. As a Soviet authority puts it, "the party indicates the goals and elaborates the means for achieving them" and then sees to it "that all governmental and nongovernmental institutions actually follow the set policy."[5] According to the same authority, furthermore, Party decisions are "given legal form in laws and decrees and other acts of the higher bodies of state authority."[6] Thus, it is the Party's decisions, not really the state laws that govern the country.

This arrangement means that no power or right enumerated in the Constitution, be this in the field of the judiciary, federalism or elections, can be interpreted without reference to the "supremacy clause" of Art. 126 (new Art. 6). Such reading, in turn, indicates that the Soviet Constitution allows much less individual freedom than conventional wisdom assumes. For example, Art. 125 (it became Art. 50 in the Constitution of 1977) that guaranteed freedom of speech, press, assembly and demonstrations, secured these rights "in the interests of the working people and for the strengthening of the Socialist system." (The equivalent Art. 52 of the new Constitution reads: "in accordance with the interests of the people and in order to strengthen and develop the Socialist system.") This seemingly innocuous qualification gains a very ominous sound when considered in conjunction with Art. 126 (Art. 6). According to this latter article, any group or institution that would interpret the meaning of "the interests of the working people" or what "strengthens the Socialist system" is party-controlled. In other words, the scope of these fundamental rights is not determined by a state institution, say, a court, but by the Party. The conclusion is clear; only the speech that serves the Party's needs will be allowed. Thus, when Pavel Litvinoff, the grandson of Stalin's foreign minister, invoked Art. 125 in defense of his right to speak against the Soviet invasion of Czechoslovakia, the court that tried him on charges of slandering the Soviet Union declared the argument "irrelevant."[7] Soviet dissidents, especially the *Khronika tekushchikh sobytii* (Chronicle of Current Events), have challenged this orthodox Soviet doctrine, but so far without success. The reason for their failure to breathe new life into Art. 125 (Art. 50) is found in the fact that an interpretation without reference to Art. 126 (Art. 6) would undermine the foundations of the Soviet system; it would challenge the Communist control of society. Litvinoff, thus, was convicted and sentenced, as were the others who claimed this constitutional protection.

It is within this context that the legal principles concerning religion must be interpreted; the law expresses the Party's policy. When in 1975, Msgr. Česlovas Krivaitis, the administrator of the Vilnius diocese, declared in New York that in Lithuania the Church functions "within the law,"[8] he meant that it flourishes within the existential perimeters set by the Party. In turn, the law limits the Church, restrains the government apparatus, but does not oblige the Party.

The Soviets, as it must be clear from this brief discussion, have devised very flexible institutional mechanisms for implementing the wishes of their absolute ruler. The government, outwardly resting on an electoral structure, inwardly controlled by the Communist "nucleus," is one such instrument. Thus, it is no contradiction, from a Soviet point of view, for the government to consider religion "a private affair" while at the same time the Party seeks to abolish it altogether. In 1954, the Party's Central Committee, to allay doubts that arose after Stalin's death, insisted that the Party can not remain neutral toward religion while the government may treat it as a private matter.[9]

In 1961, furthermore, the revised party statutes specifically listed an active participation in the "decisive struggle" to eliminate "religious prejudices" as a duty of individual party members.[10] Similarly, the Khrushchevite party program, adopted in the same year, obliged the party organization "systematically to conduct broad scientific-atheist propaganda."[11] These statements suggest a different from conventional Soviet interpretation of the concept of religion as a private affair — as well as of freedom of conscience and separation of church and state — the latter two expressly listed constitutional principles of Art. 124 (Art. 52 in the constitution of 1977).

In effect, while claiming governmental protection for religious rights, the Soviets have allotted to it a very marginal place and both the party and the government consider religion an enemy of the system. According to a Soviet Lithuanian writer, "the church in our land is the only legally functioning organization with an ideology that is inimical to us."[12] Therefore, religion has no future in a Communist society. In the words of the same author, "the remnants of religion in our country are condemned to disappearance. In the land of science and liberty that has produced the first man and woman cosmonauts and that is engaged in building communism, there can be no place for any remnants of spiritual suppression. It is a patriotic duty of every conscientious Soviet citizen to help quicken the process of their disappearance."[13]

This hostility has been incorporated into Soviet law. Shortly after seizing power in 1917, the Bolsheviks issued their famous decrees on peace, land, and the rights of nationalities, all asserting some positive gains for various segments of society. Religious institutions, however, were not among the beneficiaries. On the contrary, the decree of separation of church and state of January 28th, 1918, triggered off a series of measures, one more severe than the other, that eventually led to persecution of religion. The decree itself, while on the one hand initiating the long needed separation of the Russian Orthodox church from the state, on the other banished all churches from society altogether; the churches lost the rights of legal person. Electoral laws visually demonstrated their intended isolation by depriving the clergy of the right to vote, a right that already then possessed dubious value to a citizen, but nevertheless made him count as a member of Soviet society. By the decree of 1918, furthermore, Lenin's government took over the church buildings, vestments, and liturgical implements and in this manner, made the very performance of liturgy dependent on the government's willingness to cooperate. The liberal streak in Lenin's largely fanatical personality showed itself in the addition he made to the proposed draft of the decree which promised a free use of church facilities and other property for the performance of religious services. This provision, however, was soon made obsolete by the required land taxes and insurance fees and by special utility rates the congregations were required to pay to the government.

In time, furthermore, the regime strictly narrowed the concept of freedom of religion. While the decree of 1918 spoke merely of liturgical rites and specifically forbade the teaching of religion in state schools, it nevertheless equally specifically allowed religion learning and religion teaching in a private manner. The early Soviet constitutions, those of 1918 and 1924, included a specific right of "religious propaganda."[14] It is possible that Lenin's early views on the matter had to do with these now long forgotten provisions. In *Village Poverty* (1908), Lenin had maintained that "every person should have full freedom not only to be a member of the faith he likes but also to propagandize it, to express this faith as well as to change it."[15] This dictum was used by Father Juozas Šeškevičius, a Lithuanian Jesuit, as a defense argument in his trial on September 8th–9th, 1970. The priest was charged with illegal teaching of religion, but contended having committed no crime because Lenin had intended the constitutional right of worship to include the right of teaching as well.[16]

This is not the case, however, in current Soviet jurisprudence. Freedom of religious "propaganda" was first eliminated in 1929, in the Russian republic,[17] and in 1936, it was not included in the Stalin constitution. Art. 124 of this Constitution spoke only of "freedom of religious worship" which was compensated by "freedom of anti-religious propaganda." Thus, the concept of freedom of religion excluded the right of organization, publication, social work or teaching and is confined to the mere performance of religious ceremonies. As a consequence, the role of the clergyman was completely emasculated. His function is, as Soviet writers explain, "solely the performance of religious rites."[18] Anti-religious propaganda, on the other hand, was equated with the right to hold liturgical services. Thus the law on religious and anti-religious freedoms is asymmetric. It establishes a basic inequality between the churches on the one hand and the atheists on the other, with the balance set heavily in favor of the latter group. This is not an oversight, nor does this discrimination result from purely administrative willfulness or ignorance as it is frequently assumed, but represents a consciously devised policy that seeks, by legal provisions, to choke off all church activities and religion itself.

Laws that Govern the Churches and their Administration

While today there still exist some differences in the application and enforcement of religious laws between the dominant Russian Republic and Lithuania, on the whole, the same rules apply in Lithuania as anywhere else in the Soviet Union. They are derived (1) from the already discussed decree of separation of church and state of January 23rd, 1918, and (2) from the Stalin Constitution of December 5th, 1936, and the Brezhnev Constitution of October 7th, 1977. The detailed laws for controlling religion, however, were basically worked out in (3) the law of religious associations of April 8th, 1929, as amended by the Russian Republic authorities on June 23rd, 1975.[19] The Lithuanian version of this law was passed by the republic's Supreme Soviet on July 28th, 1976.[20] Furthermore, the churches are regulated by (4) decrees, instructions and regulations issued by councils of ministers, ministers of finance and other government institutions. Many of these are secret. Copies of such instructions are distributed only to appropriate government agencies for guidance, not to the public for its knowledge. Lithuanian Catholics and Russian dissident Igor Shafarevich had time and again referred to the existence of secret instructions to which neither the clergymen nor believers had access.[21] One such secret, "for official use only," document has been published in Moscow under the title of *Zakonodatel'stvo o religioznykh kultakch* (Legislation on Religious Cults, 1971).[22] It contains excerpts from the writings of Karl Marx and Lenin, and the Paris Commune decisions, and in 329 pages lists decrees on religious law enforcement, the taxing of clergymen, administration of cemeteries, teaching of religion, and a host of other pertinent matters. Much of the material that this text contains, for example, the secret Khrushchev instructions of 1961, have never been printed for public use. In Lithuania, the Commissioner for Religious Affairs similarly publishes "clarifications" about "the application of laws concerning religious cults." The latest known "clarification" — implementing the law of 1929 and the decrees of the post Stalin period — was published in 1969.[23] Actually, this was a translation of pertinent parts of the Russian "instruction on the application of legislation on religious cults" that was issued by the federal councils on religious and Russian Orthodox cults on March 16th, 1961.[24] The brochure was mimeographed in an edition of 600 copies, obviously insufficient for public information purposes because the edition was smaller than the number of Catholic priests in the republic, not to speak about other denominations or Catholic parish committees and other vitally involved participants.

However, a portion of these instructions, excluding limitations on the social and educational activities of the clergy and of religious associations, on February 6th, 1969, was summarized in *Valstiečių laikraštis,* a paper the regime publishes for rural readers.[25] Afterwards, reminders of restrictions that govern the churches, though in selective fashion, have been revealed by infrequent newspaper articles and an occasional pamphlet.[26] In addition to these public or undisclosed laws, churches in the Soviet Union are regulated (5) by laws that do not specifically deal with religion and finally, (6) by Criminal codes that do. In the Lithuanian code, first adopted in 1961 as a result of Khrushchev's attempts to revitalize federalism, provisions that pertain to religion are found in Articles 143, 144 and 145.[27] In 1966, the meaning of these articles was authoritatively interpreted by a decree of the republic's Supreme Soviet. These articles, as well as interpretations, are identical with the respective regulations in the Russian, Ukrainian and other republic codes — in the Russian code they are numbered 142, 143, and 144 — but since there is no national criminal code in the Soviet Union, each republic publishes its own, usually in conformity with the federal principles of criminal legislation of 1958 and actually following the amendments of the Russian Republic code.

The administration of church affairs in the Soviet Union has taken different forms. Since December 8th, 1965, it has been placed in a single Council of Religious Affairs that is attached to the Council of Ministers of the USSR.[28] On March 17th, 1966, this Council was subdivided into four administrative units and three church divisions, one for the Orthodox churches, another for Moslems and Buddhists, the third for Christians and Jews, including the Catholics and the Armenian church. The Council is a central agency. Its subdivisions have no policy making autonomy and its representatives — republic Commissioners or "Ministers" for religious affairs — are subordinated to Moscow, though attached to republic councils of ministers. The powers of the national Council are extensive.[29] It licenses religious associations or decides their abolition from which there is no appeal. It controls how the churches conform to religious legislation, prepares such legislation for adoption, issues "clarifications," informs the government of church activities, guides church relations on the international scene, acts as a government liaison to the churches, advises republic governments on church legislation, identifies individuals who violate laws on religion. Its jurisdiction seems to be broader than that of the Tsarist College that was charged with similar duties.

Monitoring and control, however, does not end with either the federal councils or their republican branches. The daily supervision is placed in the hands of local governments that in the 1960s received institutional aid for the task. Lithuania's Supreme Soviet formally provided it on February 12th, 1965.[30] Accordingly, each city and district government was obliged to create a commission to help the Soviet to oversee church observance of religious legislation and to aid in informing the population about regulations on religion. Such committees, now in existence throughout the republic, consist of deputies of local government councils, employees of cultural-educational institutions, of financial agencies and the school district. Pensioners "and other activists" may also be appointed to this group. This definition has brought to the membership of these committees many atheist propagandists and promoters, opening the groups to a justified charge that the supervision of religious legislation has been placed in atheist hands. The deputy chairman of the executive committee of local (city or district) government serves as the chairman of this group.

The Scope of Religious Freedom

With small changes, the basic law that regulates church activities in the Soviet Union remains the law on religious associations of 1929, as revised in 1975–76.[31] This law, purportedly derived from the practice of the Paris Commune of 1871, established the associational principle for the existence of churches and set up the local religious association as the basic church unit so recognized by the government. Twenty people over 18 years of age can form such an association and request recognition from the state. If the government agrees to registration, the group's existence becomes legal. It then can enter into contract with the local soviet, that is, city or district government, on the use of church buildings and implements needed for religious services. Registration is not a mere formality because it can be denied. Some religious groups are outrightly barred and thus the Uniates, the Jehovah's Witnesses, Adventists-Reformists, reformed Baptists *(Initsiativniki)*, True Orthodox Christians, Pentecostals and several others are refused registration.[32] According to Soviet sources, 1,200 such sectarian groups operate illegally.[33] The Catholics, too, have difficulties with registration, and not only in diaspora, but in Lithuania itself as well.[34]

The revised law made it more difficult to register and easier to forfeit registration than was the case in earlier days. However, the new legislation has acknowledged the existence and the rights of "religious centers" which now are allowed some pseudo-legal rights. Art. 20 of the Russian republic law of 1975 (for the 1976 Lithuanian law equivalents of articles cited in this discussion see Appendix A) permits "religious centers and diocesan boards" the right "to produce church utensils and articles of the religious cult and to sell them to societies of believers." They also have the right to "acquire means of transport and to rent, build or buy buildings for their own needs in accordance with the procedure established by the law." Religious associations, however, have the right to acquire only "property necessary for the performance of the cult." (Art. 25). In neither case does the right to "acquire" translate into the right to "own." These new provisions seem to legalize a situation that at least partly has existed for many years. In the case of the Russian Orthodox church, many portions of the law of 1929 were suspended as a result of its historical agreement with Stalin during World War II. Its hierarchy was restored by the election of the Patriarch. Full rights of legal person were never granted to it, but the Church was allowed to own transport and housing, in effect, to have what now is guaranteed by Art. 20 of the new legislation. In the past, this provision, apparently, has not been fully applied to either the Moslems, the Lutherans or the Catholics, not to speak about the others. The Catholic church as a united organization is not a legal entity in the Soviet Union. Catholics are represented by "six independent from each other religious centers."[35] These centers presumably mean administrative diocesan units, though this is not clear. If so, then two of these are found in Latvia, but are actually governed by a single bishop. In Lithuania, its six dioceses are still governed as four administrative units. The sixth "religious center" possibly means the Latin rite church in the Ukraine (Ukrainians, Hungarians and the Poles) and Belorussia, though no bishop or administrator in charge of it resides within Soviet territory. Diocesan administrators, as generally the hierarchy, appoint the priests; however, in the eyes of Soviet law, the bishops have no legal right to control parish pastors. Their appointment is regarded only as a traditional "practice" that is merely tolerated.[36] According to the law, the parish committee, in other words, the representatives of the group of twenty adults who officially register the congregation (the group is popularly known as *dvatsatka*), hires and fires the clergy,[37] and pastors can not be appointed by "religious centers" without the *dvatsatka's* consent.

After the victorious completion of the war, the Kremlin endeavored to impose the associational principle on the Lithuanian church organization. This, however, was not fully accomplished in Stalin's time. After Stalin's death, furthermore, the clergyman's influence rebounded in Russia's *dvatsatkas*. The new, more radical regulations that were forced on the Russian Orthodox church in 1961 restored their position and even went beyond the law of 1929 in excluding the priests from these committees. The *dvatsatka* was, moreover, empowered to act without consulting the congregation. These new rules further limited church contacts with the youth and also demanded that the priests register the passports and civil marriage certificates of those participating in church baptisms and marriages. At the same time, the authorities intensified supervision of church work at the local level.[38]

These stricter new regulations soon afterwards arrived in Lithuania, although their implementation and enforcement was gradual and still remains incomplete. Basic rules of religious life in the republic are nevertheless contained in the legislation of 1975/1976, but this legislation apparently does not list all prohibitions and regulations. For example, it does not define the *dvatsatka's* authority of hiring "servants of the cult," nor does it list all required taxes and fees. These latter are fixed in federal statutes,[39] and in contracts *dvatsatkas* conclude with local governments. None of these regulations have been rescinded by the legislation of 1975/76.

Thus, the law establishes the *dvatsatka* as the controlling unit of church organization. This group functions as a sort of intermediary between the authorities on the one hand, and the clergy and the believers on the other.

Its role, however, is strictly circumscribed. According to authoritative Soviet writers, it is licensed only "for the performance of the cults."[40] The *dvatsatka* therefore essentially differs, these Soviet authorities say, from labor unions, cultural, educational, sports or any other secular associations registered with the government. Religious institutions do not possess the rights of legal person. This allows the government to discriminate against the churches, the clergy, and parish employees in a manner analogous to the discrimination against the country's private economic sector. Thus, for example, clergymen are legally excluded from state sponsored old age pension plans, while at the same time required to pay higher income taxes. Similarly, the churches are charged higher utility rates, etc.

The *dvatsatka* works through its executive committee that consists of three elected members. This group can not, however, act as a collective body to hire watchmen, repair church buildings or purchase products needed for religious ceremonies. These arrangements must be made individually by a member or members of the executive committee. (Art. 11). Commercial or industrial contracts are forbidden. (Art. 11).

The law requires that members of the executive committee be acceptable to the authorities. Government directives, issued on April 15th, 1974, obliged local governments to remove from the *dvatsatka* membership "all those persons who have a record of court sentence, who have been deported or who are generally reactionaries."[41] Similarly, instructions of 1961 (Art. 4)/1969 (Art. 9) specifically denied a similar right of screening to the local clergy or to the hierarchy.[42] The priests thus have no defense or protection against infiltration of the *dvatsatka,* or of its executive group by unbelievers or straight government agents. The new regulations, furthermore, exclude the clergymen from serving on executive committees.

The legislation and instructions that were adopted in the decade of the sixties both under Khrushchev's and Brezhnev's leadership sought more efficiently than the legislation of 1929 to bar the clergy from any participation in the management of parish affairs. The priests are financially dependent on the *dvatsatkas* that pay their salaries; parochial accounting books must be open to government inspectors for checking the income of the clergymen. The rate of income tax charged to clergymen is higher than that imposed in regular cooperative or state employment. In addition, they pay bachelor's taxes and special taxes, if they own means of transportation.[43] The priest must secure approval for most of his activities, for some from his own religious group, for others from the government. This includes the administration of the sacraments. For example, the pastors are forbidden to use liturgical implements at their sole discretion; they can not direct parochial financial affairs, and are even barred from personally passing a collection plate during the services in the church. In 1974, Father Antanas Šeškevičius, back in pastoral work after serving a sentence for teaching catechism to children, protested such prohibition to the representative of the Council on Religious Affairs in Vilnius. "I was told," the priest reported, "that a clergyman can participate in the collection but under no circumstances can he carry the collection plate."[44] Šeškevičius regarded such prohibition as violating Art. 96 of Soviet Lithuania's constitution on the separation of church and state. "In this case, the state directs the collection of offerings in the church," complained the priest. It must be added that, by law, the pastor is forbidden to prescribe any obligations either to the parish committee or to the parishioners.

The regulations further require that the priest celebrate liturgy only in the parish to which he is assigned. Any pastoral activity outside the boundaries of the congregation requires permission from the local soviet. In 1974, the district government of Utena in Lithuania ordered local soviets in advance to secure the calendar of church festivities for the entire year together with the list of priests who will officiate at these festivities.[45] For inviting "outside" priests to participate in parish retreat activities, for example, Father Bronius Laurinavičius of Adutiškis was administratively sentenced as violating a provision of May 12th, 1966, that concerns organization of religious meetings.[46] This latter prohibition, it will be remembered, was enforced by Tsarist officials during the second half of the XIX century. An exception to this rule was authorized in 1973 when after a twenty year ban, the priests were allowed to participate in deanery conferences. Clergy gatherings are also allowed at the funerals of clerical colleagues. This at least partly explains why, in Lithuania, these funerals attract literally dozens of priests from near and far. The funeral of Dean Alfonsas Sirus in April, 1975, for example, was attended not only by thousands of Catholics, but also by 140, or twenty percent of all of Lithuania's priests.[47] As the traditional wake in Catholic countries, these occasions serve for business communications for which the regime otherwise allows very limited official institutional channels.

Finally, religious associations themselves — and this of course includes the clergymen as servants of these associations — are subjected to numerous and broad regulations. Teaching of religion is permitted only in theological seminaries. As previously explained, religious education otherwise is not included in the right to worship. Similarly, the old and the new laws have severely circumscribed the scope of permissible pastoral activities. The law actually cuts every social, financial, and communications dimension from this work. Taken *verbatim* from the law of 1929, Art. 17 of the amended law forbids religious associations:

> (a) to create mutual aid funds, cooperatives, or commercial unions, or in general to use property at their disposal other than for the satisfaction of religious need; (b) to provide members with material support; (c) to organize special prayer and other meetings for children, young people, and women; or general meetings, groups, circles, and sections for Bible, literary, handicraft, catechetical, and other work; or to arrange excursions and set up children's playgrounds, open libraries and reading rooms, or organize sanitariums or medical aid.

In addition, the Lithuanian law expressly outlaws clerical visitations to believers (Arts. 17, 45). Religious worship, too, is confined to specially designated places — churches or approved buildings — and is prohibited on state, public or cooperative (for example, collective farm) enterprises, including hospitals unless "in specially isolated premises or at the request of the dying or the gravely ill who are in hospitals or places of detention" (Art. 58).

While in Lithuania the principle of *dvatsatka* was originally accepted by the only surviving bishop, Paltarokas, the supremacy of parish committees until recently was refused and the requirement of contractual relations with the local government for a long time was quietly overlooked. Parish committees do not yet dictate to the clergy in pastoral matters nor do local governments exercise as complete a control over local churches as is the case in the Russian Republic.[48] The republic's representative of the Council on Religious Affairs, Kazimieras Tumėnas, has urged their more energetic role and also the activation of standing commissions of local government agencies charged with monitoring the observance of the laws. Tumėnas conceded however that "in some religious committees the role of local soviets is still negligent."[49] To augment it, secret measures were taken in the 1970s to pressure parish pastors into signing contracts for the operation of the churches. This was done without the official knowledge of the bishops. The proposed contracts were drafted in ambiguous language designed to allow the government wide latitude, especially on the possible closing of the church, and many pastors refused to accept them. Approval of such agreements would mean, the clandestine *Lietuvos Katalikų Bažnyčios Kronika* (The Chronicle of the Catholic Church of Lithuania) has maintained, "the transfer of church jurisdiction to the intimidated members of church committees."[50] Church canons would not allow the clergymen to elevate parish committees over themselves in any case, while under the existing circumstances where the authorities can dominate these committees, acceptance of such contracts doubtlessly would promote a stricter compliance with limitations of pastoral work that the government has imposed by law. In order to forestall vocal opposition, local soviets have proceeded with discretion, and as the *Chronicle* has acknowledged, have scored successes with the less concerned and more frustrated pastors.[51] Many of them, however, have refused to honor this requirement, as they have similarly disregarded the demand to register passports or civil marriage certificates of spouses and witnesses in baptisms and church wedding ceremonies.

Pressures for contracts with local government were, however, renewed after the passage of the revised law on religious associations in the summer of 1976. This law specified that all religious groups had to sign new contracts within a year.

The contract signed by the *dvatsatka* actually is a lease that stipulates under what conditions a religious association can use church buildings and liturgical implements.[52] These belong to the state, together with any newly acquired or donated additions and revert to the state in case the license is withdrawn from the *dvatsatka*. Rent for their use is not required, but according to the law of 1975/76, the terms of the lease oblige the parish to pay insurance premiums, fees for policing, that is, guarding the building, and "other collections," usually, local taxes, dues, etc. (Art. 29 and 33). Building insurance benefits, however, must be signed over to the executive committee of local, be it rural or city, government. (Art. 33). The *dvatsatka* thus pays the premium, but is not the beneficiary of insurance proceeds. The association, furthermore, must keep up the building at its own expense, repair it when needed, and pay all the utilities. Utility rates, however, are six times higher than for any other private user.[53] Members of the *dvatsatka*, finally, individually share the responsibility for any damage to state property that was caused by its use or its loss. Inventory of all possessions must be available for inspection by the local government. At the same time, the local authorities may take from parish records "any information needed for the imposition of taxes on the servants of the cult and on other persons." Finally, the church building and other property can be used only "for the purposes of religious cult." In case of noncompliance with these terms, the local government may terminate the lease. The agreement, ultimately, may be squashed if "according to established regulations," none of which are specified, the government finds it necessary to close down the building that the parish has leased.

Strictly formally speaking, the current lease agreement is about the same as "contracts" enforced in the Stalinist epoch. In 1948, the signed agreement allowed the *dvatsatka* itself to terminate the agreement on a seven day notice, thus presumably exempting its members from any financial liability. However, in Stalin's day such agreement specifically forbade the use of the church building by priests who were not registered with the Commissioner for Religious Affairs. These are, however, minor differences of formulation. At present, *dvatsatka* members are allowed to withdraw on an individual basis, while unregistered clergymen can not function in public anyway. The two contracts indicate the regime's persistence in religious policy, conceived actually more than two generations ago.

Criminal Code and Religion since 1966

Originally, in 1961, the Criminal code of the Lithuanian SSR incorporated three articles concerning religion. These specified a year's prison sentence or a hundred rouble fine for violating the laws on the separation of church and state (Art. 143); further provided three to five year sentences for group activity that under "the pretense of propagation of religion" hurt public health or induced citizens to disregard their political or civil obligations (Art. 144); and finally, the code offered protection to religious cults by setting a year's prison sentence or a hundred rouble fine to those who would "obstruct the performance of religious rites as far as these did not break public order or were not connected with attempts to threaten the rights of citizens." (Art. 145). None of these articles, however, listed specific actions that violated the code. Thus, they were subjected to very arbitrary interpretations that in the Lithuanian case were not always illiberal, as applied by local soviets.

The situation changed in 1966 when many of the offenses were spelled out. On March 18th, 1966, the Supreme Soviet of the Russian Republic took the initiative to clarify the criminal code by listing prohibited religious activities and by providing higher sentences for repeated violations.[54] This Russian action was soon echoed around the Soviet empire and on May 12th, 1966, Lithuania's Supreme Soviet passed identical legislation.[55] Its purpose, in the Russian as well as the Lithuanian case, was to combat the reviving religious commitment that had produced more generous financial support of the churches, spurred petitions of grievances, led to massive attendance of religious holy places. In Lithuania, this religious revival encompassed the doggedly stubborn insistence on teaching religion to the young. In practice, such activities, with the exception of petitions and letters, have been already prohibited by various instructions. These, however, were largely semi- or totally secret. In 1966, the list of transgressions was made public possibly as a warning to the insecure members of religious groups and the clergy, possibly as an effort of "normalizing" government relations with the churches. Thus, the broad injunction against "the violation of the laws concerning the separation of church from the state and school from the church" contained in Art. 143 of the Lithuanian republic's code was interpreted by specifying what constituted such violations. According to the new legislation, it was illegal: (a) to impose church fees or taxes for the use by religious associations or for the benefit of the "servants of the cult"; (b) to produce or massively to distribute petitions, letters or other documents containing appeals to disobey the laws on religion; (c) fraudulently to "incite religious superstitions" in the masses of population; (d) to organize religious meetings, demonstrations or ritual services that violate "public order"; (e) to organize and systematically conduct religion teaching of those under age, in violation of legal rules. All these transgressions could draw court sentences from one to three years, depending on the gravity and frequency of violation. In addition, the Supreme Soviet of the Lithuanian SSR made public another list of crimes that provided administrative punishment up to fifty roubles by administrative commissions of the local soviets for lesser, but apparently more frequently occurring, transgressions. These, too, had already been listed in the instructions of the Council on Relisgous Affairs of 1961, but for the first time were published as a clarifying corollary of the criminal code. Thus, a person could draw a fine for (a) avoiding registration of religious associations, (b) violating the laws on the organization of religious meetings, demonstrations and "other" religious rites, (c) for organizing children and teenagers to meet in study groups of literature or other subjects that have no connection "to the performance of religious cult."

After the publication of these decrees, the Chairman of the Council on Religious Affairs, V. Kuroedov, became upset that in the West the published prohibitions were interpreted as a further encroachment on the freedom of conscience. He claimed that they merely forbade "illegal activity on the part of the church."[56] A decade later, in 1976, he claimed this to be the sole limitation of religious freedom in the entire law on religious associations that the Russian republic had redrafted and republished the previous year.[57] Kuroedov also insisted that the decrees of 1966, in addition to listing illegal activities, strengthened the rights of the believers by forbidding discrimination based on religion at work or in school. Indeed the decree, in addition to listing offences, made it a crime to deny employment or admission to school or unequal treatment in factories or schools on the basis of a person's attitude toward religion. Thus, protection against the obstruction of religious services was now supplemented by formal security on the job or in education.

These new decrees had a threefold effect on the Church in Lithuania. First, they formally narrowed down the perimeters of the clergy's freedom and imposed stricter punishment for their violations. Second, they removed some arbitrariness as well as discretion until then possible for supervisory agencies with the result that local governments now had to take action where previously they could afford selectively not to see the alleged transgressions.[58] On the positive side, however, the listing of specific violations provided formal grounds for legal defense of the remaining rights or disputed actions against the increasing activism of government agencies. Unexpectedly, as a result of this reform, the government found itself challenged by both the clergy and the believers. They now contested administrative and court decisions. In these actions the believers were aided by the provisions of the criminal code that sought to protect them against discrimination in employment and to secure the undisturbed integrity of religious services. *The Chronicle of the Catholic Church of Lithuania* reported a case where Lithuania's Supreme Court, in 1970, ordered the reinstatement of a teacher fired from her position because of her religious convictions.[59] Soon, however, it appeared that like other laws that presumably protect the citizen, this one, too, was meaningless without the Party's approval. Mrs. Ona Brilienė, a teacher in the secondary school of Vilkaviškis, while saved by the court, was nevertheless barred from the classroom by the school's principal. After refusing to resign, as the judge of the local court had suggested to her, she soon was dismissed at the request of the teachers' union at her institution. In addition, she was refused any kind of job in her home town and, finally, her husband, a civil engineer in the local enterprise, was forced to resign his position as well. The law has been applied in the same manner in relation to the guaranteed safety of religious services. In 1969, a comradely court of a collective farm near Ratnyčia, on the testimony of local police, admonished a married couple as "hooligans" for threatening to kill the priest during services, stripping the priest of liturgical garments, and just about chasing him out of the church. But the district prosecutor refused to confirm the court's decision and returned the case for retrial. This time the police were not allowed to testify on the priest's behalf, one of the witnesses changed his story, testimony of a witness who was not in the church at the time was produced against the priest, and the comradely court reversed its decision. The court, furthermore, incurred additional displeasure, this time from the Communist party's daily *Tiesa,* for not publicizing the change of its verdict.[60] Similarly capricious remains the interpretation of Art. 144 that forbids interference with the rights of citizens by the believers or the clergy under the guise of performing religious rites. This is construed so narrowly that any distribution of religious literature is regarded a crime of interference. Indeed, in 1973, the court in Klaipėda so read this article in sentencing eight Jehovah's Witnesses for receiving and distributing religious literature sent to them by their headquarters in Brooklyn.[61] It seems that the protections of 1966, of which Kuroedov was so proud, still have yet to prove their worth.

The Other Rules

This discussion of legal regulations of religion in Soviet Lithuania would be incomplete without adding that these various limitations, enumerated in the criminal code, or the Council's instructions, or only orally transmitted are further supplemented by provisions of the criminal and civil codes that have nothing to do with religious beliefs or activities. Thus, the clergymen and civilians who cooperated in the construction of the new church in Klaipėda in 1959 were convicted under articles forbidding abuse of official position, conspiracy to steal state property, speculation, and illegal trade.[62] In a number of cases, especially those that involve the sale of religious devotionals — for example, rosaries — prison sentences and fines have been imposed for illegal trade.[63] The old Lithuanian custom of erecting crosses in the gardens and frontyards has drawn fines for the alleged violation of architectural codes of the republic.[64] If the crosses were not removed, they were usually destroyed. Special mention should be made of the new Family code, adopted in 1968, which requires the parents to educate their children "in conjunction with public education in the spirit of loyalty to the Fatherland." The parents are further charged with educating a "Communist attitude toward work" and, finally, "preparing children for an active participation in the construction of Communist society."[65] In case parents disagree between themselves on children's education, the dispute is resolved, the code says, by an agency of local government. Such formulations did not exist in the discarded old code. They give the government an increased opportunity to enter family relations and to influence the education of children.[66] In 1974, for example, Mrs. Birutė Paškiene of Kaunas, a Pentecostalist, was deprived of her maternal rights to her three children because she openly taught them her religion.[67] Thus, the full weight of legal strictures, not merely those that specifically deal with religion or politics, is brought to bear on the believers and the clergy. At the same time, they are denied means of resisting the colossus of state apparatus that is skillfully manipulated by the Communist party against its main ideological enemy.

VIII

Atheism: Apparatus and Methods of Promotion

However stringent the legal limitations on the life of the churches in the Soviet Union, they comprise only a part of the measures the Communist party has worked out for the elimination of religion from society. The other part consists of activities that promote the atheist philosophy of life. "We have already separated the church from the state," Lenin has said, "but we have not yet separated religion from the people."[1] Atheist activities aim at attaining this goal.

Atheism, Ideology, and Society

The Soviets offer several reasons for the maintenance of an enormous institutional apparatus concerned with atheist activities. First, promotion of atheism helps to quicken the disappearance of the "remnants" of religious beliefs.[2] The speeding up of this process is regarded to be a duty of every Soviet citizen. This obligation exists because religion draws away loyalties from the Party and its established system, interferes with the integration of young people into it, encourages anti-Soviet values and serves as a communication tube for subversive foreign ideas.[3] According to the Marxist-Leninist doctrine, the churches have lost their strength with the destruction of capitalism and can have no future in the Soviet Union because "in the Socialist system of production, religion has no social roots."[4] Nevertheless, religious traditions, practices, and beliefs have survived. These have shown an unexpected tenacity because they are nurtured, according to Soviet ideologists, by the habits of behavior inherited from the capitalist past. These habits include a penchant for private possessions, parasitism, stealing of state property, and bourgeois nationalism. They all feed on the "remnants" of religion.[5] In recent years, however, some Lithuanian theoreticians began to doubt that religiosity is a phenomenon of merely socio-economic origins, and Antanas Gaidys, a Vilnius university lecturer, has suggested that religion is not dying as expected because it is a psychological, that is, a more permanent phenomenon. "Religion reproduces itself," he wrote, "not only as a simple remnant of the past, but also as a need with the help of an illusion to overcome the contradictions between personality and the environment."[6] Atheism should help to resolve these contradictions, similarly as involvement in atheist activities should help people to shake off the "remnants" of old thinking and old habits. Another established student of Catholicism and religion, J. Minkevičius, has even denied the central Communist objection to religion, namely, the idea that religion is "unscientific" and therefore contradicts the "scientific" Marxist-Leninist philosophy. According to Minkevičius, "the confrontation between religion and science is not absolute either historically or logically." Religion has its own "inner gnoseological and social reserves that are independent from the development of science, sometimes even encouraged by it."[7]

These views indicate the theoretical difficulties that have arisen for Soviet philosophers in recent years and reflect, on the one hand, the existing strength of religious convictions in society, and the problems the propagators of atheism have to confront on the other. This fact, however, has not dampened atheist activism; on the contrary, it has convinced the government of the necessity of broader, deeper, and more sophisticated atheist work.

The regime's commitment to it is not changing largely because atheism, in addition to the tearing down of religion, serves the Soviets a very positive and integrating purpose as well. It is an instrument of political socialization and the cornerstone of the "scientific" materialist ideology *(Weltanschauung)* of the new Soviet man.[8] Thus it is functional to the Soviet system as a tool used for the indoctrination of the population and their mobilization for Communist development. Atheism encourages the citizens "actively to participate in the work and in politics" of society and strengthen their "ties with the collective."[9] In 1959, at the time Khrushchev initiated a new developmental stage, the so-called transition from socialism to communism, the Communist party began a new ideological drive which featured an attack on the churches and religion. In 1959–61, the salty Communist leader unveiled comprehensive ambitious goals. He proposed to achieve full communism in the Soviet Union by outstripping the United States in economic production and thus guaranteeing his people consumer's affluence. He also reckoned that for this new society the party will need a "new man" and thus demanded the education of "the man of the future."[10] Khrushchev's party program of 1961 stressed the need for this new man and even designed a "moral code" of the "builder of communism." This code reflected a sharp difference between the dreams the old revolutionaries entertained about the transformation of human nature and the requirements that current Communist leaders built into the Soviet ethics. Instead of the liberated individual of the Marxist vision who works in the morning and fishes in the afternoon and otherwise pursues what he desires, the present rulers appeared to seek the education of a laborious and disciplined materialist of Victorian morals who does not eat if he does not work.[11] It may be said that for the man of Marxist dreams, Khrushchev substituted an "operational citizen" equipped for living in a totalitarian party-oriented society. If there ever existed a Platonic effort of educating people into citizens of a specifically designed system, it has been this adamant Soviet commitment to the creation of the new man.

Atheist indoctrination has an immense role to play in this unparalleled Soviet attempt at social engineering. In other words, the Kremlin does not take atheism as just another theoretical doctrine but as a behavioral philosophy that shapes political and ethical behavior. Paraphrasing Marx and Lenin on religion, it can be said that Soviet atheism is the "scientific materialist" religion the Kremlin's ruling establishment has decreed for its people to help overcome systemic difficulties and to create an illusion of their perfect social integration.

There is, finally, a very specific reason for the propagation of atheism in Lithuania that has special social significance generally to non-Russian Soviet regions. Soviet sociologists and politicians believe that an atheist commitment helps not only with the education of the ideologically suitable citizen, but also promotes homogeneity of world outlook without regard to race or ethnic background, and in this manner paves the way for a smoother integration and assimilation of Soviet nationalities. In Western studies of Soviet nationality processes, the instrumental importance of atheism has been barely noticed and even less investigated. A. I. Kholmogorov, a Soviet sociologist who has empirically studied "internationalization" in Latvia and Lithuania, has included in his research a statistical survey of changing religious attitudes to show that the atheist "struggle" against religion ultimately helps "to overcome ethnic isolation and residues of nationalism and chauvinism."[12] A Khazak writer, M. I. Fazylov, is even more explicit on this point. He charges that "religion is one of the factors that negatively influence the rapprochement among nations," and furthermore, that "religion and nationalism continue to nurse each other" and that therefore, "internationalist" education — which promotes bilingualism, mixed marriages, uniform world view, assimilated life style, economic interdependence, and a centrally run state system, dominated by Russian personnel — requires atheism. "Atheist and internationalist education," he suggests, "are two interconnected sides of the same task."[13] The same theme in recent years has been stressed by the authoritative *Voprosy nauchnogo ateizma*. Atheist indoctrination, in other words, has an integrative and assimilationist role among nationalities of Catholic, Protestant, Judaic or Moslem background, whose religious traditions set them apart from the Russians and from each other.[14]

In this and other respects, Soviet atheism differs from the traditional freethinker philosophy which had strong adherents and activists in independent Lithuania. The purpose of Dr. Jonas Šliūpas, the acknowledged leader of the free-thinker movement in prewar Lithuania, was to establish a wall of separation between church and state, and to secularize society. For Soviet atheism, the struggle against religion "is not the purpose in itself."[15] It is "subordinated to the tasks of the proletarian class" and "proletarian revolution"; in other words, it is subordinated to the needs of the Communist party and the Communist state. While Šliūpas believed in freedom of conscience for all, including the religious people, the Communists consider that only their system allows for the practice of such freedom. Thus, in independent Lithuania, the free-thinker movement provided a haven for crypto-Communists of the day; however, after the Kremlin's takeover, organized Communist life frequently eschewed traditional freethinkers because their atheism, generally speaking, was democratic. In the literary journal *Pergalė* (Victory), in 1972, a young writer has pictured such a traditionalist working on the repairs of a church building that, before the war, he had attempted to dynamite.[16] Caught and imprisoned by Smetona's police for this action, he later was deported by the Communists and now would have nothing to do with them. Traditional freethinkers, furthermore, did not deny nationalism. It is no accident that Lithuanian party secretary A. Sniečkus warned at the 12th party conference in March of 1960 that "bourgeois" atheists should not be used in atheist propaganda because they might merely popularize bourgeois ideologists and thus hurt the Communist indoctrination.[17]

Atheist Activities: Emphasis since 1963

Atheist work in the Soviet Union has a long history. While antireligious terror accompanied the revolution and the civil war, an organized atheist activity began only in 1922.[18] It never subsided since that time with the exception of the German-Soviet war in 1941–45, when Stalin had suspended anti-religious propaganda and even made concessions to religion. The curve of intensity with which atheism was promoted varied, and sometimes, as in early 1954, it may even have been an issue in the struggle for power in the Kremlin.[19]

In Stalin's epoch, Lithuanian atheist activities were of a brazenly militant character, directed mainly against the clergy and the Church. This atheist propaganda and action consisted of an essentially anti-clerical, not philosophically anti-religious work.[20] Frequently it was vulgar, and as many other Stalinist practices, incorporated a direct use of force. From about 1952, and especially after the dictator's death, in 1954, the party decided to elevate atheist work to a "scientific" level, to propagandize atheist ideology with the help of academic personnel, and to employ peaceful means of persuasion. This peaceful approach, however, was understood Marxistically; it did not eliminate political or social pressure or the so-called individualized education. On the contrary, social pressure was found to be more productive than force. Since that time, intimidation, exposure, discrimination, and similar methods have been elaborated into a fine network of conditioned persuasion that is institutionalized in the fabric of society. In 1959, Khrushchev's ambition of establishing a technological base for communism produced a considerably sharpened atheist war. Its first victim was the Russian Orthodox church. Its second casualty, it appears, was the Catholic church. Soon after the Khrushchevite church closings in Russia, the Lithuanian Communist party's Central Committee in January of 1963, outlined a new program for atheist work which showed how extensive was the regime's commitment to this endeavor.

The Lithuanian party's edict was issued half a year ahead of Moscow's proclamation of a new, more comprehensive and stricter national anti-religious policy in the Central Committee's plenary session of June, 1963.[21] This was most unusual. Moscow, possibly, wanted first to experiment in Lithuania. More likely, the Kremlin considered Lithuanian Catholicism to be a special target that required a separate and quick action. The Lithuanian leadership visualized a frontal upgrading and extension of atheist education. This involved, basically, three programs: the improvement of such education and preparation of atheist propagandists; a better use of the media; and a development of new atheist traditions and customs. The list of institutions to be involved was very long and showed the comprehensiveness and scope of the project. It began with the Academy of Sciences, included social science departments of schools of higher education, mentioned the Communist party's district and city committees, and then enumerated the Ministry of Education, the Ministry of Culture, the Ministry of Higher and Specialized Education, the republican society of "Žinija" (*Znanie*), the Central Committee of the League of Communist Youth of Lithuania, and the republican Council of trade unions. These establishments were so to perfect their scientific and educational endeavor that every "institute, university, technological school graduate, teacher, medical worker, agricultural specialist, engineer or technician not only himself become an atheist but also be a propagandist capable of organizing atheist work among the working people."[22] Moscow's Central Committee soon added some new tools to this work by requiring that in addition to the already obligatory course on Marxism-Leninism, students of all higher learning institutions take a course on the principles of scientific atheism. Furthermore, the party established an Institute of Scientific Atheism attached to the Central Committee that soon afterwards began to publish *Voprosy nauchnogo ateizma,* a philosophical and sociological journal dedicated to the study of religion and atheism in the USSR.[23]

The media, or as the party edict called them "the means of ideological influence," included the press, publishing houses, radio and television, cinema, stage theater, museums, literature, music and the arts, in other words, just about everything. In 1961, the government founded and, in 1965, opened up a museum of atheism, the second such museum in the Soviet Union after Leningrad.[24] As in the Russian metropolis, the Lithuanian museum is housed in one of the most distinguished local churches. In Leningrad, it is the former Kazan cathedral. In Vilnius, the museum is located in St. Casimir's, better to say, in a church that bears the name of Lithuania's patron saint and ruler of past centuries. In 1965, the State Opera House staged an atheist opera entitled "The City of the Sun." Drama theaters and the republican movie studio have produced scores of plays, pictures, and documentaries on anti-religious themes. Prizes in literature, journalism, and the arts are provided for the best atheist books, articles, and productions of the year.

The decree of 1963, it should be emphasized, did not start this activity, but merely provided a comprehensive framework for it. The rising curve of Soviet preoccupation with atheist indoctrination can be demonstrated by the record of the Lithuania branch of *Znanie* ("Žinija"), the Association for the Promotion of Political and Scientific

Information that, in 1948, replaced Emelian Yaroslavsky's old League of Atheists. The association has sixteen divisions, one of which propagandizes in the combined fields of philosophy and atheism.[25] In 1948, the group had 100 members.[26] By 1960, its membership increased to 12,000. The next decade witnessed further growth, and in 1970 the number rose to 30,000. In the next three years, it jumped to 37,000, and by 1977, the association had about 50,000 members. This membership is highly educated. All members of the Lithuanian Academy of Sciences belong to it, as do eighty-three percent of all professors and doctors of science; furthermore, seventy percent of all candidates of science and college lecturers are members. In 1958, these members gave 3,228 lectures on scientific atheism. This represented more than a threefold increase from 1951 and compared to 1,068 on economics, 1,365 on technological matters, and 2,519 given on agriculture. The number of lectures on combined atheist and philosophical topics grew even more' phenomenally from 1,892 in 1951 to 40,000 in 1970. This actually means that about one-fourth of all lectures given in that year were on anti-religious topics. In 1958, a proportion of such topics constituted just over eight percent of the total. The number of atheist lectures was doubled between 1972 and 1977, thus further increasing the percentage of atheist topics among the total.[27] Finally, in 20 years, 1945–65, the periodical press published 2,270 articles, brochures, and feature stories on "scientific materialistic *Weltanschauung*." Of 3,389 various letters, articles, and stories published during that time, two-thirds, or 2,123, dealt with religion or methods of struggling against it.[28] These figures omit books, radio, TV, and other media.

While much of this enormous increase occurred after Khrushchev began his anti-religious campaign in 1959, it has nevertheless continued unabated and was even intensified under Brezhnev's leadership. In the spring of 1974, the republican Coordinating Council on Atheism re-emphasized the importance of atheist work among the youth and the women, and became very agitated over the fact that "a handful of reactionary clergymen" were attempting to revise "principal provisions of the Soviet constitution on the question of separation of state from church and the church from school."[29] In 1975, the Lithuanian party's Central Committee issued another decree on atheist education in factories, stressing that it should go hand in hand with the improvement of working conditions — it then would be more popular — and calling for the "unmasking" of people who bring out into the open the practices of legal discrimination against believers and who seek to broaden the constitutional Soviet concept of "freedom of conscience."[30] There followed the inevitable denunciation of "bourgeois émigré nationalists," allegedly responsible for difficulties in Lithuania — that in reality the regime has created for itself — and then repeated many of the same ideas the party had advanced in 1963. This time the committee emphasized the need to increase the number of branches of the association "Žinija." The matter did not stop there. In 1975, the Lithuanian Komsomol leadership decreed the integration of "foundations of scientific atheism" into the political education system of the organization.[31] This new program started with the 1976/77 school year. Finally, in 1977, the Central Committee, increasingly irritated by the success of the "reactionary" — as they are officially labeled — clergy among the youth, issued new orders for intensified atheist education in schools and severely criticized the ministries of common and of higher and specialized education for their "neglect." The leadership of the Lithuanian Komsomol, too, was chided for "minimal" interest in the atheist education of its membership.[32]

In atheist work, the association "Žinija" and other groups of course play only a partial and specified role. Anti-religious activities are the party's responsibility, and involve therefore not only public, but also state and party, organizations. The current Communist emphasis on this endeavor can be gauged from the fact that in the Lithuanian party's XXV conference that met in January of 1975, Jonas Aničas, the chief theoretician of Lithuanian atheism, was appointed chief of the Central Committee's division on scientific and educational institutions.

The party's concern begins at the local level. Already in 1963, the Lithuanian party ordered each primary Communist organization to appoint a member for specifically promoting atheist activities in his school or factory.[33] A coordinating council for such activities exists on top, at the party's Central Committee. Special commissions are kept at larger party organizations. While the party thus originates, plans, and monitors atheist work, it acts through the republican Coordinating Council on Atheism that has branches in local districts. The chief of the party's Agitprop doubles up as the chairman of this council. This group, on a republican as well as on a local level, combines representatives of the media with various educational and governmental institutions. In the populous district of Panevėžys, a diocesan Catholic capital, such a council in 1975 was composed of eleven members who represented the Communist party, the government, the Komsomol, the local press, education, medical profession, culture, agriculture, "Žinija" association, and the council for the development of Socialist traditions.[34] On the local level, the council is directed by the vice-chairman of the district (county) government, who also presides over the local commission that supervises church observance of laws on religion.[35] Thus, this official has considerable discretion in handling not just atheist work, but the activities of the churchmen and their congregations. The membership of these coordinating councils on atheism seems partly to overlap with commissions that control church compliance with the laws. In this way, atheist activists can check church activities on a daily basis.[36] In other words, atheists interpret the laws on religion.

Many atheist activities are concentrated in educational institutions that follow their own curricula and prepare their own personnel. However, very many enterprises, collective farms, and offices have their own atheist clubs, groups, houses, or councils.[37] The apparatus of atheist work, in other words, overlaps with the "public," as distinguished from the strictly "governmental" sector of society. It furthermore reaches not only into social institutions but also private homes. Atheist attitudes and behavior are promoted only partially by professionals employed full time in various segments of activity. There is a paid "scientific" and administrative staff at the museum of atheism in Vilnius that, incidentally, has a budget to buy what remains of religious folk art; there exist university and institute chairs specially for the study of religion and atheist methodology; and the association "Žinija" also maintains its own staff. However, the party prefers that atheist propaganda outside of educational institutions be conducted by people whose major occupation is not related to strict propagandistic — either atheist or party — work. As a result, physicians, agronomists, astronomers, that is, people who represent scientifically reputable professions and have close relations to their clients, are drawn into atheist circles.

These special lecturers and propagandists are prepared primarily by the association "Žinija." The association runs a part-time training school for lecturers that takes a year to complete. Additionally, in 1975, the association started two-year schools in various republic localities. Trainees may enroll, but usually they are selected from suitable professions. To attract needed candidates, they are freed from other "public obligations and from study in schools of the party's educational system, seminars or people's universities."[38] A program of fifty-one hours is covered in periodical meetings in which the physicians and agricultural specialists study "Marxism-Leninism as the highest form of atheism," then concentrate on Catholicism and finally analyze methods of atheist work. During the first year, twenty out of thirty-two hours are spent on the history and work of the Catholic church in Lithuania. During the second year, the school offers lectures on the incompatibility of Communist and religious ideologies and discusses church relations with nationalism, anti-communism, and public morals. Finally, several hours are spent on Soviet legislation concerning religion and on methods of atheist indoctrination.

There exists no estimate of public expenditures on all these activities, but all work in schools, the media, and other means of communication must require millions of roubles that are disbursed from the Vilnius, not Moscow's, budget under various ministries and enterprises. Only a minor fraction of atheist work can be financed from dues or income from publications and services because the dues are very low while publications are extremely cheap. Visits to atheist museums, exhibits, or festivities are free.

Targets and Methods of Atheist Work

Despite the atheist commitment to promoting a positive "materialist" understanding of the world, their work through the years has possessed a largely negative, restrictive and polemical character. This still remains the situation — though a need is seen for different approaches — largely because of the traditional Soviet commitment to the conflict theory of social change and education. This theory assumes an ongoing struggle between antagonistic social forces that are supposedly reflected in opposing opinions and ideologies. The interpretation is somewhat stultified by assertions that the class struggle in the Soviet Union has ended with the victory of socialism, but it regains functional importance when society is found to harbor still very many remnants of the bourgeois past, bourgeois consciousness and behavior. Therefore the inculcation of positive values is interrelated with the destruction of the negative, old, "bourgeois" views. Thus, in atheist activities, as in other fields of endeavor, the scientific-materialistic philosophy is not promoted by merely praising its superior advantages, but proceeds with the tearing down and the attacking of the opposing views, with the aggressiveness of the "fighting atheists," that for so many years has characterized Soviet philosophical treatises, political pamphlets, or even routine educational programs.

In the theoretical-philosophical field, the list of subjects so aggressively handled begins with the existence of God and the creation of the world. It encompasses natural sciences that are considered especially weighty for atheist indoctrination, then it includes history, liturgy, religious practices, the Church's social doctrine, aesthetics (which is part of Soviet philosophy), and the Church's and religion's ability to modernize, that is, to adapt itself to industrialized modern society, especially under Soviet rule. Each year, state publishing houses bring out much seriously-intended and popularly written literature on these questions.

The other targets represent social groups. The oldest (and perennial) target is the clergy. For obvious reasons, the Soviets have consistently sought to reduce both its size and its influence. While on the whole the clergymen were left alone until the end of 1945, media attacks on them escalated very quickly afterwards, and on July 9th, 1948, the Lithuanian Communist party's Central Committee almost retroactively adopted a decree "on the duties of party organizations in unmasking the inimical activities of the reactionary Catholic clergy."[39] This decree was fortified by another passed in June of 1950 on the matter of "improving cultural-educational work in the village."[40] In these early years of the Soviet regime, the clergy were attacked basically for their political views, for their alleged opposition to the Soviet rule, and the involvement in the nationalist underground. Historical literature published since that time has invariably pictured it as the traditional enemy of the Lithuanian people. Lithuanian defense against the expansion of the Teutonic Knights in the XIII–XV centuries and the armed efforts by the Knights to christianize Lithuania have continuously supplied ammunition to tie in the clergy, the Nazi aggressors (heirs to Teutonic Knights), the Vatican and the Pope, who had chartered Teutonic activities in the Baltic area. In other words, atheist propaganda has sought to appeal — sometimes successfully — to Lithuanian patriotic feelings and thus has attempted to harness nationalism against the clergy and the Church.

Anti-clerical propaganda died down after Stalin's death — officially in 1952 — but was again in full swing after 1958. This time, especially in 1964–65, the theme of alleged clerical collaboration with the underground was resumed, but it was supplemented by various attacks on the personal integrity of the priests. Individual priests, identified by name, were denounced as drunkards, men of corrupt morals, speculators, embezzlers, and so on.[41] They were "drunkards" if liquor was served in the rectory at dinner on religious holidays; "immoral" if they asked boys or girls to serve in religious processions or at mass; "speculators" if they distributed home-made religious articles; "embezzlers" if they registered a new parish house in their own name instead of that of the church (which had no rights of legal person), etc. This kind of anti-clerical campaign went so far that a teachers' newspaper warned the atheists to beware that "such criticisms of the clergy would not become a struggle for educating a good priest."[42] In other words, this kind of propaganda produced effects opposite from those intended. In a regular social situation, such charges generally can be at least answered, if not explained. However, the single party press and the media have denied the right of response. Even the correction of obviously falsified records has not been allowed. In 1967, for example, Rev. V. Gelgota objected to being pictured as a murderer of a Soviet official during the guerilla war of the 1940s and demanded a retraction from the author of the offending pamphlet. Otherwise, the priest said, he would go to court against the slanderer; the Supreme Court had long ago exonerated him of all charges and he had been rehabilitated.[43] The author wanted to comply with the priest's request, but neither the publishing house, nor any newspaper, would accept his correction. In another case, the atheist museum in Vilnius for years exhibited a five cornered star made of steel needles that was allegedly used by Father Antanas Ylius, a sentenced member of the underground, to torture Communist activists.[44] It took the priest a very long time to have the charge corrected. The response to complaints often is deafening. In the earlier days, the very attempt to pierce the wall of isolation by official means was dangerous. On December 24th, 1960, Jesuit Father A. Markaitis succeeded in publishing a letter in *Literatūra ir Menas,* the literary weekly of the republic, that defended fellow Jesuit Father Paukštys' missionary activities in Yakutiia which the paper had criticized. Paukštys' activities in that Siberian land had been compared to the "machinations" of the Middle Ages, and Markaitis simply said that such interpretation showed the backwardness of Soviet scholarship. Markaitis apparently wrote more than one such letter, but succeeded in publishing only once. Soon afterwards, he was sent back to a Mordovian camp from which he had been released after Stalin's death.[45]

Such corrections now begin to appear in the *Chronicle of the Catholic Church of Lithuania.* Their publication in this underground journal seems to exert an unexpected influence on the authorities, despite the fact that the reading of the *Chronicle* is regarded as tantamount to a crime against the state. On March 1st, 1974, the daily *Kauno Tiesa,* a newspaper of the second largest Lithuanian city, labeled Father Pranas Račiūnas a spy of the Vatican and of the United States for contacting Father Laberge of the American Embassy in Moscow sometime in the early postwar period. This charge was based on a story entitled "Mutiny of the Vampyres" that was published in a literary journal in 1961. Father Račiūnas wrote a letter to the author in which he explained that he had visited Moscow with the permission of the authorities and that his conviction for espionage was reversed decades later and that he had been rehabilitated.[46] He mailed copies of the letter to Bishops Labukas and Povilonis, Foreign Minister Andrei Gromyko, representative of Religious Council Tumėnas, and to Jonas Kubilius, the rector of Vilnius University where the author was a lecturer. Retraction of the falsehood was not printed by the official press, though its author for the time being disappeared from the roster of the university faculty.

If the clergy represent a target the Soviets would like to destroy, the youth is the prize they intend to capture. Education of children and teenagers "in the spirit of materialist ideology" is considered to be an objective of the first priority. This interest in the youth, needless to say, is directly connected with the regime's enmity to the Church. In March of 1972, P. Mišutis, then the chief of Lithuanian Agitprop, suggested that "to free the young generation from religious influence means to deprive the church of the future."[47] Competition for the loyalties of the youth has led the authorities to the choice of two other subordinate targets; namely, the pensioners, the old generation of the grandfathers and especially the grandmothers, and then women. The grandmother in the Soviet Union generally is a social institution. For many practical reasons, the grandparents in Lithuania usually live with their sons and daughters, and the grandmother is relied upon as the educator of the grandchildren. A Soviet Lithuanian official, when once asked why he is not caring for his children's religious education — he could not do so because of his position — retorted that "we have a grandmother at home." According to Mišutis, the grandparents are "the main source from which children receive their first religious notions." Women, on the other hand, not only have enormous influence on children but also "constitute a majority of the believers."

Education, needless to say, belongs exclusively to Communist jurisdiction. In Lithuania, Soviet concern with the atheist slant of the children's secular education was immediate. Since in the early days of Soviet rule teaching personnel did not possess Soviet training, its reeducation was the first order of business. Already in April of 1945, the party decided on measures for mobilizing the yet wavering teachers in the struggle against "bourgeois" ideology. A year later, in 1946, party activists of Kaunas impatiently complained that classes in chemistry, physics, and astronomy had not yet become "instruments of anti-religious education."[48] The regime never had any tolerance for a teacher who held "objectivist" views.[49] Periodically checking their performance, the Ministry of Education continues dismissing such teachers, especially from grade schools and kindergartens.[50] At school, the teacher must teach in an anti-religious spirit; after hours he must sponsor extracurricular activities such as plays or excursions to atheist museums. Furthermore, the educator has to watch and guide the student and, if necessary, is expected to use social pressure to get compliance. Such pressure has been well documented by the *Chronicle of the Catholic Church of Lithuania* and occasionally emerges in the pages of the Communist press itself. In a typical case,[51] for example, teachers of a South Lithuanian locality publicly ridiculed religious children for their religious beliefs, and in a less typical manner, a woman teacher forced a child to take off his pants to be spanked for attending church. The school's newspaper taunted a number of other students as "God worshippers" who "humiliate themselves, their reputation and then also besmirch the name of the school." What especially galled the school administrators was the discovery that these students were members of Pioneer and Communist Youth organizations. "They are," the newspaper editorialized, "two-faced hypocrites who attempt to accommodate themselves to church and to school, who are Pioneers and altar boys at the same time and who are paid a couple of kopeiks by the priest for their chameleonic activities." To stop their church attendance, a teacher threatened and then pleaded with the parents that if the children would continue as "God worshippers" the teacher might lose her pension rights. The parents nevertheless complained to higher authorities and upon investigation received oral assurances that their children had the right to go to church though they should read more atheist books. Such response by the inspector of the Ministry of Education was unusual and unique. More generally, the parents don't dare to complain and the ministries don't reverse decisions. In the locality of Baisogala,[52] in 1973, two graduating high school girls carried flowers in the Easter procession and for such participation in religious ceremonies had their grade for conduct reduced below the required "excellent." Evaluation of a student's behavior by a grade is traditional in some East European schools and basically means appraisal of the student's honesty and integrity. If this grade falls below "excellent," the student always has difficulties in applying to other schools or for scholarships. The graduating teenagers defended themselves by blaming their mothers' insistence on their walking in the procession, to which the teacher merely retorted that "the next time your mother will probably order you to bed with the pastor." A note was entered into their school documents stating that "notwithstanding their membership in the Communist Youth League, the girls did not develop an atheist ideology because in their senior year they attended the church." This note meant the students' automatic exclusion from university education and from a number of career choices. In still another school, a high school junior was warned ahead of time of difficulties she would have as a graduate if she continued attending church.[53] She may be excluded from the school; she had better join the Communist Youth League that now embraces virtually all graduating secondary school seniors. Cases of pressure to join the Pioneers or Komsomol are too numerous to mention. The *Chronicle* has reported that sometimes teachers physically remove children from church services or religious processions and then interrogate them. At some of these interrogations, teenagers have been beaten by police officers.[54]

The teachers and officials are especially upset when they discover that a high school senior, and a very good student at that, decides to enter the theological seminary.[55] The student himself becomes a subject to pleadings, threats, and offers from his teachers. Preparation of various certificates he needs from the police and other authorities is delayed and he has to fend off new attacks of "persuasion"; and even his parents are approached with a view of influencing the young man's decision.

Atheism and "Socialist" Traditions

Since atheist indoctrination has not only a theoretical, but also a behavioral dimension, still another aspect of atheist work consists of the promotion of secular and Communist traditions as substitutes for religious celebrations. With this activity the atheists seek to penetrate family and group life and give it a symbolic Communist or atheist meaning. In a fashion that Christianity functionalized many ancient pagan rituals, the Communists now attempt similarly to transform Christian traditions. Lithuanian atheists, one of them recently wrote, for a long time did not pay sufficient attention to these matters.[56] They forgot, this author said, that since religion has three composite parts — ideology, the cult, and psychology — each of these parts has a place in social life. Atheist work has been too much concentrated on the education of a scientific ideology *(Weltanschauung)* and on "the negative criticisms of religion." The importance of religious traditions was disregarded. These traditions were simply criticized and then discarded.

The Soviets however have rediscovered the importance of ceremonies. The existence of a variety of rituals is now acknowledged,
among them family, youth, socio-political, family-political traditions.
They are, furthermore, not only accepted but also considered indispensable as performing an important "ideological-educational" function.[57] Specifically in the ideological field, these new Socialist traditions are now appraised as "effective means for overcoming the
influence of religion."[58]

In Lithuania, most family festivities or traditions have historically
been of a religious nature, but according to Soviet writers, they are no
longer purely such; they have become "people's" traditions. A new,
Socialist economic system, according to a "traditions" specialist, P.
Pečiūra, has produced new festivities or is helping to change the
meaning of the old. Thus, there is hope, he asserts, for the transformation of Catholic into Communist traditions.

This attitude, however, is still relatively new. In 1957–59, Lithuanian ideologists thought that church traditions and rituals should be
replaced by ancient Lithuanian people's festivities and traditions. It is
interesting to note that the Nazis in Germany, too, attempted to
replace Christian traditions with those of pagan German tribes. It did
not work in Germany, and the attempts in Lithuania did not bring
much success either. In the already discussed decrees of 1963, the party
ordered a fresh start. A command was given to create "civic traditions
and habits of behavior that should push out religious rituals and by the
same token diminish the influence of the church." However, no agreement on what to do could be reached for five years until finally, in
1968, the newly appointed Minister of Culture, Lionginas Šepetys, a
sophisticated party *apparatchik,* established in his Ministry a council
for the fostering of people's traditions.

This Council has made some progress, and today the list of various
"Socialist," as distinguished from Catholic or "Capitalist," festivities is
already quite long. It includes state and revolutionary holidays, professional occasions, celebrations that are related to work, and traditional as well as family festivities.[59] These latter overlap or replace
religious commemorations. It was relatively easy to order the replacement of Christmas by the New Year and Santa Claus by Father Frost.
But Communists have found it more difficult to fight the celebration
of Easter because it always falls on a Sunday. A "spring" celebration
has been invented as a substitute though it has not yet taken roots.
Furthermore, instead of the All Souls Day for the commemoration of
the dead there now exists simply "a day for honoring the dead."

Similarly, since religious family traditions that center around birth, death, and marriage refuse to die, the Soviets decided against their elimination; instead, they have tried to secularize their character. Thus, wedding palaces were established to enliven the frequently colorless civil marriage ceremony; baptismal rites (with a party afterwards) have been rearranged into a "name giving" ritual (with the party following as in the old days); name days and birthdays are nowadays celebrated with official approval. There exists a substitute for confirmation — important especially in the Protestant case — and the funerals have been given a ritual that rivals the religious ceremony. State-sponsored funeral homes finally began to appear that do not allow religious ceremony. In brief, the Soviets in Lithuania have decided on the remaking, rather than total rejection, of the old traditions and rituals.

The task of implanting these new ceremonies has not been understood as a purely atheist task or a duty of just the professional atheists. It is an activity that, in the estimation of the new ritual makers, requires contributions from sociologists, historians, ethnographers, psychologists, poets, writers, composers, artists, and even economists.[60] Thus, like a film production, it involves anyone who can help to create illusions with which the people can best identify. The managers of these illusions in Moscow hope in this manner better to integrate and strengthen the system that they dominate.

A Look from the Inside

The questions of atheist indoctrination and religion's role in society have been discussed not only by various Soviet propagandists and policy makers, but also have found their way into literature, and not always in strict conformity with the canons of Socialist realism or the Communist dogma. As is true elsewhere, a writer frequently captures the reality better than a scholar because he can depict the feeling and the atmosphere; he can paint a sharper imagery of the emotions and agony of the people caught in the web of social or ideological conflicts. Therefore, an additional dimension of the syndrome of atheism and the context of conflict in Lithuania can be gained from a story by a well-known Lithuanian writer, Jonas Mikelinskas, that was published in the literary journal *Pergalė* in 1968.[61] In this story, entitled "Three Days and Three Nights," the author pictures a godforsaken provincial Lithuanian town to which there comes an inspector of the Ministry of Education to check on complaints made about the quality of education at the local school. While there, the inspector is surprised to discover that a close friend of his high school days also lives in the small town. He is the local Catholic pastor, and he invites the inspector for a chat. The school principal encourages the inspector to go, and after considerable vacillation, not sure how the visit would affect his career in the Ministry (as it turns out, it is hurt), the inspector finally meets the priest. The priest's mother lives with him, and in a way it is like old times except that the friends now find themselves on the opposite sides of the barricades.

The inspector is surprised to discover that quite contrary to the officially publicized image of the priest, his old friend is the most educated, collected, and sane person in the entire place. The town otherwise exhibits nothing else but violence, deceit, drunkenness and brawls in the local tavern, which is the sole social center of its life. At the parish house, the priest's bookshelves bulge with volumes of scholarship, beginning with Aristotle and including Marx as well as Lenin. After a sip of tea, they begin talking about what is on the pastor's mind, and little by little the inspector is drawn into a discussion of science, religion, and atheism. To his amazement and distress, he soon discovers that he is ideologically disarmed; he can only make official statements, but he cannot win an argument. The priest explains that his library is so complete because "the pastor of the Twentieth Century must be armed with a book, not with a stick." "Naturally," the priest continues, "it is necessary for us to know our opponent, his theses, his assertions, his reasoning, his arguments and motifs, the entire arsenal of his wisdom. Unfortunately, we do not always have the possibility for propagating our truths and in cases of need for defending them." "Why don't you use the pulpit?" suggests the inspector. "The pulpit?" asks the priest, at the same time curious and surprised. "Blessed naiveté! We don't live in times, my friend, before Guttenberg's invention of the printing press. How much can preaching from some dozens of pulpits mean against the flow of lava from the press, schools, television, radio, movie theaters, organization enterprises, lecture halls, various festivals and speakers' platforms?" As the inspector has no answer, the priest continues: "Frankly speaking, I am sorry for the person who tries to prove the atheist point of view in the press or from the speaker's stand but does not reflect that the king, as Andersen has said, is naked, that is, that his opponent's lips are forcibly sealed. There is not much honor in being righteous over a person who is made deaf and dumb. That's why I believe that a thinking person should not become an atheist at least until the time someone very powerful and just will say: let us hear out the other side as well — *audiatur et altera pars."* The discussion then shifts to the merits of religion. "The atheists," continues the priest to the increasingly nervous inspector, "reduce everything to earthly concerns; with a lantern they search for the social roots of religion; they try to explain this emotion as an expression of man's weakness when confronted with the elements, et cetera. They call it a remnant, a superstition, but the thought does not occur to them that faith is man's road to eternity, to the absolute, that it embodies man's natural thirst for extending his existence beyond the grave. This may be an illusion, but it is a holy illusion; it reflects man's nature, his essence; it helps him to exist and avoid becoming an animal." The inspector then protests and defends the atheist concept of man, freedom, and morality (Dostoyevski's "if there is no God, then everything is allowed" is used by the priest for an answer) and finally asks whether his friend has no doubts about his priestly vocation. The pastor answers slowly, but affirmatively, and then explains his reason for continuing in the priesthood. "If there were anyone who could gnash my doubts, I would immediately take off my soutane. But there is no such person and there will not be. No. We [priests] will be needed as long as man will remain mortal but will dream about immortality and will strive toward it. And if, with the help of science, to his own misfortune, he will tame immortality, we will leave the scene without a murmur. Until this happens, it is our duty to remind the man: *sursum corda* (lift up your hearts)."

Two years later the author of this narrative was severely criticized for writing the story and the editor of the journal for publishing it. The editor was demoted, the writer fell into temporary disfavor. Party chiefs did not like it because it showed atheist indoctrination and life in Soviet Lithuania for what it really is: namely, not a competition between scientific and religious forces, as it is claimed, but a monologue by the omnipotent ruler who opposes ideas different from his own for fear of the exposure of his own inner weakness. As suggested earlier, Soviet philosophers and propagandists — at least in Lithuania — are beginning to see that polarization between science and religion is artificial and that consequently, practical atheist work, as conducted until this day, no longer satisfies the needs of modern Soviet society. It goes on, however, unabated.

IX

Emergence of Religious Protest Movement: The Struggle for Liberal Society

It would have been unrealistic to expect that the heavyhanded Soviet treatment of religion would not provoke complaints, resistance, confrontation with the Communist party, and appeals for help. The first such appeal reached the West a generation ago, in 1948. It was a letter by Lithuanian Catholics to Pope Pius XII written on September 20th, 1947, and brought to the West by Lithuanian nationalist partisans who clandestinely pierced the Iron Curtain in the deep winter of that year. It was delivered to the Pope on October 1st, 1948. In Switzerland, where it was published in German translation, it was entitled "A Cry for Help from a Dying Nation."[1]

Lithuania, however, did not expire. Its Roman Catholicism survived. In 1959, the West gained a glimpse into the depth of the resurgent Lithuanian faith from a prayerbook written by four young Lithuanian exiles in Siberia and smuggled to the West. The little book served as a small, but luminous, witness of the strength of Catholic convictions. It was translated into nine languages, including English and Chinese, and its publication of about a million copies very much upset Soviet authorities.[2]

While in the West until then, our knowledge of Catholic testimonials or complaints was limited to clandestinely received works such as the Siberian *Marija, gelbėki mus* (*Mary, save us*) or to letters telling about pastoral conditions, or indeed to occasional literary pieces, in Lithuania itself accumulated grievances reached the government as well. In 1955-61, for example, there is evidence of a letter writing practice to Communist newspapers to criticize the treatment of priests or of religious subjects or even to encourage a more liberal religious policy.[3] In the 1960s, clergymen began protesting their condition to the Commissioner for Religious Affairs.

The Emergence of Lithuanian Dissent

However, an organized, collective expression of grievances and an articulated defense of vital Catholic interests did not come until 1968. This was the watershed year that marked the beginning of the battle of petitions, arrests, trials, and that culminated in the emergence of the underground press, especially the *Chronicle of the Catholic Church of Lithuania*. In 1971–72, this activity reached massive proportions and was followed by street demonstrations and by an open defiance of authorities. For the first time since the country's occupation in 1940, the religious issue put the Soviet government on the defensive; Soviet suppression of religion functioned as a catalyst for the accumulation of various other complaints, and consequently produced such outbursts of pent-up emotions that was not sought by the Catholics, nor expected by the Communists.

Thus, between 1968 and 1972, there rose in Lithuania a broadly supported religious dissent movement. In its closeness to the average man and his family it rivaled the Crimean Tartar struggle for the return to the homeland. In its ability spontaneously to engage both the intellectual and the worker, the senior citizen and the youth, it became the envy of Russian dissidents. Discrimination against religion was an issue that united people of different social and educational backgrounds and produced popular support for a constitutional opposition to the authorities and their laws. In Russia, the dissidents could find this only among the intellectuals; in Lithuania the participation of common people was massive. Since the demand of rights for religion was bsaed on the broad constitutional demand of freedoms for everyone, religious dissent served as a rallying point for people and groups with kindred grievances. In an amazing combination of viewpoint, the traditional, strong, and generally conservative Roman Catholicism became the champion of liberal constitutionalism and of ideas usually associated with secular and even anti-religious West European liberalism. Even more striking was its demonstrated ability practically to work and identify with people of different religious and national backgrounds.

The Rise of Dissent in Russia and Lithuania

A search for reasons why the Lithuanian dissent appeared on the scene only in 1968 produces two seemingly contradictory, but actually convergent, explanations. First, while in the late 1950s the hope of improvement in religious conditions was still alive, in the 1960s the prospects of amelioration diminished. In 1961, Khrushchev passed new restrictive church legislation that first hit the Russian Orthodox and Baptist churches, but that soon affected the Catholics. Two years later, the new restrictions on the clergy were followed by a specially designed atheist campaign that eventually put the local supervision of parish activities in the hands of local atheists. The next year, in 1966, there came the criminal legislation that increased punishment especially for religious teaching and that clearly sought completely to isolate the clergy from society, especially from school age children and teenagers. Thus, the squeeze not only continued, but the ax cut much closer to the bone. The Soviets were ready, as the former chief of the Lithuanian Agitprop, P. Mišutis, had said, to sever the church from its future, the youth.

At the same time, while the party's religious policy turned more reactionary, the general political atmosphere in the country remained several degrees brighter. De-Stalinization of the 1950s had bridled the secret police, reduced fear, restored a semblance of legal normalcy, allowed more intellectual freedom. By distancing the country away from the Stalinist system, Khrushchev had released the genie of freedom that later neither he, nor his successors, were able to lure back into the bottle. In the late fifties and the early sixties, Khrushchev attempted to persuade the intellectuals voluntarily to accept the party's supremacy over the arts, but Soviet writers and artists could not be bought off. The permission, in 1962, to publish Alexander Solzhenitsyn's *One Day in the Life of Ivan Denisovich* did not help either. Actually, its appearance in the pages of *Novyi mir* was a white elephant; censorship, though generally it had been eased, continued strict prior to Solzhenitsyn's achievement and remained so afterwards. Already in 1960, many younger writers could not find acceptance in the official press, and this gave birth to literary *samizdat,* a semi-legal private duplication of manuscripts, etc., that the KGB very shortly began to treat as a criminal activity. A literary journal *Syntaxis* that appeared in *samizdat* in 1959 was followed by *Boomerang* in 1960 that was, in a manner of speaking, succeeded by Yuri Galanskov's *Phoenix* in 1961. Writers, furthermore, began smuggling their works for publication in the West. About a year after Khrushchev's overthrow, two of them, Andrei Siniavski and Yuri Daniel, were caught and in 1966, sentenced to long years of labor camp for the "slandering" of the Soviet Union that is prohibited by Art. 70 of the Russian republic's criminal code.[4]

The case against Daniel and Siniavski gave the Kremlin an excuse to go after dissident writers and to clamp down on liberalization in the intellectual-literary field. This Soviet decision thus signified another turning point in domestic development. After the strike against religion, the Kremlin now reestablished control over the intellectual life. This also meant that the government did not intend more broadly to interpret substantive or procedural rights that the Khrushchevite reform of "Socialist legality" seemed to promise. Normalization of legal procedures did not ensure freedom, but a mere protection from summary justice by the secret police. Now, as Andrei Amalrik so colorfully described in the *Involuntary Journey to Sibera,* the transgressors were sentenced by regular courts that followed regularized procedures. After Siniavsky and Daniel, arrest and sentence came for Vladimir Bukovsky, Andrei Dobrovolski, Vyacheslav Chornovil, Alexander Ginsburg, Yuri Galanskov, and others, including the protestors of the Soviet invasion of Czechoslovakia in 1968. In September of 1967, Major General Petr Grigorenko was confined to an insane asylum. These actions showed the party's determination to tame and control the intellectuals by force. Liberalization, in other words, was aborted; it did not lead the country closer to a system based on law. The party had become very impatient and struck down the challenges that the writers presented to its arbitrary rule.

The intellectuals, however, at first did not cave in. They reacted to the persecution by mobilizing opinion. As a result, the Stalinist resumption of police measures against the mere words of criticism backfired. Underground publications increased in number and size, and now, instead of publishing just poetry or literary essays, *samizdat* ripped into the arbitrary administration of the law, violation of the fragile procedural protections, the inhuman conditions of political prisoners, the wanton persecution of religious believers and their priests, the prohibition to emigrate to Israel. In April of 1968, to celebrate the international year of human rights that was declared by the United Nations, there appeared the *Chronicle of Current Events,* in 1968–72 and from 1974 until the present the chief journal of the Russian dissent movement.

In addition to publications, the advocates of civil rights now engaged two other methods to help the incarcerated or harassed people. These were petitions to central government officials and their publicity not only at home but also abroad. A host of letters was sent to government officials asking freedom for the convicted writers, requesting exit permits from the Soviet Union, protesting what prisoners regarded their unjust arrests, demanding — as the Crimean

Tartars did in 1968 — the right to live in their old homeland. In various ways, texts of those documents reached the West and the publicity they received frequently helped to nudge the Soviet government into more leniency.

Religious protest, too, was heard rather loudly. In 1965, Anatoli E. Levitin-Krasnov, who had been agitating since 1960, demanded "free religion and free atheism" and would not retreat from this stand under questioning by a group consisting of a KGB representative, a man from the national Council on Religious Affairs, a member of the staff of *Nauka i religiia,* and others.[5] Baptist reformers refused to accept the limitations of 1961 and after the Baptist congress of 1963 the *Initsiativniki* continued the struggle for their rights. Arrests and sentences followed. These, in turn, were appealed to state prosecutors or other government agencies. Complaints were sent to the United Nations. In December of 1965, two Russian Orthodox priests, Nicholas Eshliman and Gleb Yakunin, wrote an open letter to the Patriarch of Moscow accusing him of subservience to the state that hurt the Church. They also mailed a statement to the Council for the Affairs of the Russian Orthodox church protesting its "unlawful actions."[6]

The government felt the pressure. As a result, mainly because of this and other articulated, but disregarded, dissatisfactions, on April 12th, 1968, the Supreme Soviet of the USSR passed a decree "on the procedure for the examination of proposals, declarations and grievances by the citizens."[7] The decree acknowledged that some government agencies did not pay sufficient attention to petitions, but ordered that these be sent to local, rather than higher governmental, institutions that now were besieged. This was a proper procedure, the decree specified, because the higher agencies return the petitions for examination to local institutions anyway. In a typically Soviet fashion, the decree contained a safety valve for the government; it forbade "slanderous" petitions and statements and, furthermore, made their authors punishable for such appeals. In effect, the Kremlin guaranteed the right of petition on the one hand, but reserved the right to decide which of them it would tolerate on the other.

All of these developments, the growing suppression especially of religious teaching, the groundswell of demands that raised hopes of reforms, the government's recognition of the right of petition helped to ignite the Lithuanian religious protest movement. The Lithuanian clergymen and parishioners had waited for two years after the passage of the restrictive legislation of 1966. They gave a chance to the initially trusted new Bishop Matulaitis-Labukas to positively influence the situation, but he quickly proved a disappointment. The reformers felt they were losing precious time.[8] It is possible, but doubtful, that the Lithuanian choice of tactics was influenced by the Ukrainian or Russian Baptist practice — there were very few Baptists in Lithuania and traditionally, Catholic relations with the Baptists were not very close — but it is more likely that the inspiration came from the *Chronicle of Current Events* that offered a philosophy of civil rights akin to the Western — a fact that the Western-oriented Lithuanian Catholics could readily appreciate — and that encouraged the use of information as a tool for constitutional reform.

The Battle of Petitions: The Clergy Leads the Protest

Petitions were sponsored by the clergy, the members of the *dvatsatkas* who were usually elder persons with nothing to lose, women, and mothers predominantly in rural areas; also, by secret members of convents and monasteries. Some petitions without much doubt were inspired by the priests themselves. This was a familiar tactic. Already in the XIX century, Tsarist governors complained that what Bishop Valančius could not get from the government directly, he sought to gain by way of people's petitions.[9]

The first petitions of grievances were sent to Moscow in the summer of 1968. Rev. Vladas Šlevas of the Telšiai diocese in Western Lithuania wrote a letter to the Chairman of the Council of Ministers, Alexei Kosygin, in which he asked that Kosygin lift "certain restrictions and deficiencies" that are imposed on the Church by "the representatives of the government of our [Lithuanian] republic."[10] He listed three requests: ordination of more priests, ending of discrimination in charging electricity rates for churches and, third, publication of the already prepared "liturgical prayerbook" that had been authorized but that could not be printed because of an alleged shortage of paper. As for utility rates, Father Šlevas said that members of collective farms paid 4 kopeiks per kwh while the churches were required to pay 25. Written communications to the government were for this priest a familiar practice. In 1960, Father Šlevas had penned letters to Lithuanian papers urging them to support freedom of religious instruction in schools. He was criticized for such activity and now went over the heads of republic authorities. The pastor's younger friend, Alfonsas Pridotkas, of the same diocese wrote a similar letter.[11]

These two letters, conceivably, were considered by their colleagues as trial balloons. The government had permitted petitions for redress of grievances; will clerical requests be respected? The answer came in two months. It was not in the form of a letter from Kosygin, but an invitation to appear before the Commissioner for Religious Affairs in Vilnius. On October 7th, 1968, both priests were severely reprimanded for their action and shortly afterwards transferred to smaller parishes.[12]

The clergy, however, would not be discouraged. Many merely regretted that so much time was lost without defending the eroding rights of their Church. The next move was collective and had two targets: their own church administration and the government. On the last day of 1968, sixty-three priests of the diocese of Vilkaviškis that, as previously explained, is administered by the bishop of Kaunas, signed a letter to all Lithuanian bishops that dealt basically with the state of the theological seminary. If the government will continue denying admission of more candidates, they said, the number of priests will shrink so much that "shortly almost none will be left for pastoral work."[13] The signers introduced a constitutional point by suggesting that the government's restrictions on admissions and also its various extra-legal efforts to prevent young men from entering the seminary directly interfered with the affairs of the Church. Such interference, the petitioners claimed, was outlawed by Art. 124 of the Soviet constitution which separates the state from the church. About a week later, a similar message, with a copy for Lithuanian bishops, was sent to the Chairman of the Council of Ministers in Moscow and the all-union Commissioner for Religious Affairs.[14]

Lithuanian church administrators were again reproached in September of 1970 by fifty-nine priests of the same diocese of Vilkaviškis.[15] Their declaration now was endorsed by forty-nine colleagues of the Vilnius archdiocese as well. This memorandum was much longer, the language was more direct, the contents dealt not only with theological studies and the secular atmosphere of the seminary that, the authors said, will make the school "to serve other than its own purposes," but also with the various questionable practices of the church administrators themselves. The hierarchs were accused, for example, of refusing to answer the clergy's petition that objected to the appointment of Dr. Butkus as the seminary's rector. Furthermore, the memorandum revealed that secretly, without any explanation to the priests or the believers, church administrators had donated thousands of church roubles to the Soviet "peace fund." They also reneged on the pledge given during their visit to Rome to support the restoration of the two exiled bishops of Kaišiadorys and Vilnius. After returning from the Eternal city, the memorandum said, the hierarchs refused to sign a petition to the Soviet government requesting the reinstallment of the removed prelates. Their relations with the clergy were said to be poor at best. Priests who strictly complied with canon law in the performance of their duties were not protected; they were punished instead. Finally, together with some clergymen, the diocesan chanceries not only displayed a hostile attitude toward government-persecuted clerics, but also criticized them for allegedly "wrecking the unity of the Catholic church in Lithuania."

The petitioners suggested that the basis for disunity was created rather by the "spirit of injustice, fear and subservience that is reflected in interview statements" given to the radio and foreign Communist press by church dignitaries. Virtually all high church functionaries were listed as authors of such statements. They included Bishops Matulaitis-Labukas and Pletkus, Msgr. Krivaitis, Chancellor of Telšiai Dr. Barauskas, Rector of the seminary Dr. Butkus. This unity was further hurt, the memorandum stated, by anonymous letters mailed to republic church administrators and the resident Lithuanian bishop in Western Europe, Antanas Deksnys. The signers finally deplored the lack of support diocesan chanceries gave to petitions that priests had sent to the government though copies of such petitions were provided to the administrators. The signers found the hierarchy's attitude toward petition writing and petition sponsors disdainful. In this manner, the bishops showed that they did not appreciate the clergy's sacrifice and dedication. The hierarchs thus were not true church leaders. "We expect," the signers said, "our pastors to be real *Pastores et Patres* (pastors and fathers) of both the religious people and the priests. We the clergy do not want to be revolutionaries but your collaborators in working for the welfare of the Church [underlined]."

These charges were almost as serious as those by the Russian Orthodox priests Eshliman and Yakunin against the Orthodox Patriarch of Moscow and indicated the increasing distance between the hierarchy and the clergy.

The majority of clerical petitions, however, were addressed to various governmental agencies, including the Chairman of the Council of Ministers, the Secretary General of the Communist party, the Commissioner for Religious Affairs. In August of 1969, forty priests of Vilnius archdiocese signed a memorandum to Kosygin in which they complained of several discriminating restrictions.[16] The conditions of the theological seminary came first; provincial exile of the two deposed bishops was next. Then the petitioners listed various prohibitions and discriminatory practices. These included obstacles for receiving the sacrament of confirmation; prohibition of spiritual and canonically prescribed retreats for priests; absence of prayerbooks and "even the most elementary religious textbook"; fines for catechisation of children; punishment of intellectuals who secretly marry in church or baptize their children; the firing of religious teachers; and the omission of the clergy and church servants, including organists and sacristans, from the coverage of the Pension Act of 1956. Then the Vilnius priests also revealed that two of their colleagues of Vilkaviškis, Fathers Zdebskis and Tamkevičius, who pursued with the government the earlier petition to the diocesan administrators, had their work permits taken away in punishment.

The priests of Vilnius invoked the constitutional guarantee of the freedom of religion and quoted Lenin who once had written that "every person must have full liberty to freely profess any religion."

About two years later, on December 24th, 1971, after repeated clerical convictions for the teaching of religion, forty-seven priests of Vilnius archdiocese again wrote to both Brezhnev and Kosygin, making six similar demands.[17] A new element was a request of a working permit for all the priests who live in Lithuania, including the Ukrainian, with whom apparently there had developed a close cooperation. The Vilnius priests, furthermore, asked the government to revoke the published interpretation of Art. 143 of the Lithuanian criminal code that makes it a crime to organize minors for the "practices of religious education." This provision, the petitioners explained, is not only abused by local courts, but also incompatible with the constitution of the Soviet Union and with an international convention of November 15th, 1961. The signers also asked Brezhnev and Kosygin to abolish all unwritten and secret instructions concerning the control of religious life and to review the cases of people "sentenced for the faith."

Similar petitions were also sent from Panevėžys and Telšiai dioceses. In 1969, the Telšiai petition was signed by 56, or about 35%, of the priests of the jurisdiction. Two years later, toward the end of 1971, 134 out of 159 priests of Panevėžys sent a request, asking the government to allow the exiled Bishop of Vilnius to act as bishop of their diocese. On July 30th, 1974, 45 out of 74 priests of the Kaišiadorys diocese asked for the return of their exiled bishop, Sladkevičius.

Altogether, during 1968–74, Lithuania's clergymen signed 21 collective petitions.[18] The number of attached signatures was 704. With the exception of three statements that were interdiocesan, all the others came from individual dioceses and thus the signatures did not overlap. Most petitions (8) came from the archdiocese of Vilnius; there were none from Kaunas, the diocese of the old Bishop Labukas. Four each originated in Telšiai and Panevėžys; one was from Kaišiadorys. The percentage of petitioners varied between 35 and 85% of diocesan priests, an amazingly high number considering the risks involved. After each signing some priests, presumably those suspected of being organizers, were harassed, reprimanded, transferred or even temporarily deprived of their work permits. Almost in each case, these priests were told by the Commissioner for Religious Affairs that the writing of such petitions was "senseless" since "no attention will be paid to them."[19] Indeed, the receipt of petitions usually was not acknowledged despite the pious promise made in the decree of 1968 that citizens' complaints will be answered within thirty days.

X

Confrontation with the Government and Mobilization of Public Opinion

The regime's immediate response to the initial clerical appeals was harsh. The government retaliated by hitting hardest where it knew it would hurt the most, namely, the religious education of the children. Instead of abolishing penalties for such teaching as requested by the Vilnius priests, the Communists now brought the alleged violators to trial. Four major trials were held in sixteen months, between September of 1970 and January of 1972; one in a small Eastern Lithuanian town of Molėtai on September 8th–9th, 1970; two others in Central Lithuania on November 12th, 1971; and the fourth in the Northern Lithuanian town of Naujoji Akmenė on January 13th, 1972. In the first three cases, the defendants were clergymen; in the last, an old woman lay teacher.

The Trial of Šeškevičius: God Comes Before Caesar

The defendant in the first trial was Rev. Juozas Šeškevičius, a Jesuit priest, born in 1914, and an alumnus of Soviet prisons and camps. He had been first sentenced to twenty-five years under Stalin. In 1956, he was released and worked in the Altai region as an unregistered priest. For this he was re-arrested and banished as a "parasite" under Khrushchev's law against criminal idleness. In 1963, he was given another seven years for "black marketeering," which consisted of manufacturing and distributing religious picture cards, rosaries, and devotionals.[1]
Back home again, in 1970, Šeškevičius was charged with violation of the laws on religion; namely, with teaching children catechism in violation of Art. 143 of the Lithuanian criminal code.
The trial lasted two days. Most of the seats in the court room were taken by "civilians" — police agents and Komsomol members — and the defendant was not allowed to present his own witnesses. It was difficult to hire an attorney for the priest, but Nijolė Sadūnaitė, a secret nun, together with the clergyman's relatives, succeeded in picking their own choice, though they were threatened for this initia-

tive by secret police officers.[2] The attorney argued that the evidence of the alleged crime was insufficient to prove the charges and requested that the case be returned to a pre-trial investigation better to determine the facts. This was, however, a vain plea. Šeškevičius was found guilty. Free during the trial, he was arrested after sentencing and spent about a year in a labor camp. An appeal of the conviction did not help. The case showed that the authorities chose to interpret the prohibition against teaching very arbitrarily.

The law and the instructions of diocesan administrators prohibit "systematic" and "organized" teaching of religion, but allow individual examination of the knowledge of children taught at home. Father Šeškevičius sat in the confessional of his church, dressed in surplice and stole, as required by diocesan instructions, and thus examined the children.[3] He sent some of them home to learn more about certain subjects to qualify for the first communion. The authorities found seventeen children in the church. Later at school, these children were interrogated and several were forced to sign depositions against the priest. Then a pre-trial investigation was held and the trial followed.

Šeškevičius defended himself with eloquence. Though his speech was interrupted and could not be fully delivered in the court room, it was written in advance, distributed as *samizdat,* and smuggled out to the West. The Jesuit, in fact, outlined the philosophy of church-state relations, not only for his own defense but also for the entire Catholic protest movement. In a paradoxical manner, like Luther in his day or Thomas More in his, Šeškevičius in so many words said the same; here I stand, I can do no other.

The priest first questioned the facts of the case; he did not "organize" the teaching, he said, nor did he conduct "systematic" teaching. Second, he challenged the legality of Art. 143 that prohibits the teaching. This article, Šeškevičius said, contradicts Art. 96 of the constitution of the Lithuanian SSR which guarantees the "freedom of the practice of religious cults." Third, the defendant maintained, this article was vague; it established no rules to define what constituted systematic or unsystematic teaching and thus no one could know whether he violated the law. In the pre-trial investigation, the priest continued, the investigator cited a Russian instruction on the subject dated March 16th, 1961, but the priest could not find it published by the Lithuanian Supreme Soviet.[4] Thus, the instruction was unknown and as such, had to be null and void on Lithuanian territory. The prohibition to teach, furthermore, ran against Leninist teachings, the priest insisted. He cited the already familiar Lenin passage from the latter's *Village Poverty* on the right to confess any religion and then suggested that even the decree of 1918 that separated state from church did not banish religion teaching as such. Lenin's decree outlawed religion teaching in schools but allowed it "by private means." This principle is still observed in countries where Leninism is followed, as for example, in Poland or East Germany, but is disregarded in Albania and China, the obviously deviationist nations.

Finally, the priest said, the prohibition of religion teaching violates the Universal Declaration of Human Rights of December 10th, 1948, and the international convention against discrimination in education that was adopted in Paris on December 14th–15th, 1960. The Soviet Union is a signatory to both of these documents. The first declaration guarantees freedom of religion and religious teaching, while the second obligates the states to rescind any legislative or administrative decrees that discriminate in "education of all types and degrees."

Thus, the priest concluded, religion teaching has been sanctioned by man-made law. At the same time, it is an obligation made by divine law. As a priest, Šeškevičius said, I am obligated by God (Matt. 28: 19–20) and by the Church (Canon 1329) to teach catechism to children. The government therefore "is trying me not for a crime but for the performance of my pastoral duty, and an incomplete performance at that." On both counts he felt he did not violate Soviet laws. "I would not be violating them even if I fully taught religion" because the Soviet constitution and international agreements allow it. And if the government insisted on forcing him to choose between obedience to the state and his duty as a priest, "I have to obey God rather than men."

He thus drew the lines of conflict in the classical style of jurisdictional division between the spiritual and temporal realms. In clarity, the strength of intellectual argument and the power of feeling there is no equal to this statement in religious or secular Soviet *samizdat*.

The sentencing of Father Šeškevičius served as a warning to clergymen and to priests very strictly to observe the vague prohibitions of 1966, but it failed to achieve the intended effect. Neither the priests nor the people were intimidated. Three delegations of parishioners went to Moscow in search of justice for Šeškevičius. On Sundays, the sentenced man's church filled with people openly praying for their pastor. Clergymen of three dioceses appealed to the Central Committee of the Communist party for his release. The appeals were signed by 32 priests of Kaišiadorys, 72 of Vilkaviškis, and 126 of Panevėžys.[5] Demands were made to abolish secret instructions forbidding religious teaching that Father Šeškevičius had discovered during the pre-trial investigation. The sentenced man's colleague Father Gediminas Blynas wrote a long "open" letter to the trial judge in which he denounced the procedures by which the Jesuit had been tried. He declared the trial "an act of force against the convictions of the people perpetrated by those who are supposed to defend the inviolability of the freedom of conscience and religion."[6] It will insult religious people, he said, hurt the reputation of the Soviet Union, and provide water for the anti-Soviet propaganda mill.

The Trials of Zdebskis and Bubnys:
Soviet Law — Instrument of the Atheists

The second case was transferred to the city of Kaunas from a small Southern Lithuanian town of Prienai, with a population of less than 10,000. On July 16th, 1971, a group of officials found Father Juozas Zdebskis, the assistant pastor, in church with a group of about 70 children and 50 mothers.[7] As in the previous case, pictures and depositions were taken, Zdebskis' quarters were searched and, in disregard of an appeal to Moscow by 89 parents that on August 26th asked to permit catechisation, the priest was invited by the prosecuting investigator "for a visit" from which he did not return. Three days later, 350 parishioners signed a petition to the Soviet Union's Prosecutor General, the Communist Party's Control Commission, chaired by Arvids Pelše, and the Prosecutor of the Lithuanian republic requesting the priest's release on the grounds that performance of clerical duties did not constitute a crime. The Soviet constitution, the petitioners said, guaranteed "freedom of conscience and the cult." The signers charged that the law was violated, not by the priest, but rather by those who arrested him. In a parish of 8,000 souls that annually sends 300–400 children to their first communion it is physically impossible, the petitioners said, for the priest to "examine" the children on an individual basis as required by the regulations. The priest, the petitioners said, was helping the parents in what was their right and obligation. "Why should the authorities want to provoke and incite the people?" they demanded to know.

This letter was delivered to the republic prosecutor's office where the parishioners were promised that the matter would be investigated. On August 30th, however, Zdebskis was quickly removed from Prienai to Vilnius. Rumors spread that the priest was not detained for religion teaching, but that he had a hidden radio transmitter, etc. Yet the people would not be misled. Within two weeks, on September 12th, 2,010 believers signed a petition to the Party's Central Committee denouncing as hypocritical government statements on religious freedom for arresting a priest who was doing his duty. The believers again demanded the release of their pastor.[8] This petition was fortified by yet another, signed by 1,190 people from a neighboring parish of Santaika that had no resident priest, but now asked that Zdebskis be appointed their pastor.[9]

Yet these pressures did not help, and with a bare warning of a day, on November 12th, Father Zdebskis was brought to trial in Kaunas, about 20 miles north from his parish. But this hurried schedule failed to prevent demonstrations in front of the court house where a crowd of 500–600 people gathered with flowers to greet the arrested priest and his mother. Many were beaten up by the police. A number were arrested and then released. One was sent for psychiatric examination and then imprisoned for two weeks.[10]

As in the previous case, children and officials testified as government witnesses at the trial. A mother said, however, that she had taken her children to the church "freely"; the government-appointed defense attorney suggested that a fine, instead of a prison sentence, might be sufficient, but the court — since it had its instructions — decided otherwise. The priest was sentenced to a year in a common regime camp.

Father Zdebskis was a man in his forties who had decided on a priestly vocation during the dark years of Stalin's rule and was ordained in 1952. Already in 1969, his work book, that is, his license to work as a priest, was temporarily suspended by the Commissioner for Religious Affairs for demanding that the church administration act on clerical petitions of December, 1968, and January, 1969. Once he already had been sentenced for the teaching of religion, but since apparently this had happened in a more lenient day, the republic's supreme court had overturned his conviction. A week before the officials invaded Zdebskis' church in search of evidence, they had warned him against teaching, but the priest responded in the manner of Šeškevičius: "In case of a conflict between the laws of God and Church on the one hand and those of the state on the other, it is necessary to obey God." In his defense speech,[11] again like Šeškevičius, he pointed to the dilemma of the priest placed between two kinds of laws, and utilized legal arguments that were borrowed from his Jesuit colleague. Zdebskis, however, went further and stressed the actual power play. He declared that the Soviet constitution does not really separate the church from the state, but "subordinates it to the interests of the atheists" and "frequently it does so by force and deceit."

Religious people and the atheists are not equal before the law, he said. While Art. 143 of the criminal code forbids refusal of employment, dismissal, or discrimination on the job or in school for religious reasons, documented violations of this provision are not prosecuted. However, employees and students faithful to their religion invariably are made to suffer. Furthermore, while the constitution guarantees the church's freedom, the atheists attempt to nullify it from within:

> While creating an impression that the bishops function, that instructions which govern church life are produced in diocesan chanceries, the atheists dictate both the clerical appointments and the governing rules; they attempt to reduce the Lithuanian Catholic church to the condition similar to that of the Orthodox church.

The atheists, the priest additionally charged, compromise certain clerics and even bishops before the believers and even in the eyes of the Vatican. They further attempt to deceive the public by allowing the existence of the seminary on the one hand, but limiting admission of candidates on the other. In a similar fashion, "examination" of children's knowledge of religion is permitted, but the unwritten requirement that the priest examine only one child at a time turns such examination into a mere formality or even makes it physically impossible altogether. In view of such double dealing:

> Is this [practice] not a deceitful attempt quietly to take the children away from the parents? Then the atheists will be able to say: we have freedom of conscience, people voluntarily denounce religion. . . . But such freedom of the faith is similar to a permission to live when forbidden to be born.

Zdebskis concluded that the clergy can not accept "cooperation with the atheists" on such terms. The only alternative left for the clergymen was to perform the priestly duties "as required by Christ and the church law," even if it means prison.

In Raseiniai, 35 miles north of Kaunas, Father Prosperas Bubnys, pastor of the neighboring Girkalnis on trial for the same offense, expressed similar views. He put the conflict over religion teaching in deeper historical perspective:

> If I confessed that by teaching religion I committed a crime [he said], I would commit a crime against mankind; I would deny the spiritual progress that has been historically made and the ennobled concept of man that with great difficulties has been achieved in the past.[12]

The revelations of the fourth trial supported both Zdebskis' charges of legal Soviet hostility to religion and Bubny's assertion of its inhumanity to believers. The case involved a seventy-year old woman resident of Žagarė, a small town at the very northern tip of Lithuanian territory that became known as a place of banishment for Bishop Steponavičius. She was tried in the provincial town of Naujoji Akmenė on charges of organizing religious instruction to prepare children for the first communion. Ms. Kleopa Bičiučaitė confessed teaching them prayers at the request of their parents and was given a year's sentence in prison. At the trial the prosecutor did not dwell merely on legalities, but straight from the shoulder declared that "the Soviet system fights religion" and furthermore that the system can not tolerate that "someone would teach children differently from what they are taught in school."[13] This was at least a candid statement admitting that Soviet courts were politically manipulated for the advantage of the enemies of religion.

The trials of both priests, as the record shows, were managed from behind the scenes. In both cases the charge was the same, the procedure was the same, the date for the trial was identical, and the sentence differed only in that Bubnys was given a year in a camp of strict regime prison.[14] The fact that Zdebskis' trial was produced and directed by the party and the secret police has been confirmed, while the management of Bubnys' case can be inferred from the noted coincidences of its handling. The manipulation of Zdebskis' trial has been revealed by Zigmas Butkus, a former judge and chairman of the Juridical Consultancy (government board of attorneys) in the city of Kaunas, who since the trial has fled to the West. At the start of the trial, the party secretary of Kaunas told Butkus to appoint for Zdebskis an attorney different from the one that was selected by the priest's relatives. When Butkus complained that it would be difficult to make the change because the family already had a lawyer and had "paid his fee," the first secretary of the Kaunas party organization told him that "those are the orders." They were issued by the party and the KGB.[15]

The unrepentant behavior of all sentenced dependents indicated that the Catholic religion teachers did not intend to retreat from the drawn battle lines. The clergymen both challenged and exposed the Soviet concept of separation of church and state as an instrument of religious suppression. On the other hand, the trials demonstrated the government's unaltered opposition to the classical division between temporal and spiritual powers. It also showed determination to willy-nilly break up the teaching of religion in the land. If other priests or laymen were not taken to court, efforts were redoubled to dissuade them from teaching by administrative fines, imposed for a variety of violations listed under Art. 143 of the penal code.[16] Thus, for example, fines of fifty or thirty rubles (up to half a month's salary for many workers) were imposed for preparing children for their first confession (Father Liesis on May 27th, 1973), for teaching religion (Father Žvinys, summer of 1973), for allowing children to serve as altar boys (Father Keina on September 28th, 1970), for permitting children in a religious procession (Father Šauklys on April 20th, 1972) and similar activities. Father Petras Orlickas was fined 50 rubles even for playing volleyball with school children (December 3rd, 1973). This, too, was considered a crime under Art. 143. Fathers Liesis, Keina, Šauklys appealed their administrative punishment to people's courts, but did not win. Such administrative punishment seems to have flourished in 1970–71, then until the middle of 1972, and again since the middle of 1973 when their incidence increased.[17] During the exempted year, instead of fines, local government agencies would issue mere warnings. As it will be explained later, the government had good reasons for such "leniency."

Appeal to the United Nations:
Mobilizing Mass Opinion and Foreign Support

The heavy hand of the government, however, did not silence the protest, but provoked louder and more massive complaints.

In December of 1971, that is, shortly after the conviction of Father Zdebskis and Bubnys, a group of Catholics, obviously in response to the court action, took the initiative for the most organized and massive petition yet written by the Lithuanians. It was addressed to Secretary General Leonid Brezhnev.[18] In it, the petitioners declared that the Soviet government "restricts religious freedom and persecutes the Church." As evidence, the memorandum listed the removal and exile of Bishops Steponavičius and Sladkevičius; the sentencing of Zdebskis and Bubnys; "a forced indoctrination" of atheism to children of religious parents; a shortage of priests caused by government restrictions on admissions to the seminary; government control of clerical appointments; dismissal from jobs on religious grounds; prohibition to rebuild churches gutted by fire. The petitioners said that they "could list many more cases of painful persecution that embitter our life and create a deep disappointment in the Soviet constitution and the laws." The signers then asked the Soviet government:

. . . to grant us freedom of conscience that is guaranteed by the constitution but so far has not been secured in practice. We don't want beautiful words in the press or over the radio; we ask for serious governmental efforts to make us, Catholics, feel that we have equal rights as Soviet citizens.

Signatures were gathered after services outside the churches; the text of the memorandum was printed on each signature sheet; people copied it from one another, and in this way the petition was signed by 17,054, the largest number ever in the Soviet Union with the possible exception of the Crimean Tartars, a nationality group that is trying to recover the right to live in their homeland. It took the organizers two months to collect the signatures. In the appendix that was added after the petition was signed, the sponsors explained that the KGB used all possible means to obstruct the gathering of signatures, thus making it possible for only "an insignificant part of Catholics" to support it. The signers urged Brezhnev to give serious consideration to their request for improvement because otherwise "we will be forced to appeal to international organizations." The Pope and the United Nations were indicated as institutions to which further petitions would be sent.

Thus invoking international public opinion, the sponsors of the petition sent their memorandum to Brezhnev through Kurt Wald-heim, the Secretary General of the United Nations. "We are addressing ourselves to you," their letter to Waldheim stated, "because the religious people of our republic have no opportunity of using the rights listed in paragraph 18 of the Universal Declaration of Human Rights."

The petition reached Waldheim toward the end of March. The procedural mechanism of the United nations does not allow direct reception of petitions from individuals. All such appeals must pass through member state institutions. Thus, the Lithuanian petition most likely was never transmitted to Soviet representatives. Secretary Waldheim declined to comment on it altogether.[19] The purpose of the petition, however, was partially achieved. The Lithuanians sought improvement through publicity in the West. For the moment, they won at least the publicity. The memorandum became first page news. "Lithuanians Rip Russians" headlined the *Chicago Sun-Times*.[20]

While the petition to Brezhnev and the United Nations best adver-tised the plight of Lithuanian Catholics, it was not the only such massively sponsored memorandum addressed to the authorities. About a year later, in May of 1973, two other petitions were sent: one to the Ministry of Education of the Lithuanian SSR, the other to the

Commissioner on Religious Affairs.[21] After a month and a half of work, this time seeking people out in private homes and again harassed as well as obstructed by the secret police, the sponsors collected a total of 31,404 signatures. The letter to the Ministry was signed by 14,604 people, one fourth of whom were students, while the letter to the Commissioner was endorsed by 16,800 signers. The first letter complained of forcible atheist indoctrination at schools, of compelled membership in student atheist clubs, ridicule of religious students, seizure of religious articles, religious discrimination in grading and in letters of reference, pressure against public expression of religiosity, and compelled participation in surveys of religious attitudes. The Ministry was asked "to make such practices impossible in our schools so that no one obstructs the students' freedom of conscience."

The memorandum to the Commissioner commented on the statement by Bishop Krikščiūnas that was published in *Gimtasis kraštas,* a Soviet weekly for Lithuanian emigration, who expressed satisfaction at the publication of liturgical texts, a prayerbook, collection of decisions of Vatican II Council, and a fresh — and superbly executed — translation of the New Testament. The petitioners approved of these publications but complained that there still was no catechism for children and that regular persons could not buy these books because even the New Testament was printed in an edition of merely 10,000 copies, including exports to Lithuanian diasporas abroad. Could the government — since it was the government, not the bishops who published these works — print more copies of these publications?

Dozens of other petitions followed the trial of Šeškevičius and especially the Brezhnev-Waldheim document. They were signed by just 18 parents as in Adutiškis (April, 1972)[22] or more frequently by a thousand parishioners — including members of the "dvatsatkas" — as in Mielagėnai (1973),[23] 1,709 in Ceikiniai (September 5th, 1972),[24] 1,100 in Vilnius (July 16th, 1972),[25] 1,025 in Ignalina (March 14th, 1971),[26] or 190 in the parish of Stirniai.[27] Virtually all petitions asked for the right to teach religion to children, for an unlimited admission to the theological seminary, for the return of exiled bishops, and for the freedom of religious press. Many complained of atheist pressures in their local schools. Some demanded the release of Šeškevičius and the other arrested priests. Still others protested the denial of a permit to build a parish warehouse (Ceikiniai), or objected to interrogation of children at school (Varėna). At least one petition, endorsed by 540 people and dated August 31st, 1973, sought the relief not just of a particular concrete grievance, as most of them did, but outlined a program which alone, the petitioners implied, could restore equality for Catholics and prevent religious discrimination in Lithuania. For this, the Catholics needed: 1. to be able to further their beliefs through the media of communications (the press, lectures, radio, TV), 2. to be able to organize religious organizations of public-social character; 3. to publish newspapers and books of religious contents; 4. to have permission for students to attend church without fear of persecution or punishment; 5. to establish an open-admissions policy to the theological seminary; 6. to restrain all religious discrimination. Poland and some other Communist countries were listed as examples of Socialist societies where such freedoms were allowed.[28]

A great majority of the local petitions came from Southern and Eastern Lithuania, that is, the archdiocese of Vilnius and the dioceses of Vilkaviškis and Kaišiadorys. However, massive support for such action was found in the other parts of the small country as well. Thus, in 1972, the Catholics of Klaipėda sent two petitions with a total of more than 5,000 signatures asking either the return of the newly built church that was seized in 1958, or at least a substitute facility.[29] Generally, more theoretical letters originated in Southern Lithuania, while their frequency was greater in localities that had current and concrete complaints.

Most of these petitions and memoranda were pigeonholed at their destination. If answers came to the sponsors who usually indicated their name and address, it was either negative or as in Ceikiniai, a promise of a building permit if the parish committee would restrain children from participating in religious services. Sometimes, the receipt of petition would be acknowledged, but a decision would never come. In Klaipėda, where this happened, the second petition to Brezhnev in the summer of 1972 brought to the city the Commissioner of Religious Affairs, who orally denied the request for the return of the church. In many other cases the petitioners had to explain themselves not to the Commissioner, but to the secret police.

The Kremlin's Answer

In Soviet conditions, the method of petition writing was the only formally legal way of aggregating interest and building up support for the believers' point of view. The authorities apparently were unprepared for the size of approval these petitions received and were completely surprised by the Brezhnev-Waldheim memorandum. The party thus was pressed for a spontaneous answer. It responded by intensifying its foreign propaganda on the "normal" state of church affairs in the Soviet Union. At home, however, it did not retaliate by drastic administrative measures, but sought instead to contain and minimize the petition's impact on the Lithuanian population. For this purpose the authorities now used the church hierarchy.

Within two weeks after the publication of the Brezhnev-Waldheim memorandum in the West, the bishops and administrators issued a pastoral letter which stressed the theme of unity within the church and then condemned the memorandum and certain other practices.[30] It was a broadside against the petitioning priests and their supporters in the parishes. The bishops said:

> Order, unity, consensus, mutual trust, trust in our supreme pastor, the Pope, and in individual church pastors remains the essential characteristic of our Church, but some priests and believers hastily and carelessly appraise diverse facts that emerge from the particular moment of history in which the Church lives in our days. Concerned with the individual difficulties that the Church today experiences, some people become pessimistic, draw shortsighted conclusions, begin to distrust even the Providence of God, Christ himself, as if He would not be concerned and would not be taking care of his Spouse the Church. Without any legal right to act, such people take inexcusable actions, as if they were not concerned with the Church's future.

Thus rationalizing their inactivity and submission to the government and raising the specter of further government punishment for resistance, the bishops took the occasion for a criticism of three activities among which the memorandum to Waldheim was only the last, though currently the most important one. First, the bishops disapproved of parishes that did not accept their appointed pastors but conducted "apostolate" (the letter put the word in quotes) beside and even against their pastor or priest. This obviously referred to the underground church. Second, the bishops admonished the parishioners not to voice displeasure with clerical transfers because priests were appointed for the "best spiritual advantage" of the believers. Finally, the administrators addressed themselves to the issue at hand:

> In some parishes [they said] irresponsible persons, acting in the name of the clergy and the believers, collect signatures outside of churches, in churches and in private homes on sheets with the text as if of a petition — or even without any text — for the transfer of a priest, not to close a church, to appoint a priest, not to remove the pastor or his assistant, etc. The signature collectors later change or write in their

own text and add to it the collected signatures. But this is a falsification. We are very surprised that there are believers who sign without knowing why, what for, and without thinking about the deed's consequence.

This slightly veiled threat of reprisals came out openly in the next sentence:

We should not forget that the signing of irresponsible writings has an influence on Church relations with the State; that it creates misunderstandings. Such actions cannot bring the Church anything good.

The letter was drafted on April 11th, in a meeting with the Lithuanian Commissioner for Religious Affairs Rugienis and the Moscow representative Orlov. The clergymen were ordered to read it in all churches on April 30th.

What should they do? The letter contained falsehoods about the collection of signatures — people saw what they signed, and the texts were not changed — but the letter came from church authorities. As such, it had to be read. But the authorities were widely disobeyed. Before the designated day, many priests received a note — obviously produced by the sponsors of the Brezhnev-Waldheim memorandum— which declared the pastoral letter to be a slur on the integrity of "the best sons and daughters of the Lithuanian Catholic church who had the courage to sign this memorandum." Such an appeal, the letter said, compromises the reputation of the bishops. "The priests," the letter continued, "are obligated to obedience only within the canonical law. No one can obligate the priest to read a slander. Conscientious priests will not read this letter even if this refusal requires sacrifices."[31] *The Chronicle* reported that most of the priests omitted the reading; many read only the religious part that admonished to unity. In its entirety, the letter was read by "an insignificant part of the clergy." Nevertheless it became known in the country because Soviet propagandists continue to quote it as an argument against the "reactionary" priests.

The Chronicle of the Catholic Church of Lithuania: The Voice of the Movement

The matter did not rest with the publicity that the Brezhnev-Waldheim petition brought to the cause of the Lithuanian church in the world. The memorandum was still on its way to New York when, on St. Joseph's day, March 19th, 1972, there appeared the first issue of the Lithuanian *samizdat* journal, *Lietuvos Katalikų Bažnyčios kronika* (*The Chronicle of the Catholic Church of Lithuania*) which immediately became the main spokesman for the Lithuanian civil rights movement. It was the first regular underground publication in twenty years since the liquidation of the nationalist guerillas and their press.

The *Chronicle* was typewritten, approximately between 40 and 70 singlespaced, folded sheet pages. It appeared in Lithuanian, but many issues were translated into Russian and distributed beyond Lithuanian borders. Some issues were reproduced on an electric copying machine that had been reconditioned primarily for a clandestine printing of prayerbooks and other religious materials.[1] Others were mimeographed or typewritten. In 1973, the editors of the *Chronicle* encouraged rewriting by hand but warned the readers to distribute only correctly copied and clearly legible issues.[2] In five years, 1972–77, the *Chronicle* published thirty issues that contain over 1,700 folded sheet pages of single-spaced typewritten material. Thus, it is a treasure of information especially about religious life in Lithuania. In the first and second year of publication there appeared four annual issues. In 1974, there were five, in 1975 the number rose to seven, in 1976 it was five, in 1977, five.

Government officials have suggested that the *Chronicle* is edited by the exiled Bishop Steponavičius, though sometimes an accusing finger has been pointed at Father Zdebskis who remains strictly supervised and is periodically searched not only at home but especially when travelling. These officials, similarly, have explained that only few issues of the journal are duplicated in Lithuania itself. The rest, allegedly, are reprinted in Poland and then sent to Western countries.

These allegations have been reported but not confirmed by the *Chronicle.*[3]

The Origins of the Chronicle and Dissident Catholic Ties with Russian Liberals

The *Chronicle's* publication was inspired by several concerns. First, the sponsors of massive petition drives scored meager successes with Soviet authorities, thus showing that this practice was as inadequate as it was risky. Petitions did not stop trials of any of the priests charged with the teaching of religion. The government simply would not be moved by mere complaints and demands of corrective action. As Ms. Nijole Sadūnaitė, the convicted sponsor of the *Chronicle,* put it, the turning point came with the sentencing of Father Šeškevičius. "The trial opened my eyes," she said.[4] Massive petition writing indeed came to an end within a year after the appearance of the first issue of the *Chronicle.*[5] Second, religious discrimination of which the believers complained in their open letters continued unabated, especially in the schools. The *Chronicle's* publication, according to its editors, was provoked by the continued "vulgar outbursts against the believers, especially the children."[6] In other words, since petitions did not help they had to be exchanged for a sharper weapon in the struggle for the freedom of religious education. If this education were free, the *Chronicle* most likely would not exist. Third, the sponsors of the *Chronicle* became extremely worried and even agitated by the Vatican's policy of detente with the Soviet Union that, in their view, signified a sellout of Lithuanian Catholics. Catholic apprehension further grew after Archbishop Casaroli's visit to Moscow in February of 1971. The Vatican seemed to be running into the Kremlin's embrace and there thus existed a desperate need to tell the Pope where this road might lead.

The method for communication was borrowed from the Russian dissident experience. It was a reportorial approach. Instead of petitions, concerned Catholics now published a journal of information that registered government actions and generally provided a record of the entire civil rights movement instead of the scattered complaints written down by the petitioners. By necessity, this made the Lithuanian protest more anonymous because the journal would reveal neither the names nor the addresses of its contributors. There existed legal sanction for petition signatures, not for an uncensored publication. This meant, of course, that the sponsors of the new venture had decided that it was necessary for the rights movement to go deeper into the underground. Finally, the *Chronicle* emerged from the need to mobilize not only the believers but also secular publics in support of religious freedoms. In this way, the *Chronicle* became a catalyst for mobilizing ideologically diverse sympathies; this, in turn, extended the journal's concern from religious to national and social rights. While the new journal shared in the best traditions of Lithuanian underground publishing, it was modeled on the modern Russian *samizdat*. As the choice of the title indicated, the Lithuanian *Chronicle* drew its inspiration from the Russian *Chronicle of Current Events*. With this choice, the Lithuanians both expressed their solidarity with the mainstream of liberal Russian dissent and betrayed their ties with the Russian dissenters.

The *samizdat,* as well as official Soviet revelations, confirm this relationship. These show that the Lithuanian-Russian communication did not develop in 1968, at the start of the Lithuanian civil rights struggle, but only two years later, in 1970. The coverage of the Russian *Khronika tekushchikh sobytii* reveals that the Russians first had contacts only in the Ukraine. These were followed by Central Asia, and then by Riga and Tallinn in the Baltic republics. The first news that Moscow's *Chronicle* printed about the Lithuanians was not from Lithuania, but about Lithuanian prisoners in Soviet labor camps.[7] Nevertheless, from the end of 1970, the Russian *Chronicle* began regularly to report Lithuanian events, mostly cases of religious discrimination and trials, and the Jewish difficulties with emigration to Israel. After the appearance of the Lithuanian publication, the Russian *Chronicle* frequently took information from the pages of its sister journal. It is therefore not surprising that Lithuanian *samizdat* materials, in this case the speech by the sentenced sailor, Simas Kudirka, was found among the possessions of the editor of Moscow's *Chronicle,* Petr Yakir, who was arrested on June 21st, 1972, and on September 2nd, 1973, convicted for its publication.[8] Issues of the Lithuanian *Chronicle* were further recovered from the home of Russian biologist, doctor of science Sergei Kovalëv, who was arrested on December 27th, 1974. He was charged with diverse dissident activities, among them the use of the Lithuanian journal for the Russian *Khronika tekushchikh sobytii.*[9] Searches for further Moscow-Lithuanian connections were made in other homes of the capital, but yielded for the Lithuanian KGB, the official instigator of the inquest, no additional prisoners. Kovalëv, a prominent scientist, was one of the original members of Academician Sakharov's Committee for the Defense of Human Rights that became the Soviet branch of Amnesty International. In 1974, together with others, he publicly assumed responsibility for the continued publication of the Russian *Chronicle*. Upon arrest, he was taken to a prison in Vilnius where a year later, on December 9th–12th, 1975, he was also tried in a Lithuanian court. It is very likely, as suggested by Sakharov in the Lithuanian *Chronicle,* that Kovalëv was removed for the pre-trial investigation and the trial to a provincial capital to keep him away from friends and to suppress the news of his arrest, but Sakharov himself has acknowledged Kovalëv's help to the Lithuanians and doctor of sciences Yuri Golfand has recorded Kovalëv's relations with the Lithuanian Catholics.[10]

Thus, in addition to the *Chronicle of Current Events,* the Lithuanians had connections with Academician Sakharov and his group of intellectuals, Kovalëv among them. On October 24th, 1971, the then secretary of Sakharov's Committee for the Defense of Human Rights, Valerii Chalidze, protested to the Presidium of the Lithuanian Supreme Soviet the arrest of Father Zdebskis and furthermore wrote a letter to René Mailliot, Director-General of UNESCO, informing him of "the absence in the USSR of an effective procedure for applying the norms" of the Convention on the Struggle Against Discrimination in the Field of Education, that Chalidze said was conspicuous in the case of the Lithuanian priest.[11] Sakharov further publicized the appeal by five Lithuanian priests asking for help to free Lithuanians arrested in 1973–74 as alleged collaborators of the Lithuanian *Chronicle.*[12] He also interceded on behalf of the Lithuanian sailor, Simas Kudirka, who was ultimately helped by Kovalëv.[13] The Academician's friend and the new secretary of the human rights group, Andrei Tverdekhebov, on November 27th–28th, 1974, was arrested and interrogated in connection with the case that the Lithuanian KGB had instituted against the Lithuanian *Chronicle.*[14] The secret police wanted to know whether Tverdokhlebov had been to Lithuania, whether he had friends there, and what he altogether knew about the Lithuanian publication.

Lithuanian cooperation with Russian dissidents continued after the arrest of Yakir, Kovalëv, and Tverdokhlebov, the exile of Chalidze, and emigration of others. Thus, on June 20th, 1976, two Lithuanian clergymen, and six laymen, together with twenty other representatives of five Christian denominations, signed the first ecumenical appeal to Soviet authorities asking for a revision of its policies toward religion.[15] The Lithuanians, too, actively participated in "public" committees that monitored Soviet compliance with the Helsinki agreement of 1975. In addition to a committee in Moscow, such groups existed in the Ukraine, Georgia, and Lithuania. To announce its formation, on

December 1st, 1976, the Lithuanian group held a press conference in Moscow. The committee consisted of five members: Jesuit priest Rev. Father Garuckas, well known in the circles of religious dissidents; Mrs. Ona Lukauskaite-Poškienė, a poet, then 71 years old; Viktoras Petkus, a prominent Catholic layman, dissident, and alumnus of Soviet labor camps; Tomas Venclova, a poet and translator, the son of the late Communist writer Antanas Venclova. His father, the senior Venclova, for years had held important positions in Lithuania's Communist administrations and dominated the Lithuanian Writers Association. The fifth member of the group was Eithan Finkelshtein [Eitanas Finkelšteinas], a doctor of physical sciences and a Jewish activist in Vilnius.

Most of the members of the Moscow group have been either arrested or forced to emigrate. On August 14th, 1977, the KGB arrested the Lithuanian group's founding member, Viktoras Petkus, called in for warning Mrs. Poškienė, and began harassing Dr. Finkelshtein, who for years had sought to emigrate to Israel. In January of 1977, Tomas Venclova was removed from the scene by the issuance of a five year visa to teach at the University of California; on June 14th, 1977, he was deprived of Soviet citizenship. The Lithuanian Helsinki group has collected considerable evidence of violations of civil rights (some of this evidence overlaps with facts published in the *Chronicle of the Catholic Church of Lithuania*), drawing attention to the separation of families, denial of the right of emigration for the Volga Germans, harassment of Estonian political prisoners. Its first statement, dated April 10th, 1977, however, concerned the situation of the Catholic church and believers in Lithuania. This document on institutionalized religious persecution was co-signed by the Russian Helsinki group of Moscow.[16]

Only future historians, of course, will be able to tell what actual influence the Russians had, or did not have, on the Lithuanian ideas. The Lithuanians, it seems clear from published materials, have closely followed Sakharov's and Solzhenitsyn's struggle for freedom and closely identified with it. Both Solzhenitzyn and Sakharov have been congratulated for their achievements. On the occasion of Sakharov's winning the Nobel peace prize, the editors of the Lithuanian *Chronicle* reported:

. . . the joy of all Lithuanians of good will with the honor bestowed upon you for your courageous struggle for truth, freedom and human decency . . . your noble and self sacrificing example will encourage many others to dedicate themselves to the struggle for human rights; respect for these rights constitutes the foundation of a firm peace.[17]

After the arrest of Sergei Kovalëv, these editors volunteered an admission that the work of liberal Russian intellectuals had "compelled the Lithuanian Catholics to take another look at the Russian nation."[18] Those familiar with the deeply seated Lithuanian suspicions of the Russians will be much impressed by this statement; it could be made only on the basis of a rather intimate knowledge of these intellectuals.

The Philosophy and Goals of the Chronicle

It is therefore not surprising that the general publication philosophy of the Lithuanian *Chronicle* was akin to that of the Russian. The Russian *Chronicle* subscribed to the view that information constituted power and therefore was an instrument of constitutional reform. The Universal Declaration of Human Rights, it wrote, guarantees each person a right to the freedom of his convictions and to their free expression, and also a right to receive, as well as to distribute, information. The Moscow *Chronicle* did not even consider itself illegal but, it said, it had to publish clandestinely because of a "peculiar interpretation of the legality of freedom of information that has been worked out through many years by certain Soviet organs."[19]

The Lithuanian *Chronicle,* too, rejected the official Soviet interpretation of the freedom of the press. It understood Art. 125 (which grants qualified freedom of expression) in a literal sense and also believed that Art. 124 (on religious freedom) grants some, though very unsatisfactory, rights to the churches. It sought reform, but first of all, it desired to bring about the government's compliance even with those limited freedoms. In 1974, the *Chronicle* vowed that it would stop publication "only after the government will grant the Church and the believers at least as much freedom as guaranteed by the constitution."[20] Generally, in the view of the *Chronicle,* the actual Soviet application of constitutional rights must be judged in accordance with the Universal Declaration of Human Rights:

> As long as the Lord will permit its existence [its editors wrote celebrating three years of publication], the *Chronicle of the Catholic Church of Lithuania* will continue to present facts about Soviet observance and practice of the Universal Declaration of Human Rights and the spirit as well as the letter of the decisions of the Helsinki conference of 1975.[21]

The Lithuanian *Chronicle,* in other words, subscribed to the Western concept of freedoms of expression and religion. Its publishers further believed that Soviet compliance with their own constitution and the laws can be achieved through the exposure of various violations of the latter.

The journal's language was somewhat more direct than that of the Russian *Chronicle;* sometimes it was sarcastic and angry, but the *Chronicle* always observed the rules of evidence. For example, it often took issue with government statements on religious freedom, but its rebuttals were factual, in many cases, simply statistical. Otherwise, it scrupulously kept to the strictly reportorial style and disassociated itself from the opinionated, loud approach that was adopted by others. In the fall of 1976, for example, commenting on the just published first issue of another *samizdat* journal, *Dievas ir tėvynė* (God and Country), the *Chronicle* severely criticized it for the tone of its language: it was "too sharp"; it "insulted people who held different opinions." "We must show respect for others if we want to be respected ourselves," the editors said, and wished that the new publication "live up to the nobility of its title."[22]

The *Chronicle* appeared to have two basic purposes for this reasoned and precise exposition of factual information. One was to mobilize public opinion at home and abroad, and the second, to provide information and testimony for the Vatican. The Lithuanians were convinced, as were the Russian dissenters, that especially Western and world opinion could influence domestic Soviet behavior:

> You can not expect concessions from the atheists by way of negotiations; [the editors of the *Chronicle* wrote in 1974.] The Lithuanian Catholics will have only as much freedom as they will be able to win by struggling for it. The truth of this view has been proven by the several concessions already won in this manner. Lithuanian Catholics however [the *Chronicle* stressed] will be capable of making gains only if they will be more widely supported by world opinion and by the high ranking hierarchy of the Catholic church.[23]

The publishers of the journal felt sure, for example, that if world bishops and Catholics had reacted in time, Bishop Borisevičius would have been saved from death. Thus, the *Chronicle's* chief target was the Vatican that traditionally had supported Catholics, but that now was perceived as seduced by pro-Soviet informants. This perception seemed to serve as one of the dominant motives, if not *the* reason for the *Chronicle's* publication. The *Chronicle's* future sponsors first suspected the Vatican in the sixties when Rome conferred honorific church titles on "loyal" Lithuanian administrators; this action was interpreted as papal approval of their behavior.[24] The distrust grew enormously after the Roman appointment of "government nominees" as new bishops in 1969. An alarm was sounded: "The checkists have penetrated the Roman chancery. We have been betrayed."[25] Then, according to the *Chronicle* editors, the only alternative left was "to trust the Providence of God and to search for ways on how to pass correct information to the Vatican and the world."[26] The *Chronicle* specifically listed several bishops and administrators as such "misinformants," and tongue in cheek — an attitude that betrayed the editors' sense of humor even in this difficult situation — dedicated its issue No. 8 (1974) to this "small group" of clergymen.[27] "Lithuanian Catholics and priests," the *Chronicle* said later in the year, "feel a great need to pray that more objective information reach the Holy See."[28]

The journal further specifically solicited aid from the Lithuanian emigration and from world Catholics everywhere. In 1975, its editors pleaded with Lithuanian diasporas abroad and "with all our friends in the world" to spare no effort in informing national societies and governments of Soviet violations of human rights in Lithuania. Their "input of energy and sacrifice is vital to us," the editorial said in issue No. 15 (1975),[29] after reporting a wave of arrests and sentences of people connected with the *Chronicle's* production and distribution. The journal wondered why world Catholics did not defend the already incarcerated members of the Catholic dissent movement with the diligence and tenacity the Communists displayed in protecting their own people in the West. Silence, it suggested, "makes it easier [for the Soviets] to deal with the arrested."[30]

The Social Roles of the Chronicle

The journal began with the printing of only hard news without any editorial explanation or preface, and only in the second issue the editors added a postscript requesting the readers' help with the collection of "exact facts from current life."[31] The readers were further asked to protect the *Chronicle* from seizure by the secret police. The first three issues contained nothing but documentation of Soviet conduct, texts of petitions and of speeches made at the earlier held trials. The editorial postscript in the fifth issue appealed for information "about the condition of the persecuted Church."[32] In the sixth and seventh issues, the editors stressed the importance of factual precision; all facts should be "thoroughly checked, clear, correct."[33] "The *Chronicle,"* the editors said, "will not use information that is not concrete or facts that are not exact."[34] With the seventh issue, approximately in the fall of

1973, the editors broadened the scope of the journal to include also "the history and the current status of our nation."[35] Then they solicited information about "the discrimination against Lithuania's believers and their resistance to Russification (denationalization) as well as to their atheist indoctrination."[36]

In this respect, the Lithuanian *Chronicle* differed from the Russian. The Moscow publication concentrated almost exclusively on individual cases of violations of substantive or procedural rights, news from prison camps and related matters. The Lithuanian publication, while reporting violations, arrests, or difficulties the believers experienced, further extended its coverage to the national scene to include strikes, social problems, and last but not least, efforts at maintaining Lithuanian culture free of ideological Communist demands and restraints. The *Chronicle* became, as *Soviet Analyst* has put it, the "uncensored voice" of Lithuania.[37] It assumed, in effect, the role of a people's tribune or ombudsman in sensitive matters of national or religious policy and in some cases, even of personal difficulties with the government. It also reported small vignettes of life that illustrate the operation of the Soviet system.

The journal's role as representative of Lithuanian national interests emerges especially clearly from the coverage of activities, arrests, and trial reports of ethnographic and amateur film making groups. Commitment to the defense of these interests is further clarified in the journal's editorials. It points to the convergence of national and religious philosophy in the work of Catholic dissenters. Thus, for example, the *Chronicle's* view of the political, as differentiated from ideological, function of atheism shows the conviction that, as in the XIX century, Catholicism strongly enhances the survival of Lithuanian nationality. The *Chronicle's* concept of the atheist function, paradoxically enough, is strikingly similar to the official Soviet view, namely, that atheist indoctrination is an essential part of the "internationalization" of the Soviet population. The *Chronicle* put the idea in the following way:

> Seeking to destroy religious faith, the atheists want to become absolute rulers over the people's spiritual world so that faith in God and religious ethics do not interfere with their purposes. Atheist Marxism seeks to make all people think, speak and act in conformity with the Communist party's program. By fighting religion in Lithuania, the atheists attempt to break the spirit of the Lithuanian nation, to deprive it of its spiritual values, to enslave the Lithuanian's personality and to de-nationalize the believing people. When Lithu-

anians will become atheists, start entering into mixed marriages, disparage their own Christian culture, then conditions will be achieved for them to submerge in a homogeneous mass of people who adopt Lenin's native language.[38]

In other words, atheism prepares the way for Russification. The inference is obvious: the Lithuanians will not endanger their identity only if they remain religious or respect Christian ethics and culture.

The journal's attitude toward Moscow's leadership was best expressed in an essay on environmental problems which summarized an appeal that twenty-one intellectuals sent to Lithuanian party and government leaders on March 22nd, 1966. In that appeal, the authorities were asked to protect the republic's water resources, especially the delta of the republic's chief river, Nemunas, and of Lithuania's Baltic seacoast. The memorandum revealed pollution of rivers, loss of water through various amelioration projects, and asked the squashing of a project to construct an oil refinery on the banks of the river Nemunas. [This appeal was heeded to the extent that the site for the refinery was moved to northern Lithuania, closer to the Latvian border.] The *Chronicle* added its own commentary on national parks in Lithuania and the expected effects that the atomic power plant, now under construction in a very beautiful east Lithuanian lake area, was likely to have on the environment. Then the *Chronicle* concluded:

> Moscow treats our environment like a stepmother. Thousands of our compatriots were killed or deported to Siberia. It would be naive to think therefore that Moscow would value our environment. Moscow occupied Lithuania to satisfy its imperialist appetite. In our environment, too, it sees only economic gains. The oil refinery and the atomic power plant are constructed primarily for military and political reasons, namely, (1) in case of war, Lithuania would become an oil base and a substation of electric energy; (2) Lithuania would be even more tightly integrated into Russian economy; (3) Lithuania's northwest districts [the site of the oil refinery] and the already somewhat Russified parts of northeastern Lithuania would be newly flooded with Russian immigrants.[39]

The *Chronicle's* reports on individual cases of disaffection have told much about the cultural and ideological conditions that prevail in the land. Thus, for example, the published appeals to the Communist leadership that were written by Tomas Venclova, a writer, and Vladislovas Žilius, an artist, have revealed the stringency of recent conditions of censorship.[40] Both petitioners had asked for the permit to emigrate on the grounds that they could no longer endure political restrictions on their work. Venclova's application, it seems, was helped by the publication of this appeal in the *Chronicle*. In January of 1977, after a two year delay, he was granted a five year visa to teach at the University of California in Berkeley, though in June, the Supreme Soviet stripped him of Soviet citizenship. In May of the same year, the government allowed the emigration of former political prisoner Kęstutis Jokubynas, who had been held up for years without hope or explanation. In 1975, his appeal to Podgorny was published in the *Chronicle* and in 1977, he was allowed to join his brother in Canada.[41] The tight control of the news media, furthermore, was pictured by several priests whose protests against their continued denunciation by the official press were published by the *Chronicle*.[42] At the same time, while the offending newspapers did not retract the falsehoods, their further dissemination was stopped.

The *Chronicle*, furthermore, has published evidence to confirm the reports about the still strong nationalist spirit among Lithuania's students and young professionals. It has also discussed the practice of Soviet nationality policy in the republic as well as beyond its borders. In Belorussia, according to the *Chronicle*, local officials do not allow the use of the Lithuanian language or religious services in Lithuanian.[43] In the vicinity of the city of Šiauliai, on the other hand, students have organized a cross-carrying marathon to the hill of crosses "to expiate the humiliation of the cross [the authorities had repeatedly destroyed crosses on the hill] and the sins of the nation."[44] The nine foot long wooden cross that the young men and women carried was symbolically adorned with a heart pierced by two swords and then by a *Hagenkreuz* at one end and the Communist star on the other, that symbolized Lithuania's sufferings inflicted by both the Nazis and the Soviets.

The *Chronicle*, finally, has registered some social developments and pictured the population's responses to especially ideological demands of the regime. For example, it reported a secret order issued by the Ministry of Health, in 1975, to convert a mental hospital into a facility for the treatment of venereal diseases.[45] It also supplied rarely, if ever, published figures on alcohol consumption in the republic. Again, the journal has noted continued resistance to ideological indoctrination, concluding that the people "are absolutely disappointed in Marxism."[46] Workers' strikes, too, have been reported.[47] A news item from Girdžiai told of a mother who burned her daughter's Komsomol membership card because, she said, the girl was forced to join the organization.[48] In another rather amusing situation — though it probably was deadly serious in real life — a wife burned the Communist party card of her husband, declaring that "two [ideological] parties can not sleep under the same blanket."[49]

However, the editors of the journal have suggested that their primary purpose is to report on the religious situation. They covered the national and social scene to fill the existing information gap. The *Chronicle* therefore welcomed the appearance of *Aušra,* an underground journal of kindred ideology, that since 1975 has published nine issues on political, economic, and cultural developments in Lithuania.[50] In 1976, in No. 24, the editors of the *Chronicle* announced that because of the new underground publications — *Aušra* and the much criticized *Dievas ir tėvynė,* the journal "in the future will confine itself to matters that pertain to the Church and the believers."[51]

The Chronicle *and the Government*

Despite its clandestine character, neither the *Chronicle,* nor its individual supporters, perceived it to be an anti-government publication. As Rev. Bronius Laurinavičius, the pastor of Adutiškis, in March of 1972, wrote to the Commissioner for Religious Affairs, "Lithuanian priests want to work within the limits of Soviet laws, but the Soviet government itself breaks these laws."[52] The five priests who wrote an appeal to Sakharov's Committee on Human Rights asking help for the sentenced *Chronicle* people explained that:

> The Chronicle of the Catholic Church of Lithuania does not have the aim of overthrowing or weakening the Soviet regime in Lithuania. As the only free voice it merely reports facts on the violations of Soviet laws, and tries to eliminate such violations. Thus, the CLCC does not harm society or the Soviet system but, on the contrary, helps them.[53]

The Rev. Vladas Šlevas, the priest of Telšiai who started clerical petition writing, assured Kosygin that "neither the clergy nor the priests generally are opposed to the present state system."[54] The editors of the *Chronicle* termed it "a diplomatic expression." They were somewhat less positive about the system. In 1975, the *Chronicle* took an inventory of what the Soviet rule brought to Lithuania, and identified the fruits as physical destruction of the population, their denationalization (Russification), and their moral decay. In the latter category, it listed alcoholism, juvenile crime and venereal disease, abortions, divorces and concluded that "the moral balance [of the 30 years of Soviet rule] is indeed sad."[55] It is clear from this editorial that the *Chronicle* considers the system unsatisfactory and possibly evil, yet at the same time inescapable and therefore endurable. This realistic attitude and the belief that the Soviet legal structure eventually is capable of securing rights of religion is conveyed in the determination to publish the *Chronicle* until "the government will grant the Church and the believers at least as much freedom as guaranteed by the constitution." It is of course clear, as explained earlier, that the *Chronicle's* interpretation of this article is, generally, Western. It widely differs from the view held by the Soviet government for which "freedom of conscience" means freedom from religion; for the *Chronicle* this article guarantees freedom from the Communist caesaropapism. In this sense, the *Chronicle* seems to consider religious beliefs to be a private affair while the Communist party does not, the government's statements to the contrary notwithstanding.

While the *Chronicle* has not formally articulated its philosophy on church-state relations and their respective rights, it seems that generally it subscribes to the theory of two realms as defined by Fathers Šeškevičius and Zdebskis in the courtroom. The rights of the religious realm, the *Chronicle* has explained in its pages, include the following: (1) the right of free self-administration in appointments, in internal legislation, and in clerical government, including a free Vatican choice of their hierarchy; non-interference in church affairs by any subterfuge; (2) an unencumbered teaching of children as well as theology students; (3) the right to publications necessary for this purpose; (4) guarantee of practical equality of the believers before the law. The *Chronicle* has published long pages of evidence that suggest the limits for the government's control of church activities. The journal's documentation shows how not only narrowly, but also arbitrarily, the government interprets the already very limited rights of the priests and believers, and second, how the government disregards even its own laws, thus institutionalizing discrimination on religious grounds. The journal, for example, has listed names of women dismissed from their jobs because of suspected membership in secret convents, of workers who lost their positions because of religious convictions, of believers discriminated against on the job because they provided transportation or other help to the church, etc.[56] The journal has publicized the work of local administrative commissions that supervise church activities and impose fines for suspected teaching of religion to children. It has stressed the government's interference in the affairs of the theological seminary and revealed the intensified efforts of the KGB to recruit agents among its students.[57] It further has reported church fires, religious art robberies, vandalism for which, even in documented cases, the perpetrators were not punished as the law requires.[58] Finally, it has repeatedly demanded the restoration to their positions of the deposed Bishops Steponavičius and Sladkevičius.[59]

Does the *Chronicle* really believe the government will eventually stop from thus interfering in the work of the Church? The journal's views on the question seem to have mellowed. In 1972, it seemed to reject the possibility of a dialogue with the Soviet government altogether. However in 1975, even after the arrests and convictions of the *Chronicle* people, the journal editorially said that "We still want to believe that the government of the soviets will understand that it is committing a major error in supporting the atheist minority [in the republic] and thus inciting the Catholic masses against itself."[60] It thus still saw a flickering hope of detente with the Kremlin, based on the idea that Moscow needs an improved accommodation with the Church in its own interest.

The Chronicle *and the Vatican*

The *Chronicle's* message to Rome is similarly clear. The journal has disapproved of "certain unfavorable decisions"[61] the Vatican has made in the past, has criticized the silence it thought Rome had kept about the persecution in Lithuania, and has objected to Vatican concessions that make it easier for the Commissioner for Religious Affairs to interfere in clerical appointments. The *Chronicle,* furthermore, has opposed favors granted to "loyal" priests and disapproved of certain episcopal and administrative appointments because of their considered harmfulness to the Church. The editors of the *Chronicle* were also deeply worried that even Cardinal Bengsch of East Berlin, who visited Lithuania with a staff of four clergymen on August 22nd-26th, 1975, would be misinformed about the situation in Lithuania because neither of the deposed bishops, nor "those who could have told you much about the real condition of the church," were allowed in the Cardinal's vicinity.[62]

The basic message that the *Chronicle* stressed again and again was the conviction that "the Soviet government has intensified the drive to strangle the Lithuanian Catholic church with the hands of our own clergymen and believers."[63] In other words, the Kremlin was trying to destroy the Church from within. Lithuanian Catholics, the *Chronicle* said, even risked the publication of a clandestine journal to warn the Vatican that it is not persecution, but the self-tied hangman's rope, that presents the greatest danger to the Church. The journal further complained that clergymen who actually work for the secret police are frequently considered as people "who know how to adapt to conditions of persecution." These clergymen advocate a "dialogue" with the government, but the Vatican "does not understand the meaning of this dialogue [through such people]. It signifies capitulation. It means a complete betrayal of the interests of the Church."[64] Thus condemning the dialogue furthered and directed by government controlled administrators, the *Chronicle* did not oppose Vatican communications with the Communists as such. "The Catholics are convinced of the necessity of a dialogue, but without illusions. It can be useful if good will is displayed on both sides."[65] It is wrong, however, to assume the existence of such an attitude on the Communist side.

The *Chronicle* finally criticized the perceived Vatican prescription for the solution of Lithuanian problems. The Roman Curia, the publication suggested, thought it possible to normalize the situation by reestablishing church organization, concretely, by appointing more bishops and then by adopting an appeasing stand toward the Soviet government. In Lithuania's situation, however, the number of bishops is sufficient "and new appointments are not wanted."[66] The *Chronicle* again underlined this conviction five years later, in its distress signal of March, 1977:

> Lithuania does not need new bishops, but new priests. . . . The future of Catholicism in Lithuania [the publication's editors stressed] depends not on the number of bishops or administrators, but the work of dedicated rookie priests on the pastoral front. At present, the atheist government seeks to conceal the tragedy of the Lithuanian Catholic church before the world public opinion by using the episcopal violet [robes].[67]

If the atheist rulers desire to show good will, let them permit the deposed bishops to function as administrators. The Lithuanian clergy and the believers "implore the Holy Father and the Roman Curia," the same editorial said: (1) not to appoint new bishops from among those who appease the government; (2) to check the suitability of new nominees with the Lithuanian bishops in exile; (3) to refuse diplomatic concessions to the Kremlin just on the basis of faith in its good will. In an address to Cardinal Bengsch, the *Chronicle* criticized the alleged Vatican advice to Lithuanian Catholics not to engage in conflict with Soviet authorities:

> We do not know whether this really is the advice of the Holy See, but if this principle for relations with the Soviet government would

prevail, we would need to abandon essential pastoral duties, for example, the catechisation of children. This would create a source of continuous conflict with our conscience. We would then become real "servants of the cult," as the Soviet government wants to have it.[68]

Thus criticizing the Vatican's policy of detente, the *Chronicle* cautioned Cardinal Bengsch himself:

We believe that by its diplomatic activity the Holy See sincerely wants to help the persecuted Church. However, because of the lack of knowledge of concrete circumstances, in some situations the Holy See may find itself helping the interests of only the atheists. We therefore dare to warn you: do not believe the promises of the Soviet government because they will not be fulfilled. Do not believe those who officially come from the Soviet Union — all of them more or less are obliged to execute the assignments of the party and the KGB.[69]

At the same time, the editors predicted the consequences of the Vatican policy:

Because of the persecution of the faith [they said], pastoral work is already partially conducted in the conditions of the catacombs, and the Soviet government, with good reason, is afraid of underground work because it can not control it. The more the government restricts official church activities, the more intensive becomes the secretly conducted pastoral work. Government-inspired priests attempt to picture this work as harmful and destructive of church unity as well as of normal church-state relations. However, if at this time the Catholic church in Lithuania would not adapt itself to the underground work conditions, she would be threatened by the fate of the Russian Orthodox church; this church has been almost completely smothered.[70]

The Vatican thus was informed that unless Rome helps to widen the liberties of the visible church, the latter will become invisible. The government, too, was warned that persecution will bring diminishing returns and thus will be counterproductive from its own point of view.

Formula for Survival

Toward the fall of 1977, the *Chronicle* further defended its philosophy of firmness toward the government and the necessity of underground religious activities by citing the experiences of diverse religious groups in the Soviet Union. In the process, the editors of the journal formulated their own theory for the survival of the Church under the Kremlin's rule.

The journal noted that the strongest and the most vigorous religious Soviet communities were those which did not sway away from their principles, especially from the duty to evangelize. Such were "the secretly or semi-secretly active Baptists, Pentecostals, Jehovah's Witnesses and other religious groups."[71] Contrariwise, religious groups that made substantive concessions to the government lost their strength and their following. The best such example was the Russian Orthodox Church. Instead of gaining from submission to uncanonical government dictates, this Church merely demoralized its clergy and hierarchy. "For this reason," the *Chronicle* wrote, "there are today in Russia very few committed, conscious believers."[72]

The journal suggested a similar pattern of development among the Soviet Catholics. Comparing Belorussia, Latvia, the Ukraine, and the German and Polish diasporas, the editors of the *Chronicle* found the worst situation among groups that did not keep catacomb churches. These included the Latvians, but especially the Belorussians. "Where there is no catacomb activity," the journal said, "the Catholic church has completely disappeared or exists only in stagnation."[73]

For the survival of the Catholic church in the Soviet Union, the editors of the *Chronicle* concluded, it is imperative that the Vatican does not legitimize the existing conditions but instead supports the evangelization of the country. Concretely, the journal had two sets of suggestions for the Holy See. One concerned solely the Lithuanian situation, and included a petition to speed up the canonization of God's Servant Jurgis Matulaitis, and the beatification of Bishops Matulionis and Borisevičius, who had suffered defending the Church's independence from Stalin. The Vatican was further reminded not to honor or support as bishops clergymen who have compromised themselves "morally or politically."[74] The second and longer set of requests dealt with the broader Soviet scene. The dissidents asked the Vatican:

(1) to encourage greater concern with the evangelization of the Soviet Union; (2) to make a strenuous effort to win the right for all Catholics of Belorussia and the Ukraine to establish their own theological seminary; (3) to secure the opening of churches and appointment of priests, at least in the large Soviet cities, as for example, Kiev, Minsk, Novosibirsk, Krasnoyarsk, Omsk, Tomsk; (4) to issue pastoral decrees that would allow the evangelization of the Soviet Union, effective on the date of their announcement, and to broadcast such decrees over the radio; (5) to warn local bishops not to interfere with thus authorized evangelization; (6) to allow priests, who have not violated church discipline, to hear confessions in private apartments of lay people and religious sisters without regard to diocesan boundaries.[75]

The *Chronicle* prefaced this important statement concerning the religious situation and policy by an expression of gratitude to Western Catholic bishops, American congressmen, Russian dissidents, Jewish journalists for their support of Lithuania's "freedom of faith" and their Lithuanian "prisoners for faith and freedom." The journal finally stressed the unity with the Pope who, the journal hoped, "in appreciation of our loyalty and devotion [to the Holy See] will show us more confidence and, according to possibilities, will grant us our requests."[76]

The journal ended by suggesting that the "decisions of the Helsinki conference [have] created favorable conditions for the defense of the harassed and persecuted believers in the entire world, and especially in the Soviet Union."[77]

XII

Catholicism and Nationalism in the 1970s

It would be an understatement to suggest that the Soviets found the *Chronicle's* voice much more inconvenient than any petition sent to Moscow. Domestically, the journal demanded constitutional reform that would allow "private" rights and the co-existence of a social institution not penetrated by the party, thus possibly threatening the party's monopoly on ideology and power. In foreign affairs, the *Chronicle* threw a monkey wrench into the smoothly-proceeding Soviet accommodation with the Vatican that the Kremlin found useful for international purposes. Thus, the *Chronicle* had to be silenced.

However, before the KGB had time to stretch out its dragnet to catch the organizers of petitions and the sponsors of the *Chronicle,* the Communist party's attention was distracted by a nationalist upheaval of Lithuanian youth that culminated in the self-immolation of a young man and massive demonstrations in the city of Kaunas, the second largest in the republic with a population of 300,000 at that time. The revolt of the youth followed not only in the footsteps of the Catholic protest movement, but also criticisms by liberal intellectuals, displaying a possibility of snowballing opposition. This upheaval induced the government, at least temporarily, to ease its church policy. Even more important, the events of the restless Lithuanian spring demonstrated a new kind of convergence between nationalism and Catholicism, the twin forces that Soviets had thought deeply dormant, if not yet dead, thus again raising for the Kremlin the specter of nationalist Lithuanian resistance.

Liberalization and the Rebirth of Nationalism

The new Lithuanian nationalism and the events that produced improvement in the Church's condition need to be explained in the perspective of post-Stalinist liberalization. At the time of the XX Party Congress, at which Khrushchev denounced Stalin for his crimes, militant Lithuanian nationalism as an organized force was not only exhausted but also destroyed. Thousands had perished in the guerilla war, 1944–52, while those who survived were either repressed or reeducated. In this situation, the perennial First Party Secretary Antanas Sniečkus smoothly directed Lithuania's transition from the Stalinist suppression of both nationality and religion to the new age of party-directed liberalization. On the one hand, Sniečkus eased pressures, while on the other he firmly contained the outpourings of nationalist, religious, and social dissatisfaction that visibly reappeared and struck the fear of God in local Communists after the Hungarian events of 1956.[1] As a result, the Lithuanians were able to take advantage of Khrushchev's temporary relaxation in cultural affairs without abrasively challenging Moscow's economic or personnel policies. Thus, while in 1958–61 for serious "national" Communist deviations, Khrushchev extensively purged the top party and government leadership in Latvia, the Lithuanian republic experienced relatively minor shake-ups necessitated by Russian complaints of discriminatory self-assertion by the Lithuanian cadres. Some personnel were dismissed, some arrested and tried, but within a decade the disgraced officials and academicians resurfaced in different capacities. It was clear that while on the one hand, Sniečkus controlled demands of national autonomy, on the other he protected, as much as he apparently could, those who strove for it. As a result, the Khrushchevite liberalization in Lithuania lasted somewhat longer than, for example, in the Ukraine and in Russia. In these two major republics, intellectual suppression began with the arrests of 1965 and 1966 respectively. In Lithuania, the period then was not yet over. The Lithuanian and generally Baltic enjoyment of relative intellectual freedom not merely lasted longer; it also was richer in ideas because the Balts were permitted partially to rediscover their historical memory, namely, their ties to prewar culture which on the whole was steeped in Western traditions. Furthermore, these republics now had closer contacts with the modern West through contacts with the Baltic emigration. Thus, the late fifties and sixties witnessed a certain rebirth and reassertion of native culture and of its Western antecedents as well as proclivities.[2]

These conditions, in the sixties, allowed a discernible articulation of three nationalist Lithuanian attitudes among its younger intelligentsia.[3] The first was the "autonomist" nationalism of loyalists who sought neither separation from the Soviet state nor the elimination of the system, but who seriously took Lenin's teachings on the nationality question. Wherever it was not too dangerous to employ salami tactics of acquisition, these loyalists inched toward greater republic autonomy in domestic affairs. The second variety asserted "national" Communism, which shared many "autonomist" views, but preferred independence in a manner of at least a Socialist Poland. They believed that it was not Moscow's policies but Lithuanian skills and energy that explained the improvement of economic and cultural life in Lithuania. They were further convinced that history was made by nations, not by social classes as the official ideology insisted. In 1971, Sniečkus was urged to accept a euphemistic definition of this principle, but refused.[4] "National" Communists were committed to national survival and for this reason, were supportive of the Catholic church as an institution that was helping this objective. The views of the "autonomists" toward the Church were not clear, but likely less generous. "National" Communists in Lithuania have been quietly purged in the past, but they apparently were found even in the ranks of the party itself.[5]

There appeared, finally, a variety of nationalism whose ideological underpinnings were not related to Communism. The Soviets denounced it as "bourgeois" nationalism, but actually, this variety did not originate from the already destroyed bourgeois classes, nor did it have much to do with the capitalist economic system. This nationalistic attitude, as it soon appeared, was shared not only by the older and the middle generation of Lithuanians, but also by the teenagers and young adults who showed even more determination than their elders. The philosophical texture of this attitude overlapped with liberalism, democratic socialism, and religion, that is, Catholicism. It has been articulated in *samizdat* literature — the underground journal *Aušra* that started publication in 1975 belongs to this latter category. Its existence has been confirmed by official sources and by publications of non-Lithuanian origins, and before the Kaunas events of 1972, it was succinctly formulated by Simas Kudirka, a Lithuanian sailor, during his trial for treason.

Kudirka, a radio operator in the Soviet merchant marine, on November 23rd, 1970, tried to defect to the United States by jumping from his ship, the *Sovetskaia Litva,* to the U.S. Coast Guard cutter *Vigilant* that was moored alongside the Soviet ship at Martha's Vineyard in Massachusetts.[6] Inexplicably, after Kudirka safely landed on the American ship, the Soviets were allowed to board it and forcibly seize the defector. He was beaten up and then brought back to Lithuania for trial on charges of illegally attempting to leave the country. According to Soviet law, this is treason. Kudirka's forcible return to the Soviets stirred up a storm in the United States, caused the retirement of some Coast Guard officers, and inspired a congressional investigation. None of this, however, helped Kudirka who in June of 1971 was sentenced to ten years in a strict regime camp.

Feeling that he would receive no mercy from the court, Kudirka engaged in an uninhibited political discussion with the judge, while pleading innocent from the standpoint of the Universal Declaration of Human Rights and of the Soviet constitution. He denounced the physical annihilation of Lithuanians in Stalin's years, condemned the Russification that was conducted currently, and declared himself in favor of an independent Lithuania. When asked how he understood it, Kudirka answered: "An independent Lithuania, in my opinion, has a sovereign government and is not occupied by any army. The Government has a national administration, its own legal system and a free democratic system of elections."[7] He also confessed to be "a devout Catholic." Expecting to be sentenced to death, he requested the court to allow a priest "to give me the last rites of the Catholic church."

Kudirka articulated what many felt. The Soviets, it appeared, faced a reborn anti-Communist nationalism. Nationalist strivings ran so deep that Genrikas Zimanas, editor of the party's main journal and an old ally of Sniečkus, in 1969 discovered them "disguised as the party's policy."[8]

Intellectual Retrenchment and the Youth

Kudirka's attempt to defect occurred in a politically very disquieting atmosphere among Lithuania's intellectuals and youth. From the Soviet point of view, Lithuania's climate had been poisoned by burgeoning deviationist ideas widely tolerated by the permissive behavior of republic authorities. Actually, Kudirka's jump to freedom and the young intelligentsia's heretical ramblings represented a reaction to the political and intellectual retrenchment that Moscow ordered after the trials of Daniel and Siniavsky in 1966. Following the Kremlin's crackdown on the Russian writers, Lionginas Šepetys, the chief of the Lithuanian Communist party Central Committee's division of culture, was appointed the republic's Minister of Culture. Šepetys had a reputation of liberal *apparatchik* and by appointing him, Sniečkus may have sought to shield the creative intelligentsia from Daniel and Siniavski's fate by restraining the more unorthodox behavior. But in 1969, the new Minister turned into a strict political commissar who imposed a heavy hand on intellectual life. At first, the tightened controls resulted only in replacements of the more liberal editors and other managers of cultural life with the more dogmatic and fanatical Communists. Then, on November 12th, 1970, a former chief of the republic's secret police became the Minister of Justice. At the same time, the intelligentsia were taught a lesson of obedience that by its stark reminder of Stalinist practices shook up even the establishment intellectuals.

The involved victim was Professor Jonas Kazlauskas, an internationally known specialist of Baltic linguistics.[9] On October 8th, 1970, he mysteriously disappeared on a Vilnius street, and on November 17th, his body was lifted from the river Neris that flows through the city. Since he was the Dean of the Linguistics Faculty at the Kapsukas University and an internationally known man, a medical team was organized to announce that he had drowned in the river. Despite the fact that he was a ranking university administrator, a doctor of sciences, a full professor, and a party member, the party newspaper *Tiesa* did not carry a necrology as usually is the case, and neither university nor party representatives offered the customary eulogy at the funeral. The best available circumstantial evidence suggested that the forty-year old scholar had a conflict with the authorities, but since his linguistic work posthumously was rewarded with a state prize, his difficulties possibly were not with the party, but with the KGB which mishandled the case.

Other measures against the intellectuals were not as drastic as those taken against Kazlauskas. In the winter and spring of 1971/72, some poets, critics, and editors, especially those connected with *Nemunas,* a youth publication in Kaunas, were publicly criticized for rejecting Socialist realism as the sole artistic criterion, for advocating objectivist, apolitical principles of aesthetics that in Sniečkus' earlier interpretation constituted disguised elements of the nationalist "single stream" theory of history [teaching that national loyalties are stronger than class divisions]. In April, one of the main literary culprits, the critic V. Kubilius, had to make a nowadays very rare public confession of ideological errors. He also publicly apologized to "those who were insulted by my lack of tact and inconsiderate cleverness."[10]

By focusing on *Nemunas,* the authorities actually concentrated on the condition of the Lithuanian youth. The party had good reason to be concerned with it. Despite the claims that this youth had learned "to live and work like Lenin,"[11] the Komsomol of the republic had been plagued by grave problems that on occasion had led to wholesale removal of the entire leadership of the organization. Western studies of the early 1960s showed that nationalist attitudes remained strong even among the Komsomols and that in terms of religious views, many of the young people had become agnostic but not atheist. Many still attended church and married there. The youth "revolution" and fashions of the 1960s that shook the West reached the Soviet Union as well, but while the Western youth voiced Leftist revolutionary demands, the Lithuanians displayed nostalgic longings for the non-Communist past. In 1971/72, for example, the most popular music in private gatherings of Kaunas consisted of romances and music of the independent Lithuanian period. Popular Lithuanian music from the emigration also was a great hit, as was the American Jesus Christ Superstar. The reason for nostalgia and for Western music rested not only in the spirit of youthful protest, but also in the search for the traditions of their native land that the regime had suppressed. For the Soviets, this was especially dangerous because Lithuanian traditions included national independence and relatively broad intellectual freedom. Thus, some youth organized ethnographic study groups that explored historical places and collected documentation (sometimes on anti-Soviet guerillas). Others defied society by wearing long hair and walking barefooted, in an obvious imitation of Western youth. Groups of "beatles" promoted Western music; "hippies," the more philosophical rebels, practiced poverty in the style of St. Francis of Assisi though without Catholic overtones.

Self-Immolation of Romas Kalanta and the Youth Rebellion in Kaunas

Sometime in the spring of 1972, these non-conformist youth conceived of the idea of making the Lithuanian struggle for freedom known to the world. The Lithuanians already had a Czech example. Twenty year old Jan Palach, unable to fight directly against the Soviet occupant, in January of 1969 sacrificed himself in the center of the city of Prague. This form of resistance threatened to catch on in the Soviet Union where within a month, on February 10th, 1969, a forty-five year old alumnus of Stalinist camps and a father of three children, Nikolai Berislavski, tried self-immolation in Kiev. He protested the Russification of the Ukraine.[12] Within the next two months, on April 13th, 1969, the same feat was repeated in Riga, Latvia, by a twenty year old Jewish student, Ilya Rips. At the obelisk of freedom where he lit himself on fire, he carried a placard that demanded freedom for Czechoslovakia and also freedom from discrimination of the Jews and freedom to emigrate to Israel.[13] The Lithuanians adopted this method of protest in the spring of 1972. A group of young rebels, apparently, drew lots, and a nineteen-year old evening high school student, Romas Kalanta, prepared for the sacrifice.[14]

The event was apparently planned to coincide with President Nixon's visit to Moscow in May of 1972. The self-immolation thus occurred on May 14th, 1972, in the park of the musical theater that is situated in the center of Kaunas.[15] On a quiet, clear Sunday afternoon, at about one o'clock, when a matinee performance went on in the theater, a young long-haired youth wrote some notes (never recovered), took off his shirt, poured over his body some liquid and with a deliberate strike of a second match burst into a living torch. He refused help from bystanders and the police because, he insisted, "I am dying for the freedom of Lithuania." After the initial shock, the police extinguished the flames, and the young man was taken to a hospital where to his interrogators he kept repeating his vow to die for Lithuania's freedom. Then he lost consciousness. His burns were too extensive and he died within hours.

The police apparently did not find out anything from Kalanta except that his self-immolation was a political act. Thus they had a reason to become apprehensive, especially after learning from the Moscow KGB, as they must have, that this was not the first, though the first successful, sacrifice of self-immolation in the Soviet Union. Thus, the action of Romas Kalanta in Kaunas could trigger off a chain reaction, if other nationality youth were involved. Unconfirmed reports indicate that the city was filled with young people not only of Lithuanian, but also Estonian, Latvian, Ukrainian, and even Russian background. Jonas Jurašas, the former artistic director of the Kaunas theater, has reported to the Sakharov Commission in Copenhagen that a Latvian and an Estonian "intended to sacrifice themselves together with Romas Kalanta, but were arrested on the train on their way to Kaunas."[16] Thus, the police mobilized and prepared to outsmart the congregating people.

Kalanta's funeral was set for May 18th, at two o'clock in the afternoon. However, in hopes of diffusing possible disturbances, the police ordered a secret family burial two hours ahead of the promised schedule in another cemetery far out of town. The masses of young people gathered in front of Kalanta's home quickly learned of this deceit, but instead of dispersing as the police had expected, became angry, locked arms and marched on to the main thoroughfare of the city that led past the square of the self-immolation. They disregarded a government spokesman who asked them to go home, applauded their own men and women speakers who denounced Moscow's rule over Lithuania, and then began to move again on the thoroughfare that, ironically, from the old times, still carried the name of Freedom Boulevard. Placards that the youth carried stressed the same theme.[17] One intoned Kalanta's "Freedom for Lithuania." Another more diplomatically declared that "We are not against socialism but for a free Lithuania." A third called for "Freedom for the Jews." The youth, furthermore, chanted slogans; the streets resounded from the calls "liars," "freedom for Lithuania," "freedom for the youth," "freedom for Romas' father" (the rumor had spread that he was arrested). Slogans demanding freedom of religion were heard as well.[18] Then the chanting human waves of the thousands confronted the police. At first the police did not frontally attack the crowd, which overturned one or two police vehicles, threw a Molotov cocktail into Communist party offices and hoisted the old, "bourgeois" Lithuanian flag on the church roof near the police headquarters that the crowd momentarily reached. Their singing of the national anthem, however, was interrupted; the police finally moved in to beat the demonstrators.

The night of the 18th was restless, and on the afternoon of the 19th, special security forces arrived to help control the crowds. About five hundred people were arrested. Police and demonstrator deaths were reported. Of the arrested, about three hundred were released in a short time and ultimately only eight were held for trial. Police movie cameras that reeled pictures during demonstrations doubtlessly showed — as confirmed by the official press — that the demonstrators almost totally were very young, in their late teens and early twenties, and that the crowd represented workers from Kaunas factories and students from several schools, primarily the Polytechnical Institute of Kaunas that trains engineers and a high school that ironically bears the name of the Komsomol.[19]

The flames ignited by Kalanta literally did not die for some time. Shortly afterwards, Moscow's dissidents reported three more self-immolations, one on May 28th, by a young sanitary technician Stonys, born in 1949, another on June 3rd in Kaunas by Andriuškevičius, a sixty-year old worker, and the third on June 10th, by a sixty-two-year old street worker Zaličkauskas in the town of Kapsukas, some forty miles south of Kaunas.[20] Stonys and Andriuškevičius succeeded, Zaličkauskas did not. The number of confirmed self-sacrifices was larger than this; Jurašas' report to the Sakharov hearings in Copenhagen mentions ten self-immolations that followed Kalanta's.[21] Their purpose was the same: to protest the Soviet rule. Their motivation, according to conflicting reports, was not in each case as idealistic as Kalanta's.

Youth demonstrations, too, did not subside immediately. The next outburst of pent-up emotions occurred in Vilnius, the capital city, in a different setting, namely, an international sports competition. The spectator youth jeered the Soviet volley ball team, cheered the foreigners, and furthermore, refused to stand up for the playing of the Soviet anthem. Party secretary Antanas Barkauskas denounced these demonstrators as "hooligans."[22]

The Soviets were quick to suppress the Kaunas demonstrations, but at a loss in explaining the event. Information of Kalanta's self-immolation and the subsequent rebellion reached the West through dissident sources in Moscow and Western radio stations broadcast the news on May 20th. Locally, in Lithuania, the republic party daily published an announcement only on May 21st. Until then, it was treated as purely the affair of the city of Kaunas. However, the news of the rebellious demonstration could not be contained in this manner. Thus, a medical commission was established and announced that upon examining Kalanta's papers and hearing the testimony of his parents, teachers and friends, it found the young man "a mentally ill person who committed suicide while in a sickly condition."[23] Moscow's reaction did not come until May 26th, when Western correspondents in Moscow were finally told to expect a longer statement. But the Kremlin, obviously annoyed at the embarrassing world publicity the event received just before President Nixon's visit to the Soviet Union, decided to minimize its importance and issued only a terse release declaring that Kalanta was mentally ill, while the demonstrations were staged by vandals and thieves. There were, TASS said, "no political motives or political aspects to this affair."[24]

The Soviet propaganda machine, however, did not believe its own story. After the Kaunas events, its foreign broadcasts did not flail the "hooligans," but conspicuously stressed the freedom of religious life and cultural as well as economic accomplishments under the Soviet rule. These were credited to Soviet nationality policy. In this way, Moscow attempted to counter the Western interpretation of the Kaunas self-immolation and rebellion as a religious and nationalist event.

The Western press interpreted Kalanta's self-immolation and the youth demonstrations, in the main, as a part of the Catholic protest movement. The Lithuanian *Chronicle,* on the other hand, considered the May confrontation on the streets of Kaunas as an event "more of a national [patriotic] character."[25] In Kalanta's personal case, available evidence overwhelmingly points to his nationalistic, rather than specifically religious, commitment. In an official interview, the young man's mother predictably asserted her son's suffering from a nervous condition, and in a special reference to Western imputation of religious motive, denied her son's religious beliefs.[26] Indeed, Kalanta grew up in a Communist family. His father, a World War II veteran, was a party member. His elder brothers, as well as he himself, were members of the Komsomol. His younger brother was a Pioneer. The official version of young Romas' a-religiosity has been confirmed by private communications. It appears that he was neither mentally disturbed, nor a church going Catholic, but primarily a patriotic nonconformist and rebellious youth. Since Catholic teaching disapproves of suicide, Kalanta's Catholic indoctrination is not likely. At the same time, there is no evidence of his anti-religious attitudes either. Suicide was an accepted way out for Lithuanian nationalist guerillas — in situations where escape from capture was impossible. Thus, not only the Czechs, but the guerillas of the past generation may have determined the method for Kalanta's protest.

Moscow's Response: Purges and Arrests

It is not surprising that the upheaval in Kaunas and the flickering flames throughout the land seized the immediate attention of Communist authorities, and in terms of action priorities, overshadowed the concern with petitions for religious rights and the *Chronicle*. The search for the originators of petition drives and the journal continued, but the KGB was now absorbed in the task of discovering and punishing all the culprits of the Kaunas events. The Communist response to the youthful May provocation tells much about the character of the new Lithuanian nationalists and their relationship to the Church.

The Kremlin's answer to Kalanta's drama emerged in the meeting that Lithuanian party leaders held in Kaunas on June 2nd, together with M. Morozov and P. Korotkov, the representatives of the Central Committee's Agitprop in Moscow.[27] At this, and other meetings that were held in Kaunas schools and factories from which the demonstrators drew their massive support, party secretary Antanas Sniečkus blamed "bourgeois" ideology — not just nationalism — which "directs its main punch against the friendship of nations [read: acceptance of Russian domination]." "This ideology," he said, "attempts to poison the consciousness of the working people with the poison of nationalism, attempts to inculcate national egoism, isolationism and nihilism."[28] Thus, the old and ailing party chief identified nationalism — not "hooliganism" as Moscow originally had announced — as responsible for the events in Kaunas. Sniečkus, an experienced bureaucrat, had a three-tier program for the handling of the upheaval. To soothe Moscow and his own hard-liners, he stressed the ideological effort that ultimately called for the use of social pressure at the place of work to straighten the "deviations from the norms of our life that are exhibited by individual people."[29] Under the cover of such verbal assault, he apparently intended to make some managerial changes and only then leave the field free for the KGB to isolate the incorrigible nationalist activists. As a result, the regime's immediate reaction to the youthful rejection of the system was relatively mild. This course of action, however, soon toughened; it seems that Sniečkus' essentially verbal response undermined his own position so that his Russian deputy, Valerii Kharazov, took over the actual management of the party — and anti-nationalist policy — before Sniečkus' death in January of 1974.

The old secretary began his last propaganda battle by angrily denouncing the protestors and demanding education "of order and self-discipline" that however "should not end with the 'problem' of long hair."[30] At the republic women's conference in June — obviously referring to groups with which Kalanta was associated — he characterized the youthful dissidents as "the overgrown nauseating half-growns [i.e., teenagers] who have lost the appearance of human beings."[31] This tirade was accompanied by salvos of other propagandists who zeroed in on nonconformity in Lithuanian literature. The critic Vitas Areška attacked "the poetization of chaos," especially by Sigitas Geda, a distinguished poet of the postwar generation, which indicated, according to the critic, a desire to run away from life, while literature should struggle "for the truth, for man, for a Communist future."[32] Another critic reminded the writers of their "civic duty" to work as "helpers" of the Communist party.[33] They should reject the theories of "single stream," of "art for art's sake," of "metaphoric interpretation," of estheticism. Party secretary for propaganda Antanas Barkauskas added to this list some other transgressions, namely, formalism, idealization of the "patriarchical" village, preference for the old moral norms, an "anarchistic" concept, in his view, of creative talent. All of these, and many other deviations, the secretary said, made the artists and the editors forget that they must serve communism.[34]

Secretary Barkauskas then trained his guns on the remaining social sins of the unnamed members of society who bedevilled its smooth operation. These sins included: localism [preference for local rather than national Russian interests], alcoholism, amorality, bribe taking, imitation of bourgeois fashions, especially the "hippism," and last but not least, nationalism. This enemy, he said:

. . . masks itself in various colors, wears different disguises. In some places it pretends to fight for the preservation of national heritage, elsewhere it flirts with religion, still in other places it speculates with the love for the native country or mourns the passing of thatched roof farm houses or undrained bogs and swamps [to read: village tradition] or again it encourages the mood for emigration.[35]

The root of all this trouble, Barkauskas said six weeks after the bloody confrontation between the youth and the police in Kaunas, was "liberalism, the atmosphere of reconciliation with all of these evils."[36]

Shortly afterwards, the authorities quietly demoted — though did not destroy — several officials who, by definition, failed to prevent these disastrous attitudes from developing. Thus, the chief of the Lithuanian Agitprop, P. Mišutis, became a counselor to the Lithuanian Council of Ministers. Then fell Antanas Drilinga, the editor of the Kaunas youth magazine *Nemunas* that had printed deviationist articles. These were followed by the editors of another Kaunas journal, *Kultūros barai,* a popular magazine of national culture, and the editors of the publishing house *Vaga* in Vilnius. Ultimately, even party secretary Barkauskas, responsible for propaganda, was removed from party management and kicked upstairs to the position of chairman of the Lithuanian Supreme Soviet. In early 1976, Lionginas Šepetys, who had supervised the retrenchment in Lithuanian cultural life as Minister of Culture, returned to the party apparatus as a replacement for Barkauskas. Jonas Aničas, the chief atheist propagandist, became the chief of the Central Committee's division for science and education.

At the same time, the official press began a hunt for nationalist witches. The list of all the cases would be too long to repeat in these pages. It first found them among historians who had dared to reprint the Lithuanian declaration of independence of 1918 in one historical anthology.[37] Three years later, in 1975, Genrikas Zimanas' journal, *Komunistas,* found nationalist deviations even in the memoirs of Justas Paleckis, the original Soviet-selected president of Lithuania, then chairman of the Presidium of the Supreme Soviet of Lithuania and the Soviet Union's House of Nationalities (1966–70). These memoirs were published in Moscow by a Russian publishing house and their sin was a favorable view of independent Lithuania's democratic Leftist leaders.[38]

These developments were accompanied by police action. At first there came the trial of the alleged eight leaders of the Kaunas demonstration. Formally, they were not charged with conspiracy or action against the state. The charges were disturbance of public order, destruction of public property and hooliganism (Articles 99 (3), 199 and 225 of the Lithuanian penal code respectively). The trial was held at the beginning of October of 1972, and the eight were sentenced from one to three years of strict and common incarceration. The oldest of the defendants, the twenty-five year old Vytautas Kaladė, a theater stage worker, received the highest sentence.[39]

Then the secret police destroyed ethnographic study groups that, according to secretary Barkauskas, masked nationalist activities. Obviously ethnocentrically-oriented, these groups have functioned not only in Lithuania, but also Latvia,[40], Armenia,[41] and possibly elsewhere in the national republics. On March 27th, 1973, the KGB arrested more than one hundred activists in Lithuania (Vilnius and Kaunas) and in Riga (Latvia).[42] Some of the arrested were let go after signing a pledge that they would no longer participate in these activities. The KGB interrogators nevertheless wanted to know about their excursions, their relations with similar groups in other republics, the alleged gathering of documentation about the anti-Soviet partisan war in Lithuania, the organization of the anniversary of Kalanta's death, preparation and distribution of anti-Soviet literature. These questions indicated the scope of activities such groups were suspected of conducting.

Five of the arrested ethnographists were detained, charged and on February 18–March 5, 1974, tried for anti-Soviet activities as defined by Art. 68 of the criminal code.[43] In terms of age, these five were older than the previously sentenced eight demonstration leaders, but with the exception of a medical doctor born in 1911, the oldest was 36, the youngest 24 years of age. They were also better educated. One of them, Š. Žukauskas, was a graduating medical student; another, A. Sakalauskas, was a teacher of German at the Polytechnical Institute in Kaunas, who, in 1957, had been sentenced to two years for an attempt to flee the Soviet Union by boat; the third, V. Povilonis, was a technological engineer who had actively aided many Komsomol programs; and the fourth, A. Macevičius, was a student at the Polytechnical Institute and a former candidate member of the Communist party. Activities charged to the group included distribution of anti-Soviet leaflets, establishment of an underground publication, *Naujasis Varpas* (The New Bell; its first issue with a slightly changed title — *Varpas* — was reported published in 1976), financial support of the family of the imprisoned sailor Simas Kudirka. The accused drew sentences from two to six years of strict regime camp. The youngest, however, was sent to a regular camp.

The ethnographists were not left alone even after the trial. A number lost their positions, still others had to sign promises of good behavior or were dismissed from the schools. This group represented the young Lithuanian intelligentsia, the doctoral candidates, young instructors at schools of higher learning, professionals. Some had ties to one or another clergyman. Some were members of the Komsomol, as was Š. Žukauskas, who drew the heaviest six year sentence in the trial. The group included religious people. Its alleged preparation to issue the *New Bell* would put them in the tradition of the moderate democratic Lithuanian Left that began with the publication of the clandestine original *Bell* under the Tsarist rule.

Further KGB action was directed against individual dissenters of nationalist and anti-Communist leanings. One of those was Antanas Terleckas, obviously suspected of aiding both the nationalist groups and the *Chronicle*. On December 19th–20th, 1973, he was tried by the court of the Lenin district in Vilnius. At that time, Terleckas managed product storage in the confectionery division of the state company that administers Vilnius' restaurants and other dining facilities.[44] A graduate economist, he had been sentenced in 1958 and served a four year term for alleged anti-Soviet agitation. Afterwards, as a history student at Vilnius university he wrote a graduate thesis on "Lithuania under the Russian Rule, 1795–1915." But as in the case of the more famous Andrei Amalrik in Moscow, his thesis was rejected; however, it was returned to him not by his faculty advisor, but by the KGB. The police warned the student not to show it to anyone because it was "full of hatred for Russia."[45] Since his contacts with the dissidents in Lithuania and Russia could not be proven, the secret police framed him in a case that involved the stealing of state property. He was sentenced to a year of strict regime camp for thefts from his warehouse. The sentence was mild, the judge explained, because Terleckas had an ill wife and three children to support. Since he was arrested in May of 1973, he completed his incarceration in May of 1974, and at the end of 1975, Terleckas was taking care of Andrei Sakharov's visit to Vilnius and signing protests against Sergei Kovalëv's trial.[46] In August of 1977, however, he was re-arrested, this time in connection with the work of the Lithuanian Helsinki group.[47]

XIII

The Kremlin vs. the *Chronicle:*
Personalities of the Protest Movement

By the end of the summer of 1972, it became clear that the immediate beneficiary of this national and cultural upheaval was the Catholic church. The Soviets usually avoid total confrontation. Challenged by the forces of Lithuania's reborn nationalism, they temporarily eased the condition of religion in order to have time to deal with the nationalist danger. Thus, at least for the time being, the Lithuanians witnessed a reversal of the historical roles of Catholicism and nationalism. If at the end of the XIX century, Lithuanian peasants, by their forceful defense of the Kražiai parish church, strengthened the rising movement of Lithuania's national awakening, the nationalist demonstration of Kaunas relieved the pressures on the Church. Soviet authorities made immediate concessions not to the strong demands of freedom for Lithuania that were voiced in Kaunas, but to the less heard cries of freedom for religion.

The Easing of the Atmosphere

The first signal of the relaxation of the critically tense relations was sounded on August 12th, 1972, by K. Rimaitis, an authoritative writer on religion, who spoke of the "further necessity of strengthening the struggle against religious influence." More important, in the article he published in *Sovetskaia Litva,* this writer warned that in the antireligious activities

> . . . administrative attacks and any insults of the feelings of the believers can do irreparable damage. Incorrect methods of struggle against religion not only do not undermine the basis for its expansion but on the contrary, lead to the intensification of religious fanaticism, to disguised and secret services and rites; they encourage distrust and dissatisfaction among the believers and embitter their attitude.[1]

The government noted, in other words, that religious persecution had rekindled religious beliefs, driven the church into the underground, and further alienated the Catholic population from the Communist system.

This article revealed the Communist decision to mollify the Church, and indeed its appearance was followed by a string of actions, some small, others conspicuous, to improve the atmosphere. Some of these measures were reported in the official press. The *Chronicle*, too, confirmed that during the second half of 1972, the Lithuanian situation became more peaceful.[2] New trials for the teaching of religion were not organized, although this teaching continued. Administrative penalties also fell out for about a year. After serving their terms, the sentenced priests Zdebskis and Bubnys were at first allowed to work in their old parishes. This stood in marked contrast to 1971, when the similarly released Father Šeškevičius was shunted around and told to look for a different profession because his clerical work permit would not be restored to him. The change in political climate was followed by further improvements. In 1972 and 1973, the regime allowed the publication of the long prepared translation of the New Testament and of the Psalms, though the Bible was published only in a small edition of 10,000. In 1973, deanery retreats and meetings, with episcopal participation, were allowed for the first time after the war, and shortly afterwards the authorities made a small concession on admissions to the theological seminary. The procedure for application was not changed, but the *numerus clausus* for the 1974/75 school year was raised to fifty. In 1976, a concession was made to Communist visits in church. While in the earlier day, the escorting of a parent's bier to church funeral services was sufficient cause for losing party membership, now the propagandist party journal allowed that a party member may pay the last respects to the deceased even in church, but he must behave "like a Communist," that is, he should not participate in the liturgical rituals.[3]

Hand in hand with these concessions and relaxation went changes in personnel. As earlier explained, in the summer of 1972 the party demoted P. Mišutis, the chief of the Central Committee's division of agitation of propaganda. In February of 1973 the authorities pensioned off Commissioner for Religious Affairs Justas Rugienis. He was replaced by the suave and more tactful Kazimieras Tumėnas.[4] The new officer had a university education and a reputation of a propagandist-diplomat.

Western newspapers interpreted the new attitude as "a more subtle attack on religion" and even "a shift of the anti-religious policy in Lithuania."[5] The republic's laymen leaders, according to Western journalistic sources, urged Catholics not to "unnecessarily embarrass the government with new petitions or demonstrations" in hopes that the authorities will further tolerate the quickly spreading Bible study sessions in private homes and ultimately will treat the Church in Poland's manner. These laymen leaders had agreed, it was reported, even to loosen their ties to Moscow's dissidents in exchange for relaxation and accommodation.[6]

As later events demonstrated, this high optimism was only partially warranted. Priests were no longer tried, but now the turn came for the lay Catholics and for Moscow's dissidents who helped the Lithuanians. The laws of punishment for religious instruction were not revoked and the practice of administrative fines was restored within a year. Further religious publications were held up although ready for the printer. Nevertheless, the atmosphere continued to improve.[7] Pressures eased on one of the exiled bishops, Msgr. Sladkevičius. In 1976, a mixed delegation of "loyal" and "reactionary" priests was allowed to attend the Eucharistic congress in Philadelphia. In January of 1977, Sladkevičius was permitted to preach at a locally-held commemoration of the death of God's Servant Archbishop Jurgis Matulaitis and to praise him as the founder of the currently forbidden Marian congregation.[8] The Communist party, furthermore, in its May, 1977, appeal for a further atheization of school children and the youth several times stressed the need "not to hurt the freedom of conscience of believers."[9] Exposure of vulgarity and arbitrariness apparently was helping to normalize administration of religious laws, if not to broaden religious freedoms themselves. The *Chronicle* saw in the limited gains between the summer of 1972 and the spring of 1973 and in the continued easing of the atmosphere a justification of its pressure based on the reportorial approach.[10] Its tactic, anyway, did not prove calamitous as Commissioner Tumėnas and some anonymous clergymen had suggested.

Persuasion with Stick and Carrot

While extending an olive branch with one hand, the Soviets nevertheless sought to undermine and to destroy the Catholic protest movement with the other. The *Chronicle* and its suspected circle of friends became a target both of Soviet domestic diplomacy and of the KGB.

Thus, the new Commissioner for Religious Affairs tried a stick and carrot approach. On May 8th, 1973, he convened the bishops and administrators and, after promising aid for the publication of a catechism and for the manufacture of some religious devotionals, denounced the *Chronicle*. The KGB had been at work; the Commissioner had in his possession the fifth issue of the journal that he declared to be a slanderous work of some clergymen. "Someone will have to pay for this," he prophesied,[11] knowing that at this very time, the secret police were searching for the journal's sponsors. Commissioner Tumėnas further disapproved of petition writing. He repeated the same warning to clergymen in deanery conferences that in the spring of 1973 were allowed to convene for the first time after the war. At approximately the same time, Bishop Matulaitis-Labukas was asked publicly to condemn and disavow the *Chronicle*. However, the bishop unexpectedly refused. He explained to the authorities that such condemnation would merely hurt the bishops by tarnishing their reputation even more than their letter which denounced the Brezhnev-Waldheim memorandum.[12]

Since the hierarchs refused to condemn the publication, the authorities attempted to organize pressure among the clergy demanding such episcopal action. Anonymous unsigned letters to Bishop Labukas and to other bishops, even abroad, explained the alleged harm the *Chronicle* was doing to the Church. One letter was signed by the "group of priests of Vilkaviškis." In an unusual public reference to such letters, on November 22nd, 1972, Commissioner Tumėnas interpreted them as a genuine clerical voice.[13] It is, however, doubtful that it was. At the trial of the supporters of the *Chronicle* that was soon to follow one of the defendants, Jonas Stašaitis, on the first day of the trial refused to apologize for helping the *Chronicle*, but later regretted it for reasons that were identical with those of the anonymous letters. The *Chronicle*, Stašaitis said, hurts Catholic unity; it has caused the destruction of clandestine shops that manufacture religious literature. Catholics can best help themselves by a "rapprochement" with the atheists.[14] Stašaitis' point concerning the status of religious publications provided a strong lever for Tumėnas' and the KGB's persuasion campaign. Since a free official printing of prayerbooks is forbidden, old texts are reproduced in clandestine printing shops. Paulius Petronis, another defendant in the *Chronicle* trial, revealed that in six years time, 1968–74, he had printed more than 20,000 of them and had distributed 16,000 copies.[15] The publication of the *Chronicle* could hurt this effort because the authorities could destroy these shops in retaliation for the continued printing of the *Chronicle* as the KGB in fact did in 1974.

Unable to persuade church authorities and the clergy to abandon the *Chronicle*, the government sought to contain its influence by destroying its factual reliability. With the help of the KGB, some people whose difficulties were reported in the *Chronicle* were forced to sign denials of the reported facts that then were used to defame the journal's reportorial integrity.[16] Similarly, the official press intensified its attacks on the Vatican radio that broadcast the text of the *Chronicle* in which individual items reported in the journal were declared distorted, untrue, or invented. Such articles never mentioned the *Chronicle,* but served to warn the Vatican not to rely on the *Chronicle's* facts. Domestically, in atheist groups and also in the press, atheist propagandists sought to blacken the Catholic efforts to achieve constitutional improvements and accused "propaganda by reactionary clergy" [read the *Chronicle*] of deception. Jonas Aničas insisted that this alleged propaganda "falsifies the process of Lithuania's atheist education, distorts the condition of the priests, churches and believers, and falsifies the results and fruits of atheist indoctrination."[17]

Finally, in meetings with the clergy, Commissioner Tuménas insisted that the publication of the *Chronicle* hurts good church-state relations and that the government will not permit publication of catechism nor make any other concessions if the journal continues. He asked clerical deans to refuse support of the *Chronicle.*[18] The police, on the other hand, began harassing priests suspected of sponsoring the offending publication. Thus, for example, Fathers Zdebskis and Tamkevičius had their driver's licenses suspended on the basis of manufactured traffic violations.[19]

Simultaneously with these political efforts, the authorities engaged the KGB. The secret police began its searches in the spring of 1972,[20] but was interrupted by the self-immolation of Kalanta. The investigation was intensified in early 1973. In several provincial districts the authorities demanded that all offices, enterprises and organizations, including religious communities, supply samples of the typeprint of their typewriters.[21] This request, so reminiscent of Stalinist legislation and practice, was to help to trace, it appeared, not only religious dissenters but also the authors of anti-Soviet leaflets that were later attributed to members of arrested ethnographic study groups sentenced in March of 1973.[22]

Later in the year — according to the *Chronicle,* it happened on November 14th, 1973 — the agency decided to silence the journal by crushing the clandestine printing shops that so far had successfully duplicated religious literature. Manufacturers of such literature had been arrested in the past, thus, the police had leads. A week later, on

November 20th, 1973, the KGB seized Boleslovas Kulikauskas who had once been sentenced for the printing of prayerbooks and again was manufacturing them. But he appeared to have no connection with the *Chronicle*.[23]

The first and the most massive wave of searches affected over forty persons, mostly lay Catholics, but also several Lithuanian and Ukrainian priests. These searches yielded copies of prewar religious journals, old and new theological and philosophical books, thousands of bound and especially unbound copies of prayerbooks, a copy of the Brezhnev-Waldheim petition with signatures. A printset for a substantial book was also found, as was electrographic printing equipment and other duplicating tools. Further materials included *samizdat* brochures on Bishop Matulionis, on the trial of Simas Kudirka, an essay "Between the Laws," and others.[24] The confiscated literature probably created a pile as high as the one the Nazis burned in front of the University of Berlin on May 10th, 1933. At the parish house and the church of Rev. Boleslovas Babrauskas of Smilgiai in north central Lithuania, for example, the KGB men hauled away ten burlap sacks of literature, including the *Chronicle* and the prewar edition of the Bible. Police discoveries showed that religious Lithuanian *samizdat* was widespread, and furthermore, indicated that *samizdat* readers had communications with Moscow's dissidents on the one hand, and Western sources on the other. Both the works of Solzhenitsyn and Medvedev in Russia and the studies by Lithuanian philosophers A. Maceina and J. Girnius in the West were confiscated by the police. As a result of these raids, the Lithuanian KGB succeeded in closing down almost all clandestine centers that manufactured prayerbooks and catechisms.[25] This destruction, without much doubt, was the punishment the secret police meted out to clerical and lay Catholic leaders for their shielding and supporting of the *Chronicle*.

The executed searches and interrogations also led to a number of arrests. It is interesting to note that people were not charged merely for the possession of an issue of the *Chronicle,* a copy of a petition, or a *samizdat* manuscript. Therefore while interrogations and detentions were numerous, charges were preferred only against nine people. Public interest in the unseen but felt KGB raids was so keen that on December 23rd, five weeks after the arrest of Petras Pliuira-Plumpa, Povilas Petronis, and Jonas Stašaitis, the official press, in an unusual announcement, revealed that the three men were detained and charged "with illegal manufacturing and duplication of various publications, among them materials of a reactionary nature."[26] This included the

Chronicle, though the daily did not name it. The newspaper also said that the investigation was continuing. Indeed, on April 4th, the KGB arrested Virgilijus Jaugelis. Three weeks later, on April 24th, the police took Juozas Gražys, and on August 27th, it came for Nijolė Sadūnaitė.[27] The seizure of A. Patriubavičius completed the set. To these, the arrest of Sergei Kovalëv was added in Moscow, though it came more than a year later, on December 27th, 1974, after the Lithuanian prisoners were already tried and sentenced.[28]

Two of the accused Lithuanians, the already mentioned Kulikauskas and his friend Ivanauskas, were charged with the stealing of state property — though they manufactured prayerbooks — and a year later, on September 18th, 1974, the Supreme Court of the Lithuanian SSR sentenced them to three and a half and to two years of labor camp respectively.[29] The other seven were tried in case No. 395 for the reproduction and distribution of the *Chronicle* and other religious and non-religious materials. The first five were grouped together while Gražys and Sadūnaitė were given individual consideration.

The Chronicle *Before the Soviet Bar*

Case No. 395 was tried before the Lithuanian Supreme Court in Vilnius.[30] The trial lasted twelve days. It began on December 2nd, 1974, and ended on Christmas Eve, December 24th, with the pronouncement of sentences. Two of the defendants, Plumpa-Pliuira and Petronis, were charged with the violation of Articles 68 and 70 of the penal code. The remaining three, Jaugelis, Stašaitis, and Patriubavičius, were accused of violating Art. 199 of the same code. Art. 68 forbids any "agitation or propaganda that seeks to undercut or weaken Soviet government or that seeks to commit especially dangerous individual crimes against the state." It also outlaws "the spreading of slanderous fabrications that humiliate the Soviet state and social system." Art. 70 punishes three actions: "organized activity that seeks to prepare or commit especially dangerous crimes against the state; formation of an organization with the purpose of committing such crimes and also participation in an anti-Soviet organization." Art. 199 outlaws a "systematic oral dissemination of fabrications that humiliate the Soviet state and social system and also a manufacture and circulation of works of the same nature in printed or any other form." Thus, the duplication and distribution of the *Chronicle* was treated as a state crime rather than a violation of statutes on religion. The cases, then, were political though the *Chronicle* did not preach or incite any anti-government actions.

The trial of the five transpired without surprises. The public was not allowed into the court room though immediate relatives could attend. Only Patriubavičius pleaded guilty. Jaugelis who was accused of duplicating and distributing No. 6 of the *Chronicle* and also collecting signatures for the Brezhnev-Waldheim memorandum said he was innocent. His plea, however, seemed to be based on the philosophical proposition that freedom of speech was not a crime. Actually, he said, "the prosecutors should sit in the chairs of the defendants."[31] Stašaitis partially confessed, but disagreed with the motivation that the prosecution imputed. Petronis and Plumpa agreed only partially to the factual accusations, though Petronis pleaded misinterpretation of his motivation.

The prosecution regarded Plumpa as the chief criminal. He had assembled two electrographic duplication machines and printed four issues of the *Chronicle* and some other *samizdat* literature. He was further charged with the falsification of his passport. Because of his camp record in Mordovia, Plumpa could get neither desired housing nor work, and to be able to settle down to a married life, he tampered with his passport though later he informed the Mordovian authorities. The Lithuanians, too, were in the process of issuing him a passport in his own name. He received the maximum sentence of seven years for the violation of Art. 68 and Art. 70, and an additional three years for falsification of documents (Art. 212). The court sent him to eight years of hard labor. Petronis, in view of his old age, was given four years of strict regime camp. Jaugelis was sentenced to two years in a common regime institution. Stašaitis regretted his actions and was sentenced for the length of time he already had spent in prison, and thus was freed after the trial. Charges against Patriubavičius were changed to causing an auto accident that resulted in injuries to two young passengers (Art. 246). He regretted his part in the duplication of the *Chronicle* and, like Stašaitis, was sentenced and let go. Unlike Stašaitis, he was omitted from the report in the party daily *Tiesa* that summarized the results of the case.[32]

The trial of Juozas Gražys was held on March 11th–17th, 1975. He was charged with the violation of Art. 68 and was sentenced to three years of labor camp.[33] The case of Sadūnaitė, the only woman in the group, was separated out of Case 395 and her trial was held on June 16th–17th of the same year. She also received a three-year sentence, but in a camp of strict regime. An additional three years of exile from Lithuania were added to the prison sentence, thus banishing her for six years from home.[34]

These dry facts depict neither the drama of the courtroom nor the personalities of the sentenced supporters of the *Chronicle*. If anything, the trial revealed the ways by which Soviet authorities estrange their own people and then punish them for demands to be reinstated into society. The defendants, generally, belonged to the rejected group of citizenry. The degree of their alienation was revealed in their self-identification to the court. Only Patriubavičius, a man with two years of primary education, identified himself as a "citizen of the USSR." The attitude of Gražys and Sadūnaitė has not been recorded. Petronis and Stašaitis were "citizens of the Lithuanian SSR," Jaugelis — "citizen of Lithuania," and Plumpa said that he was a Lithuanian without citizenship.[35] Plumpa said he could not be a citizen of a country that does not allow him to hold a job to support a family. This identification showed that the degree of their socialization in the Soviet system varied; only the uneducated Patriubavičius spoke the official language. Others showed autonomist and also nationalist loyalties. Yet, the defendants did not fit the category of class enemies, as the regime prefers to paint its critics and opponents. On the whole, they represented a solid, sophisticated working class stratum with, for that group, good education.

Petronis, the sixty-three year old man, was the oldest defendant. The youngest was Jaugelis, then 28. Plumpa was in his mid-thirties, Stašaitis over fifty, and Patriubavičius close to forty. Gražys' age is not known though most likely he belonged to the senior generation, while Sadūnaitė was 37. Actually, three of the accused (Jaugelis, born in 1948, Plumpa, born in 1939, and Sadūnaitė, born in 1938) were products of the Soviet system. They were educated in Soviet schools. With one exception, all defendants had secondary education. Petronis, in addition, had a specialty of paramedic (feldsher). Their social background is not well known, but for the most part the seven were of poor farmer or working class background. Petronis had started hiring out for farm work as an eight year old boy. Jaugelis had been a truck driver; Plumpa worked at various heavy manual jobs. Only Sadūnaitė came from a professional's family. Her father had been a professor of the Agricultural Academy. After receiving secondary education, however, Sadūnaitė did not pursue formal studies but stayed home to nurse her sick parents. She was, reputedly, a secret nun, who organized Father Šeškevičius' legal defense.

Two other defendants once aspired to religious vocation. Before World War II Petronis had managed to travel to Italy to enter a school of Salezian Fathers, while Jaugelis sought admission to the theological seminary in Kaunas; his application, however, did not pass the scrutiny of the government. All were deeply religious and dedicated men, though Patriubavičius said he manufactured prayerbooks because he could make a profit from it. Gražys and Plumpa had "previous records"; the first had been already twice sentenced for "political" crimes and in camp had contracted an incurable intestinal disease, while the second had been convicted for secretly harboring "weapons," which consisted of several rusted relics of World War II that all teenagers then collected. Actually, he had participated in patriotic demonstrations on the traditional All Souls evening sometime in the fifties, most likely at the time of the Hungarian revolution in 1956, and had raised, with friends, a Lithuanian flag. The KGB caught up with him in 1958 and he received a seven year sentence in a labor camp. In the camp, he said, he became deeply religious.

It would be natural to expect that the promoters of the *Chronicle* would harbor nationalist Lithuanian views. Their self-identification betrayed this proclivity; however, in court they denied "nationalist" charges. This they did, it may be surmised, because the Soviets attach to the term "nationalism" a notoriety that may identify the suspect with "bourgeois" nationalists who allegedly seek to overturn the Soviet system in collaboration with Western "imperialists." Nevertheless, Jaugelis tried to recite patriotic poetry — nationalism and patriotism being two different attitudes — and the court found it difficult to squelch his rhymed expressions of love for the homeland. But his speeches did not deal with nationalist or even nationality issues — as Kudirka's famous court address in 1970 did — but with freedom of religion and the Universal Declaration of Human Rights. Plumpa, though denying Soviet citizenship, professed to the overriding bond of humanity, not nationality. In camp, he said, his best friends were not Lithuanians but "a Jew, a Georgian, a Latvian and two Russians."[36] Petronis, who since 1968 had quit his regular job to be able to manufacture prayerbooks and other religious literature, ministered equally to all, including the Russians, as a Russian witness testified. In Lithuanian conditions, this otherwise innocuous praise of a man's moral integrity indicates an attitude diametrically opposed to nationalism. Sadūnaitė, too, dwelt on mainly religious issues. "This day," she declared, "is the happiest day in my life because I am tried for the *Chronicle of the Catholic Church of Lithuania* which struggles against any physical and spiritual tyranny over men."[37] This was her description of the journal she had helped to type. Such manner of argument — as also others found in the pages of the *Chronicle* — indicates a curious parallelism and even blending of ideas of Lithuanian religious dissenters with those of the past philosophers of civil rights, philosophers who were hostile to Catholicism. Historical fate and individualized experiences had so transposed the positions of Catholics who once believed in church domination over secular affairs and of their old opponents whose religiosity was nondenominational, that two hundred years later in Sadūnaitė's exclamation one could hear Thomas Jefferson writing to Benjamin Rush that "upon the altar of God [he had] sworn eternal hostility against every form of tyranny over the mind of man."[38] Jefferson opposed the establishment of religion; Sadūnaitė fought the establishment of atheism. The bond that united them was the idea of freedom for all.

The Trial of Moscow's Kovalëv and the Death of Tamonis

The next trial of a prominent supporter of the *Chronicle* was held on December 9th–12th, 1975.[39] The defendant was the Russian scholar Sergei A. Kovalëv, a member of Sakharov's group of civil rights advocates, and a self-confessed editor of several issues of the Russian *Khronika tekushchikh sobytii.* Kovalëv lived and worked in Moscow where he was arrested on December 27th, 1974, but he had been associated with Lithuanian dissidents and was brought to prison and the subsequent trial in Vilnius. Specifically, he was charged under Art. 70 of the Russian republic's code which outlaws information that humiliates or slanders the Soviet system. Concretely, in addition to various other Moscow activities, this included the proven possession and use of three issues of the Lithuanian *Chronicle.* While the alleged crime was committed in Russia and the biologist was accused of violating the Russian republic's law, his trial by the Lithuanian Supreme Court provided a glimpse into the working of the Soviet federal system; as we understand federation, it really does not exist in the Soviet Union.

During the three days, the court heard twenty-two witnesses but refused to call Yakir and Krasin, the earlier sentenced editors of the Russian *Khronika,* as Kovalëv had demanded. It similarly refused Kovalëv's request to have his own lawyers and forbade the use of the text of the Universal Declaration of Human Rights. Kovalëv protested against the removal of his witnesses from the court room and the refusal to allow Academician Andrei Sakharov, who had come from Moscow, to attend the trial. But the protest did not help. In response, Kovalëv refused to participate in further proceedings and was removed from the room. He then declared a hunger strike. Nevertheless, the court continued without the defendant and sentenced him to the highest possible term, seven years of strict regime camp and three additional years of exile. Canadian correspondent M. Levi could only report the sentence but not the trial since he, too, was barred from attending. Many Lithuanian dissidents were similarly pushed away. The *Chronicle* considered Kovalëv a man of the utmost altruistic convictions whose "sacrifice helped Lithuania a great deal." The journal saw a further rapprochement between the Lithuanian and Russian dissidents emerging as a result of the case against the Russian: "The court process and persecution shows that the secret police is capable of bringing closer together the Lithuanian and Russian nations."[40] "When he returns from prison," the journal concluded after reporting his trial, "we will welcome Russian scholar S. Kovalëv like our brother and best friend."[41]

In the meantime, the *Chronicle* continued publication, increasing the number of annual issues to six. The secret police continued its probe that, however, took some time in producing new results.

The KGB did not catch any new *Chronicle* supporters until the end of 1976. On October 19th–20th, 1976, the organization's agents searched the apartments of J. Matulionis and V. Lapienis in Kaunas and of Ms. O. Pranckūnaitė in Panevėžys.[42] The police confiscated several typewriters, 20 kilograms of paper, some issues of the *Chronicle,* various religious literature and works of *samizdat,* including the Lithuanian translation of Solzhenitzyn's *Gulag.* The men were arrested immediately, while the woman was arrested on January 7th, 1977.[43] Ms. Pranckūnaitė, a 37 year old worker in the local textile factory, was first imprisoned in 1951, at the age of 15. The crime for which she had been sentenced to 10 years in Siberian camps was the writing of a ditty critical of collective farms. Matulionis was a 45 year old university graduate with a major in Lithuanian language and literature. He had also studied in the musical conservatory, from which he was excluded for singing in a church choir. Some time ago he was fired from his position as director of the Picture Gallery in Vilnius. Lieponis, a graduate economist, was the oldest of the three, born in 1909. The police had searched him previously, in connection with petitions and letters published in the *Chronicle.* These three were tried on July 20th–25th and received predictable, though shorter, sentences than Kovalëv, Plumpa-Pliuira, and the others. Matulionis was put on a two-year probation (he "regretted" his involvement). Lapienis was sent for two years to a strict regime camp and the woman, Pranckūnaitė, was sentenced to two years in a camp of "common" regime.[44]

Police methods, used against the supporters of the *Chronicle,* generally were the same as those employed in Moscow, including the use of psychiatric treatment. The journal had recorded cases of referral to a psychiatric hospital for examination. It also related a celebrated case of Mindaugas Tamonis, a candidate (an approximate equivalent of Ph.D. degree) of technological sciences whom the *Chronicle* posthumously praised as a hero of his generation.[45]

Tamonis was born in 1940, the year the Soviets occupied Lithuania. He was married and as an avocation wrote poetry which he published in the official press. The young man worked at the Institute for the Conservation of Monuments. His difficulties began in 1974 when he refused to repair a monument to the Red Army the Liberator that had been erected at an important crossroads in the Western part of Lithuania. He objected to this assignment, he said, because he did not recognize as legal the present political status of Lithuania. He further demanded the correction of the consequences of Stalinist rule in the Baltic republics, including mass deportations and the destruction of Baltic independence. As a condition for cooperation, he demanded the building of monuments to the victims of the Stalinist regime, the implementation of the constitutional provision that allows republic self-determiantion, and the establishment — if people so desire — of the same kind of cultural and economic independence that is enjoyed by other Socialist nations. Finally, he wanted freedom for the Social and Christian Democratic, and other parties, with their own press and with "really" democratic elections. These reforms, he suggested, would make a democratic system possible and effective "within the framework of socialism." A short while after he wrote this letter, Tamonis was confined to a psychiatric hospital in Vilnius where he received strong injections of insulin and other drugs. This treatment, according to the *Chronicle,* damaged his metabolism and his nervous system. Released from the hospital, on June 25th, 1975, he wrote a letter to the Communist party's Central Committee in Moscow where he elaborated his proposals for the removal of the consequences of the Stalinist and Khrushchevite rule. But as soon as this letter was mailed, he was returned to the *psikhushka.* This turn of events contributed to the death of his mother. A month later, on July 25th, he was released from the hospital but had to agree periodically to return for injections of the drug moditen. Now, according to the journal, he was isolated at work and the KGB put pressures on his relatives and family to make life impossible for him. On November 5th, 1975, he was found killed by a passing train, an apparent suicide. The *Chronicle* suggested, however, that his death was the result of the KGB's intentional drive through pressure and blackmail to terminate his life.

The *Chronicle's* publication was not affected by any of these arrests, deaths or confiscations. It continued as in the earlier day, and in March of 1977, in addition to the textual material, the journal began printing illustrations of destroyed religious art, photographs of arrested supporters, and other documentary pictures. The fact that the journal did not succumb to the very intense political pressures and police attacks in all probability shows that the editors and producers of the *Chronicle* operate very deeply in the underground where they enjoy strong support.

Effects of Soviet Religious Policy on the Church: An Institutional Balance Sheet

A generation of Soviet rule, it is anticlimactic to say, brought revolutionary changes to Lithuania's Catholic church. The nation's oldest institution found itself slated for extinction and thus registered considerable losses. These included not only properties, status, influence in public affairs, especially education and publishing, but losses that affect, so to speak, its vital statistics, namely, the churches, the clergy, the membership. Has the Church been sufficiently injured to hope for survival? Has it lost the youth? Have there been no gains and no signs of new vitality? The current state of information does not permit the composition of a complete statistical picture, but nevertheless allows a reasonable statement on the institution's basic inventory to separate fact from fiction on this controversial, and from the Soviet point of view politically explosive, subject. A statistical profile usually gives some indication of institutional viability that no political arguments can deny.

The Churches and Chapels

In 1940, at the time of the Soviet invasion of Lithuania, the country's six dioceses, covering the Lithuanian part of the Vilnius archdiocese and the Klaipėda prelature, had 708 active churches and 314 chapels in convents, hospitals, prisons, cemeteries, and orphanages.[1] The majority of the chapels were closed by the authorities in a very short time. The last to be physically destroyed were the thirty-five chapels of the Calvary in the Verkiai hills near Vilnius. They were dynamited and removed shortly before the celebration of Soviet Lithuania's 25th anniversary in 1965.[2]

Most church closings took place before the ascendancy of Leonid Brezhnev in 1964. In 1954, by reporting that 688 churches were still active, Bishop Paltarokas suggested that in Stalin's years only 20 churches were lost to services.[3] A larger number were closed under Khrushchev, 1957–64, and the number dropped to 608 in 1965. In the next decade, some closed churches were apparently reopened or "temporary" places of worship constructed, at least for limited services,[4] and the reported number in 1974 stood at 628. Of these, 554 churches had resident priests while the rest were served by neighboring pastors. The number of such churches is quickly growing. In 1974 it stood at 74. In 1975 it increased to 85.[5] The largest percentage of churches is found in cities that in the meantime have swollen in population. By 1973, for example, the citizenry of Kaunas and Vilnius almost doubled respectively to 330,000 and 410,000; however, the number of Catholic churches in Vilnius had been cut from thirty-one to nine, if the chapel of the Eastern Gate is included in the total, while in Kaunas the authorities closed down all but three churches. Of the total of 80 churches withdrawn from religious use since 1940, thirty-seven were found just in these two cities. It may be added that in these two largest Lithuanian towns there is not a single Protestant church left — they were closed down — though the closings apparently did not affect the Russian Orthodox churches.[6]

The usual Soviet explanation for church closings is the diminishing number of believers. It is possible, though it has never been reported, that some churches collapsed under the burden of use taxes, insurance payments, and utility rates. Their support by believers usually has been firm. Some more conspicuous temples, as the cathedral-basilica in Vilnius, very likely were secularized because of their central position in the city that gave it a sort of religious appearance. In Vilnius, the Communist party headquarters are located almost on the same square, and the Communist leaders apparently could not accept this proximity. In contrast, Estonian government leaders, in a similar situation, have tolerated a Russian Orthodox church in the upper town of Tallinn. In the Lithuanian case, the cathedral was converted into a picture gallery and a concert hall.

Only very few of the seized churches have been razed; most have been turned over to other uses.[7] Thus, the church of St. Casimir houses the museum of atheism, the church of All Saints in Vilnius has become a gallery of folk art, the Garrison church in Kaunas, seized already under Brezhnev's rule, has been converted into a museum of sculpture and stained glass. Some, as the Church of the Resurrection in Kaunas, today function as factories; still others, as the former church of the Jesuits in the same city, as a sports hall. Many of the buildings, however, for many years have been used as warehouses for medical and paper supplies, opera and ballet decorations, and merchandise.

Still others today serve as movie theaters, laboratories, archival storage facilities, social clubs, and restaurants. One of the oldest and architecturally most famous Lithuanian churches, that of St. John's in Vilnius, built in 1387, was used as a newsprint warehouse for the Communist daily *Tiesa,* and for a time was leased to a Belorussian movie company as a film studio.[8] The Belorussians filmed in it a war picture and very realistically exploded real hand grenades and artillery shells. Many old and artistically valuable sculptures, stained glass windows and frescoes were damaged beyond repair. A similar fate befell the art of a number of churches, some because of neglect and others because of wanton destruction. In the early sixties, the local party leadership allowed restoration of some of the damaged churches as "national monuments." In 1961, however, Khrushchev ordered such activity stopped.[9] After Khrushchev's demise, restoration was continued on a more selective basis and at a slower pace, but several churches — for example, the historic monastery church of Pažaislis, the church of the Holy Cross in Vilnius, and ultimately the much damaged church of St. John's — have been renovated for secular use. St. John's will house a concert hall and a museum of "progressive thought." Its administration has been returned to the University of Vilnius to which the church historically has belonged.

The surviving churches, generally, have been kept up in recent years largely through the enterprising efforts of their pastors who understood how to secure "deficit" materials, that is those that can not be easily obtained because of their shortage.[10] For any repairs a permission must be secured from the local government and the Council on Religious Affairs; "cooperative" priests are granted the permission more easily than the others. Since 1974, it has become more difficult to secure such permission. Since, however, the priests are banned from educational and pastoral activities that in the past consumed their time, they eagerly work on the churches, sometimes with the help of the local youths,[11] and most of today's provincial churches, though modest, are kept spic and span. Diocesan administrators, too, stress this activity. For example, of the 223 questions in the pastoral survey that the administrator of the Vilnius archdiocese asked the pastors to answer, 128 concerned church buildings, 7 liturgical vestments and vessels.[12] Village churches have been electrified; some larger churches have been equipped with loudspeakers, installed either just for the occasion of a festive celebration or even permanently.

In recent years, several provincial churches have burned down under mysterious circumstances that have suggested arson. Church thieves and vandals, searching for liturgical vessels and religious art items (these are bought by government museums and by private collectors) have become a problem and Bishop Matulaitis-Labukas on December 12th, 1972, issued to his pastors a directive asking not to keep any liturgical vessels in the church unless the church was guarded in the night time.[13] The caught perpetrators, however, are either not prosecuted by the government,[14] or are treated very leniently by the courts.[15]

The Clergy

The number of buildings, though pointing to the Church's institutional ability to keep the operation going and indicative of the support it has among the Catholic population, still reveals much less about the institution's condition than the data on the clergy. A major consequence of the Soviet religious policy has been a substantial decline in the numbers of the priests and, furthermore, their diminishing ability to serve because of old age and limited life expectancy.[16] In 1940, the total of diocesan and monastic clergymen was 1,451. By the end of the war, in the fall of 1944, it had dropped to about 1,200. This decline was caused by the withdrawal of 253 priests to the West. An estimated 180 priests were deported to Siberian and other camps where about one-third of them perished and some dozens stayed on for pastoral work. Possibly about 150 priests of Polish nationality emigrated to Poland. In 1954, at any rate, Bishop Paltarokas reported the survival of 741 clergymen. With the returnees from the camps and exile, and with some newly ordained, the number in 1965 was 869. By then, however, the group was already declining. The reason was very simple; more priests annually died than the government allowed to be ordained. In the two following years, 1966–67, the number went down to 848; in 1971 it diminished to 794; in October of 1974 it further decreased to 772. This figure includes clergymen who were ordained after World War II, 1945–74. Of these, there were 390, or on the average about 13 annually. Actually, a larger number was ordained in the immediate postwar period while in the sixties and seventies the median figure was about six. Six were ordained in 1968, three in 1969, eight in 1970, four in 1971, six in 1972, five in 1973 and eight in 1974. In other words, during the six-year period 40 young men became priests. Within the same time span, however, almost 120 clergymen died.

As the table indicates, the net balance is grossly negative. While the republic's Catholic population is steadily increasing, the number of priests is catastrophically diminishing. In 1974,[17] the city of Kaunas

Number of Priests in Lithuania, 1940-74

Diocese	1940	1965	1974
Kaišiadorys	101	83	73
Kaunas	298	199	171
Panevėžys	241	173	159
Telšiai[1]	245	171	154
Vilkaviškis	214	136	118
Vilnius	184	107	95
Sub-total	1,283	869	772
Priests of			
monastic orders	163	---	---
	1,451	869	772

Sources: Lithuanian Religious Information in Rome, including list of sources in footnote 1.

[1] The figure for 1940 does not include the priests of Klaipėda prelature, figures for 1965 and 1974 do.

had 37 clergymen, Vilnius — 23, Panevėžys — a city of 84,000, had 10, Šiauliai — a city of 100,000, had 7, Telšiai — a diocesan seat with a population of 22,000, had 5, while many country churches could no longer claim a resident priest because of their shortage. To put these figures in perspective, we can compare the Kaunas figures with the number of Lithuanian priests in Lithuanian diasporas abroad. Thus, in 1974, Chicago had 77 Lithuanian priests who served a much smaller number of Catholics; Brooklyn had 21; Sao Paulo in Brazil — 15; and Philadelphia — 13.[18]

A table showing the breakdown by age of the clerical corps further conspicuously demonstrates the great and quickening decline of its actuarial strength.

At this rate of decline, in 1986, the total number of priests, in round numbers, will be only slightly higher than 500 or less than it was more than a hundred years ago.

This shortage in Lithuania is not the result of desertions — only 21 priests have left the priesthood since 1945 — but the result of highly restrictive policies the authorities have imposed on admissions to the sole theological seminary of the country.[19] The number of semi-

Catholic Clergymen in Lithuania by Age
1965-1974

| | Age Groups | | | | |
	24-29	30-39	40-59	60-90	Total
1965	18	122	434	295	869
1974	9	61	320	377	772

Source:

For 1965 — Lithuanian Religious Information in Rome
1974 — *World Lithuanian Roman Catholic Directory* (ed. by Rev. Casimir Pugevicius) (Putnam: Lithuanian Roman Catholic Priests' League of America, 1975).

narians, from 1946 kept at 150, was reduced to 60 in 1949 and though two years later it was increased to 75, where it stayed between 75 and 80 until 1959, it again was cut to 60 and gradually was mowed down until it reached 25 in 1965-66. Afterwards the set *numerus clausus* became 30; in 1974 it was increased to 50. During the 1977-78 school year it had 66 students. Candidates have great difficulties in admission, and in recent years only one in four of those who had the courage to apply could hope to reach his goal. In 1962, the authorities allowed 5 new admissions, in 1963 again only 5; in 1964 the number was 4; in 1965 it was 5 again; in 1966 — 8; in 1967 — 7; in 1968 — 6; and afterwards — ten a year until 1974 when it was closer to fifteen. The quota, not always allowed to be filled, since 1976 was set at 19.[20] Knowledgeable Lithuanian Catholics estimate that each year between 100 and 150 candidates would apply, if application were free. As it is, even the priests are forbidden to advertise the seminary or otherwise encourage priestly vocations.

Church in the Underground?

Surprisingly enough, the Soviets have reaped from this decline only mixed benefits. While the shrinking of the numbers was welcome, it was accompanied by a startling and an apparently unexpected phenomenon that has created a substantial problem. Instead of choking off the supply of clergymen, the strict Soviet policy has encouraged theological preparation in the underground, and, in effect, has provoked the emergence of an incipient underground church. Little is known about its existence, but allusions made to it in the official press and in the *Chronicle* are unmistakable. In 1972, K. Rimaitis suggested in *Sovetskaia Litva* that the government's church policy drove many Catholics underground.[21] The *Chronicle* reported that almost two decades ago, in 1960, a seminarian who was denied ordination on government orders was nevertheless ordained "in an illegal way."[22] While refused a professional work permit that is required of all active priests, he was promised a parish appointment by the secret police if he would reveal who ordained him, where he said the Mass, in what localities he preached, in other words, where and with whom he worked. The *Chronicle* has not denied the existence of such pastoral activity. The so-called *podpolshchiki* (from Russian "undergrounders") apparently are a fact of life. Allegations have been made that these secret priests are trained in an underground seminary; these Soviet inspired suspicions have been neither confirmed nor denied by the publishers of the *Chronicle,* who favor preparation of the priests in the underground if it can not be properly done in the "official" seminary and who praise underground priests as "examples of faith, courage and sacrifice."[23]

The underground church includes monastic organizations as well. While all convents and monasteries were officially closed in 1948, their institutional life apparently did not stop. In 1960, *Ogonëk,* a Russian periodical of Moscow, reported and pictorially illustrated the existence of two secret convents in the city of Kaunas.[24] The nuns, the authors of the article said, worked as teachers, nurses, laboratory technicians. Since that time, while these particular monasteries were disbanded, the idea of monastic life apparently could not be suppressed. Their recent existence was confirmed by the former chief of Lithuanian Agitprop Mišutis in 1974.[25] In February of 1976, in an atheist seminar held in Vilnius, government speakers suggested that in Lithuania there are about 1,500 secret nuns who work mostly as medical sisters.[26] This number is much larger than convent membership in 1940 when it was 629. Furthermore, the very intensive propaganda against the Jesuits, Marians, and other monastic orders that has been prominently featured in the press[27] suggests that the authorities assume their continued existence and growth though their numbers have not been anywhere revealed. Why else propagandize — out of the blue sky, so to speak — against institutions that presumably have died thirty years ago?

In addition to the secret convents and monasteries, the underground Church includes lay circles that study the Bible, teach children, duplicate prayerbooks, read and spread theological literature. Still other Catholics participate in very loosely connected, unofficial — since not licensed — but really not secret or "undercover" groups which further individual religiosity. An example of such groups is the Movement of the Friends of the Eucharist that promotes daily contemplation, church attendance, and secular virtues of patience, industry, integrity, and abstinence from liquor.[28] The group does not hold any meetings.

Despite the complaints of the government, "official" Catholic authorities in Lithuania do not seem to consider the underground activities as contrary to the functioning of the official church. While some aspects of underground involvement have led to disagreements among the clergymen — these will be explored in the coming pages — the underground has not caused a division of the Church itself. According to the *Chronicle,* the secretly or unofficially operating part of the Church "does not obstruct the officially functioning local church, does not seek to impair [church] discipline or to divide it [the Church], but [instead] makes every effort to supplement its work."[29] It would appear that the relationship between the "official" and "unofficial" portion of the Church is somewhat similar to the condition of Islam in Central Asia.

Lithuania's religious underground has been totally the product of Moscow's anti-religious policies. The search for an "unofficial" pursuit of clerical or monastic vocation was clearly encouraged by the regime's very strictly circumscribed "official" sphere of religious life, the very tightly controlled theological education at the Kaunas seminary and a total absence of religious literature and education for adults as well as children. The authorities, however, seem to prefer the current course in hopes that these stringent controls will cut the historical continuity between generations. Furthermore, by blotting out historical memory, they apparently expect to loosen and destroy traditional clerical loyalties to the Church as a religious and national institution. Indeed, within a decade, a large majority of Lithuanian priests will have received their secular and theological education under Soviet rule. Despite the official claims that the existing seminary trains theology students in conformity with a Western, Vatican approved curriculum, because of a lack of literature and faculty preparation, the students most likely do not receive an up-to-date philosophical and theological education. The canons of the Church, that is, the legal backbone of the Church's organizational principles, are interpreted to comply to the Communist party's totalitarian supremacy. The teaching of universal and Lithuanian church history is lagging. Finally, students do not have textbooks. They have to rely on notes taken in classes and neither the students nor their teachers have access to Western theological literature. Instead, students are required to take courses on Marxism-Leninism and Soviet constitutional law, which of course is needed but hardly as a substitute for Catholic writings.

The worsening of the seminary's situation has coincided with the appointment of Rev. Viktoras Butkus as its rector. While the past rectors have changed very frequently because of forced resignations, Msgr. Butkus has survived for more than a decade. His appointment followed a confict over the hierarchy's influence on the seminary that brought the Bishop of Vilnius Steponavičius to a confrontation with the Commissioner for Religious Affairs, Rugienis. The bishop lost, and with him any autonomy that was left in the seminary's management. Butkus, just returned from Rome where he graduated from the Lateran university with a doctor's degree, was appointed to direct the seminary in the stringent new spirit dictated by Moscow's new chief of religious affairs V. Kuroedov. Butkus favored administrative training over the philosophical and theological education to make the future clergymen capable of functioning as confined servants of the cult in the bureaucratic Soviet system. This educational philosophy diametrically contradicts the goals of the Catholic protest movement which has been highly critical of Butkus' leadership. The Rector has retaliated to the protesters and the *Chronicle* by forbidding his students to associate with "reactionary" priests. Nevertheless, concerned with the *Chronicle's* surmised influence in the Vatican, Msgr. Butkus has remained very sensitive to the journal's criticisms and, as a result of a possible collusion with the Soviet government, has directly tried to combat and neutralize the journal's opposition to him in the Papal Curia.[30]

Soviet authorities apparently expect that the severely limited educational life and experience will produce clergymen of a substantially different orientation than in the past. The backbone of the clerical corps of today, as seen from their composition by age, still consists of people who have received much or all of their secular and theological education in free or relatively unfettered circumstances. As a result, they combine a loyalty to the Church with Western cultural and social values. Furthermore, these clergymen are deeply rooted in Lithuanian national history and traditions. This middle-aged group, however, will be gone in ten to twenty years, a fact that makes the Soviet prospects look rather promising and the apprehensions of the outgoing group very real.

Conflict in the Clergy

Another result of the "pressure cooker" Soviet policy toward religion — this one purposefully aimed at — has been the creation of discord among the clergymen. Confronted by a Communist iron hand, the clerics and their hierarchs were bound to respond differently to the squeeze, and these different responses have been exploited by the regime for creating conflict and division within the clerical ranks.

The Soviets began their "divide and rule" tactic very early and collected the first fruits already in 1947–48 when they succeeded in persuading several Vilnius pastors to accept the Soviet type parish committee — the *dvatsatka* — as the parish manager. Although the committee's superiority has not been fully enforced, this division ultimately led Bishop Paltarokas to accept the system for the entire church province. The subsequent machinations for the establishment of a national Lithuanian church and the denunciation of Pope Pius XII did not succeed; only 19 clergymen out of 1,000 signed the anti-Papal declaration.[31] Yet the issues of guerilla warfare, of government interference in parish affairs, instruction in catechism, support of Soviet "peace movements," and removal of bishops provided issues that helped to create differences of opinion and ultimately, as the Soviets say, to "differentiate" the clergy into "loyalist" and "reactionary" priests. In the seventies, the authorities no longer question the civil clerical loyalty to the Soviet system as was the case in Stalin's epoch. In the Soviet view, the clergy had no choice but to accept it as "an essential condition for the continued existence of the church."[32] Therefore, to be a "loyalist" means not just loyalty to the Soviet system, but acceptance of the narrow function for religion that the Soviet law has prescribed. "Reactionary," on the other hand, is interpreted as an attitude of a traditional priest who insists on the Church's independent right to teach, preach, and freely administer the sacraments. "Reactionary" priests, too, assume the role of protectors of Lithuania's national culture.[33] In practical terms, the first group consists of "obedient" and status quo priests; the second of "disobedient" clerics who seek to change Soviet laws, if not attitudes, to make more room for religious life.

If the "disobedient" group is more or less homogeneous, the "obedient" class is not at all monolithic. It includes, first of all, some very few who have gone all the way over: not only to the side of the government but also that of the secret police. The KGB has its informers among clergymen; occasionally, a cleric is found who will testify against colleagues in court about crimes he never saw them commit. Many of the "obedient" group belong to the administrative pyramid and are caught between their dedication to the Church and subservience to the state. They attempt therefore to live a life of compromise which involves both cooperation and independence, frequently in a mixture that makes the clergyman's actions ambiguous, to say the least. This group encompasses some regular pastors who, without their superiors' knowledge, sign church contracts with the local government or treat children's catechism instruction in a casual manner. It further includes church administrators and dignitaries who sign political statements; it also includes priests who are tired of struggling though they frequently sign petitions asking for more religious freedom. *Tiesos kelias,* a new underground publication that demands a high level of activism from clergymen, characterized these latter as "resigned" priests. They are good clergymen but have lost hope. They feel that it is "useless to blow against the wind."[34] According to *Tiesos kelias,* this attitude allegedly characterizes the majority of Lithuania's clerics, leaving the "disobedient" group in a minority.

Division lines have again sharpened as a result of the government's attempts to exploit the inevitable differences of opinion among the clergy on the tactics and goals of the protest movement and the *Chronicle.* Since a "loyalist," pro-government position remains extremely unpopular, opposition has been voiced by anonymous letters. In one of the unsigned communications that allegedly a group of clergymen of the diocese of Vilkaviškis sent to the bishops in 1974, the anonymous authors complained about the "lack of unity" among the clergy that is incited by the "so-called patriot priests, 'the fighters for the church's and religion's freedom.'" "These priests," the letter said, "in various ways seek to turn back the clock of history; they are hungry for publicity over foreign radio and press; they want to become uncrowned martyrs and in this way to satisfy their unbridled egoism and vanity."[35] The letter, written on September 1st, 1974, claimed that churches are now better taken care of than in the years before the war and that the "so-called secret theological seminary," underground priests, and the publication of the *Chronicle* hurt the Church. The secret authors appealed to the bishops to condemn such activities and to react against the "chauvinist propaganda that is conducted by priests-reactionaries." In the view of Commissioner Tumėnas, such letters showed that "more and more clergymen dissociate themselves from activities of this kind."[36] Such public endorsement, as well as the language used in one of the letters ("priests-reactionaries," "turning back the clock of history"), showed that it could be written only with government help and most likely at its inspiration.

Failing to silence the "reactionaries" by such missives to Church hierarchs, the KGB organized its own "public opinion" campaign in the underground. In 1977, it published a *samizdat* "anti-*Chronicle.*" This was a 30 page typewritten publication entitled *Bažnyčia ir LKB Kronika* (The Church and the Chronicle of LCC). In appearance, it resembled the *Chronicle,* but in content it was hotly belligerent and polemical. Speaking in the name of the "steady readers of the *Chronicle,*" and alternating between quotations of biblical passages on peace on the one hand and vehement denunciations of the *Chronicle's* criticisms of clergymen who totally submitted to the government, on the other, the publication suggested that the *Chronicle* was a KGB product because "the *Chronicle'*[s] criticisms are destructive of the Church of our country and [because the *Chronicle*] is breaking to pieces [the Church's] unity."[37] Politically, the publication conveyed the disappointment of the authorities that the relaxation of the religious situation after the Kaunas events of 1972 did not restrain the *Chronicle's* activism. With the possible help of some ex-priests or still active clerics, the government now sought to convince the Catholic dissenters that the *Chronicle* behaved irresponsibly and that by its continued critical attitude toward the government and pro-government clergymen the journal really sought to divide and thus to destroy the Church from within. The "anti-*Chronicle,*" in other words, attempted to turn the *Chronicle's* arguments against the dissident journal itself.

Church Administration

The new conflict over tactics in relations with the state, as in the immediate postwar period, could not help but deeply involve church administrators. The old generation of church leaders had expired in 1961, with the removal of Bishop Steponavičius of Vilnius. Lithuania again was left with only one reigning bishop, namely, Msgr. Petras Maželis of Telšiai, a literate priest who, like a personage from Victor Hugo's *Les Miserables* lived for the poor, completely oblivious of political conflicts and involvements that surrounded him. Steponavičius was replaced by Rev. Česlovas Krivaitis, whose appointment was approved by the Vatican. Krivaitis was given the rank of Monsignor though the Kremlin apparently sought for him the title of bishop. The new administrator, born in 1921 and educated in Lithuania, reputedly lives in a villa on the shores of the river Neris in Vilnius; for a long time, he has acted as the regime's main spokesman on Catholicism in Lithuania. As a result, he became a controversial person at home and abroad. Although a very flexible man, he appears a partisan of the "obedient" approach. The main reason for his selection may have been exactly his training in such obedience; for eight years he served as chancellor to Bishop Paltarokas whose cooperation and temperament in the fifties the Kremlin found acceptable.[38]

In December of 1965, the government and the Vatican agreed on a replacement for the Kaunas and Vilkaviškis dioceses. Their administrator, Msgr. Stankevičius, though he loyally had carried out Communist wishes, after a trip to Rome became to the government inconvenient to keep and consequently resigned the position.[39] The new leader was Msgr. Juozas Matulaitis-Labukas, who was consecrated bishop while on a visit in Rome. At that time, Matulaitis was seventy years old. He was educated in Lithuania and Western Europe and had spent most of his pastoral life as diocesan chancellor or vicar general, that is, as church administrator in the diocese of Kaišiadorys which he for a year, moreover, administered until Bishop Matulionis was appointed ordinary in 1943. In 1946, he was arrested together with the bishop and sent to a camp from which he was allowed to return only in 1955. A man of long and varied experience, the bishop had witnessed the destruction of Matulionis and apparently became convinced that the tactic of opposition and confrontation produces no results. As many another older Lithuanian priest, at first he had hopes that the Western powers would roll back the curtain, but as a result of the so-called confrontation over Cuba during the Kennedy administration, decided that Lithuania's occupation by the Soviets would not terminate in the foreseeable future. Tired of personal persecution and pessimistic about chances of successful resistance to the authorities, he apparently chose a role of resigned non-provocative administrator.

With the consecration of Matulaitis-Labukas, Lithuania now had four bishops: two deposed and sent to provincial exile and the other two functioning as diocesan administrators. However, within months, the second bishop, Msgr. Petras Maželis of Telšiai, died as a result of a grave illness, and on June 15th, 1966, the diocesan council was allowed to elect a successor who was confirmed both by the Soviets and the Vatican. He was the Rev. Juozas Pletkus, a small town parish pastor, who at that time was already seventy years old. Both appointments had to be viewed as temporary compromise solutions because of the prelates' age. Their interregnum, however, extended for a longer time. As a result, four years later, in December of 1969, Labukas was given authority to consecrate two new bishops, an older — apparently to please the middle-aged traditional clerical generation — and a young man who was a Soviet product. In this manner, apparently, the government thought it possible both to appease the traditionalists and gradually to replace church leadership with clerics of Soviet sponsorship.

The older prelate was Rev. Liudas Povilonis, a fifty-nine year old, wholly Lithuanian-educated former member of the outlawed Marian congregation. Povilonis was well known in Lithuania and in Moscow. In 1958, he had built the new church of Mary Queen of Peace in the port city of Klaipėda and upon the church's completion was tried and in 1962 sentenced to an eight-year prison term.[40] He obviously did not serve the full punishment because seven years later he was made bishop. An affable man, reputedly capable of making friends in unlikely places, he most probably was able to get permission to build the church, and then be saved and elevated to episcopal rank because of this talent. His appointment nevertheless raised many eyebrows; transition from a prison cell to the bishop's cathedral was a prize that the Soviets usually grant only to their favorites. Povilonis therefore was widely regarded as a convert to the regime's position of obedience. He was first sent to Telšiai as an assistant to the old Bishop Pletkus.

Together with Povilonis, Bishop Labukas consecrated Rev. Romualdas Krikščiūnas, who had until then been Matulaitis' chief assistant in administering the archdiocese of Kaunas. This bishop was a young, Soviet-educated cleric, born in 1930, ordained in 1954, who for four years, 1959–63, studied on a Soviet scholarship at the Lateran University in Rome.[41] There he earned a doctor's degree in canonical law.

Krikščiūnas had frequently made statements for the Western or Lithuanian language press in the United States and elsewhere in which he had defended Soviet laws on religion and criticized Soviet critics. There seems to be little doubt that the new bishop has rather closely cooperated with Soviet authorities and enjoyed their support. At first, Krikščiūnas was left in his old position in Kaunas, but in 1973, he was transferred to Panevėžys as administrator of the old diocese of Bishop Paltarokas. At the same time, Povilonis replaced Krikščiūnas as vicar general of Kaunas.

While thus restoring church leadership, the Soviets — and the Vatican — nevertheless ran into further appointment difficulties. On

September 29th, 1975, Bishop Pletkus died after a long illness, and three days later was buried with honors in the presence of the government representative for religious affairs, the Lithuanian and Latvian hierarchs, 273 Catholic priests and leaders of Lithuania's Orthodox, Calvinist and Lutheran churches. Seven thousand people on a regular working day attended the funeral. His passing raised the question of a new appointment, and his funeral newly reminded all participants of the problem of the two deposed bishops; the chief celebrant of the memorial rites was Bishop Sladkevičius, banished from the Kaišiadorys diocese almost two decades ago. Pletkus' burial was clearly a demonstration of the unity of the Lithuanian clergy. The memorial mass was concelebrated by the three reigning bishops. It has been reported that some years ago the authorities had offered to solve Bishop Sladkevičius' problem by allowing him to take over a pastorate of a church near Vilnius, but he refused out of solidarity with Bishop Steponavičius whose banishment would continue. This remains the regime's attitude. The provincial exile of these two bishops continues to be a thorn in church-state relations and adds fuel to anti-Soviet feeling. It also nurses divisions within the clerical ranks.

The hierarchs and administrators who were appointed in the decade of the sixties proved to be less stubborn and more pliable than their predecessors of the previous decades. Time and again they were persuaded to issue bland or even incorrect statements about the condition of their dioceses and especially about the freedom of religion in the Soviet Union. Bishop Matulaitis-Labukas and the others have closely followed the wishes of the representative of the Council on Religion in pastoral appointments and on other issues. On government demand, the bishop has suspended priests from preaching or altogether from pastoral duties for transgressions to which the government objected.[42] Pastors who were "too diligent" have been transferred to smaller, more obscure, and less populous parishes.[43] In a statement to Cardinal Alfred Bengsch, who on behalf of the Vatican visited in Lithuania on August 22th–26th, 1975, the publishers of the *Chronicle* suggested that "in pastoral work there has developed the style of appeasement and concessions to the government. Diocesan administrators considered those priests as exemplary who know 'how to get along with the government,' in other words, those priests who blindly obeyed government officials, who lightly regarded their priestly obligations, and who appeased church and civil authorities."[44]

It must be said that most church administrators, at one time or another, found it necessary to bow to the will of the government or at least to compromise. Bishops Paltarokas and Maželis participated in "peace" meetings, wrote demanded semi-political statements, and complied with the *dvatsatka* principle. Msgr. Stankevičius of Kaunas issued orders that most clearly contradicted canon law. Thus, he forbade the preparation of children for the first communion, acceptance of children as altar boys, the annual Christmas season visitations to parish families, the blessing of crosses erected by private persons, etc. Bishop Matulaitis-Labukas, pressured by Representative Rugienis, requested from the Vatican and on November 19th, 1970, received a dispensation from strictly following canonical law in the appointment of pastors.[45] On March 30th, 1971, furthermore, he denied the clergymen the right of hearing confession and preaching outside the jurisdiction of their own diocese.[46] These ordinances made church regulations better conform to the government laws on the internal operation of the churches, but they also chipped further powers away from the priests and the bishop himself; by doing this, Labukas accepted greater government interference in the personnel policies and the movement of the priests. These actions offended a large group of clergymen who considered them as directly damaging to religious apostolate. About a year later, finally, the bishops and administrators were persuaded to condemn the petition that 17,054 Lithuanian Catholics signed for Secretary Brezhnev and the United Nations Secretary General Kurt Waldheim in which the Lithuanians complained of religious persecution.[47] More than anything else, this event betrayed the existence of occasionally serious disagreements, forced by the government, between the church managers and the parish priests. Thus, after the visit of Cardinal Bengsch, the *Chronicle* issued a statement to the Cardinal in which the publishers of the dissenting journal warned the Vatican's envoy that in Lithuania, surrounded as he was by diocesan administrators, he heard only about the "official," not the "real," condition of the Church.[48] Thus, there exists a split though its seriousness can not be determined. Pope Paul VI apparently considered it deep enough in his April 6th, 1976, letter to Bishop Matulaitis-Labukas to urge unity while commemorating the 50th anniversary of the Lithuanian church province.[49]

At the same time it must be said that while the church leadership has generally exhibited the tendency to comply with government pressures, they are not blind instruments in the hands of the Communist rulers. Bishop Matulaitis, for example, has refused publicly to condemn the *Chronicle of the Catholic Church of Lithuania.*[50] Similarly, church administrators so far have held out against the complete supremacy of the *dvatsatkas* as the law requires. They attempt, furthermore, to make their own appointments and do not give in without a bureaucratic struggle.[51] Their situation, admittedly, is excruciatingly difficult because they have to walk the fence between the government on the one hand, and the clergy as well as the practicing Catholic population on the other. The interests of the two sides are so sharply contradictory that it is reasonable to question whether Moscow's current anti-religious policy allows for them any other choice but complete compliance or complete opposition. Since the first alternative is more realistic, the *Chronicle* and Catholic dissidents do not want any new episcopal appointments.

The Catholic People

If statistics on churches and the clergy are rather definitive, statistical data about the Catholic people in Lithuania are contradictory and disputed. All sources, Catholic and Communist, agree that the church lost membership, but no one can answer what the losses actually were. What is the number of Catholics in Lithuania? How many people practice religion by participating in services and the sacraments? Have the atheists won the youth? These and similar questions cannot be answered with statistical precision; membership lists have never been kept, and currently, many priests refuse to register baptisms, marriages, and other partaking in the sacraments for fear of government reprisal against the involved people and their relatives. Thus, information is incomplete, and even ambiguous; sorting it out, however, is necessary because it helps better to understand the church's concerns and situation that led to the movement of dissent and confrontation.

The lowest figure of Catholics in Lithuania is found in the Vatican's *Raccolta di Tabele Statistiche 1969,* the papal statistical summary, where the number stands at 420,000. This is an exceedingly small figure and since its publication, the then Vatican's Secretary of State Archbishop J. Benelli declared it to have been a "typographical error."[52] The other standard papal publication, the *Annuario Pontificio,* that usually gives data supplied by local bishops, has not printed any new figures, with the exception of the diocese of Telšiai that, in 1975, was reported to have 385,000 Catholics, a number identical with the figure published by the Lithuanian church directory of 1939. The Lithuanian Human Rights Commission in the United States has reported 83.5% of the Republic's population or 2,724,000 Catholics for 1975, thus registering a very slight and unrealistic decline from

1940 when the percentage was established at 85%.[53] Professor Bohdan Bociurkiw, a Canadian specialist on religion in the Soviet Union, has compiled a statistical table that gives the figure of 2,330,495 for 1971, but he had to take his information from the Vatican's *Annuario Pontificio* 1969-75, that has published data of 1944 vintage.[54] An English correspondent, David Satter of the *Financial Times,* in 1977 brought back an estimate of one and a half million Catholic believers (or approximately 47% of the total population).[55] These widely differing figures indicate the difficulties in producing a correct appraisal. Even the Soviets, otherwise very eager to speculate with percentages, claim that they do not know but are researching;[56] in their view, possibly, any of these figures would be too high and thus politically inconvenient.

A recent Soviet estimate, nevertheless, has been reported by an East German source, the editor of *Begegnung,* a journal of "progressive" Catholics in East Berlin who wrote, in 1969, that the "majority of the population in the Lithuanian Socialist Republic confess to the Catholic faith," and then specified that this majority means an estimated 75 percent of the total republic's population.[57] Hubertus Guske, the editor, was given this figure on his official travels in Lithuania, and while it is not clear whether it was supplied by the government or by church authorities, its publication undoubtedly had official sanction. At any rate, the percentage is rather high, and if it is to be accepted, it means that of the usually Catholic Lithuanian and Polish population that constitutes 88 percent of the republic's total, only 13 percent would not classify themselves as Catholic. The prewar estimated Catholic percentage was 85 percent, most of which virtually identifying themselves as such. The estimated loss, in other words, would be about 13 percent of church membership, a decline not unusual in modernizing countries and understandable in a country where church communion disqualifies people from many careers and a chance for professional progress and position of leadership. In 1969, seventy-five percent of the total republic population constituted approximately 2,250,000 people, a number close to the figure Bociurkiw reports for 1944. Such a figure has never been directly or indirectly confirmed by Soviet authorities, who stress the country's increasing de-Christianization, but neither has it been denied, and Guske's description of Catholic life, though without the percentages he gave, has been frequently used by the Soviets for domestic and foreign propaganda purposes.

Editor Guske has further reported that the number of practicing

Catholics stands between 50 and 80 percent, the lower figure in the cities, the higher in the villages. In many respects, this is basically confirmed by official Soviet data though the Communists emphasize the allegedly consistent decline.

Participation in Sacraments and Religious Rites in Lithuania

	Baptisms in %	Marriages in %	Burials in %
1958	80	60	79
1964	58	38	60
1968	81	64	79
1969–70	51	30	58
1972	46	25	51

Sources:
1958, 1964 V. Pomerantsev, "Vchera i segodnia," *Nauka i religiia,* No. 4 (April, 1966), p. 5 ff.
1968, 1972 P. Mišutis, "The Church and Religiosity in our Days," *Kalba Vilnius,* No. 5, 1974, p. 13; cited in K. Surblys, *Lietuvos KP veikla ugdant socialistinę darbininkų klasę* (Vilnius: Mintis, 1976), p. 82.
1969–70 A. S. Barkauskas, "Osushchestvlenie Leninskikh ideii ob ateisticheskom vospitanii v prakticheskoi deiatel' nosti partiinnikh organizatsii," *Voprosy nauchnogo ateizma,* Vol. 10 (Moscow: Mysl', 1970), p. 162.

These Soviet figures, especially taking into consideration that the Soviets love to lower ideologically embarrassing percentages, would tend to support the higher American Lithuanian estimates of over 80% Catholic membership in Lithuania just a decade ago. However, as the table above shows, Soviet data is questionable because it registers unrealistic statistical fluctuation (see 1958–68 data). Furthermore, only funeral registration may be assumed to be complete. According to Soviet figures, the major decline has occurred after 1968, that is, the year Catholic protest movements began and five years after the start of a very comprehensive atheist war. Most of the claimed decline has occurred in the cities. According to the data of *Nauka i religiia,* in 1964, in Kaunas, the second largest city, 58 percent of babies were baptized, 50 percent of all funerals were held with church services and a mere 13 percent of marriages were contracted in the churches.[58] In smaller towns and districts, like Kretinga in the western part of Lithuania, official figures were much higher than for the republic as a whole. In 1972, respective figures were 58, 76, and 53 percent.[59] Party or government representatives usually speak of slightly over a half of practicing Catholic population.[60]

The veracity of Soviet figures for the republic, at least for the year 1969, can be, albeit imperfectly, checked in connection with baptisms. According to *Annuario Pontificio* of 1972, in 1970, 21,888 baptisms were administered in Lithuanian dioceses, with the exception of Vilnius for which the figures were not published. This diocese, it can be reasonably assumed, has as many baptisms as the diocese of Vilkaviškis, smaller in population, but similar in numbers of priests and churches and well known for its religious orientation. This would make a total of 26,129 baptisms.[61] In 1970, the number of babies born in the republic was 55,500,[62] of whom, if the entire Lithuanian and Polish population were considered Catholic, 48,840 would be born in Catholic families. That would mean that 53 percent of all possibly Catholic babies were reported baptized. If Guske's percentage of Catholics is used, the percentage of baptized babies would rise to 62. Either calculation suggests that the Soviets have a tendency to lower the figures that show religiosity. In addition, a good number of babies and children are baptized secretly and their baptism is nowhere recorded, thus further raising the actual percentage of those who were baptized.

Information also conflicts on the question of children's religious education. According to the earlier quoted former chief of Agitprop Mišutis, in 1972, about 20,000 children received first communion.[63] The *Chronicle* contradicts Mišutis and suggests that not less than 44,000 children annually prepare for the first communion though, in this estimate, about 50,000 actually should be participating.[64] The *Chronicle,* apparently, considers the total Lithuanian and Polish population "Catholic," and therefore suggests that a larger number should be preparing for the first communion than it estimates actually to be the case. If the Communist figures are correct, it would mean that 40 percent of eligible children annually study catechism, while if the *Chronicle* is right, 88 percent of children do so. Guske's total figures, again, would suggest 47 percent, if Mišutis is right on the numbers attending, and virtually one hundred percent participation if the *Chronicle's* estimate is correct. As in the case of baptisms, the official Soviet figures do not take into account deficiencies in reporting. Since 1973, the government requires the clergy to report the number of studying children, but some priests refuse to do so altogether, while others submit "information of the type the atheist government desires in order that 'it would not pain its heart.'"[65] Mišutis' figures, too, are a mere estimate. Nevertheless, all of these figures show that at least 12 percent of children from traditionally Catholic families do not participate in the early religious education, an estimate that in turn bolsters Guske's figure of 75 percent as the total Catholic population for Lithuania.

Further difficulties surround the appraisal of the religiosity of the youth. Thus, a poll conducted by the Communist party daily *Tiesa,* in 1972, showed that only between 14 and 17 percent of people between 16 and 30 years of age classified themselves as believers, their religiosity sinking between the ages of 21 and 25 but jumping up between 26 and 30.[66] This last group also had the largest number of "don't knows," almost 32 percent. The percentage of un-believers (not necessarily atheists) among this group was 50 percent. It was larger among the 21–25 age group and largest among the youth between 16 and 20. While this was a mere questionnaire to the readers of *Tiesa,* who are more likely to be pro-Communist and non-believing, it nevertheless showed the tendency of young adults to recover from the indoctrination received in the teenage years. Among the secondary school youth, the percentage of "un-believers, atheists, and fighting atheists" was reported in one sociological study to be about 63 in rural areas and 74–76 percent among city youths.[67] The *Chronicle* disputes evidence of this kind by giving concrete examples of schools where, for instance, sixteen out of twenty graduating seniors, all Komsomol members, told the teacher that they believed in God.[68]

The Communists are not very sure themselves. In the East Lithuanian town of Utena, survey research showed that 60 percent of those asked did not have an opinion about the social role of religion, about 40 percent said that "religion is neither useful nor harmful" and 20 percent said they did not know. Only 19–20 percent of people between 18 and 29 declared religion to be harmful.[69] Such research shows, according to a lecturer in philosophy and atheism, Antanas Gaidys, that "the ideology of a considerable part of the youth is yet indefinite, that it is indifferent to religion and does not comprehend its harmfulness."[70] The present chairman of the Lithuanian Supreme Soviet, Antanas Barkauskas, who previously served as the party secretary for ideological affairs, spoke at the Communist youth conference of February, 1974, of the "rising religious fanaticism" and complained that it was very painful to see a part of the young generation getting married in church, and even more painful to see that not a small part of Komsomol and party members availed themselves of the clergy's services.[71] The former director of the Kaunas drama theater, Jonas Jurašas, has reported a privately given estimate by a very high party functionary that in the party's estimate, 70 percent of the Lithuanian youth are church communicants.[72] The new theological-professional underground journal *Tiesos Kelias,* obviously published by the supporters of the *Chronicle,* decried, on the other hand, "the loss of the youth" for the Church.[73] While all these claims and counterclaims make it difficult to come up with reliably definite figures of religiosity, it is, it seems, quite clear that the atheist point of view has not yet won and that there has arisen doubt that it ever will. Already in the 1960s, it appeared that the most that the Soviets were able to achieve with the portion of youth alienated from the Church was their agnosticism.[74] Today the Soviets themselves consider religious indifference a conspicuous phenomenon. It is very likely, furthermore, that in many cases this indifference is a facade that hides general, if not denominational, religiosity.

The effect of this ideological development is twofold. On the one hand, the Communists are frustrated at their failure to capture the youth, while on the other, the Catholics are fearful of losing the youth, either totally or partly to atheism or a-religiosity. This intensifies the conflict between Communism and religion, state and church, and constitutes the reason why religious education and participation of the youth has emerged as one of the most crucial, if not the ultimate, issue in the recently inflamed conflict.

Another phenomenon that was predictable in the sixties was the rise of the importance of Catholic laymen.[75] With priests so much handicapped in pastoral work, a greater involvement of the laity was bound to come. Indeed, lay people play a considerable part in religious education. These consist mostly of women: retired grandmothers, secret nuns and workers. This phenomenon is not new, and the Soviets have tried to scare such people away from religion teaching by intimidation and even by prison sentences. However, so far this has not helped. Laymen, furthermore, have played the leading role in the recent years of conflict with the government, and according to Michael Parks of the *Baltimore Sun,* these laymen "increasingly took over Catholic leadership."[76] This role, it will be remembered, is not new to Lithuanian lay Catholics. The Catholic intelligentsia had become extremely influential in independent Lithuania. The phenomenon apparently was reborn. Among the people so far arrested and tried for the publication of the *Chronicle of the Catholic Church of Lithuania* there was not a single clergyman.

These statistical inputs suggest that the Church has not been crushed, as Pozdniakov predicted to Bishop Brizgys in the winter of 1940, and that statistical gains have been made for convents; there arose a very important "worker-nun" phenomenon that no doubt provides enormous spiritual and organizational strength for the Church. On the other hand, the disastrous decline of the numbers and the intellectual preparation of the clergy and a jealous control of admission to the priesthood is likely to allow doctrinal and religious devastation of the Catholic people whose numbers, too, are not growing with the population, but shrinking, though the sympathies of many a-religious people very likely remain with the Church. The statistical profile of the institution, in other words, shows a church that is still strong by any comparison except with its own past, but whose condition can very quickly go from worse to desperate.

XV

Communism and Catholicism in the Soviet State: Is Co-existence Possible?

In the preceding pages we examined historical forces that have influenced the development of the Catholic church in Lithuania; we then analyzed the modern conflict between Communism and Catholicism in the Soviet state. Is a peaceful and accommodating resolution of this conflict possible? Is it in sight? Some answers, appropriate for the conclusion of this volume, may be gained from appraising the tenacity and continuity of these historical influences.

In the XIX and XX centuries, especially since the insurrection of 1863, the character of Lithuania's oldest societal institution has been shaped, in the main, by four influences: the rulers of Russia; the religious commitment and resilience of the clergy and believers; Lithuania's strong ethnic self-identification and nationalism; and last but not least, the Vatican.

The modern rulers in Moscow have created a new model of church-state relations unknown either in the past or in modern times. The theory of two realms, the temporal and the spiritual, that has dominated the historical development of the West and has survived the rise of the nation-state, and the ensuing secularization of society does not exist in the Soviet Union. It is not recognized perhaps not only because of ideological Communist reasons, but also because the traditional Russia never experienced the social evolution of the Middle Ages. In this respect, Russia's historical development was hardly interrupted by the Bolshevik revolution that very shortly — paraphrasing Leszek Kolakowski — replaced the Orthodox church with the Communist party. The revolutionary disestablishment of religion was converted to an establishment of Communist ideology.

In Marxist-Leninist terms, religion is not only useless, but also harmful, and as such has no place in the Soviet system, nor has the clergyman in Soviet society. This traditional attitude, though punctured by temporary concessions since 1941, has never changed. The dualism between law and power in institutional arrangements similarly has been fully reasserted. The state continues to regard religion as a private affair, but the party, that is, the ruler of the Soviet state, remains hostile to it not only within its own ranks but also in society.[1] The party still feels it has to fight religion as an "unscientific" ideology and to replace it with "scientific," that is, an atheist view of the world that conforms to the dogmas of established Communism. This principle remains enshrined in the new Soviet constitution that was drafted in 1977 after sixteen years of procrastination. This constitution further enhances the importance of the Communist party and in addition, more clearly establishes its control over the newly centralized government. In the sphere of civil rights, it keeps ideological qualifications. In the field of religion, it reasserts the same asymmetric distribution of rights. Art. 52 grants only the freedom to perform religious cult to believers, while conferring the right of propaganda to the atheists. The same Art. 52 ends with an innocent sounding, though potentially ominous, phrase that forbids the "incitement of hostility and hatred in relation to religious beliefs."[2] This of course can cut like a two-edged sword, but there is little doubt that the sentence is directed against religious dissenters who in the past have been accused of fomenting disunity, distrust, and mutual hatred among believers.

The position of churches, thus, is not changed by the new constitution. The new document, indeed, excludes the possibility of dissident interpretation of constitutional principles by more clearly relating the enjoyment of rights to the goals of the Communist party and the Soviet system.

The views of Communist rulers, furthermore, have not changed on the role of the clergy nor the need for atheist indoctrination. As is well known, Soviet population censuses of 1959 and 1970 did not publish the figures on clergymen among the professions, in this manner reaffirming the earlier view that clergymen are social outcasts. This official attitude conforms to current opinion, recently expressed by an authoritative representative of the Soviet intellectual establishment, M. Rutkevich, the Director of the USSR Academy of Sciences' Institute for Sociological Research. In an article published in *Voprosy filosofii* in 1975, he asserted that "the process of achieving the Socialist Way of Life [that consists, partly, of the overcoming of the 'remnants of the past']" requires "the elimination of . . . ministers of various religions who use, for their own purposes, the survival of religious feelings among a part of the population."[3] The ministers are listed immediately after "hardened criminals," a fact that indicates how totally unacceptable to the Communists a clergyman is. It may be added that the same attitude applies to places of worship. Soviet urban designers, for example, do not provide a place or location for church construction sites in either the cities or collective farm villages.

The efforts of atheist indoctrination by education, social pressure, and religious discrimination have hardly lessened. The edict of the Lithuanian Communist party's Central Committee that was announced on May 13th, 1977, in *Tarybinis mokytojas* calls for an extremely comprehensive new program and shows no signs of seeking any *modus vivendi* with clergymen to teach religion. These clergymen, the edict says, must be "unmasked."[4] The party order further denies any positive characteristics of religion. The Catholic church, the party predictably insists, "is not a defender of Lithuanian people's national interests and culture."[5] Less predictably, the Church is not even a "defender of universal human culture, ethics, and morality";[6] Christian "religion and morality are all lies and hypocrisy."[7] The schools, finally, were admonished not to compromise with students who seek to conform to school rules on the one hand, but privately practice religion on the other.

Yet, since the summer of 1972, the authorities have exercised restraint and the atmosphere has eased. The regime made no principal concession to the role or legal position of religion, but allowed publication of the New Testament and some liturgical and Church texts. Secret laws, for the most part, were spelled out in the newly amended law of 1929, thus revealing a standard of behavior, however disadvantageous to churches, but at least known to all concerned. In the calls for intensified atheist education, the authorities urged "respect" for the feelings and "freedom of conscience" of believers and, finally, representatives of Moscow's Council on Religious Affairs counseled moderation.[8] At the same time, fines replaced court sentences for the continued teaching of religion to children. Clergymen were treated more politely.

This relative relaxation showed that Moscow will, when necessary, subordinate its ideological policies to current needs of national policy. To a large degree, the easing of the atmosphere, the synthetic "normalization," represented the regime's response to the widely heard voices of the dissent movement in Lithuania and to Moscow's need of rapprochement with the Vatican. In Lithuania, the year of 1972 witnessed not only an upsurge of Catholic dissent by massive petitioning and the publication of the *Chronicle,* but also an explosion of nationalist feelings in the Kaunas demonstration of the youth. Thus, the twin social forces of the past, the Catholic commitment and

Lithuanian nationalism, made a stark reappearance on the scene. The Catholic dissent movement conspicuously demonstrated to the regime that, first, the very tight controls of religion, instead of destroying the Church, will take the believers underground, that is, beyond the normally possible supervision on which the Soviets very jealously insist in all spheres of life, and second, that religious beliefs in Lithuania were far from smothered. The massive petition movement and the ability of the *Chronicle* to survive — it became the oldest continuously published *samizdat* journal in the Soviet Union, not broken by waves of arrests — brought home the fact that religious beliefs were more tenacious than assumed and continued much stronger than expected. These beliefs were nursed, according to Soviet sociologists, by deficiencies found in Soviet life that included differences of standards of living between the city and the village, the position of women in society, economic shortages, inadequate services, and arbitrary behavior of administrators. In addition, foreign subversion and nationalism, too, allegedly encouraged religion. In the main, however, religion survived, the Soviets now say, because psychologically man needs "faith" that atheism has not yet succeeded in replacing and, finally, because the Church has modernized, thus making itself more acceptable to the "scientific" Soviet people.[9] In gnoseological terms, indeed, at least one Soviet Lithuanian philosopher discovered that religion does not contradict science altogether.[10] Such a conclusion raised the specter of failure of atheist indoctrination. Consequently, the disappearance of religion, like of nationality, now is postponed until the ultimate development of Communist society. This indicates, of course, that no quick or "final" solution of the religious question in Lithuania is possible.

The Catholic dissent movement, no doubt, helped to mitigate the disposition of the authorities. The Soviet Union, needless to say, gets a black eye every time world newspapers report that the teaching of catechism is punished by a prison sentence or that prayerbooks have to be printed in clandestine shops. Furthermore, the hundreds of pages of facts of discrimination against lay Catholics that have been compiled by the *Chronicle* had to have at least some adverse effect on the Vatican's moves in its *Ostpolitik*. The regime, in other words, felt the sting of publicity that was made possible by the risky reportorial enterprise of the *samizdat* and was helped by Western radios whose rebroadcasting of information to Lithuania has been essential to the undertaking's success.

The dissent movement in Lithuania, furthermore, has strength not found elsewhere in the Soviet Union. It is a mass movement, the first and the largest in the Soviet empire.[11] In the 1970s, it became more articulate and grew in scope. By 1977, Lithuanian dissenters periodically published seven underground journals, each duplicating 2–5 issues of 40–60 typewritten pages a year. In addition to the *Chronicle of the Catholic Church of Lithuania,* the Lithuanians published *Aušra* (The Dawn), *Varpas* (The Bell), *Tiesos kelias* (The Way of the Truth), *Dievas ir tėvynė* (God and Homeland), *Laisves šauklys* (The Herald of Freedom), *Rūpintojėlis* (an idiomatic Lithuanian term referring to a wood-carved sitting figure of the sorrowful Christ the Provider which serves as a religious-national Lithuanian symbol). While not all these journals were church-oriented, all of them were strongly Catholic. This growing strength of the Lithuanian dissent movement can be explained by the depth of the people's religious commitment, the convergence of religious and national traditions and finally — as at least one Western scholar has put it — by the high degree of modernization that the Lithuanian Catholic church has achieved.[12] The Soviet side, too, has noted this fact with special concern, insisting that while this is true, both ends of modernization allegedly beat the Church.[13] Nevertheless, in their view, the Church has kept up philosophically and intellectually, and even in economic and social policy, large segments of the Catholic clergy are reported as holding "progressive" views. In the ability to modernize, it may be added, the Lithuanian church had a unique advantage over the Russian Orthodox in that it enjoyed a free existence in independent Lithuania.

Finally, the Catholic dissent movement has been aided by the new stirrings of Lithuanian nationalism. The events of 1972 showed that the Communists did not succeed in eradicating anti-Soviet nationalism. Anatole Shub is probably correct in asserting that "the Lithuanian [nationalist] protest movement may well be the most difficult with which Brezhnev and his colleagues have yet had to deal."[14] As explained in Chapter XII, the demonstrated vitality of nationalism deflected the attacks on the Church. This upheaval, furthermore, confirmed the survival of a still large convergence between Catholicism and nationalism that was inherited from the previous generation. It provoked the regime's fear of the "clericalization of nationalism *(klerikalizatsiia natsionalizma),*" a newly coined phrase to describe a phenomenon of utmost concern, primarily because it eschews atheist education as anti-Lithuanian.[15] Time is needed to untangle, as a Soviet commentator put it, the "clericalization of nationalism on the one hand, and the introduction of elements of nationalism into religious consciousness of the people on the other."[16] Hence the continued easing of the atmosphere.

In the XIX century, by fighting Catholicism with uncannily similar, though less efficient, legal and administrative means, the Tsarist officialdom helped to articulate not only the dormant Lithuanian nationality but also the national awakening with eventually far-reaching political consequences. Today, nationalism serves as a protective shield for Catholicism. Whether the relationship between the Catholic and national traditions is "essential" or "accidental," as the Soviets prefer to view it, in the republic and beyond its borders in the Soviet Union, Catholicism is perceived as a part of the Lithuanian national tradition. In Lithuania, the Church becomes by degree the more cherished the less the regime allows an articulation of spontaneous national values in communications, society, and in public policy. Thus, in dealing with Catholicism and nationality in Lithuania the Soviets fell into a vicious circle: further suppression of the Church intensifies nationalism, while an easing of nationality policy in Lithuania raises demands for more autonomy in republic affairs, more elbow room for the arts and literature, more freedom from the ideological strait jacket. These latter demands, however, have been rejected by the Party, thus making strong measures against Catholicism that much more difficult and risky to adopt.

In 1972, the regime eased pressures on Catholicism in hopes of blunting, or even dissipating, the Catholic dissent movement so it does not serve as a catalyst for the rising nationalist feelings, liberal intellectual stirrings, and other oppression. The Soviets, therefore, may feel inclined to further improve the Church's situation, allowing a larger number of clerical candidates to train for the priesthood, for example, if this preparation can be taken out of the cultural Lithuanian context. At least partially, this may be possible by normalizing church-state relations on a union-wide basis, without regard to jurisdictional boundaries or diocesan jurisdictions of the Lithuanian or Latvian church provinces or Ukrainian and Belorussian dioceses. An establishment of a single Catholic church organization for the entire Soviet Union with bureaucratic leadership somewhere in Moscow, or in its vicinity, and with the training of priests in a single seminary where nationality differences would need to be submerged by the adoption of Russian as the *lingua franca,* could be expected to reduce the importance of national culture in the doctrinal Catholic training. It would help to loosen the connections the Church now has with national traditions, with the current concerns of its people and, generally, with the national idiom of Lithuanian culture.

This may be one of the most difficult issues to be resolved in the protracted Moscow negotiations with the Vatican and one solution that the Catholic dissent movement, it can be expected, would vigorously oppose.

Indeed, toward the end of 1977, the editors of the *Chronicle* suggested that such an arrangement would not help the faith but would constitute "the first step toward a religious schism,"[17] that is, an organizational separation of Soviet Catholics from Rome. The Papal Curia, needless to add, has undeniably high stakes riding with the improvement of Catholic rights in the Soviet Union. Its interest in a solution of Catholic difficulties that would hurt neither ethnic communities nor their ties to Rome, while not much publicized, should be judged to be less than enormously intense only if it were assumed that the Curia is resigned to a permanent loss of Lithuanian, Latvian, Ukrainian, and other Catholics.[18]

Historically, the Vatican has influenced the life of the Lithuanian church in a moderate measure, chiefly by making episcopal appointments (one wonders what would have become of Lithuania had the Vatican in the middle of the last century agreed to the candidate for the Samogitian diocese that the Russians originally preferred) and also by negotiating conditions for its work. For periods at a time, papal agreements with the Tsars mitigated the behavior of Russian bureaucracies.

In the current state of affairs, the Vatican has more leverage with the Kremlin than it had with St. Petersburg. This unexpected influence rests in Moscow's interest in the developments of Italian and European Communism, and generally in Catholic attitudes especially throughout Latin America where the Soviets expect the revolutionary situation to ripen in the near future. The Vatican, on the other hand, no doubt has been encouraged by the visits that Soviet leaders Podgorny and Gromyko, and then Tito, Zhivkov, Kadar and Gierek of Eastern Europe have paid to the Pope. In Eastern Europe, as it is generally known, the Church can exercise limited teaching apostolate. In Hungary it maintains some private schools. In East Germany, it publishes religious literature and has sisters serving especially in the medical social field. In Poland, theological studies are free. However constrained these Eastern European freedoms of religion may look in comparison to the industrialized Western societies, the Lithuanians perceive them as an ideal to be achieved. The *Chronicle* and generally the Catholic dissenters seek to "Polonize" the Lithuanian religious situation. The existence of relative freedom in Poland and other East European lands inspires hopes that similar arrangements are possible with the Soviets. The Eastern European examples encourage the struggle for broader rights and inspire the Lithuanian protest movement not as a voice of desperation and fanaticism, but of hope and accommodation.

The Vatican thus has an opportunity for a favorable input into the Lithuanian situation. As a German church paper put it, after giving the Lithuanian church good marks as a result of a visit by Cardinal Bengsch, a wise policy of the Vatican can further improve the conditions.[19]

On the other hand, the *Chronicle's* dissidents may be expecting more than the Vatican can deliver. After all, the situation is firmly in the hands of the Communist rulers. There is not a shred of evidence — and the disssenters know it — that Moscow will in any immediate future alter its very narrow and limited view of the place of religion in society. Any arrangement between the Vatican and Moscow — whatever the long term expectations generally for Christianity in the Soviet Union that the Vatican may hold — would be made under this ideological handicap and thus would be only of a very limited stop-gap nature. Should the Church accept such terms? There exists a view among Western scholars, put forward by Professor William Fletcher, a specialist on the Russian Orthodox church, that to survive, the churches in the Soviet Union must accept the role of the ritual performer that the system has assigned to them.[20] For the Catholic church in Lithuania, as this study, hopefully, demonstrates, and possibly for many other smaller evangelical churches, this does not offer hope because essential to their continued viable existence is not just the freedom of liturgy but freedom of communications. This, in effect, constitutes the core of the conflict between the churches and the Communists. We know Soviet sensitivity on this question. It is not likely that Moscow would grant it as a right. Such freedom, that is, freedom of communications inside and outside the church, or an adjustment — however imperfect — of the asymmetric rights granted to the believers and the atheists is not anywhere in the cards. Historical Russian experience, finally, does not offer sufficient precedent to hope for such change. The only times that the Communist party made more or less substantial concessions to the churches involved periods of national danger or shock, as was World War II and Stalin's death. In prerevolutionary days, churches and clergymen won civil rights, in the main, only as a result of the shake-up of the autocratic system that occurred during the revolution of 1905. The Kremlin seems to be determined to run the risks of accumulated confrontations rather than accommodation that would grant the Church, as Father Zdebskis said at his trial, the right to be born. Any future prospect of improvement, it seems, should be judged in this perspective of Russia's historical experience.

Appendix

A. The Main Constitutional and Legal
Statements on Religion in the
Soviet Union and in the
Lithuanian SSR

B. Selected Documents of Lithuanian
Catholic Dissent

A

1. *Federal Constitutional Provisions*[1]

The Constitution of 1936
(The Stalin Constitution)

Art. 124. In order to ensure to citizens freedom of conscience, the church in the U.S.S.R. is separated from the state, and the school from the church. Freedom of religious worship and freedom of anti-religious propaganda is recognized for all citizens.

Art. 125. In conformity with the interests of the working people, and in order to strengthen the socialist system, the citizens of the U.S.S.R. are guaranteed by law: (a) freedom of speech; (b) freedom of the press; (c) freedom of assembly, including the holding of mass meetings; (d) freedom of street processions and demonstrations.

These civil rights are ensured by placing at the disposal of the working people and their organizations printing presses, stocks of paper, public buildings, the streets, communications facilities and other material requisites for the exercise of these rights.

Art. 126. In conformity with the interests of the working people, and in order to develop the organizational initiative and political activity of the masses of the people,

The Constitution of 1977
(The Brezhnev Constitution)

Art. 52. Citizens of the USSR are guaranteed freedom of conscience, that is, the right to profess or not to profess any religion, and to conduct religious worship or atheistic propaganda. Incitement of hostility or hatred on religious grounds is prohibited.

Art. 50. In accordance with the interests of the people and in order to strengthen and develop the socialist system, citizens of the USSR are guaranteed freedom of speech, of the press, and of assembly, meetings, street processions and demonstrations.

Exercise of these political freedoms is ensured by putting public buildings, streets and squares at the disposal of the working people and their organizations, by broad dissemination of information, and by the opportunity to use the press, television, and radio.

Art. 6. The leading and guiding force of Soviet society and the nucleus of its political system, of all state organizations and public organizations, is the Communist citizens of the U.S.S.R. are guaranteed the right to unite in public organizations: trade unions, co-operative societies, youth organizations, sport and defense organizations, cultural, technical and scientific societies; and the most active and politically-conscious citizens in the ranks of the working class, working peasants and working intelligentsia voluntarily unite in the Communist Party of the Soviet Union, which is the vanguard of the working people in their struggle to build communist society and is the leading core of all organizations of the working people, both public and state.

Art. 135. Elections of deputies are universal: all citizens of the U.S.S.R. who have reached the age of eighteen, irrespective of race or nationality, sex, religion, education, domicile, social origin, property status or past activities, have the right to vote in the election of deputies, with the exception of insane persons and persons who have been convicted by a court of law and whose sentences include deprivation of electoral rights.

Every citizen of the U.S.S.R. who has reached the age of twenty-three is eligible for election to the Supreme Soviet of the U.S.S.R., irrespective of race or nationality, sex, religion, education, domicile, social origin, property status or past activities.

[The differently formulated equivalent had no reference to "attitude on religion"]

Party of the Soviet Union. The CPSU exists for the people and serves the people.

The Communist Party, armed with Marxism-Leninism, determines the general perspectives of the development of society and the course of the home and foreign policy of the USSR, directs the great constructive work of the Soviet people, and imparts a planned, systematic and theoretically substantiated character to their struggle for the victory of communism.

All Party organizations shall function within the framework of the Constitution of the USSR.

[Mention of religion omitted in the 1977 equivalent]

Art. 34. Citizens of the USSR are equal before the law, without distinction of origin, social or property status, race or nationality, sex, education, language, attitude to religion, type and nature of occupation, domicile, or other status.

The equal rights of citizens of the USSR are guaranteed in all fields of economic, political, social, and cultural life.

2. *Constitution of the Lithuanian SSR of 1940*[2]

Article 96. In order to ensure citizens freedom of conscience, the church in the Lithuanian SSR is separated from the state and the school from the church. Freedom to perform religious rites and the freedom of antireligious propaganda are recognized for all citizens.

Article 97. In accordance with the interests of the workers and in order to strengthen the socialist system, citizens of the Lithuanian SSR are guaranteed by law: (a) freedom of speech; (b) freedom of the press; (c) freedom of assembly and mass meetings; (d) freedom of street processions and demonstrations.

These rights of citizens are ensured by placing at the disposal of the workers and their organizations printing presses, supplies of paper, public buildings, the streets, the means of communications, and other material requisites for their exercise.

Article 98. In accordance with the interests of the workers and in order to develop the organizational initiative and political activity of the masses of the people, citizens of the Lithuanian SSR are guaranteed the right to unite in public organizations: trade unions, cooperative associations, youth organizations, sports and defense organizations, cultural, technical and scientific societies; and the most active and conscious citizens from the ranks of the working class, working peasants and working intelligentsia voluntarily unite in the Communist Party of the Soviet Union, which is the vanguard of the workers in their struggle for construction of the Communist society and which serves as the leading core of all organizations of workers, both governmental and nongovernmental.

Art. 107. Elections of deputies are universal: all citizens of the Lithuanian SSR having reached the age of 18, regardless of racial or national affiliation, sex, religion, educational qualification, residence, social origin, property status or past activities have the right to participate in the elections of deputies and to be elected, with the exception of those persons acknowledged by the established legal procedures to be insane.

Each citizen of the Lithuanian SSR having reached the age of 21 years, regardless of racial or national affiliation, sex, religion, educational qualification, residence, social origin, property status or past activities, can be elected a deputy to the Supreme Soviet of the Lithuanian SSR.

Article 31. The Presidium of the Supreme Soviet of the Lithuanian SSR: (a) convenes sessions of the Supreme Soviet of the Lithuanian SSR; (b) issues decrees; (c) gives interpretations of the laws of the Lithuanian SSR; . . .

3. Decree on the Separation of Church from State and School

Adopted by the Council of Peoples Commissars on January 23, 1918[3]

1. The Church is separate from the State.
2. It is prohibited to enact on the territory of the Republic local laws or regulations which would put any restraint upon, or limit freedom of conscience or establish any advantages or privileges on the grounds of the religion of citizens.
3. Each citizen may confess any religion or no religion at all. Loss of any rights as the result of the confession of a religion or the absence of a religion shall be revoked.

    The mention in official papers of the religion of a citizen is not allowed.
4. The actions of the Government or other organizations of public law may not be accompanied by any religious rites or ceremonies.
5. The free performance of religious rites shall be granted so long as it does not disturb the public order and infringe upon the rights of

the citizens of the Soviet Republic. In such cases, the local agencies are entitled to take the necessary measures to secure public order and safety.

6. No person may evade his citizen's duties on the grounds of his religion.

Exceptions to this provision, and only under the condition that a certain duty of a citizen shall be substituted by another, may be permitted by the decision of the people's courts.

7. Religious oaths shall be abolished.

In cases where it is necessary only a solemn vow may be given.

8. The acts of civil status shall be kept solely by civil [status] agencies.

9. The school shall be separate from the Church.

The teaching of religion is prohibited in all state, municipal or private educational institutions where a general education is given.

Citizens may give and receive religious instruction privately.

10. All ecclesiastical and religious associations are subject to regulations pertaining to private societies and unions, and shall not enjoy any advantages or receive any subsidies either from the State or from local self-governing institutions.

11. The compulsory exaction of fees or impositions to benefit ecclesiastical and religious associations as well as any kind of coercion or infliction of punishment by these associations upon their members is prohibited.

12. No ecclesiastical or religious associations shall have the right to own property. Such associations shall not enjoy the rights of a legal entity.

13. All property belonging to churches and religious associations existing in Russia shall become public property.

Buildings and objects intended especially for religious worship shall be handed over by special decision of local or central authorities, free of charge, for use by the religious associations concerned.

4. Statute on Religious Associations of April 8, 1924
(as amended January 1, 1932)[4]

1. Churches, religious groups, sects, religious movements, and other associations for any cult or any denomination come under the Decree of January 23, 1918, on the separation of the Church from the

State and the School from the Church (Collection of Laws No. 18, 1918, text No. 203).

2. Religious associations of believers of all denominations shall be registered as religious societies or groups of believers.

A citizen may be a member of only one religious association (society or group).

3. A religious society is a local association of not less than 20 believers who are 18 years of age or over and belong to the same cult, faith or sect, united for the common satisfaction of their religious needs. Believers who are not numerous enough to organize a religious society may form a group of believers.

Religious societies and groups do not enjoy the rights of a legal entity.

4. A religious society or group of believers may start its activities only after the registration of the society or group by the committee for religious matters at the proper city or district (raion) soviet.

5. In order to register a religious society at least 20 initiators must submit to the agencies mentioned in the previous Article an application in accordance with the form determined by the Permanent Committee for Religious Matters at the [Council of Ministers].

6. In order to register a group of believers, the representative of the group (Art. 13) must submit an application to the agencies mentioned in Article 4 of the city or district where the group is located in accordance with the form determined by the Permanent Committee for Religious Matters at the [Council of Ministers].

7. The registration agencies shall register the society or group within one month, or inform the initiators of the denial of the registration.

8. The registration agencies shall be informed on the composition of the society, as well as on their executive and accounting bodies and on the clergy, within the period and in accordance with the forms determined by the Permanent Committee for Religious Matters at the [Council of Ministers].

9. In the list of members of religious societies or groups of believers only believers who expressed consent thereto may be included.

10. For the satisfaction of their religious needs, the believers who have formed a religious society may receive from the district or city soviet, under a contract, free of charge, special prayer buildings and objects intended exclusively for the cult.

Besides that, the believers who have formed a religious society or group of believers may use for prayer meetings other premises left to them by private persons or local soviets on lease. Such premises shall be subject to all regulations provided for in the present Law relating to prayer buildings; the contracts for the use of such premises shall be concluded by individual believers on their personal responsibility. Such premises shall be subject to technical and sanitary regulations. A religious society or group of believers may use only one prayer building or [complex of] premises.

11. Transactions for the management and use of religious property, such as the hiring of watchmen, buying of fuel, repairing of the building and objects destined for the rite, purchasing of products or property necessary for a religious rite or ceremony, and other transactions closely and directly connected with the doctrine and ritual of the cult, as well as for the renting of premises for prayer meetings, may be made by individual citizens who are members of the executive body of religious societies or are representatives of groups of believers.

No contract embodying such arrangements may contain in its text any reference to commercial or industrial transactions, even if these acts are of a kind directly connected with the affairs of the cult, such as the renting of a candle factory or a printing establishment for the printing of religious books, etc.

12. For each general assembly of a religious society or group of believers, permission shall be obtained: in cities from committees for religious matters of the city soviets, and in rural areas from the executive committees of the district.

13. For the accomplishment of functions connected with the management and use of the religious property (Art. 11), and for outside representation, the religious associations elect at their general assemblies executive bodies from among their members by open ballot — a religious society, an executive body of three members, and a group of believers with one representative.

14. The registration agencies are entitled to remove individual members from the executive body of a religious society or the representative elected by a group of believers.

15. The general assembly may elect an auditing committee of no more than three members for the examination of religious property and money collected by religious associations from their members as donations or voluntary offerings.

16. No permission of the government authorities is necessary for the meetings of the executive and auditing organs.

17. Religious associations may not: (a) create mutual credit societies, cooperative or commercial undertakings, or in general, use

property at their disposal for other than religious purposes; (b) give material help to their members; (c) organize for children, young people, and women special prayer or other meetings, circles, groups, departments for Biblical or literary study, sewing, working or the teaching of religion, etc., excursions, children's playgrounds, libraries, reading rooms, sanatoria, or medical care.

Only books necessary for the purpose of the cult may be kept in the prayer buildings and premises.

18. Teaching of any kind of the religious cult in schools, boarding schools, or preschool establishments maintained by the State, public institutions or private persons is prohibited. Such teaching may be given exclusively in religious courses created by the citizens of the USSR with the special permission of the Permanent Committee for Religious Matters at the [Council of Ministers].

19. The activities of the clergymen, preachers, preceptors and the like shall be restricted to the area in which the members of the religious association reside and in the area where the prayer building or premises are situated.

The activities of clergymen, preachers and preceptors who permanently serve two or more religious associations shall be restricted to the area of residence of the believers who are members of such religious associations.

20. The religious societies and groups of believers may organize local, All-Russian or All-Union religious conventions or conferences by special permission issued separately for each case by

a. the Permanent Committee for Religious Matters at the [Council of Ministers] if an All-Russian or All-Union convention or congress on the territory of the RSFSR is supposed to be convoked;

b. the local Committee for Religious Matters, if a local convention is supposed to be convoked.

The permission for convocation of republican conventions and conferences shall be granted by the Committee for Religious Matters of the appropriate republic.

21. Local, All-Russian and All-Union religious conventions and conferences may elect from among their members executive bodies in implementation of the decisions of the convention or conference. The list of members of the elected executive bodies shall be submitted simultaneously with the materials of the convention or conference to the authority which granted the permission for organizing the convention or conference in two copies in accordance with the form determined by the Permanent Committee for Religious Matters at the [Council of Ministers].

22. Religious congresses [and conventions] and executive bodies elected by them do not possess the rights of a legal entity and, in addition, may not:

    a. form any kind of central fund for the collection of voluntary gifts from believers;

    b. make any kind of obligatory collection;

    c. own religious property, receive the same by contract, obtain the same by purchase, or hire premises for religious meetings;

    d. conclude any kind of contracts or legal transactions.

23. The executive bodies of religious societies or groups, as well as religious conferences [and conventions], may use exclusively in religious matters stamps, seals and stationery with the imprint of their names. Such stamps, seals and stationery may not include emblems or slogans established for Soviet agencies.

24. Religious conventions and conferences may be initiated and convoked by religious societies and groups of believers, their executive bodies and executive bodies of religious conferences [or conventions].

25. Objects necessary for the rites of the cult, whether handed over under contract to the believers forming the religious association, acquired by them, or donated to them for the purpose of the cult, are nationalized and shall be under the control of the Committee for Religious Matters at the city or district soviet.

26. Premises used for the dwelling of a watchman which are located near the prayer building shall be leased together with other religious property to believers by contract, free of charge.

27. Prayer buildings with objects shall be leased to believers forming religious associations for use by the Committee for Religious Matters at the city or district soviet.

28. Prayer buildings with objects in these buildings shall be received by contract from the representatives of the district or city soviet by no less than 20 members of a religious society for use by all believers.

29. In the contract concluded between believers and the city or district soviet [it] shall be required that the persons who receive a prayer building and religious objects for use (Art. 28) shall:

    a. keep and take care of it as state property entrusted to them;

    b. repair the prayer building, as well as pay expenses connected with the possession and use of the building, such as heating, insurance, guarding, taxes, [state and] local, etc.;

    c. use the property exclusively for the satisfaction of religious needs;

    d. compensate for any damage caused to the State by deterioration or defects of the property;

e. keep an inventory of all religious objects, in which [inventory] shall be entered all newly obtained objects for the religious cult either by purchase, donation, transfer from other prayer buildings, etc., which are not owned by individual citizens. Objects which become unfit for use shall be excluded from the inventory with the consent of the authority which concluded the contract;

f. admit, without any hindrance, the representatives of the city or district soviet to exercise control over the property with the exception of the time when religious ceremonies are performed.

30. Prayer buildings of historical or artistic value registered as such in the Ministry of Education may be leased to believers on the same conditions, however, with the obligation to observe the regulations prescribed for registration and maintenance and the guarding of monuments of art and antiquity.

31. All local inhabitants of a corresponding faith have the right to sign the contract on the receipt of the buildings and religious objects for use and to obtain by this, after the leasing of property, similar rights of management over the property with persons who signed the original document.

32. Whoever has signed a contract may cancel his signature on the above-mentioned contract by filing the corresponding application to the agencies enumerated in article 4; this, however, does not free him from the responsibility for the good condition and safekeeping of the property during the period of the time prior to the filing of the above-mentioned application.

33. Prayer buildings shall be subject to compulsory fire insurance for the benefit of the appropriate local government at the expense of the persons who signed the contract. In case of fire, the insurance payment may be used for the reconstruction of the prayer building destroyed by fire, or upon decision of the appropriate local government for social and cultural needs of a given locality in full accordance with the Decree of August 24, 1925, on the Utilization of Insurance Payments Acquired for Prayer Buildings Destroyed by Fire.*

---

*This law, published in the collection of RSFSR laws (*Sobranie uzakoneny i rasporiazheny,* no. 58 [1925], text 470), provides that, as a rule, the insurance payments shall be used for the reconstruction of the prayer building destroyed by fire (Arts. 1 and 2). However, they may be used also for cultural needs, if the local government has made a decision on the liquidation of the prayer building in this district (Art. 3). Such decision may be appealed before higher authorities and carried out only if the higher authority has confirmed the decision of the local government. If confirmed, the money may be used for cultural needs of the district in the location of the prayer building destroyed by fire.

34. If there are no persons who wish to use a prayer building for the satisfaction of religious needs under the conditions provided for in Articles 27–33, the city or district soviet puts up a notice of this fact on the doors of the prayer building.

35. If, after the lapse of a week from the date of notice, no applications are submitted, the city or district soviet informs the higher authority. This information supplies data giving the date of the construction of the building and its condition, and the purpose for which the building is supposed to be used. The higher authority decides the further destination of the building in accordance with the provisions of Articles 40–42.

36. The transfer of a prayer building leased for the use of believers for other purposes (liquidation of the prayer building) may take place only according to a decision of the [Council of Ministers] of the autonomous republic or oblast which must be supported by reasons, in a case where the building is needed for government or public purposes. The believers who formed the religious society shall be informed regarding such decision.

37. If the believers who formed the religious society appeal to the [Council of Ministers] within two weeks from the date of the announcement of the decision, the case on the liquidation of the prayer building shall be conveyed to the Council. If the [Council] confirms the decision, the contract with the believers becomes null and void, and the property shall be taken away from them.

38. The lease of nationalized or private houses for the needs of religious associations (Art. 10, par. 2) may be broken by a court decision in accordance with the general provisions of court procedure.

39. The liquidation of prayer buildings may be carried out in some instances by the Committee for Religious Matters by order of the city or district soviet in the presence of representatives of the local finance department and other interested departments as well as the representative of the religious association.

40. The religious property of the liquidated prayer building shall be distributed as follows:

    a. all objects of platinum, gold, silver and brocade as well as jewels shall be included in the account of the State fund and transmitted for disposal by local financial agencies or the Ministry of Education, if the objects were registered there;

    b. all objects of historical, artistic or museum value shall be transferred to the Ministry of Education;

    c. other objects, such as sacred images, priestly vestments, banners, veils and the like, which have special significance for the performance of religious rites shall be entrusted to believers for use in other prayer buildings or premises; they shall be included in the inventory of religious property in accordance with the general rules;

d. such everyday objects as bells, furniture, carpets, chandeliers and the like shall be included in the account of the State fund and transmitted for disposal by local financial agencies or agencies of education if the objects were registered with these agencies;

e. so-called expendable property, such as money, frankincense, candles, oil, wine, wax, wood and coal, shall not be taken away if the religious association will continue to exist after the liquidation of the prayer building.

41. Prayer buildings and wayside shrines subject to liquidation, which are registered in special local agencies for State funds, may be transferred for use free of charge to proper executive committees or city soviets under the condition that they will be continuously considered as nationalized property and their use for other purposes than stipulated may not take place without the consent of the Ministry of Finance.

42. Special local agencies for State funds shall register only such liquidated prayer buildings as are not included in the register of the Ministry of Education, such as monuments of art, or [those which] may not be used by local soviets as cultural or educational establishments (schools, clubs, reading halls, etc.) or dwelling houses.

43. When the religious association does not observe the terms of the contract or orders of the Committee for Religious Matters (on re-registration, repair, etc.) the contract may be annulled.

The contract may also be annulled upon the presentation of lower executive committees by the [Council of Ministers] of the autonomous republic, oblast, etc.

44. When the decision of the authorities mentioned in Article 43 is appealed to the [Council of Ministers] within two weeks, the prayer building and property may actually be taken from the believers only after the final decision of [the Council].

45. The construction of new prayer buildings may take place upon the request of religious societies under the observance of the general regulations pertaining to construction and technical rules as well as the special conditions stipulated by the Permanent Committee for Religious Matters at the [Council of Ministers].

46. If the prayer building, because of dilapidation, threatens to fall apart completely or partly, the Committee for Religious Matters on

the city or district soviet may request the executive body of the religious society or the representative of the group of believers to discontinue temporarily the holding of divine services and meetings of believers in such building until examined by the technical committee.

47. Simultaneously with the requirement on the closing of the prayer building, the officials exacting such requirement shall ask the appropriate agency of construction control to make a technical examination of the building. A copy of the letter shall be given to the agency which concluded the contract upon the leasing of the building and property to believers.

If the building is registered by the Ministry of Education, a copy shall be given to the appropriate agency of the Ministry.

48. The [following persons] shall be invited with the right of deliberative vote to the examination procedure by the technical committee:

   a. the local representative of the Ministry of Education, if the building is registered by the Ministry;

   b. the representative of the Committee for Religious Matters at the appropriate city or district soviet;

   c. the representative of the religious association.

49. The decision of the technical committee stated in the examination document is binding and subject to execution.

50. If the technical committee decides that the building threatens to collapse, the committee must also indicate whether the building shall be demolished or made safe if appropriate repairs are made. In such case, the [examination] document shall describe in detail the necessary repairs for the prayer building and the date of completion. The religious association may not hold prayer or other meetings in the building until the repair work has been completed.

51. If the believers refuse to carry out the repairs as indicated in the [examination] document of the technical committee, the contract for the use of the building and religious property shall be annulled according to the decision of the [Council of Ministers] of the autonomous republic or oblast.

52. If, as required by the decision of the technical committee, the building shall be demolished, the contract for the use of the building and religious property shall be annulled according to the decision of the [Council of Ministers] of the autonomous republic or oblast.

53. [Any decision for the demolition of the prayer building] shall be carried out by the Committee for Religious Matters at the city or district soviet and the expenses defrayed from the sale of building material remaining after the demolition of the building. Any money left over shall be transferred to the Treasury.

54. The members of the groups of believers and religious societies may pool money in the prayer building or premises and outside it by voluntary collections and donations, but only among the members of the given religious association and only for the purpose of covering the expenses for the maintenance of prayer building or premises and religious property, and for the salary of the clergy and activities of the executive bodies.

Any kind of compulsory collection of money for the benefit of religious associations is punishable under the provisions of the Criminal Code.

55. It is compulsory to enter in the inventory of religious property any kind of religious property, whether donated, or purchased with the money received through voluntary donations.

The donations made for the purpose of beautifying the prayer building or religious property shall be entered in the general inventory of the religious property which is in use by the religious association free of charge.

All other donations in kind made for indefinite purposes, as well as donations in money to cover the upkeep of prayer buildings (renovation, heating, etc.), or for the benefit of the clergy shall not be subject to entry in the inventory. The donations in money shall be entered by the cashier in the account book.

56. Expenditures of donated money may be carried out by the members of the executive body in connection with the purposes for which they are donated.

57. Prayer meetings of believers who formed a society or group may be held, without notification to or permission of the authorities, in prayer buildings or specially adapted premises which comply with the technical and sanitary regulations.

Divine services may be performed in the premises not specially adapted for these purposes, if notification [is made] to the Committee for Religious Matters.

58. Any kind of religious ceremonies or rites or display of objects of the cult in the buildings belonging to the State, public, cooperative or private institutions or enterprises is prohibited.

Such prohibition does not apply to the performance of religious rites in hospitals and prisons, in specially isolated rooms, if requested by dangerously ill or dying persons, or to the performance of religious ceremonies in cemeteries and in crematoria.

59. A special permission [granted] for each case separately by the Committee for Religious Matters is required for the performance of religious processions as well as the performance of religious rites in the

open air. An application for such permission must be submitted at least two weeks prior to the ceremony.

Such permission is not required for religious processions connected with funerals.

60. Permission is not required for religious processions which are an inevitable part of the divine service and are made only around the prayer building, provided they do not disturb normal street traffic.

61. A permission of the agency which concluded the contract for the use of property is necessary for each religious procession as well as the performance of religious ceremonies outside the place where the religious association is situated. Such permission may be granted only with the agreement of the executive committee of the place where the procession or performance of ceremonies is supposed to take place.

62. A record of the religious societies and groups of believers shall be kept by agencies which register the religious association (Art. 6).

63. The registration of agencies of religious associations (Art. 6) submit data to the Committee for Religious Matters at the city and district soviets in accordance with the forms and within the period established by the Permanent Committee for Religious Matters at the [Council of Ministers].

64. Surveillance over the activities of religious associations, as well as over the maintenance of prayer buildings and property leased to religious associations, shall be exercised by registration agencies, and in rural areas by village soviets.

5. *Statute on Religious Associations of the Lithuanian SSR, Adopted by the Presidium of the Supreme Soviet of the Lithuanian SSR on July 28, 1976* [5]

[Provisions of this statute are virtually identical with the revised law on religious associations of 1929 as amended in 1932 that was adopted by the Presidium of the Supreme Soviet of the Russian Federated Soviet Socialist Republic a year earlier, that is, on June 23, 1975.]

1. The present statute applies to all religious societies and groups of believers of all faiths and religious movements, and also to religious centers, clerical and other associations of all denominations which are active on the territory of the Lithuanian SSR.

2. Religious associations of believing citizens of all cults must register as religious societies or as groups of believers.

Each citizen may be a member of only one religious-cult association (society or group).

3. A religious society is a local association of believing citizens [who are] eighteen years of age or over, of one and the same cult [denomination], faith or movement, not less than twenty persons in number who unite for a common satisfaction of their needs.

Those believing citizens who because of their small number cannot organize a religious society have a right to organize a group of believers.

Religious societies have a right to acquire church utensils, articles of religious cult, means of transport, [a right] to lease, build and buy for their needs according to procedure established by law.

4. In conformity with legislation of the Union of SS Republics, decision on the registration of a religious society or a group of believers and on the opening of a prayer building is made by the Council for the Affairs of Religion at the Council of Ministers of the USSR on the recommendation by the Council of Ministers of the Lithuanian SSR.

A religious society or a group of believers may start its activities only after the decision on the registration [has already been made].

5. To register a religious society, its founders, in number not less than twenty people, submit an application for the registration of a religious society and for the opening of a building of prayer (Catholic, Orthodox or Lutheran church and so on) to the executive committee of a district, city (city of republic subordination), council of working people's deputies which makes [its own] decision on the application, and together with the received application of believers directs it to the Council of Ministers of the Lithuanian SSR.

6. For the registration of a group of believers, the application, signed by all the believers of this group, is submitted to the executive committee of district, city (city of republic subordination), council of working people's deputies which makes [its own] decision on the given application, and together with the received application directs it to the Council of Ministers of the Lithuanian SSR.

7. After receiving registration materials of the society or group of believers, the Council of Ministers of the Lithuanian SSR considers it according to established procedure.

8. In conformity with legislation of the Union of SS Republics, the register of religious associations, houses and buildings of prayer is kept by the Council of Religious Affairs at the Council of Ministers of the

USSR which establishes the procedure for the presentation of the necessary data concerning religious associations.

9. The list of members of religious societies or groups may include only those believers who have expressed their consent to it [to the listing].

10. According to established procedure, for the satisfaction of religious needs, the believers who constitute a religious society may receive for use free of charge a special prayer building on terms laid down by a contract concluded by the religious society with the executive committee of district, city (city of republic subordination), council of working people's deputies.

For prayer meetings, believers who constitute a religious society or a group of believers may also use other premises presented to them for lease by the executive committee of district, city (city of republic subordination) council of working people's deputies or by individual persons with the consent of these executive committees. These premises are governed by the same rules which are established for prayer buildings by the present statute; contracts for the use of such premises are concluded by individual believers on their own personal responsibility. In addition, these premises must satisfy the building-technical and sanitary rules.

A religious society or a group of believers may use only single premises for prayer.

In prayer buildings and premises, [it is permitted] to keep only property of the cult, including books necessary for the performance of a given cult.

11. Transactions and agreements related to the management and use of cult property, such as, contracts on hiring cleaning women, guards, janitors, stokers — stove tenders; [such actions] on delivery of fuel, repair of the prayer building and the cult property, on acquisition of products and property for the performance of religious rites and ceremonies and similar activities which are closely and directly connected with the teachings and rituals of the given religious cult, and likewise [transactions] on the hiring of premises for prayer meetings, may be concluded by individual citizens who are members of executive organs of religious societies or by the representative of the group of believers.

Such transactions may not have as their object [such] contractual relations which though connected with the cult nevertheless pursue commercial or industrial aims.

12. General assemblies of religious societies or groups of believers

(except for prayer meetings) may take place [only] with the permission of the executive committee of the district, city (city of republic subordination) council of working people's deputies.

13. For a direct execution of functions connected with the management and the use of cult property (Art. 11), also for the purposes of outside representation, religious associations, in general assembly of believers and by open ballot, elect executive organs from among their members — [a body] of three members in religious societies, and one representative in a group of believers.

14. The executive committee of district, city (city of republic subordination) council of working people's deputies has the right to remove individual persons from the executive organ of a religious society or [the right to remove] the representative of a group of believers.

15. For the purpose of auditing cult property and sums of money which are received by way of collection of voluntary donations, religious associations, in a general assembly of believers, may elect from among its members an auditing commission [consisting] of not more than three members.

16. Meetings (sessions) of the executive and auditing organs of religious societies and groups of believers take place without notification of or permission from the organs of government.

17. Religious associations have no right to organize and conduct special children's and youth meetings [of worship] and likewise [have no right to maintain] work, literature and other circles and groups which have no relation to the performance of the cult.

18. Instruction of religious doctrines may be allowed only in clerical scholastic institutions which are founded according to an established procedure.

19. The sphere of activities of the servants of the cult or of religious preachers, etc., is restricted to the place of residence of members of the religious association which they serve and to the location of the corresponding premises of prayer.

Activities of the servants of the cult and of religious preachers who permanently serve two or several religious associations are restricted to the territory [which is] permanently inhabited by [those] believers who belong to the indicated religious associations.

20. In accordance with the legislation of the Union of SS Republics, religious centers of society or group, in each individual case with the permission of the Council for Religious Affairs at the Council of Ministers of the USSR, may convene religious congresses. Religious

centers, ecclesiastical governing boards and other organs of religious organizations which are elected in meetings, congresses, conferences [may] direct only religious (canonical) activities of associations of believers. They [these institutions] are maintained with the means secured by religious associations solely on a voluntary basis.

Religious centers, [and] diocesan administrations have the right to produce church utensils, articles of religous cult and [the right] of sale of these to societies of believers, and likewise [the right] of acquiring means of transport, [the right of] leasing, construction and purchase of buildings for their needs, according to established legal procedure.

21. Religious centers, and also executive organs of religious societies and groups of believers may make use of stamps, seals and letterhead stationery with the imprint of their name, [but] solely for matters of a religious nature. These stamps, seals and letterhead stationery may not include emblems and slogans established for institutions and organs of Soviet government.

22. Property necessary for the performance of the cult, whether handed over under a contract to the use of believers who constitute a religious society or newly acquired or donated to them for the needs of the cult, are state property and remain registered by the executive committee of district, city (city of republic subordination) council of deputies of the working people, with the exception of property which in accordance with the legislation of the Union of SS Republics may be the property of religious associations.

23. Prayer buildings and cult property are handed over to the use of believers who constitute a religious society under terms and under the procedure laid down in the contract concluded by the religious society with the executive committee of district, city (city of republic subordination) council of working people's deputies.

24. Cult buildings and their property [property located in cult buildings] are received from the executive committee of district, city (city of republic subordination) council of working people's deputies, according to the contract, by not less than twenty members of the religious society for the presentation of the named property for the use of all believers.

25. It is provided in the contract that persons who receive cult building and property for this use are obligated:

    a. to keep it up and to take care of it as state property entrusted to them;

    b. to repair cult buildings, and also to cover expenses connected with the management and the use of this property, such as heating, insurance, payment of taxes, dues, etc.;

c. to use this property exclusively for the satisfaction of religious needs;

d. to compensate for the loss caused to the state by the deterioration or [making of] defects of the property;

e. to keep an inventory description of all cult property, into which to enter all newly acquired (by purchase, donation, transfer from other prayer buildings, etc.) objects of religious cult which do not belong to individual citizens by right of personal property, and to exclude from inventory description, with the consent of the corresponding executive committee of district, city (city of republic subordination) council of working people's deputies, objects which have become unfit for use;

f. to admit, without hindrance, at any time, with the exception of the time during which religious rites are performed, authorized representatives of the executive committees of district, city/*apylinkė* [village] and locality councils of working people's deputies for the auditing and inspection of the property.

26. Buildings of the cult which have historical, artistic and archeological significance [and which are entered] in the special register of the Ministry of Culture of Lithuanian SSR, are handed over according to the same procedure and on the same terms, but with an obligatory [requirement of an] observance of established rules for the registration and upkeep of the monuments of history and culture.

27. All local inhabitants of a corresponding denomination or movement have the right to sign a contract for the receipt of buildings and property of the cult for [religious] use, acquiring, in such way, the right to participate in the administration of this property on equal terms with persons who originally signed the contract.

28. Each signer of the contract may cancel his signature by submitting a corresponding declaration about it to the executive committee of the district, city (city of republic subordination) council of working people's deputies; this, however, does not free him from responsibility for the preparation and maintenance of the property during the time until the submission of such declaration.

29. Buildings of religious cult are subject to compulsory insurance at the expense of the signers of the contract.

Insurance compensation for the burnt (damaged) buildings of prayer accrues [goes] to the corresponding executive committee of the council of working people's deputies which keeps account of these buildings.

30. The question of the closure of a prayer building in corresponding cases is considered, in an established procedure, by the Council of Ministers of the Lithuanian SSR.

The closure of prayer buildings transpires in the presence of representatives of the financial department of the executive committee of the district, city (city of republic subordination) council of working people's deputies and of other interested departments, and also [in the presence] of the representatives of the given religious association.

31. The transfer of a building of the cult, which is used by believers, to [serve] other needs (in the case of the closing of a prayer building) is allowed according to established procedure. Believers who constitute a religious society are informed of such decision.

32. The question concerning the use and reconstruction for other purposes or the demolition of prayer buildings which are subject to closure and are not under state protection as monuments of history or culture is considered, in an established procedure, by the Council of Ministers of the Lithuanian SSR.

33. The contract on the lease of premises for the needs of religious associations (Art. 10, part 2) up to the exploration of the term of contract cannot be dissolved in any other way but by court procedure on the basis provided by law.

34. At the closing of a prayer building, cult property is divided in the following manner:

a. all objects of platinum, gold, silver and brocade as well as precious stones are subject to the transfer to the disposition of local financial organs or organs of the Ministry of Culture of the Lithuanian SSR, if these objects were registered there [with the Ministry];

b. all objects of historical, artistic or museum value are handed over to the organs of the Ministry of Culture of the Lithuanian SSR;

c. remaining objects (icons, priestly vestments, gonfalons, palls, etc.), which have special significance for the performance of the cult, are handed over to the believers for transfer to other buildings of prayer of the same cult; these objects are entered into the inventory of cult property in accordance with general rules;

d. every-day objects (bells, furniture, carpets, chandeliers, etc.) are subject to be handed over to the disposition of local financial organs or organs of the Ministry of Culture of the Lithuanian SSR, if these objects were registered by them [the latter];

e. transient [expendable] property, [such as] money, and also incense, candles, oil, wine, wax and fuel, which have definite and specific significance for the fulfillment of the conditions of contract or for the performance of religious rites of the cult, is not subject to confiscation in case of the continuation of [religious] society after the closure of the buildings of prayer.

35. Registration of a religious association may be cancelled in case it violates legislation on religious cults.

The question of cancelling registration of a religious association, in an established procedure, is considered by the Council of Ministers of the Lithuanian SSR.

36. The question of rescinding the contract on the use of the prayer building or the cult property in case of non-observance of this contract by a religious association is considered, in an established procedure, by the Council of Ministers of the Lithuanian SSR.

37. [For making] substantive or routine repairs and also for other construction or repair work [of the prayer building] religious associations secure the consent of the executive committee of the district, city (city of republic subordination) council of working people's deputies which [had] concluded the contract on the use of the cult building.

38. Application of religious associations asking for permission for the construction of new prayer buildings with the means of the believers, in individual cases are considered, in an established procedure, by the Council of Ministers of the Lithuanian SSR.

39. If because of its decaying condition, the prayer building threatens fully or partially to collapse, the executive committee of the district, city, *apylinkė* [village] or locality council of working people's deputies has a right to propose to the executive organ of the religious association or the representative of the group of believers temporarily to discontinue the holding of religious services and meetings in it, until a special technical commission inspects the building.

At the same time, the corresponding executive committee informs the Ministry of Culture of the Lithuanian SSR of its decision temporarily to close the prayer building, if the cult building has historical, artistic or archeological significance and is protected as a monument of history and culture.

40. A representative of religious association is invited to the technical commission that is established by the executive committee of the district, city (city of republic subordination) council of working people's deputies.

41. In case the technical commission recognizes [decides] that the building is threatening to collapse, it is necessary to indicate in the adopted report whether the building is to be demolished or [whether] it is sufficient appropriately to repair it. In the latter case, the report must

indicate exactly what repairs of the prayer building need to be carried out and the [length of] time necessary for the carrying out of repairs. Religious associations have no right to allow the holding of religious services and meetings of believers in the building until the completion of repairs.

42. Decision by the executive committee of the district, city (city of republic subordination) council of working people's deputies [which is] made on the basis of the inspection report of the technical commission, is obligatory and is subject to execution.

43. In case the believers refuse to carry out the repairs indicated in the report of inspection, [its] contract concerning the use of the building and cult property becomes subject to be rescinded according to established procedure.

44. In case the executive committee of the district, city (city of republic subordination) council of working people's deputies decides to recognize [approve] the inspection report of the technical commission that the prayer building is subject to demolition, [its] contract with the believers on the assigned use of this building is rescinded according to established procedure.

45. For purposes connected with the maintenance of the prayer building, cult property, the hiring of the servants of the cult and the maintenance [to meet the costs] of the executive organ of religious association, religious associations and members of groups of believers have a right to make collections and gather voluntary donations in the prayer building among members of the given religious association.

Religious associations have no right to create mutual aid funds, cooperatives, production associations, to use property at their disposal for any other purpose but the satisfaction of religious needs, and also [have no right to] give aid to their members.

Servants of the cult are forbidden to engage in [annual, usually, Christmas season] visitations (*koliadovaniia*) of believers.

46. Any acquired cult property is subject to an obligatory entry into the inventory description of the cult property.

Voluntary gifts (donations) which are made for the purpose of decorating the prayer building with the donated object or for the purpose of beautification of the objects of the cult, are entered into the inventory description of the entire cult property, available for free use by the religious association.

All other types of voluntary donations in kind which are not made for the above mentioned purposes, and also money donations whether [made] for the benefit of the religious society [in order] to maintain the prayer building and premises (repair, heating, etc.) or for the benefit of the servants of the cult, are not subject to be added [do not have to be listed] to the inventory description of cult property.

Voluntary cash donations by believers are accounted for in the income-expenses books kept by the treasurer of the religious association.

47. Members of the executive organs of religious associations and authorized representatives of groups of believers may spend donated sums in accordance with the purposes of managing the prayer building and the property of the cult.

48. Prayer meetings of believers organized in societies or groups may take place without notification or permission of the organs of government in buildings of religious cult or in specially adapted premises which satisfy construction-technical and sanitary regulations.

49. Performance of religious rites and ceremonies of the cult, and also the keeping of objects of the cult, is not allowed in state, public, cooperative institutions and enterprises.

The present prohibition does not extend to the performance of religious-cult rites in isolated premises at the request of the dying or critically ill [patients] in hospitals or in places of deprivation of freedom, and equally [does not extend] to the performance of religious rites in cemeteries and in crematoriums.

50. Religious processions, performance of religious rites and ceremonies under open skies and also [such performance] in apartments and houses of believers are allowed [only] by special permission, obtained each time [the rites are performed] from the executive committee of the district, city (city of republic subordination) council of working people's deputies, with the exception of the performance of religious-cult rites in apartments and houses of believers at the request of the dying and the critically ill.

Applications to obtain permission for religious processions and the performance of religious rites under open skies must be submitted not later than two weeks before the date of the fixed ceremony.

Religious processions and also performance of religious rites and ceremonies outside the location of religious association may be allowed, each time by special permission, by the organ which concludes the contract on the use of the property of the cult. Such permission may be given after [obtaining] a preliminary consent from the executive committee of that local council of working people's deputies on whose territory the holding of processions, rites or ceremonies is proposed.

51. Special permission from or notification of organs of government is not required for [holding of] religious processions which constitute an inalienable part of religious service [and which] are executed [take place] around the building of the cult in the city as well as in rural localities, under conditions that these processions do not violate normal street traffic.

52. Registration of religious societies and of groups of believers, and also supervision of their activities and of the safe-keeping of the building and cult property handed over to the use of the believers on the basis of contract in the territory of district, city of republic subordination is placed in the executive committees of district, city (cities of republic subordination) councils of working people's deputies. In rural localities, in cities of district subordination and in city-type localities such supervision is placed also in the executive committees of *apylinkė,* city, locality councils of working people's deputies.

53. Violation of the present statute draws responsibility in accordance with existing legislation.

Secretary of the Presidium of the Supreme
Soviet of the Lithuanian SSR
S. Naujalis

6. *Basic Provisions of the Criminal Code of the Lithuanian SSR concerning freedom of religion and other laws applied to believers and the clergy in Lithuania*[6]

(Equivalent, practically identical, articles in the Criminal Code of the Russian Federated Soviet Socialist Republic are the following: 70, 72, 142, 227, 143, 190[1], 190[3].)

Art. 68. Anti-Soviet Agitation and Propaganda. Agitation or propaganda that seeks to subvert or to weaken Soviet government or to commit especially dangerous individual crimes against the state or the circulation of slanderous fabrications which defame the Soviet state and social system for the same purposes, also the distribution or production or possession of literature of the same contents for the same purposes are punishable by deprivation of freedom [for a term] of six months to seven years with or without exile [consisting of additional] two to five years, or by exile from two to five years.

The same actions by a person who already has been convicted for [committing] especially dangerous crimes against the state, also [actions] committed during the war are punishable by deprivation of freedom [for a term] from three to ten years with or without [additional] exile from two to five years.

Art. 70. Organized activity which seeks to commit especially dangerous crimes against the state; also participation in an anti-Soviet organization. Organized activity that seeks to prepare or to commit especially dangerous crimes against the state, [that seeks] to recruit an organization for the purpose of committing such crimes, also participation in an anti-Soviet organization are punishable according to Arts. 62–69 of this Criminal Code [Art. 62 punishes treason, Art. 63 — espionage, Art. 64 — terrorist activities, Art. 65 — terrorism against foreign diplomats, Art. 66–67 — diversion and sabotage, Art. 68 — anti-Soviet agitation, Art. 69 — propaganda of war. Punishment ranges from a term of six months to death.].

Art. 143. Violation of laws concerning the separation of church from the state and school from the church. Violation of laws concerning the separation of church from state and school from the church is punishable by deprivation of freedom [for a term of] up to one year or [confinement for] corrective labor for the same length of time or a fine of up to one hundred roubles.

The same activity, committed by a person who had earlier been convicted for the violation of laws concerning the separation of church from the state and school from the church, and also an organized activity, aimed at the same action, is punishable by deprivation of freedom for [a term of] up to three years.

Appendix of explanation
§1. *[Decision] concerning the application of Art. 143 of the Criminal Code of the Lithuanian SSR.* The decree of May 12, 1966, passed by the Presidium of the Supreme Soviet of the Lithuanian SSR (published in *Lietuvos TSR Aukščiausios Tarybos ir Vyriausybės žinios,* No. 14–97, 1966).

Concerning questions that arise in connection with the application of Art. 143 of the Criminal Code of the Lithuanian SSR, the Presidium of the Supreme Soviet of the Lithuanian SSR, in conformity with Art. 31, Sect. c of the Constitution of the Lithuanian SSR, decrees: To explain that [the following is understood] as violation of the laws concerning separation of church from the state and school from the church, which carry criminal responsibility in conformity with Art.

143 of the Criminal Code of the Lithuanian SSR: the taking of involuntary donations and imposed fees for the benefit of religious associations or [for the benefit of] the servants of the cult; production, with the aim of massive distribution, of petitions, letters, leaflets and other documents which encourage non-compliance with the laws on religious cults, or a massive distribution of such; commission of fraudulent actions which aim at the incitement of religious superstitions among the masses of population; organization and conduct of religious meetings, processions and other rituals of the cult which violate public order; organization and systematic conduct of religious instruction practices of minors in violation of regulations established by law; refusal of employment to citizens or their admission to school, dismissal from work or expulsion from an educational institution, deprivation of citizens' advantages and privileges established by law and also other essential limitations of the rights of citizens which are made because of their attitudes toward religion.

§ 2. *Concerning administrative responsibility for the violations of laws on religious cults.* Decree of May 12, 1966, of the Presidium of the Supreme Soviet of the Lithuanian SSR (published in *Lietuvos TSR Aukščiausios Tarybos ir Vyriausybes žinios,* No. 14-98, 1966).

The Presidium of the Supreme Soviet of the Lithuanian SSR resolves to establish that the violation of laws concerning religious cults which occurs by the following actions: the evasion by leaders of religious societies of registration of societies with the organs of government; the violation of regulations established by law on the organization and conduct of religious meetings, processions and other rituals of the cult; organization and conduct by the servants of the cult and members of religious associations of special meetings for children and the youth, also the [organization and conduct] of labor, literature or other circles and groups which have no relation to the performance of the cult are punishable by a fine up to fifty roubles that is imposed by administrative commissions [attached to] the executive committees of district and city Soviets of working people's deputies.

Art. 144. Attempt to infringe on the citizens' personality and rights under the guise of performance of religious rituals. The organizing of a group, the activities of which conducted under the guise of preaching of [religious] faith or performance of religious rituals, is connected with causing harm to the citizens' health or some other attempt to infringe on the citizens' personality or rights, or [is related] to the encouragement of citizens to renounce public activities or [to refuse] the performance of civic obligations, also leadership of such group, are punishable by deprivation of freedom [for a term of] up to five years or by exile for the same length of time with or without confiscation of property.

Active participation in the activities of a group defined in the first part of this article [Art. 144], also a systematic propaganda which aims to materialize activities defined in this part are punishable by the deprivation of freedom [for a term of] up to three years or by exile for the same length of time, or [confinement to] corrective labor [for a term of] up to one year.

If acts defined in the second part of this article [Art. 144] and the persons who have committed them are not very dangerous to society, it is permissible to apply to the latter the measures of social influence [pressure].

Art. 145. Interference with Religious Rituals. Interference with religious rituals, in as much as the latter do not interfere with public order and are not attempting to infringe on the rights of citizens is punishable by deprivation of freedom [for a term of] up to one year or [confinement for] corrective labor for the same length of time or a fine [of] up to one hundred roubles.

Art. 199¹. The Circulation of fabrications known to be false which defame the Soviet state and social system. Systematic oral circulation of fabrications known as false which defame the Soviet state and social system, also production or distribution of works of the same contents in an oral, printed or another form is punishable by deprivation of freedom [for a term of] up to three years or by [confinement for] corrective labor [for a term of] up to one year, or by a fine of one hundred roubles.

Art. 199³. Organization of group activities which violate public order and an active participation in these activities. The organizing of group activities which in a coarse manner violate public order or are related to a clear disobedience to legal demands made by the representatives of the government, or which have harmed the work of transport, of state, [or] public or factory enterprises, likewise an active participation in these activities is punishable by deprivation of freedom [for a term of] up to three years or [confinement for] corrective labor [for a term of] up to one year, or a fine of up to one hundred roubles.

7. Some Other Provisions of the Criminal Code applied to religious activity in the 1960s and 1970s[7]

Art. 94 (theft of state or societal property); Art. 164 (black marketeering); Art. 177 (abuse of official position); Art. 181 (bribe giving).

B

1. Lithuanian Catholic Proposals for Constitutional Changes (1977)[8]

To L. Brezhnev,
Secretary General of the CC of the CPSU,
Chairman of the Presidium of the Supreme Soviet of the USSR,
Chairman of the Constitutional Commission of the USSR

Copies to
P. Griškevičius, Secretary of the CC of the Lithuanian CP, and Chairman of the Lithuanian Constitutional Commission
His Excellency Bishop Dr. R. Krikščiūnas, Apostolic Administrator of Panevėžys Diocese
K. Tumėnas, Lithuanian SSR Representative of the Council on Religious Affairs of the Council of Ministers of the USSR

DECLARATION
by the Priests of the Diocese of Panevėžys

We, the priests of the Panevėžys diocese who have below attached our signatures to this declaration, [being] familiar with the views of believers and making use of the right of all citizens to suggest proposals concerning the draft of the new Constitution of the USSR, hereby, express opinions about articles of the draft Constitution that relate to religion and affairs of believers, and propose a more precise [corrected] formulation of these articles.

The substantive content of Article 52 of the draft Constitution is taken from Article 124 of the current USSR Constitution. We know from experience that this latter article, for years applied to the lives of believers, is undemocratic and that it restricts personal and religious freedom of the believers. Here is a portion of the [proposed] Article 52: "Citizens of the USSR are guaranteed freedom of conscience, that is, the right to profess any religion, to perform religious rituals or not to profess any religion, to conduct atheist propaganda." This single sentence expresses a self-contradictory thought — all citizens are guaranteed the freedom of propaganda, despite the fact that for believers this propaganda is an essential element of their conscience and their religious faith. Unequally treating believers and non-believers in their relations with the state and their freedom of ideological [Weltanschauung] propaganda has brought to the believers suffering and calumny. The atheists, however, on the basis of this article, enjoy an unlimited freedom to propagate atheism. Considering their own ideology [Weltanschauung] as state ideology, they denigrate religion and the believers while the state supplies them with all means of propaganda which have been acquired partially with the funds of believers: the school, press, radio, television, theater, etc. The believers have the freedom only for the performance of and participation in religious rites (in fact, not all believers are allowed to participate), but they have no freedom publicly to defend or to propagate their convictions in society though this is an essential part of profession (testimony) of religion. The preparation of children, in church buildings, for the participation [practice] in religious rites that is conducted by clergymen is punished by imprisonment or by administratively imposed fines. For the believers, profession of religion causes persecution, degradation, obstacles for promotion, even dismissal from a job, etc. In order to be appointed to a position of greater responsibility one has to disavow one's religious convictions. Because of persecution, many believers are forced to perform their religious practices in secret. The only theological seminary of our republic, located in Kaunas, is not allowed to prepare all suitable candidates for priesthood. As a result, many parishes no longer have a priest. (This year [1977], 6 priests died in Panevėžys diocese while the seminary prepared only one new priest). Until now the freedom of performance of religious rites for the believers was but a dream because the preparation of priests is restricted by administrative means, and without priests it is not possible to perform religious rites.

Article 52 of the draft Constitution states: "Incitement of discord or hatred in relation to religious faiths is forbidden." The believers do not even have the opportunity for [such] incitement while atheists have all available opportunities. This point of Article 52 needs to be redrafted [with a view of eliminating the inequality between believers and atheists]. One more sentence from the current Constitution has been taken over into Article 52 of the [new] draft Constitution, namely, "In the USSR the Church is separated from the state and the school from the Church." If the Church is separated from the state, the Constitution should guarantee that the state will not interfere in the internal affairs of the Church, will not [attempt to] subordinate it [to itself] by making the Church dependent on the executive committees of local district soviets [government] as if they [the latter] were religious divisions; this [type of subordination] is clearly seen in the statute on religious associations approved by the decree of the Presidium of the Supreme Soviet of the Lithuanian SSR No. IX-748 adopted on July 28, 1976. Under the guise of the principle of separation of school from the Church, believer parents are seriously impeded in religiously educating their children; children are incited against religious parents, children are forbidden to practice religion. In this way, the authorities violate the inalienable right of parents to educate their children in conformity with their conscience and convictions.

To eliminate discrimination, we propose that Article 52 be revised in the following manner: "Citizens of the USSR are guaranteed freedom of religion, that is, the right guaranteed to all citizens, without regard to age or position in the state, to confess any religion, freely to perform religious practices, to learn and to teach religious doctrines or not to confess any religion, to live and to act according to atheist convictions.

For the propagation of their [respective] ideologies [Weltanschauung], the believers and the atheists have equal right to use all information media of our times: the school, radio, television, etc.

Religion and atheism are supported and maintained by the efforts and means of co-thinkers, while they conduct instruction in their own doctrines in freely maintained and supported special schools.

Incitement of discord or hatred in relation to religious or atheist convictions is forbidden."

To redraft Article 36: "Diverse nationalities, races, believers and non-believers have equal rights."

To amend Article 57: "Soviet laws protect and defend the health and life of an unborn human being — abortion is forbidden."

To amend Article 66: "Believer parents have a complete right to educate their children according to their conscience and religious convictions."

In addition, it is necessary constitutionally to guarantee that no one will be directly or indirectly forced to speak or act against one's conscience or convictions. All constitutional rights should not only be declared; it ought to be made possible practically to make use of them.

The Priests of the Diocese of Panevėžys
Signed by 120 priests and Bishop V. Sladkevičius September 12, 1977

[Very similar petition was signed by 83 priests at the Vilnius diocese and 70 priests of Vilkaviškis diocese. These percentages represent ca. 80 percent of clergymen of these dioceses].

2. The Memorandum to Brezhnev — Waldheim (1972)[9]

TO: L. Brezhnev, Secretary General of the General Committee of the Communist Party of the Soviet Union
Moscow — The Kremlin
FROM: The Roman Catholics of Lithuania

Memorandum

After World War II, nations rose from the ruins and sought permanent peace. The foundation of true peace is justice and respect for the rights of man. We, the Catholics of Lithuania, intensely deplore the fact that as of today the freedom of conscience of believers in our nation is constrained and the Church is persecuted.

Bishops J. Steponavičius and V. Sladkevičius, though they have committed no crimes, have suffered in exile for over ten years [which was decreed] without court decision and for an undetermined period of time.

In November of this year [1971] two priests, J. Zdebskis and P. Bubnys, were sentenced to a year in prison, because at the request of parents and while fulfilling their priestly duties, they explained the fundamentals of the Catholic faith to children. These priests helped to prepare children for the First Communion not in school but in church and did not use pressure on anyone — those came to study who wanted to do so.

At the same time the children of believing parents are forcibly taught atheism in schools; they are forced even to speak, write and act against their conscience. Nevertheless, no one reprimands or takes to court people who use such force.

Clergymen cannot properly serve us, believers, because there are not enough of them. In many cases, one priest serves two or sometimes three parishes. Old and sick priests are compelled to work. This [situation] exists because the affairs of the theological seminary are directed not so much by the bishop as by the representative of the state [Commissioner for Religious Affairs]. The state permits the seminary to accept only ten candidates a year.

State officials also direct the appointment of priests to parishes.

Even though the Penal Code of the Lithuanian SSR provides penalties for the persecution of believers, these penalties, in practice, are not applied. In 1970, the Vilkaviškis Education Section [school board] fired a teacher, [Mrs.] Ona Brilienė, because of her religion, and the authorities of the Vilkaviškis district refuse to rehire her even as a janitor. No one punishes these officials even though because of their willfullness the intelligentsia fear publicly to practice their faith.

State officials do not permit believers, at their own expense, to rebuild burned churches, for example, those in Sangrūda, Batakiai and Gaurė. After a great deal of difficulty, permission is granted to set up a wayside cross at one's residence but its transfer to the churchyard is absolutely forbidden.

We could cite many more examples of severe persecution which make our life bitter and bring about disappointment with the Soviet Constitution and the laws. We therefore ask the Soviet government to grant us the freedom of conscience which is guaranteed by the USSR Constitution but which up to now has not been practiced. We do not want beautiful words in the press or on the radio but evidence of serious efforts on the part of the authorities to help us, Catholics, feel that we are citizens equal to all others of the Soviet Union.

December 1971.

To the Secretary General of the Central Committee of the CPSU

(An addition to the memorandum)

Attached to this memorandum are 17,054 signatures. It must be pointed out that only a small part of the believers of Lithuania signed because the militia and KGB organs used every means available to stop the mass collection of signatures. People collecting signatures in Kapsukas, Šakiai, Išlaužas and Kapčiamiestis were arrested and the sheets with signatures found on their persons were confiscated despite the fact that the memorandum was addressed to the Soviet government.

If in the future the state organs continue to treat the complaints of believers in the same manner as they have until now, we will be forced to turn to international organizations, namely, the Pope of Rome, the Head of our Church, or to the United Nations Organization as the authoritative institution which defends the rights of man.

We also want to remind you that this memorandum is the result of a national misfortune. During the period of Soviet rule, such vices as juvenile delinquency, drunkenness, suicide, as well as divorce and abortion have increased tenfold in Lithuania. The further we drift away from our Christian heritage, the more apparent become the horrible results of forcible education in atheism and the more widespread the inhuman way of life without God and religion.

We turn to you as the supreme authority of the Communist Party asking that the facts we present be seriously and responsibly investigated and that appropriate decisions be made.

February, 1972

Representatives of Lithuania's Catholics

To Kurt Waldheim, the Secretary General of the United Nations Organization

Appeal of Lithuania's Catholics

Mr. Secretary General,

Keeping in mind that Lithuania does not have its own representation in the United Nations Organization, we, Lithuania's Catholics, are compelled to appeal to you, taking advantage of means available to us only by chance.

Our appeal to you is prompted by the fact that believers in our Republic cannot make use of the rights listed in Article 18 of the Declaration on the Universal Rights of Man. Our priests, groups of believers and individual Catholics have repeatedly brought this matter to the attention of the highest state organs of the Soviet Union demanding that violations of the rights of believers be stopped. Several petitions from believers were sent to Soviet authorities. Among these were the following: an appeal by 2,000 Catholics of Prienai, sent in September 1971; an appeal of believers from Santaika parish, Alytus District, signed by 1,190 individuals and sent October 1971; the appeal by 1,344 believers of Girkalnis parish, Raseiniai District, sent December 1971. All these appeals were sent to diverse highest ruling institutions of the USSR; however, not one of them sent an official reply even though state institutions are obliged to answer citizens' appeals within a month's time. Increased repression of believers was the unofficial reply.

The Catholics of Lithuania decided to remind Soviet leadership of their illegal status [deprivation of rights] by means of a memorandum to CPSU Secretary General Mr. Brezhnev. However, Soviet militia and the KGB stopped the massive collection of signatures by means of threats, arrests and by other special means.

Such behavior by state authorities convinced us that the memorandum signed by 17,000 believers will not reach its intended destination if it is sent by the same route as previous collective declarations.

Therefore, we, Lithuania's Catholics, appeal to the honorable Secretary General and ask that this memorandum with its signatures which we are sending to you be routed via the United Nations Organization to CPSU Secretary General Mr. Brezhnev.

January 1972

Respectfully yours,

Representatives of the Catholics of Lithuania

3. *Report on the Situation of Religion in the Soviet Union (1977)*[10]

Why Western Observers and Visitors Frequently Misunderstand the Situation

When our fellow countrymen, whether clergy or laity, meet fellow Lithuanians visiting here [in Lithuania] as tourists, or when they themselves go abroad, they note how many [visitors] have great difficulty grasping the complex questions of religious life in Lithuania. Even high-ranking clergy, with few exceptions, are unable to understand or to solve many of our problems, to say nothing of rank-and-file laity.

Some of them think that local Ordinaries can decide all religious questions, even those dealing with the secret activities of believers. They forget that the activities of many Ordinaries are restricted, and that the faithful do not dare approach some of them.

Others cannot understand how, in Lithuania, about 70% of the children can be catechized, when many priests and laity have been punished for teaching religion in Lithuania.

They have no idea how extensively in Lithuania religious education is carried out in catacomb fashion, under the direction of priests and laity who fear neither fines nor imprisonment. There have even been tourists who have wondered why Lithuanians being dragged off to Siberia did not telephone the police to prevent their exile. It is often difficult for them to tell which individuals they can trust, and which they cannot. They have no idea how people in Lithuania are engaged by the KGB to confuse trusting individuals and public opinion.

We can justify this phenomenon in part, because it is very difficult to understand our complex situation if one has not lived here longer and has not seen Siberia. Our neighbors, the bishops and believers of the Socialist states of Germany and Poland, admit that they find it difficult to understand us. All the more difficult it is for people of the western world, born in freedom and reared in freedom, to understand our situation. The problem is compounded by the cunning deceit of our nation's enemies. They are able freely to send misleading documents and publish articles abroad.

The worst thing is that [our own] spiritual leaders of various ranks contribute to this deception, albeit under pressure. Some of them, conscientiously carrying out the instructions of the atheists, even misinform the Vatican when they visit there. Thank God that at least recently that kind of deception has been seen through. Even those clergy and laity abroad who understand us better and sympathize with us complain that they are unable to obtain privileges or assistance for us. Our requests by word and in writing have till now most often remained without results. We trust that the hierarchy of the Catholic church and our fellow-countrymen will become better acquainted with our situation, and will help us more effectively.

First of all, we feel the obligation to thank the Apostolic See for establishing us as a separate ecclesiastical province. We thank our present Holy Father, Pope Paul VI, for the attention he has paid us in recent times: the meaningful broadcasts of Vatican radio, the refusal to recognize officially the occupation of Lithuania, the establishment of the College of St. Casimir in Rome, the conferral of the title of basilica on the Shrine of Our Lady of Šiluva, for the kind reception given representatives of our nation who visit the Holy Father, for the sensitive reaction to the Petition of the Seventeen Thousand, for diplomatic efforts to help us, for all the sympathy and love, and for the kind prayers.

We are grateful for the wish to help us by all means possible. We know that the strength of the Catholics of Lithuania lies in unity with the Holy Father and with the Catholic church. Our oppressors have tried in various ways to tear our bishops and individual priests away from the Apostolic See. For their loyalty they had to suffer much. In the most difficult times, the Catholics of Lithuania have demonstrated their sense of discipline and their obedience to the Holy Father.

We invite Lithuanians throughout the world and the Catholics of the entire world to show the greatest love and respect for, and confidence in, the Holy Father, to refrain from unhealthy criticism of Church leaders which is not rooted in love. We condemn any action disruptive of Church unity. We trust that the Holy Father, appreciating our loyalty and dedication, will in the future show us even more confidence and, within the realm of possibility, will satisfy our wishes.

We are grateful to the Catholics of Ireland for showing us sincere fraternal sympathy and for giving [presenting] our suffering nation the statue of the Blessed Virgin Mary.

We especially thank the Bishops of the United States, senators, and congressional representatives for their defense of Lithuanians imprisoned for the faith and freedom of Lithuania.

We are grateful to a host of bishops, clergy, and believers in Italy, Germany, France and Switzerland, who by written and spoken word defend the religious freedom of Lithuania. Moreover, we are grateful to the defenders of human rights in the Soviet Union, especially Academician Andrei Sakharov, and Doctor Sergei Kovalëv, who is imprisoned for defending that freedom.

We would like to take this opportunity to thank Jewish journalists and their newspapers for proclaiming widely to masses of readers the wrongs perpetrated on us by the atheists of the Soviet Union.

In the terrible days of the Hitler terror, a whole host of Lithuanian clergy, at the risk of their own lives, saved a good number of Jewish lives. Such facts are described in the book *Ir Be Ginklo Kariai* [Soldiers Without Weapons]. Bishop V. Brizgys, calumniated in every way by the atheists, in the Garrison church sermon in Kaunas during the Nazi occupation, publicly denounced the mass murder of Jews, as incompatible with Christian morals.

Seeing the wish of our fellow-countrymen abroad and friends of the Catholic church in Lithuania to help us, and knowing how the atheists of the Soviet Union are trying to mislead world public opinion, we are determined at least in brief outline to inform our fellow-countrymen, the believers of the entire world and people of good will, about the burning matters concerning Lithuania and its Catholic church which require speedy and forceful decisions, and about the thinking of our clergy and laity.

Regardless of the greatest risks, we are trying to do everything to see that the [Catholic] faith survives in our land.

In order that it might be easier to understand the chicanery of the atheists of the Soviet Union, we shall briefly acquaint you with the methods they are using to destroy the Orthodox church in the Soviet Union. After that we shall acquaint our readers with the problems of the Roman Catholic church throughout the Soviet Union, and especially in Lithuania.

According to Marxist theory, religion is a capitalistic, parasitic social phenomenon. In those countries where the capitalistic system is destroyed, religion is destined gradually to disappear. Religion is the opiate of the people.

Since life does not bear out this theory and religion survives in lands ruled by the Communists, they use all weapons, propagandistic, administrative, and even physical, to see that this theory is proven correct. It is therefore not surprising to find in the Soviet Union the following policy: religion is tolerated for the time being, only as a disappearing phenomenon, and it is attacked with all possible force wherever it begins to show signs of revival.

The Roman Catholic church, as a dying [destined to die] institution, is allowed by Soviet laws on [religious] cult to function in a limited way for the time being: priests are allowed to perform liturgical ceremonies and to confer the sacraments. However, even here, complete freedom does not exist. In general, the activities of religious believers are limited by all sorts of unofficial, secret or semi-secret, directives and instructions.

Most often, the methods of the Russian Tsars are slavishly copied. They [Soviet authorities] choose candidates for the episcopacy, interfere in the work of diocesan chanceries and in parish activities, placing them in the care of so-called parish committees, of which even atheists can be members. In this way the administration and activities of the Church are paralyzed from within.

The Situation of the Orthodox Church in the Soviet Union

No sooner had the Bolsheviks taken over the government of Russia

after the October Revolution, than the repression of religious believers, especially of the Orthodox church and of the Catholics began,
later becoming a bloody persecution. By newly promulgated decrees,
the Church was separated from the state and the schools were separated from the Church. As a matter of fact, the Orthodox church was
subjugated to the state, and in the schools atheistic education was
introduced, forbidding youngsters from going to church.

Over a period of years, the Soviet government became convinced
that the best way of fighting religion was not by bloody persecution,
but by attacking the Church from within. It was unfortunate that the
head of the Orthodox church lived in Russia. Moreover, the Orthodox
[believers] were accustomed to obeying civil authorities. After the
most terrible persecutions, the Orthodox church, wishing at least to
survive, was forced to make various concessions to the atheistic
government. It was forced to agree that the Church should be in charge
of individuals who agreed to carry out the orders of the atheists.

This did great damage to the Orthodox church. Its leadership, by
praising the Soviet government in all sorts of decrees and by misleading world opinion concerning the alleged freedom of religion in the
Soviet Union, and by agreeing to cooperate with security organs, lost
respect in the eyes of the believers. The Russian Orthodox church
succumbed to corruption. Bishops showed up, who helped the atheists
to close down churches.

Great numbers of Russian Orthodox clergy are poorly trained, and
given to various vices such as drunkenness and materialism. They have
developed practically no pastoral ministry, they do not catechize the
children, rarely preach, and are loath to hear confessions or visit the
sick. Most of them are satisfied to perform liturgical functions. This is
why there are in Russia very few enlightened believers.

A segment of Russian Orthodox clergy and believers pays no heed to
restrictions imposed by their leaders. They boldly proclaim the Gospel
of Christ and try to prevent the [Orthodox] faith from dying. Such
individuals are respected by the believers. On them depends the future
of the Orthodox church in the Soviet Union.

Situation of Protestant Groups

The situation is similar with Christians of other persuasions. Protes-
tants, Baptists and other sects operating out in the open usually have as
leaders individuals chosen by the atheists and trusted by them. through
whom the atheists undermine their work from within.

The most active groups, which have most successfully developed their religious activities are those persecuted by the government: Baptists, Pentecostals, Jehovah's Witnesses and other religious groups which operate clandestinely or semi-clandestinely.

The Situation of the Catholic Church in the Soviet Union

It is by the same methods that the atheists wish to destroy the Catholic church in the Soviet Union. At first they tried to destroy it by physical means, arresting and exiling Church leaders: bishops, priests and the more active laity. Currently, they are trying to destroy the Catholic church from within, by trying to see that positions in the hierarchy are filled by persons agreeing to carry out their decrees, which paralyze the activity of the Church.

Thank God, their plan has succeeded only partially. In the European part of the Russian Federation there function barely a few Catholic churches, intended not so much for ministry, as for public relations. The Church of St. Louis, in Moscow, is in the yard of the headquarters of the [State] Security Committee of the Soviet Union [KGB]. Here, even the least kind of religious activity is carefully watched by the KGB. Most visitors to the church are elderly Polish women, foreigners and members of the Russian intelligentsia.

The plight of the one remaining church in Leningrad is similar. The chairman of its parish committee is a representative of the KGB, living with another man's wife and still receiving Holy Communion. When a priest visiting from Lithuania wished to speak with local believers, the chairman would not allow it.

Local Catholics are afraid to get married in such churches. It is doubtful whether a single child has been prepared for Holy Communion all year long. The Catholic faith in Russia is doomed, unless underground activity is developed.

The situation is somewhat better in other [Catholic] churches found in the territory of the Soviet Union, among the Germans, and partly among the Poles, where there are active believers, able to function in underground fashion. Where there is no underground church activity, the Catholic church has either disappeared completely, or it is moribund (as in vast reaches of Siberia).

The Catholic Church in Belorussia

The plight of the Church is especially precarious in the Republic of

Belorussia. In no republic is the Catholic faith so persecuted as in Belorussia. There, many of the most beautiful churches have been closed, while others have been turned into warehouses, abandoned and in the final stages of delapidation (e.g., Druja [Druia], Vydžiai [Vidzy], and elsewhere). There is a great shortage of priests. One priest sometimes has to minister to the faithful of 28 former parishes.

There is no seminary, nor is any effort made to prepare any candidates for the priesthood clandestinely. When it happened that some young men expressed a wish to enter the seminary in Riga [Latvia] or Kaunas [Lithuania], the KGB began so much to persecute them in an effort of recruiting them as informers that they were forced to flee to other republics.

Moreover, the seminary in Kaunas will not accept candidates from Belorussia or the Ukraine, fearing that the KGB, instead of sending suitable candidates, will send its own agents. Candidates for the seminary here are designated by the [republic] Representative for Cult [Affairs].

Most priests in Belorussia are about seventy years old. Some must be carried to church (e.g. the pastor of Borūnai, who broke his leg and was unable to walk to church). In five to ten years, Belorussia will be without priests. It is forbidden to invite neighboring clergy to help out. The inhuman work load drives the still working priests to an early grave. It is often necessary to travel 130–200 kilometers on a sick call.

In Minsk, where there are about forty thousand Catholics, there is not a single functioning Catholic church. The government allowed Catholics to carry out services in an Orthodox church. Did the priests not make a mistake in not taking advantage of such permission?

In Gardinas [Grodno], where there are three functioning Catholic churches, there was not a single priest at Christmas, 1976, who could celebrate Mass for the believers. The believers wept when a letter from the local priest was read to those gathered for the occasion. In it they were informed that the local priest was seriously ill and did not have the strength to celebrate Mass.

The believers of Para have been keeping their beautiful church from being closed for eighteen years by performing services without a priest. For a long time, members of the church committee used to stand at the church doors, checking the identity cards of young people. The government had forbidden young persons up to the age of eighteen to go to church. Priests of parishes where young people show up in church are especially persecuted, e.g. in Breslava [Braslav].

Language poses special pastoral problems. The young people do not understand Polish. Many local priests do not wish to teach youngsters religion in Belorussian or Russian. In this way conditions are created for the spread of atheism. In Belorussia there is a specially debilitating problem of alcoholism. The Catholic Church is persecuted not so much by local people, but by Russian interlopers. The persecution of the Church there goes hand in hand with Russification of the Belorussians.

The Uniate Church in the Ukraine

In the Ukrainian Republic the predicament of western-rite Catholics is similar to that of Catholics in Belorussia: priests are dying off, and there is no local seminary. In the Ukraine there are several younger priests who are products of the seminary in Riga. Catholics of the western rite are served by priests of the eastern rite. Pastoral work is greatly hindered by national antipathy between Ukrainians and Poles.

Even more difficult is the plight of eastern rite Catholics. All their churches are closed, and the clergy are especially persecuted. There have even been sacrifices of life.

Liturgical books, vessels, and vestments are confiscated from the priests as the property of the Patriarch of Moscow. Some Orthodox clergy help persecute the Catholics. In the circumstances, the believers of the Ukrainian Eastern Rite Catholic church feel quite uneasy at seeing the excessive — in their opinion — friendship of Roman Catholics with the Patriarchate of Moscow, while not sensing much support themselves.

The Eastern Rite Ukrainian church is fortunate in being able to operate underground. Local security officials believe that in the city of Lvov [Lviv] every neighborhood has its own eastern rite priest. It is said that the security people regret having driven them underground, because they have no way of controlling their activities.

The Ukrainians have been accustomed since the days of old to being persecuted, and they have learned to work underground, making it difficult for the atheists to subjugate them. They are grateful to their beloved martyr Cardinal Slypyi, who, understanding local conditions, was able to help them.

The Catholic Church in Latvia

In Latvia, since 1940, the Soviet Union ostensibly assigned the pastoral care and evangelization of the Catholics of the entire Soviet

Union to the Archbishop of Riga. However, throughout those forty years, it has been difficult to observe signs of that pastoral care. It must be acknowledged, however, that the bishops of Latvia partially perform these duties. Having but a few priests, they send them to the few functioning Catholic churches in the Soviet Union. However, they do not carry on any broader evangelization of the Soviet Union.

Why? Latvian Catholics constitute barely a fifth of the population of Latvia. From of old, they are accustomed to accommodating themselves to the demands of the government. Now, more than ever before, they carry out the demands of the atheistic government, which restricts the activities of the Church. The religious life of Latvian Catholics in many parishes is weak. Priests are afraid of being punished by the government, and they do not trust one another; many limit themselves to liturgical functions and to ministering the sacraments to the older generation and the dying; religious education of children has been neglected. Many convents of women religious in Latvia lack apostolic spirit. They have not studied the decrees of the Second Vatican Council and are not concerned about putting them into practice. They hardly catechize the children at all, nor do they get involved in pastoral work. They are said to have received instructions from their superiors to watch and to pray.

The Catholic Church in Tadzhikistan

The situation of the Catholic church is better in the Republic of Tadzhikistan, where many zealous Catholics, especially Germans and some Poles live. Their zeal and grasp of their faith could be a source of edification to the believers of West Germany and other countries of Europe. These are wonderful examples of the working of the Holy Spirit! It is the result of the work of zealous priests, religious and third order members. They have been able to prepare their people for a life in the catacombs. The faithful have been able, without priests or bishops, to keep the [Catholic] faith. The faith is especially vigorous in those regions which have been visited by former prisoners and banished priests. A special object of their respect has been Father T. A. Šeškevičius, S.J. In the homes of many Germans in Asia, the portrait of Father Šeškevičius hangs alongside the pictures of saints.

The atheists of the Soviet Union are hatching fresh plans to destroy the Catholic church in the Soviet Union. It is said that while making certain concessions to the Holy See, they want the headquarters of the Catholic church in the Soviet Union to be established in Moscow. In charge would be a clergyman who has capitulated to the government, with the rank of Cardinal. His jurisdiction would extend to all the Catholic dioceses in the Soviet Union: those of Lithuania, the Ukraine, Belorussia and the rest. Thus the first step towards schism would be set up. Even now some Orthodox clergy are heard to say that since the Catholic church acknowledges the Patriarch of Moscow as a legitimate member of the ecclesiastical hierarchy, the time is approaching for the Catholics of the Soviet Union to renounce the Holy Father of Rome. The Patriarch of Moscow would be able to lead them.

We find it difficult to understand the recent so-called *Ostpolitik*. In our opinion, it has greatly hurt the Church in Eastern Europe. We hear such arguments: "The Soviet Union is a powerful country, whose physical power today we cannot overcome. It is necessary to seek diplomatic avenues of dialogue with that power, with the aim of defending the resident [Soviet] believers from complete annihilation."

In our opinion, it is not diplomatic efforts which keep them [the Soviets] from atrocities, but the necessity of reckoning with the might of powerful states, world and national public opinion, and fear of a new Nuremberg trial.

Representatives of the Soviet Union eagerly seek diplomatic ties with the Apostolic See, in order that, having obtained concessions from the Catholic church, they might even more subtly persecute the Church, especially at the hands of Church leaders who have capitulated to them. Bishops accommodating themselves to the atheists by their written or oral directives often interfere with the activities of especially the catacomb Church often forbidding persecuted ministers the celebration of Holy Mass in private homes, the hearing of confessions outside one's own diocese, in private apartments, and especially the confessions of women religious.

A bold defense of the faith impresses Catholics of Eastern [European] countries. If the Catholics of Lithuania can be defended [merit defense] by non-Catholics and even persons of atheistic persuasion, like Academician Andrei Sakharov or Sergei Kovalëv, at the risk of their freedom, then all the more we expect a word of intercession from our brothers the Catholic bishops and believers of other lands. Thank God, we are lately hearing their voices raised in our defense.

One gets the impression that Catholics, unwilling to spoil relations with the atheists of Moscow, have chosen the tactic of silence. One bishop of Lithuania, upon his return from Rome asserted that the Holy Father, in an audience, advised the believers of the Soviet Union: "Pray and wait quietly and patiently."

We are accustomed to being deceived, and we do not believe that the Holy Father would so have advised us. We have the Gospel, the decrees of the Second Vatican Council concerning the missions and the apostolate; we hear the words of our Holy Father, Pope Paul VI, over the radio, speaking of the duty to evangelize the world of today, without regard even for one's life. How can we be quiet and wait, when the atheists and other enemies of the Church are not quiet and do not wait? Can we calmly watch and wait when hundreds of thousands of youth, students and intellectuals are longing for the Gospel, disenchanted [both] with atheism, and with the moral rot stemming from it? If we do so, we are all guilty. The Apostle Paul cried, "Woe to me, if I did not proclaim the Gospel!" An example to us in this regard could be members of the various [Protestant] sects in the Soviet Union, [for example], the Jehova's Witnesses and the Pentecostalists. They have discovered methods suitable for [the apostolate in] the Soviet Union. Spiritually and materially, they are supported by their brothers abroad. Among their members they have developed an apostolic spirit which fears neither suffering nor death. They are provided with the latest literature, they have created a disciplined organization with leaders at various levels: the small group, the village, city community, region, republic, etc.

For long years the Catholic church in the Soviet Union was, as it were, moribund, showing no signs of greater apostolic effort. Now the situation has changed significantly. We need not soporific slogans, but words of encouragement, suitable leeway for action, and the requisite authorization, without which we do not feel we have the right to send anyone forth in the name of the Church, or to urge anyone on to apostolic work demanding heroism. Our strength lies in our unity with the Holy Father, and a bold, well-organized defense of the Church.

We can rejoice that in this regard the Catholic church has made significant progress. Thanks to those efforts, the facts regarding the persecution of the faith in the Soviet Union have forced even the Communist parties abroad to condemn the persecution of believers waged by the Soviet Union.

The Catholic Church in Lithuania

Because of its geographical situation and historical circumstances, Lithuania is the outpost of the Catholic church in the East [Eastern Europe]. It can serve humanity by creating a synthesis of the cultures of East and West. For that reason the level of religious life in Lithuania

can have extraordinary significance for the Catholic church and the
history of Europe.

For that reason the Roman Catholic church should be very concerned that Catholicism in Lithuania survives, be strengthened by its
trials and with the proper support, manifest itself in all its vigor and be
able to fulfill the mission assigned to it by Providence and by the
Church.

Lithuania is a Baltic country, the majority of whose inhabitants are
Catholics. Even now the Catholic Church there [in Lithuania] works
overtly and also covertly, in catacomb style. Its work would be even
more active, if it received the moral and material support of the rest of
the believers.

In spite of long, determined and bitter persecution by the atheists,
the Catholic faith in Lithuania is alive. We can boast to the Holy
Father that we have had very few priests among us renounce their
priesthood, there is no dearth of vocations to the priesthood or
religious life, eucharistic life is flourishing, and the sacrament of
penance is appreciated. You have plenty of data showing how cour-
ageously the clergy and faithful of Lithuania are defending their faith.
We have had a host of martyrs for the faith, and of girls who have
sacrificed their lives in defense of their chastity (Students Elena
Spirgevičiūtė, Stasė Lūšaitė, Danutė Burbaitė and others).

In our country the spirit of the apostolate is alive, thirsting to spread
the Catholic faith throughout a vast land which has been subjected to
atheism. The Catholic church is working effectively in catacomb
fashion: an underground press flourishes, catechization is conducted
on a broad scale; religious communities are active despite all kinds of
sacrifices [they have to make]. There is no lack of responsible officials
or even members of the Communist Party, who albeit secretly, hold the
faith. On their death-bed, they ask to be buried with the Catholic
liturgy. We have several bishop-martyrs: Archbishop T. Matulionis,
M. Reinys, V. Borisevičius and P. Ramanauskas. For their loyalty to
the Church, Bishops J. Steponavičius and V. Sladkevičius have been
exiled from their dioceses. About six hundred Lithuanian priests have
been imprisoned without ceasing even in prison to spread the teachings
of Christ.

However, the atheists in Lithuania do not cease by any means dis-
rupting the life of the Catholic church.

1. The first means of destroying the Catholic church in Lithuania
consists of the diligent and relentless efforts of the atheists to introduce
into the hierarchy of the Catholic church of Lithuania individuals who

would agree to carry out their directives: a) to spread abroad lies about the so-called freedom of religion in Lithuania. It is on this condition that the banished bishops have been promised that they would be allowed to return to their duties; b) to help mislead the Vatican and to help place in episcopal sees candidates acceptable to the atheists; c) to thwart pastoral efforts by ignoring the decrees of the Holy Father; d) to promote bad priests, assigning them to responsible positions; and to persecute zealous priests, assigning them to the hinterlands; e) to neglect religious education, etc.

The atheists have partly succeeded in carrying out their plans, but not entirely. The newly appointed bishops presently concern themselves with pastoral efforts as much as possible. Those who on account of age are unable to function and to resist the demands of the atheists would be acting honorably if they resigned.

2. The atheists interfere with candidates wishing to enter the seminary, they try to recruit those who enter, and they try to see that the level of education and training in the seminary is at a low level. The bishops are able freely to appoint neither the administration of the seminary, nor its faculty. They are powerless to remove from their positions individuals obviously unfit for such duties. The seminarians lack theological textbooks. The seminary library is very poor, and is not being replenished with books of a purely religious nature published abroad. It is no wonder that the level of education and of spiritual training at the seminary in Kaunas is quite low. Often, young priests revive spiritually once they begin their priestly ministry.

3. One of the greatest means of wrecking Catholicism in Lithuania is the well-organized compulsory atheistic education of the children, without regard either to the Declaration of Human Rights, or to the Final Act of the Helsinki Conference. Even now, priests are fined for teaching children catechism. Teachers in Lithuania are pressured in various ways by the Ministry of Education to educate children in atheism. A segment of opportunistic teachers performs this task zealously. According to the statistics of Lithuanian atheists, 70% of the children entering school are religious believers; only 30% finish secondary school with their faith intact. Their faith is further ruined in institutions of higher learning. All university students are required to complete a course on so-called "scientific atheism."

Since youth are forbidden to attend church, and there is a great dearth of religious literature, a great part of the young people are not so much atheist as they are religious illiterates. The fruit of atheism is a moral degeneracy among the young which has caused even the atheists concern.

4. One of the most detrimental and to the [Catholic] faith and morals of the Lithuanian people demeaning practices is the mass recruitment of people to become informers for the KGB. All possible means, such as bribery, blackmail, the threat of being discharged from work, the most attractive promises of career advancement and of higher education [are used to achieve this purpose]. Those who do not agree to become informers are threatened with all sorts of punishment. Those who agree are often pardoned for criminal offenses. All are subject to recruitment, beginning with elementary school children and ending with bishops.

It must be acknowledged that such pressure, extending over the years, produces results. Consequently, many Lithuanians today do not trust one another, fear to speak out and are constantly afraid of being betrayed.

Especially subject to such recruitment are seminarians [students in the theological seminary]. Those who do not agree to become agents of the KGB are threatened that they will not be accepted for the seminary [theological studies] or that they will not be ordained. Seminarians are placed under particular pressure during vacation. Sometimes they are required to commit themselves publicly to renounce priesthood after [ordination and] a few years as priests. Thus it was with Father Vytautas Starkus, the pastor of Sidabrava.

5. On July 28, 1976, a new law was promulgated in Lithuania which envisions a further restriction of the work of the Church. One section of the new law allows the priest to perform his ministrations only in the church for which he has been registered. According to that regulation, priests are forbidden from helping neighboring priests to hear confessions, when the latter are overwhelmed with work during feastdays or funerals.

The same law forbids the teaching of religion. The teaching of religion is allowed only in the theological seminary. All who teach children prayers or catechism must now expect new persecution — now based on the law.

The same law forbids clergy from carrying out pastoral visits — kalėdojimas — even though Canon Law requires this. The same law directs that the question of establishing new parishes be decided not by the faithful, but by the members of the executive committee of the district.

The Catholic church in Lithuania is operating on two levels: overtly and covertly. Forced to operate entirely in catacomb fashion are all religious communities of men and women; young men secretly preparing for ordination to the priesthood, almost all students and various officials who are afraid to be seen in church or to receive the sacraments, in order not to suffer for it.

A significant number of priests working with official approval are forced also to operate in catacomb style: preparing children for First Communion or Confirmation, visiting patients in hospitals where the priest is not admitted by the medical staff, and witnessing the marriages of officials.

The Catholic church is working in exclusively catacomb fashion or semi-catacomb fashion in broad areas of Russia. It is able to operate because it ignores the restrictions of the atheists. Such activity is quite difficult, since it is bitterly persecuted by the atheists. However, it is difficult to squelch, when properly organized. The Church operating overtly can be destroyed in a moment by the atheists, by closing churches and arresting bishops and priests.

However, it is very difficult to subdue the Church of the catacombs, since they are unable to keep track of its activities. The Church operating in catacomb conditions does not interfere with the local Church operating overtly, it does not try to disrupt its discipline or to divide it, but tries as much as possible to complement its work. As much as possible, it upholds the authority of the pastor [in charge of the diocese], tries to win the conditions necessary for a more free operation, defends the pastors from government persecution and pressure, and blocks misleading statements emanating from them.

As for the relationship of the Church of the catacombs with the atheistic government, the government is quite unhappy about the activity of the Church of the catacombs, because it is unable to control it. While the Church operating in the open has some privileges, the Church of the catacombs is persecuted. Therefore priests and religious operating clandestinely are termed agents of the Vatican or foreign spies.

Those making these accusations know themselves that it is not so. Even the Catholic church operating in catacomb conditions is not about to plan an uprising, nor to fight the Soviet system by force. It does not forbid Catholics to serve in the Soviet army, to participate in social action, or to work in state offices or factories. Many Catholics are exemplary, trustworthy workers. Even the sisters, who have been driven underground, are appreciated as conscientious medical personnel who conscientiously nurse Party members and security agents. The Church operating in catacomb conditions does not seek to disrupt good relations between the Apostolic See and the Soviet Union. It wants only to proclaim the doctrine of Christ to all people without hindrance.

A great pastoral error was committed when the bishops, priests and people of Lithuania were not prepared in time juridically or pastorally, for pastoral work in catacomb conditions. The more freedom of religion increases, the less will become the significance of the Church of the catacombs. The greater the persecution, the more deeply the Church will be forced to burrow into the catacombs and the more will its significance grow.

In view of these facts we trust that our Lithuanian brothers abroad and the bishops and believers of the whole world will help us to preserve the Catholic faith, will help us with their offerings and prayers, and with all their might will defend us from those who persecute us for our faith.

[We hope that] they will make better use, as much as possible, of the media of information in the hands of Catholics and of other good people. As much as possible they will try to see that the Catholic church leadership assists not only the Church operating openly, but also the Church operating in catacomb conditions.

In recent times, relations between the Apostolic See and the Soviet Union have improved. The representatives of this country regularly visit the Holy Father, Cardinals visit Moscow and Leningrad. No one denies that it is necessary to use all diplomatic channels, seeking contacts even with an atheistic government, working for world peace, justice and racial equality. The atheists eagerly seek better relations with the Apostolic See. However, by that diplomatic activity, they wish to obtain concessions which would enable them more deeply to hurt the Church.

As a rule, they [the atheists] do not honor their promises or their agreements. The pronouncements of the new bishops of Hungary or Czechoslovakia give us no joy. The atheists threaten that if their demands are not met, if the activities of diligent Catholics are not restricted, a new bloody persecution of the faithful could break out, such as took place from 1917 to 1923, and from 1930 to 1938. We do not feel threatened by bloody persecution as much as by the slow, silent strangulation throttling the Church with its own hands.

Lithuanian Catholic Petition to the Vatican

With all this in mind, we ask our brother Lithuanians abroad the following:

1. To show more concern, love, spiritual and material help, especially for the Catholic church in catacomb conditions.

2. In a suitable manner to request the Holy See:

    a. as much as possible to hasten the beatification of the Servant of God Jurgis Matulaitis-Matulevičius;

    b. to exert efforts, that the cause of beatification of new Lithuanian martyrs for faith and morals be taken up: Archbishop T. Matulionis, Bishop V. Borisevičius, and student E. Spirgevičiūtė, who showed heroism similar to that of St. Maria Goretti;

    c. to request the Holy Father not to appoint bishops and not to confer titles of honor on individuals who have compromised themselves morally and politically. Not to trust the recommendations of those who have already misled the Apostolic See;

    d. to encourage concern for the evangelization of the Soviet Union; to instruct local Ordinaries here not to pose obstacles for those who wish to do missionary work in this country;

    e. to exert efforts that the faithful of Belorussia and the Ukraine might obtain the right to open their own seminary;

    f. to try to see that churches be opened and priests assigned to them, at least in the larger cities of the Soviet Union, such as Kiev, Minsk, Novosibirsk, Krasnoyarsk, Omsk, Tomsk, etc.; to promulgate pastoral directives for radio broadcast by the Holy See, urging the evangelization of the Soviet Union, effective from the day of announcement; warn that local Ordinaries would not have the right to restrict their carrying out. To grant the right of hearing confessions to priests in good standing, without regard to diocesan boundaries, in private homes and apartments, not only of the laity, but also of religious sisters.

Decree No. 7, "Christus Dominus," of the Second Vatican Council, urges the bishops of the entire world to show particular love and concern for those priests who suffer various persecutions for Christ. It urges them to assist by prayer and support. Moreover, it urges all the faithful, especially those in higher positions, boldly to defend persecuted believers. (Cf. *Gaudium et Spes,* #75). We are waiting for these decrees to be diligently put into practice. The Helsinki Accords created favorable conditions for defending believers repressed and persecuted throughout the world, and especially in the Soviet Union.

This appeal has been drafted after appealing to the Holy Spirit for light, and listening to the opinions of many priests, religious and laity, of Lithuania. We trust that our brother Lithuanians overseas, the faithful of the entire world and people of good will, will help us as they can. We will ask the Most High that our cry for help be heard.

Notes

CHAPTER I
CATHOLICISM AND NATIONALITY: THE LITHUANIAN PERSPECTIVE

1. Soviet view of the concept found in Ia. V. Minkiavichius [Minkevičius], *Katolitsizm i natsiia* (Moscow, 1971), pp. 181 ff. Lithuanian Catholic view of the role of the Church in Lithuanian history is extensively discussed in a commemorative volume ed. by [P. Mantvydas, ed.], *Krikščionybė Lietuvoje: praeitis, dabartis, ateitis* (Kaunas: Šv. Kazimiero Dr-ja, 1938).

2. Paulius Rabikauskas, ed., *Relationes status dioecesium in Magno Ducato Lituaniae,* Vol. I (Rome: Academia Lituana Catholica Scientarum, 1971), pp. 5, 223.

3. Viktoras Gidžiūnas, "Catholic Church in the Great Duchy of Lithuania," *LE,* Vol. XV, p. 141. Most extensively, the reformation period in Lithuania has been studied by the late Zenonas Ivinskis. See his "Die Entstehung der Reformation in Litauen bis zum Erscheinen der Jesuiten (1969)," *Forschungen zur osteuropäischen Geschichte,* Vol. 12 (Berlin, 1967). His main work is the yet unpublished book-length monograph on Bishop Melchior Giedraitis.

4. P. I. Kushner, *Etnicheskie territorii i etnicheskie granitsy* (Moscow: Akademiia nauk SSSR, 1951), presents an extremely well-documented study by the Soviet Academy of Sciences of the changing demographic characteristics of East Prussia.

5. An example of an assimilated Lithuanian was Bishop Antanas Baranauskas (Antonius Baranowski). A classic Lithuanian poet in his youth, he wrote some strongly patriotic anti-Russian lyrics. He later lost any connection to Lithuanian affairs and considered himself a Pole while Bishop of an ethnically mixed diocese of Seinai (Sejny). Cf. Jerzy Ochmanski, *Litewski ruch narodowo-kulturalny w XIX wieku* (Białystok: Białostockie Towarzystwo Naukowe, 1965), p. 127.

6. Cf. Edward Crankshaw, *The Shadow of the Winter Palace* (New York: The Viking Press, 1976), pp. 90 ff.

7. Paulius Šležas, "The Relations between Church and State in the Samogitian Diocese during the Times of Valančius (1850–1875)," *Židinys* (Kaunas), Vol. XXVIII, No. 7 (July, 1938), p. 4.

8. "Katolitsizm v Rossii," *Entsiklopedicheskii slovar',* Vol. 28, p. 740.

9. From Bishop Valančius Diary *(Pastabos Pačiam Sau)* cited by Paulius Šležas, ibid.

10. Ibid.

11. The quote from Rapolas Krasauskas, "The Church during the Tsarist Occupation," *LE,* Vol. XV, p. 143. Survey of Tsarist policies in ibid. and K. Gečys, *Katalikiškoji Lietuva* (Chicago: Draugo spaustuvė, 1946), pp. 108–9.

12. Steponas Matulis, "Lithuania and the Holy See, 1795–1940," Lietuvių Katlikų Mokslo Akademija, *Suvažiavimo Darbai IV* (Rome, 1961), p. 160.

13. Antanas Alekna, *Katalikų Bažnyčia Lietuvoje* (Kaunas: šv. Kazimiero Draugija, 1936), p. 139.

14. *Dokumenty Komitetu Centralnego Narodowego i Rzadu Narodowego, 1862–1864,* ed. by E. Halicz, S. Kieniewicz, I. Miller (Wroclaw-Warszawa-Kraków: Wydanictwo Polskiej Akademii Nauk, 1968), Doc. No. 509, an appeal to the peasants, p. 539. For the most recent comprehensive Lithuanian study of the insurrection see K. R. Jurgela, *Lietuvos sukilimas 1862–1864 metais* (Boston: Lietuvių Enciklopedijos Leidykla, 1970).

15. For Muravëv's personal account of his rule and policies in the Northwestern territory see "Vsepoddanskii otchet grafa M. N. Muraveva po upravleniiu severozapadnym kraem (c 1 maia 1863g do. 17 aprelia 1865g)," *Russkaia starina* (June, 1902), pp. 486–510.

16. *Entsiklopedicheskii slovar',* Vol. 39, p. 91.

17. J. Žiugžda et al., eds., *Lietuvos TSR istorijos šaltiniai,* Vol. II (Vilnius: VPML Leidykla, 1965), pp. 123–24; S. Kenevich et al., eds., *Vosstanie v Litve i Belorussii ·1863–1864 gg.* (Moscow: Nauka, 1965), pp. 95–101.

18. Antanas Alekna, *Žemaičių vyskupas Motiejus Valančius* (Kaunas: Šv. Kazimiero Dr-ja, 1922), pp. 157–63, contains a list of those Samogitian clergymen.

19. Valančius' letter to Muravëv cited by Šležas, loc. cit., p. 56.

20. Text in the appendix of Alekna, *Žemaičių vyskupas Motiejus Valančius,* 2nd ed. (Chicago: Lituanistikos institutas, 1975), p. 293ff; see also Muravëv's report as in footnote 15.

21. *Lietuvos TSR istorijos šaltiniai,* II, p. 83. Past tense is used in the text.

22. Alekna, *Žemaičių vyskupas Motiejus Valančius,* p. 160.

23. Cf. Jerzy Ochmanski, *Historia Litwy* (Wroclaw-Warsaw-Cracow: Zakład Narodowy im. Ossolińskich-wydawnictwo, 1967), pp. 170–71; also the same author's *Litewski ruch narodowo-kulturalny w XIX wieku* (Białystok: Białostockie Towarzystwo Naukowe, 1965), pp. 115–18.

24. Cf. V. Trumpa's introductory essay in *Žemaičių vyskupas Motiejus Valančius,* 2nd ed., p. xxviiff.

25. See text of Valančius' appeal in ibid., pp. 142–43.

26. Text with Russian additions indicated in ibid., pp. 150–51.

27. For Gilferding's views see his "Vchem iskat' razresheniia pol'skogo voprosa?" and "Neskol'ko zamechanii o Litovskom i Zhmudskom plemeni" and other writings reprinted in S. Sholkovich (ed.), *Pol'skoe delo po otnosheniiu k Zapadnoi Rossii,* Vol. I (Vil'na: Tipografia A. G. Syrkina, 1885), esp. pp. 16, 37, and 101ff and Vol. II (1887). The linguist supported separate Lithuanian nationality but at the same time advocated the use of cyrillic characters for Lithuanian writing. His articles indicate that he was impressed by the German assimilation of Lithuanians in East Prussia which he assumed was helped by the use of Gothic characters for Lithuanian publication.

28. Iurii Samarin, "Sovremennyi obem pol'skogo voprosa" in Sholkovich, Vol. I, pp. 1–18. In the article Samarin discusses, among other matters, how Latin Catholicism contradicts the spirit of Orthodoxy.

29. V. K-n, "Neskol'ko slov o zhmudzkikh narodnikh knigakh," Sholkovich, Vol. II, p. 422.

30. *Entsiklopedicheskii slovar',* Vol. 39, p. 190; *Lietuvos TSR istorijos šaltiniai,* Vol. II, p. 84 (Document No. 85, a letter by Muravëv to the Minister of Internal Affairs with suggestions for additional distribution of land).

31. Cf. R. Vëbra, "Lithuanian National Movement in 1865-1883," *Lietuvos TSR Mokslų Akademijos Darbai,* Ser. A, Vol. 2 (59), p. 51 ff. The author writes: "He [Valančius] urged resistance not only against the Russification but also the Polonization of the Lithuanians, that is, [he] urged a struggle against Polish nationalism."

32. Obolenski's letter in the appendix to Alekna, *Žemaičių vyskupas Motiejus Valančius,* 2nd ed., p. 300.

33. The use of the Russian language in Catholic churches of Lithuania was forbidden in 1848, but after a long debate that showed Orthodox fears of losing believers to the Catholics if Russian is used in Catholic churches was reintroduced and promoted in 1869. The famous Conservative Slavophile Mikhail Katkov strongly supported this practice. See his "O russkom iazyke v katolicheskom Bogosluzhenii," in Sholkovich, Vol. I, pp. 221-227. In the same volume, an unnamed author asserted that the use of Russian in Catholic churches will further the Russian nationality (p. 227). The split between Catholic diocesan administrators on the question and the opposition to the use of Russian in churches by Bishop Valančius is examined by Paulius Jatulis, "Motiejus Valančius — Ideal Bishop," *Aidai* (Boston-Brooklyn), No. 5 (May, 1975), p. 206. Jatulis' study, to a large part, is based on yet unpublished Vatican archives.

34. Document No. 86, *Lietuvos TSR istorijos šaltiniai,* Vol. II, pp. 127-28. It contains the text of Kaufman's proposal to the Minister of the Interior but leaves out the governor's strongly nationalistic Russian theoretical justification for the request. This part is found translated by Jonas Matusas, "The Prohibition of Latin Alphabet," publ. in V. Bagdanavičius et al., eds., *Kovos metai dėl savosios spaudos* (Chicago: Lietuvių Bendruomenė, 1957), pp. 125-26. Professor Vaclovas Biržiška, a specialist on the problem, discusses the involved legal matters in "Prohibition of the Press Had No Legal Foundation," ibid., p. 73 ff. Since the Kaufman-Valuev decree replaced an orally-issued prohibition by Muravëv in 1864, the prohibition is considered to have lasted forty years instead of the formal thirty-nine.

35. Document No. 85, *Lietuvos istorijos šaltiniai,* Vol. II, pp. 126-27.

36. Obolenski's summary of Muravëv's and Kaufman's motives in his letter of Aug. 13, 1868. Text in the appendix of Alekna, *Žemaičių vyskupas Motiejus Valančius,* 2nd ed., pp. 296, 298.

37. Ibid., pp. 114-15.

38. Letter by Valančius to the Governor General of Vilnius, text in appendix of ibid., p. 286 ff.

39. Obolenski cited in ibid., pp. 206-7. According to Obolenski, the Samogitian diocese needed only 500 priests. Bishop Valančius insisted that he required at least 605.

40. *The Times* (London), Jan. 4, 1894, p. 5. See also *The New York Times,* Dec. 1, 1893.

41. *The Annual Reporter for the Year 1894* (London, 1895), p. 293. See also *The Times* (London), Oct. 13, 1894, p. 5.

42. Statement by Mackevičius to his interrogators, *Vosstanie v Litve i Belorussii 1863-1864 gg* (Moscow, 1965), pp. 65-66.

43. I. M. Bogdanov, *Gramotnost' i obrazovanie v dorevoliutsionnoi Rossii i v SSSR* (Moscow: Statistika, 1964), pp. 59 and 61.

44. V. K-n, "Some Words About Samogitian National Books," Sholkovich, Vol. II, p. 407.

45. *Tėvynes sargas,* No. 1, 1900, pp. 65-66; cited by R. Vėbra, *Lietuvos katalikų dvasininkija ir visuomeninis judėjimas* (Vilnius: Mintis, 1968), p. 171.

46. *De condizioni del Lituani Cattolici nella Diocesi di Vilna e gli eccessi del panpolonismo. Memorandum del Clero Lituano* (Roma, 1912), cited by Steponas Matulis in a paper on the establishment of the Lithuanian church province, delivered at the conference of the Lithuanian Catholic Academy of Sciences, Detroit, November, 1976. An argumentatively written but factually rich source on Polish nationalism in the Lithuanian church is *L'Eglise Polonaise en Lithuanie* (Paris: Bureau d'Informations de Lithuanie, n.d.) written by Rev. C. Propolanis who served in the Catholic church's hierarchy in Mogilev and then was attached to the Russian Embassy in Rome.

CHAPTER II
THE CHURCH AND THE NATIONAL STATE:
INDEPENDENT LITHUANIA, 1918-1940

1. Mykolas Vaitkus, *Keturi ganytojai* (Chicago: Lietuviškos knygos klubas, 1960) vividly describes the visit on pp. 70-76.

2. Background of his appointment in Juozas Vaišnora, "Jurgis Matulaitis' Road to the Vilnius See," *Aidai,* No. 3 (1977), pp. 97-104. To balance Polish influence in Vilnius, German occupation authorities desired the appointment of a Lithuanian and supported the candidacy of Msgr. K. Olšauskas. However, the Vatican considered him unacceptable because of his aggressively articulated struggle for Lithuanian rights in the capital. Instead, Rome proposed Rev. Matulevičius-Matulaitis, the General of the Marian Congregation. He was well known for his pastoral work in Poland and thus was considered more acceptable to Polish Catholics. The Lithuanian State Council agreed to sponsor his candidacy and an agreement on his appointment was reached between the Vatican, the Lithuanians and the Germans. Matulevičius was supported by Polish bishops but did not believe that the Vilnius Poles would accept him or allow him to serve.

3. V. Daugirdaitė-Sruogienė, *Lietuvos steigiamasis seimas* (New York: Lithuanian National Federation, 1975), p. 46. This volume summarizes and reprints excerpts from the stenographic record of the meetings of Lithuania's Constituent Assembly.

4. These parties are examined in Daugirdaitė-Sruogienė, op. cit., as well as in Royal Institute of International Affairs, *The Baltic States* (London, 1938), pp. 56-60. See also Algirdas Kasulaitis, *Lithuanian Christian Democracy* (Chicago, 1976); and Petras Maldeikis, *Mykolas Krupavičius* (Chicago: Lietuvių Krikščionių Demokratų Sąjunga, 1975).

5. Daugirdaitė-Sruogienė, *op. cit.,* p. 193. The constitution was passed by the votes of the Christian Democratic majority, six out of seven votes of the Jewish minority and one dissident vote of a non-partisan former Populist representative.

6. *Protocol of a meeting of Lithuanian bishops* on February 15, 1925, pp. 8–9. Hereafter cited as *Protocol*.

7. For example, "Victory for Some, Defeat for Others," *Lietuvis,* May 21, 1925, pp. 2–5; reprinted in Morkus Šimkus, ed., *Profesorius Augustinas Voldemaras: Raštai* (Chicago: Lietuvos Atgimimo Sąjūdis, 1973), pp. 605–611.

8. *Protocol,* p. 4.

9. Text of the constitution of 1922 in Malbone W. Graham, *New Governments of Eastern Europe* (New York: Henry Holt, 1927), pp. 720–735. Text of the constitution of 1938 in Albert Blaustein, ed., collection of world constitutions, published by Oceana, volume on special sovereignties and dependencies.

10. Dr. Šliūpas, a physician, was a firebrand activist. An editor of the chief clandestine journal of Lithuanian national awakening, *Aušra,* published in Prussia at the end of the 19th century, he distinguished himself as a very effective, though controversial, leader of American Lithuanians in the United States before World War I. A strong nationalist, in the Freethinkers Alliance he nevertheless surrounded himself with secret Communists who became party and government functionaries after Lithuania was occupied by the Soviet Union. Šliūpas refused to cooperate with the Soviets and declined to continue atheist propaganda under Communist auspices. Instead, he reestablished closer relations with churchmen though he never changed his atheist views. A former mayor of the Baltic resort town of Palanga, he returned to the mayor's office on radio instructions of the Provisional Government of Lithuania that declared Lithuania's independence after Germany attacked the Soviet Union on June 22, 1941. However, the German military *Kommandant* removed him from office after he made a public speech condemning the wholesale arrest and maltreatment of the town's Jews by German authorities. His old age saved him from further punishment. In 1944, he nevertheless retreated to Germany with his family where he died before the end of World War II. The Soviets took more than two decades to partially rehabilitate his atheistic writings; they objected to their democratic and "bourgeois nationalist" character.

11. On the Lithuanian-Polish dispute see Alfred Erich Senn, *The Emergence of Modern Lithuania* (New York: Columbia University Press, 1959) and *The Great Powers, Lithuania and the Vilna Question* (Leiden: E. J. Brill, 1966).

12. Aldona Gaigalaitė, *Klerikalizmas Lietuvoje, 1917–1940* (Vilnius: Mintis, 1970), pp. 153–55.

13. Voldemaras, loc. cit., p. 615.

14. This plan was very similar to the draft finally approved by Rome. The bishops wanted to stress the temporary administrative character of Kaišiadorys (actually, part of Vilnius diocese), but agreed to name the province after the Kaunas archdiocese. The final draft disapproved of the first proposal and made a concession to Lithuanian nationalism on the second. *Protocol* of February 15, 1926, pp. 4–6.

15. Letter to Bishop Būčys, dated March 29, 1926, cit. by Viktoras Rimšelis, "Archbishop Jurgis Matulaitis and the Lithuanian Church," *Draugas* (literary supplement), December 18, 1976, p. 4.

16. Canon Mykolas Vaitkus tells the story of the confrontation in *Keturi ganytojai: Atsiminimai* (Chicago: Lietuviškos knygos klubas, 1960), pp. 89–

90. Biographies of other bishops in *LE* (individual entries). A *samizdat* biography of Bishop Reinys was smuggled out of Lithuania and published as [no author] *Arkivyskupas Mečislovas Reinys* (Chicago: Lietuvių Krikščionių Demokratų Sąjunga, 1977).

17. *Acta Apostolicae Sedis,* Vol. XVIII, No. 4 (April 6, 1926), pp. 121–23.

18. Cited by Voldemaras, in Šimkus, op. cit., p. 619.

19. *Protocol,* October 6–8, 1926, pp. 1–2.

20. Ibid., p. 7.

21. *Protocol,* January 15–16, 1927, p. 1.

22. Text in Amedeo Giannini, *Il Concordato con La Lituania* (Rome: Anonima Romana Editoriale, 1928), pp. 15–23. Further on the political developments of 1926–27 and the new regime, see my essay in V. Stanley Vardys and Romuald R. Misiunas, eds., *The Baltic States in Peace and War, 1917–1945* (1978).

23. Gaigalaitė, *op. cit.,* p. 166.

24. *Protocol,* October 12–14, 1927, pp. 2–3.

25. *Receipts and Expenditures of the Republic of Lithuania for the Year 1938* (Kaunas, 1938), p. 53. It seems that Lithuania's authoritarian regime was more generous with religious denominations, including the Catholic church, than was its democratic predecessor. In 1925, for example, the Christian Democratic majority approved Lt 1,440,162 (appr. $243,000 in 1930s post-depression dollars) for "the support of religious institutions" (*Ministerių kabineto priimtasai Lietuvos valstybės 1925 metams biudžeto Projektas,* p. 59). Under the Populist-Socialist coalition, this amount for 1927 rose to Lt 1,575,182 (appr. $267,000). It further increased under Smetona's rule, but began dropping in 1932. For 1941, the government considered raising the expenditure by almost a million Litas, to Lt 2,600,000 ($442,000), most likely to provide help to the Catholic and Jewish institutions in the newly incorporated city and region of Vilnius (*Lietuvos aidas* (morning ed.), April 14, 1940, p. 6). Soviet authors have variously manipulated these figures to the point — never repeated — of alleging that "clergymen of all denominations received in Lithuania 18–20,000,000 Litas (3, 6–4, 0 mill. dollars) every year." (J. Dagys, "The Income of Clergymen in Bourgeois Lithuania," *Mokslas ir gyvenimas,* No. 2, 1958, p. 41.)

26. Piotr Łossowski, *Kraje bałtyckie na drodze od demokracji parlamentarnej do dyktatury (1918–1934)* (Wróclaw: Polska Akademia Nauk, 1972), pp. 142–47. Smetona's suppression of high school "Ateitis" and the imprisonment of its founder Professor Pranas Dovydaitis is well documented in Juozas Girnius, *Pranas Dovydaitis* (Chicago, 1975), pp. 412–443; 202–226.

27. Rapolas Krasauskas, "Juozapas Skvireckas, the First Archbishop and Metropolitan of Kaunas," *Lux Christi,* No. 2 (35), June 1960, p. 19.

28. "From the Notes of Kazimieras Paltarokas, Bishop of Panevėžys," *samizdat* manuscript, p. 135. The author of another *samizdat* work (see ft. 16) concluded that Svireckas was "too weak" to function as Metropolitan Archbishop (p. 54).

29. Protocol, Oct. 6–10; 20–23, 1931, pp. 5–6.

30. *XX Amžius,* May 10, 1938.

31. *Acta Apostolicae Sedis,* XXI (1939), p. 611.

32. J. Daulius, "The Hour Has Come for Closing the Ranks," *Tiesos kelias,* No. 12 (1939), p. 802.

33. *Lietuvos aidas,* April 30, 1940, p. 1.
34. *XX Amžius,* May 24, 1940, p. 3.
35. *Le Saint Siège,* Part I (1967), No. 72, the Lithuanian government's note of December 20, 1939, asking for an "honorable retirement" of Archbishop Jałbrzykowski (p. 157) because of his public hostility to the Lithuanian state. In No. 73 (pp. 158–59), the Vatican's chargé d'affaires Msgr. Giuseppe Burzio investigated the charge and reported to Rome that the archbishop lacks prudence and a "spirit of conciliation." Jałbrzykowski's self-defense is attached to this document. On December 29, Burzio reported that the archbishop's attitudes were changing for the better (No. 81, p. 175). Consequently, Cardinal Maglione on January 4, 1940, declared to Lithuanian Minister Girdvainis that Jałbrzykowski will stay, but Lithuanians will be considered for future episcopal nominations (No. 86, pp. 182–83). The archbishop then was refused Lithuanian naturalization (No. 110, p. 211), but allowed to continue in office. After several public campaigns, he finally allowed more Lithuanian language services in the churches of Vilnius. See *Lietuvos aidas,* May 8 and 19, 1940, p. 1.
36. The law was prepared and the text summarized in the press on February 10, 1940. See *Lietuvos aidas* of that date, p. 3.
37. *Elenchus omnium ecclesiarum* (1920); *Elenchus omnium ecclesiarum et universi cleri Provinciae Ecclesiasticae Lituanae. Pro Anno 1939; LE,* XV, pp. 146ff, 154ff, 158; individual entries for various statistical information on these pages. The Soviet *MLTE,* II, p. 801 lists the membership of *Pavasaris* as 90,000 instead of the 40,000 listed by *LE.*
38. See Kazimieras Pakštas in *Židinys,* No. 11 (1932), pp. 357–59; and also No. 4 (1937), p. 398.
39. Cf. M. Gregorauskas, *Tarybų Lietuvos žemės ūkis* (Vilnius: VPML Leidykla, 1960), p. 78.
40. See discussion in *Tiesos kelias,* a professional clerical journal, No. 7–8 (1939), pp. 570–72; No. 10 (1939), pp. 748–49; No. 3 (1940), pp. 119–23.
41. *Naujoji Romuva,* 1931–40, a weekly literary and public affairs magazine, was edited and published by Juozas Keliuotis, who was deported to Siberia after World War II and after Stalin's death released largely through Ilya Ehrenburg's efforts. The magazine's contributors included Catholic and Liberal intellectuals and even artists close to the Communist party. It possessed an international flavor; in 1939, it published original essays by Czeslaw Milosz, among others. *Židinys* was a monthly journal of literature and public affairs, published by literature professor Jonas Grinius and edited by Ignas Skrupskelis, who later took over the editorship of the daily *XX Amžius.* Jonas Grinius survived World War II in the West while Skrupskelis, a literary critic and journalist of note, was arrested by the Soviets in July of 1940 and perished.
42. Pranas Dičius, *Santuoka ir šeima Tarybų Lietuvoje* (Vilnius: Mintis, 1974), p. 184; *Lietuvos statistikos metraštis,* Vol. XII (Vilnius: Centralinis statistikos biuras, 1940), p. 17; *Lietuvos TSR ekonomika ir kultūra 1972 metais* (Vilnius: Mintis, 1973), p. 17.
43. *Naujoji Romuva,* November 10, 1935, p. 815.
44. F. Kemėšis, "Religion and Nationality in Our Life," *Naujoji Romuva,* December 3, 1933, p. 964.
45. Ibid., p. 966.

46. A. Maceina, "The Nation and the State," *Naujoji Romuva,* March 19, 1939, p. 229.

47. Stasys Šalkauskis, "The Importance of Catholic *Weltanschauung* for Lithuania's Future," in [P. Mantvydas, ed.], *Krikščionybė Lietuvoje:praeitis, dabartis, ateitis,* pp. 78–79.

CHAPTER III
THE COLLAPSE OF THE LITHUANIAN STATE

1. Raymond J. Sontag and James S. Beddie, eds., *Nazi-Soviet Relations, 1939–1941.* Documents from the Archives of the German Foreign Office (Washington: Department of State, 1948), pp. 114–115. Hereafter cited as *Nazi-Soviet Relations.*

2. *Nazi-Soviet Relations,* p. 78.

3. Jane Degras, ed., *Soviet Documents on Foreign Policy* (London: Oxford University Press, 1953), p. 492. Hereafter cited as *Soviet Documents.*

4. *Nazi-Soviet Relations,* pp. 1–2; *Soviet Documents,* p. 329; Winston Churchill, *The Gathering Storm* (Boston: Houghton Mifflin, 1948), p. 367 ff.

5. *Nazi-Soviet Relations,* p. 7.

6. Ibid., p. 50.

7. Ibid., p. 69 ff.

8. Ibid., pp. 102–103; 107.

9. Ibid., p. 107.

10. Ibid., p. 267; for the story, see Bronis J. Kaslas, "The Lithuanian Strip in Soviet-German Diplomacy, 1939–1941," *Journal of Baltic Studies,* No. 3 (1973), pp. 211–225.

11. For the story of "mutual assistance pacts," see Albert N. Tarulis, *Soviet Policy Toward the Baltic States* (Notre Dame: Notre Dame University Press, 1959), p. 145 ff.

12. Ibid., p. 158; reported by the Vatican chargé d'affaires in Kaunas, in Pierre Blet et al., eds., *Le Saint Siège et la Situation Religieuse en Pologne et dans les Pays Baltes, 1939–1945,* Vol. III, Part I (The Vatican, 1967), p. 122.

13. *Soviet Documents,* pp. 380–382; *The New York Times,* November 15, 1939, p. 3.

14. The conflict over the city of Vilnius most recently has been analyzed by Alfred E. Senn, *The Great Powers, Lithuania, and the Vilna Question 1920–1928.*

15. *Documents on German Foreign Policy, 1918–1945. Series D (1937–1945),* Vol. VIII (Washington: Department of State, 1954), pp. 113, 12.

16. *The New York Times,* October 9, 1939, pp. 1, 7.

17. *Nazi-Soviet Relations,* p. 147.

18. See collection of documents by Dietrich A. Loeber, *Diktierte Option* (Neumuenster: Wachholtz Verlag, 1972).

19. *Soviet Documents,* p. 454.

20. V. Stanley Vardys, ed., *Lithuania Under the Soviets* (New York: F. A. Praeger, 1965), pp. 51 ff; Leonas Sabaliūnas, *Lithuania in Crisis* (Bloomington: Indiana University Press, 1972), pp. 179, 183 ff.

21. *Tarybų Lietuva,* November 6, 1940, p. 1.

22. V. Kancevičius, *1940 metų birželis Lietuvoje* (Vilnius: Mintis, 1973), pp. 109–110.

23. K. Domaševičius, *Tarybinio valstybingumo vystymasis Lietuvoje* (Vilnius: Mintis, 1966), p. 95.

· 24. *Darbininkų žodis* (Kaunas), June 29, 1940, p. 1; *Tiesa,* June 26, 1940.

25. U.S. Congress, House of Representatives, *Third Interim Report of the Select Committee to Investigate Communist Aggression and Forced Incorporation of the Baltic States into the USSR,* 83d Cong., 2d sess., pp. 353–354. Hereafter cited as *Baltic States.*

26. X. Y. [Mykolas Roemeris], *Lietuvos sovietizacija* (Augsburgas: no publ., 1949), p. 9.

27. Ibid., pp. 11 ff.

28. Text in *Baltic States,* p. 347.

29. *XX Amžius,* June 24, 1940, p. 10.

30. *Baltic States,* pp. 453–54.

31. Ibid., p. 458.

32. H. Šadžius et al., eds., *Lietuvos TSR istorija,* Vol. IV (Vilnius: Mintis, 1975), p. 359; Kancevičius, op. cit., pp. 81–93 passim.

33. Document of this operation is translated in *Baltic States,* pp. 468–70.

34. Text in *Darbininkų žodis,* April 13, 1940, p. 3; translated in *Baltic States,* pp. 445–48.

35. *Darbo Lietuva* (Kaunas), July 17, 1940, p. 1; *Vilniaus balsas,* July 9, 1940 (No. 158).

36. *Lietuvos TSR įstatymų, Aukščiausios Tarybos Prezidiumo įsakų ir vyriausybės nutarimų chronologinis rinkinys,* Vol. I, 1940–47 (Vilnius: Valstybinė Politinės ir Mokslinės Literatūros Leidykla, 1956), pp. 5–7. Hereafter cited as *Chronologinis rinkinys.*

37. Ibid., pp. 7–8.

38. Editorial, *Darbo Lietuva* (morning edition), July 14, 1940, p. 1.

39. *Šadžius,* op. cit., pp. 17–18; *The New York Times,* August 4, 1940, p. 29.

40. *The New York Times,* July 20, 1940, p. 14.

41. Ibid., July 23, 1940, p. 8.

42. Ibid., July 24, 1940, p. 1; *Department of State Bulletin,* Vol. III, No. 57 (1940), p. 48.

CHAPTER IV
THE CATHOLICS AND THE COMMISSARS: THE FIRST EXPERIENCES

1. *Tiesa,* June 26, 1940; *Darbininkų žodis,* June 29, 1940, p. 1.

2. Walter Kolarz, *Religion in the Soviet Union* (London: Macmillan and Company, 1961), pp. 182 ff.

3. J. Daulius, *Komunizmas Lietuvoje* (Kaunas, 1938), pp. 54 ff.

4. *Le Saint Siège,* Vol. III, Part I, No. 158 (Centoz and Maglione), pp. 206–61.

5. List of various anti-religious measures from J. Aničas, *Katalikiškasis klerikalizmas Lietuvoje 1940–1944 metais* (Vilnius: Mintis, 1972), pp. 32 ff.

6. *Le Saint Siège,* Vol. III, Part I, No. 165 (Centoz to Maglione), No. 168 (Maglione to Centoz), resp. pp. 266, 270; Aničas, *op. cit.,* pp. 27 ff.

7. Notes by Bishop V. Brizgys, p. 3.

8. *Darbo Lietuva,* July 19, 1940, p. 4.

9. *Darbininkų žodis,* July 29, 1940, p. 1.

10. *Chronologinis rinkinys,* p. 57.

11. *Lietuvos aidas* (morning edition), July 2, 1940, p. 1.

12. *XX Amžius,* July 2, 1940, p. 8.

13. *Darbo Lietuva,* July 23, 1940, p. 1; *Chronologinis rinkinys,* pp. 9–10.

14. M. Gregorauskas, *Tarybų Lietuvos žemės ūkis* (Vilnius: Politinės ir mokslinės literatūros leidykla, 1960), p. 77.

15. Ibid., p. 78; *Aničas,* op. cit., p. 29.

16. *Protocol,* July 2–3, 1940.

17. *XX Amžius,* July 8, 1940, p. 10.

18. *Darbo Lietuva,* August 28, 1940, p. 3.

19. Text in *Lietuvių archyvas,* Vol. I (Kaunas: Studijų biuras, 1942), pp. 28–30.

20. Text in loc. cit., pp. 33–34.

21. Text in A. Trakiškis, "The Situation of the Church and Religious Practices in Occupied Lithuania," in the appendix of U.S. House of Representatives, 83rd cong., 1st sess., *Hearings before the Select Committee to Investigate the Incorporation of the Baltic States into the USSR* (Washington, 1954), pp. 604–605.

22. Text in ibid., pp. 605–606.

23. Notes by Bishop Brizgys, pp. 13, 26.

24. *Lietuvių archyvas,* Vol. I (Kaunas: Studijų biuras, 1942), pp. 70–73; Cf. the report of Archbishop Juozapas Skvireckas to Pope Pius XII, October 10, 1941, in *Le St. Siège,* Vol. 3, Part I, No. 316. These figures did not include the priests of Vilnius Archdiocese. Since Vilnius had constituted a part of prewar Poland, the Vatican did not recognize the annexation of Vilnius by Lithuania *de jure,* and the Archbishop of Vilnius, Romuald Jałbrzykowski, a dedicated pastor and a man of Polish nationalist convictions, kept aggressively aloof from the Lithuanian bishops and did not attend their conferences. By the Vatican's decision, his successor, Archbishop Mečislovas Reinys, too, was forbidden to participate in these conferences. Archbishop Skvireckas therefore did not report to the Pope for the entire territory in the Lithuanian republic that the Germans later administered as *Generalkommissariat Litauen.* Archbishop Jałbrzykowski on February 14, 1942, reported to Cardinal Maglione that during the Soviet occupation of his archdiocese, the Soviets had imprisoned 15 priests. Six additional priests were killed by the retreating Russian military. See *Le Saint Siège,* Vol. 3, Part II, No. 355. Partial personal listing in Trakiškis, *op. cit.,* pp. 614–616.

25. *Notes* by Bishop Brizgys, p. 2.

26. *XX Amžius,* June 24, 1940, p. 3. Original in Stasys Yla, *Nerami dabartis ir ateities perspektyvos* (Marijampolė, 1940). The book left the printer already after Lithuania's occupation by the Red Army but was seized by the Communists.

27. See *XX Amžius,* June 26, 1940, p. 3.

28. *XX Amžius,* June 24, 1940, p. 10.

29. Petras Maldeikis, *Mykolas Krupavičius,* pp. 234ff.

30. *XX Amžius,* June 26, 1940, p. 10.

31. *Protocol,* July 2–3.

32. *Le Saint Siège,* Vol. II, Part I, No. 70, p. 271.

33. Document No. 2.

34. Document No. 3.

35. V. Brizgys, "The Theological Seminary in Kaunas During the Year of Bolshevism," *Lietuvių archyvas,* No. I, p. 58; *Le Saint Siège,* Vol. III, Part I, No. 214 (Brizgys to Orsenigo), pp. 312–15.

36. Document No. 4.

37. Jonas Aničas, *Katalikiškasis klerikalizmas Lietuvoje 1940–1944 metais* (Vilnius, 1972), p. 53.

38. *Le Saint Siège,* Vol. III, Part I, No. 199 (Brizgys to Centoz), pp. 293–94.

39. Notes, p. 26; *Le Saint Siège,* Vol. III, Part I, pp. 312–15.

40. Maldeikis, op. cit., pp. 237ff; *LE,* Vol. XIII (Boston, Mass: LE Leidykla, 1958), p. 238.

41. *Le Saint Siège,* Vol. III, Part I, No. 199 (Brizgys to Centoz), pp. 293–94.

42. *Protocol,* August 28–29, 1940, p. 2.

43. *Le Saint Siège,* Vol. III, No. 241 (Brizgys to Orsenigo), p. 294.

44. Ibid., Vol. IV, No. 257, p. 380.

45. Detailed list of districts to be transferred in *Aušra (samizdat),* No. 5 (1977), pp. 24–29. Only a small part of the promised territory was shifted over to Lithuanian jurisdiction in 1940–41. The remainder was never transferred.

46. *Tarybų Lietuva,* November 26, 1940, p. 1.

47. *Tarybų Lietuva,* November 12, p. 1.

48. Mečislovas Gedvilas, *Lemiamas posūkis, 1940–1945 metai* (Memoirs; Vilnius, 1975), p. 99.

49. Jonas Aničas, "The Realization of the Ideas of the Leninist Decree of Freedom of Conscience in Lithuania in 1940–1941," *LKP istorijos klausimai,* No. 9 (1970), p. 47.

50. *Le Saint Siège,* Vol. IV, No. 227 (Orsenigo to Maglione), p. 331.

51. *Lietuvių archyvas,* Vol. I, p. 61.

52. Ibid.

53. *Protocols* of these dates.

54. Texts in Trakiškis, op. cit., pp. 592–93.

55. Document No. 5. Decision recorded in *Protocol.*

56. *Lietuvių archyvas,* Vol. I, p. 65.

57. A. Merkelis, "Massive Deportation of Lithuanians into the USSR," *Lietuvių archyvas,* Vol. II (Kaunas, 1942), pp. 15–50. The author estimated the figures as "between 35–40,000'" (p. 48). However, the final tally showed the number of 34,260. See Juozas Brazaitis, "The First Soviet Occupation (1940–1941)," LE, Vol. XV, p. 369. See also *samizdat Aušra,* No. 1, p. 22, which lists 35,000.

58. Gedvilas, op. cit., p. 178.

59. Antanas Venclova, the dean of Lithuanian Communist writers and the former Minister of Education, in 1969, wrote that many arrests for deportation were made casually "as if security agencies had been infiltrated by enemies whose purpose was to provoke opposition to Soviet power among as many inhabitants of Lithuania as possible." See his *Vidurdienio vėtra* (Vilnius: Vaga, 1969), pp. 92–93. On April 8, 1962, *Izvestiia* published a page-long letter by Latvia's former Minister of Foreign Affairs Vilhelms Munters in which the deportations were disapproved as "exceedingly strong measures."

CHAPTER V
THE IRON CURTAIN DESCENDS: THE YEARS OF STALIN

1. The brief, but stormy, period of German occupation does not belong to the scope of the current study, though it deserves more attention from historians than shown so far. In the West, German policies toward the Church in Lithuania have not been studied at all, with the exception of the work of Victor Pavalkis, one of whose articles in English has been published by the *Journal of Baltic Studies,* No. 2 (1973), pp. 130–34. It was entitled "The Attitude of the Vatican Toward the German Church Policy in Lithuania During Its Occupation, 1941–44." In Soviet Lithuania, the years of German occupation have been screened mainly for their propagandistic value. The most comprehensive study on the Church during this period has been written by Jonas Aničas. For full citation, see ft. 9.

In Western languages, there exist some studies generally of the occupation period. Alexander Dallin's *German Rule in Russia, 1941–45: A Study of Occupation Policies* (New York: Macmillan, 1957) is still the best analysis of German policies in occupied areas. It includes a chapter on the Baltic countries. Nazi organization and policies in Lithuania, in reasonable detail, have been very competently examined by Seppo Myllyniemi, a Finnish historian, in *Die Neuordnung der baltischen Länder, 1941–44* (Helsinki: Societas Historica Finlandiae, 1973). In English, the best summary of the war years in Lithuania has been written by the late Zenonas Ivinskis, "Lithuania During the War: Resistance Against the Soviet and the Nazi Occupants," publ. in V. Stanley Vardys, ed., *Lithuania Under the Soviets* (New York: Frederick A. Praeger Publishers, 1965). Its pp. 66–84 cover the Nazi period.

2. B. Vaitkevičius et al., *Lietuvos TSR Istorija,* Vol. IV (Vilnius: Mokslas, 1975), p. 130.

3. A. Venclova, *Vidurdienio vėtra* (Memoirs by a prominent Lithuanian Communist functionary and writer), (Vilnius: Vaga, 1969), pp. 485, 489–98 ff.

4. *LE,* Vol. XVI, p. 447.

5. M. Raišupis, *Dabarties kankiniai* (Chicago: Krikščionis gyvenime, 1972), p. 393. Cf. Dr. J. Savasis, *The War Against God in Lithuania* (New York: Manyland Books, 1966), p. 23. Bishop Brizgys has described the circumstances under which the Germans evacuated the bishops in his memoirs of the war years, 1940–44, entitled *Katalikų Bažnyčia Lietuvoje 1940–1944 metais* (Chicago: [no publ.], 1977), pp. 168–70.

6. Venclova, op. cit., p. 515; see also p. 93.

7. *Pravda,* February 28, 1945, p. 2.

8. Gerhard Simon, *Church, State and Opposition in the U.S.S.R.* (Berkeley: University of California Press, 1974), pp. 57–58.

9. Cf. J. Aničas, *Katalikiškasis klerikalizmas Lietuvoje 1940–1944 metais* (Vilnius: Mintis, 1972), p. 204.

10. Paul Mailleux, "Catholics in the Soviet Union," in Richard H. Marshall, Jr. et al., eds., *Aspects of Religion in the Soviet Union, 1917–1967* (Chicago: University of Chicago Press, 1971), p. 370.

11. "Letter by Lithuanian Catholics to Pope Pius XII," in J. Daumantas, *Partizanai,* 2nd enl. ed. (Chicago: Į Laisvę Fondas, 1962), pp. 431–448. This was confirmed by the British Embassy in Moscow which in April of 1945

reported to the Vatican, at the latter's request, that "externally" the Catholic church in the Baltic States existed much as it had at the time of their annexation to the Soviet Union: "the hierarchy and organization are unaffected, worship is free and seminaries are open." The report added, however, that neither religious teaching nor publication were allowed though the latter was formally legal. See *Le St. Siège,* Vol. III, Part II, No. 598, pp. 901–2. The situation was indeed comparable to 1940, but to December rather than to August, the month of formal incorporation of Lithuania into the Soviet Union.

12. *Memoirs about Archbishop M. Reinys (samizdat* manuscript in Lithuanian).

13. Ibid.

14. Letter by Archbishop M. Reinys to Chairman of the Council of Commissars M. Gedvilas, Dec. 22, 1945. From ibid.

15. *Memoirs about Archbishop M. Reinys (samizdat).*

16. Jonas Aničas, *Socialinis politinis katalikų bažnyčios vaidmuo Lietuvoje 1945–1952 metais* (Vilnius: Lietuvos TSR Mokslų Akademija, 1971), p. 123.

17. *Pro Memoria* by Matulionis to Gedvilas, summer, 1945. Cf. references to it in Jonas Aničas, *The Establishment of Socialism in Lithuania and the Catholic Church* (Vilnius: Mintis, 1975), p. 87.

18. Cf. Aničas, op. cit., 1972, p. 158.

19. *Le Saint Siège,* Vol. III, Part II, No. 355 (Jałbrzykowski to Maglione), pp. 532–33.

20. Private information.

21. *Memoirs about Archbishop Reinys.*

22. Text in ibid., pp. 218–220.

23. On the Lithuanian guerrilla movement, see V. Stanley Vardys, "The Partisan Movement in Postwar Lithuania," *Slavic Review,* Vol. XXII, No. 3 (September 1963), pp. 499–522; K. V. Tauras, *Guerrilla Warfare on the Amber Coast* (New York: Voyager Press, 1962).

24. Ibid., p. 151.

25. Polish repatriation reported by Mečislovas Gedvilas, op. cit., pp. 262–63.

26. Quoted by George Weller, *Chicago Daily News,* August 17, 1961.

27. Further see Vardys, as in ft. 23.

28. J. Jarmalavičius, "The Struggle of the LCP Against the Influence of Clericalism in the Republic During the Period of Construction of Socialism," *LKP istorijos klausimai,* No. 17 (1975), p. 106.

29. Aničas, op. cit., 1971, pp. 78–79. Amnesty proposal was repeated on June 3, 1945. Ibid.

30. Ibid., p. 81.

31. Aničas, op. cit., 1971, p. 82.

32. *Pro Memoria* to Gedvilas.

33. Record of conference, text in Andrius Baltinis, *Vyskupo Vincento Borisevičius gyvenimas ir darbai* (Roma: Lietuvių Katalikų Mokslo Akademija, 1975), pp. 142–143.

34. Aničas, op. cit., 1975, p. 60.

35. Memoirs about Archbishop Reinys.

36. Text in ibid., pp. 222–231.

37. Aničas, op. cit., 1971, p. 25.
38. Aničas, op. cit., 1975, p. 61.
39. Jarmalavičius, *LKP istorijos klausimai,* No. 17 (1975), p. 103 ff.
40. Savasis, op. cit., p. 26; Daumantas, op. cit., pp. 485–87; Raišupis, op. cit., pp. 83–93. *Encyclopedia Lituanica* (Boston), Vol. I, pp. 387–88; Baltinis gives documentation and details, op. cit., p. 142 ff.
41. Baltinis, op. cit., p. 151.
42. Ibid., p. 152; testimony by Rev. K. Balčys, who, as an American citizen, was allowed to leave the Soviet Union early after World War II, *Lux Christi,* No. 3 (October–December 1951), pp. 15–16.
43. Raišupis, op. cit., pp. 91–93, 166–172; Savasis, op. cit., p. 26; *Encyclopedia Lituanica,* Vol. IV, pp. 432–433.
44. *Memoirs about Bishop Matulionis,* Lithuanian *samizdat,* p. 100.
45. *Memoirs about Archbishop Reinys;* Savasis, op. cit., p. 26; *Encyclopedia Lituanica,* Vol. IV, pp. 461–62.
46. Philip Friedman, *Their Brothers' Keepers* (New York: Crown Publishers, 1957), pp. 140, 214.
47. *Memoirs about Archbishop Reinys,* p. 205.
48. *Private Kelley by Himself* (London: Evans Brothers Ltd., 1954), pp. 192 ff.
49. *LKBK,* No. 10, Vol. II, p. 151.
50. Savasis, op. cit., p. 27.
51. Lithuanian Religious Information in Rome. *Aušra,* No. 1, p. 22 estimated the number of deportees as 200,000, but No. 1 of *Varpas* quotes the figure of 10% of the population or ca. 300,000.
52. Walter J. Ciszek, S.J., with Daniel L. Flaherty, S.J., *With God in Russia* (New York: McGraw-Hill, 1966), pp. 248 ff.
53. Joseph Scholmer, *Vorkuta* (London: Weidenfeld and Nicolson, 1954), pp. 129 ff.
54. Joseph Hermanovičius, M.I.C., *Raudonųjų stovyklose,* Lithuanian translation by K. A. Matulaitis, M.I.C. (London: Nida Press, 1969), pp. 150–51, 155, 191, 269.
55. *Memoirs about Archbishop Reinys,* p. 216.
56. Daumantas, op. cit., p. 436.
57. Text in *LKBK,* No. 15, pp. 42–44.
58. Ibid., p. 45.
59. *Memoirs about Archbishop Reinys,* p. 215.
60. *LKBK,* No. 10, Vol. II, p. 120.
61. *Conference in Defense of Peace of All Churches and Religious Associations in the USSR,* held in Troitse-Sergiyeva Monastery, Zagorsk, on May 9–12, 1952 (Zagorsk: Moscow Patriarchate, 1952), pp. 13, 108–221.

CHAPTER VI
DESTALINIZATION AND THE CHURCH:
LIBERALIZATION WITHOUT RELIGION

1. Cf. John A. Armstrong, *The Politics of Totalitarianism* (New York: Random House, 1961), pp. 242 ff; Wolfgang Leonhard, *Kreml ohne Stalin* (Cologne, 1959), pp. 108 ff.

2. V. Stanley Vardys, "The Role of the Baltic Republics in Soviet Society," in Roman Szporluk, ed., *The Influence of East Europe and the Soviet West on the USSR* (New York: Praeger, 1976), p. 160.

3. Pastanovlenie Tsk KPSS, "O krupnykh nedostatkakh v nauchno-ateisticheskoi propagande i merakh ee uluchsheniia," *O religii i tserkvi: sbornik dokumentov* (Moscow: Izdatel'stvo politicheskoi literatury, 1965), pp. 72–73.

4. Reprinted in *Kommunisticheskaia partiia i sovetskoe pravitel'stvo o religii i tserkvi* (Moscow: Gos. Izd. Pol. Lit., 1961), pp. 84–88.

5. See ft. 3 and 4.

6. Postanovlenie Tsk KPSS, "Ob oshibkakh v provedenii nauchno-ateisticheskoi propagandy sredi naseleniia," *O religii i tserkvi: sbornik dokumentov,* pp. 77–82.

7. *Tiesa,* October 21, 1956, cit. by Savasis, op. cit., p. 29.

8. *Tiesa,* December 11, 1956, cit. ibid., p. 30.

9. Ibid.

10. *L'Osservatore Romano,* April 2, 1954.

11. Savasis, op. cit., p. 31.

12. J. Rimaitis, *Religion in Lithuania* (Vilnius: Gintaras, 1971), p. 22.

13. *Sovetskaia Moldavia,* January 29, 1960, cited by Donald A. Lowrie and William C. Fletcher, "Krushchev's Religious Policy," in Marshall, op. cit., p. 133.

14. *Sovetskaia Belorussia,* February 18, 1960, cited ibid.

15. Simon, op. cit., p. 72.

16. S. Laurinaitis, S. Bistrickas, *Jų Dievas* (Vilnius: VPML Leidykla, 1962); the pamphlet describes the construction of the church, arrest, and trial from the Soviet point of view. The trial received wide coverage in the daily press.

17. *LKBK,* No. 2, Vol. I, p. 86.

18. *La Chiesa in Lituania,* a pro-memoria submitted by Bishop Vincentas Brizgys to the Second Vatican Council, p. 15.

19. *LKBK,* No. 20, Vol. III, pp. 221–228.

20. *LKBK,* No. 23, p. 12.

21. Ibid., p. 15.

22. *LKBK,* No. 6, Vol. I, p. 268 has statistical data.

23. Cf. *LKBK,* No. 10, Vol. II, pp. 113–122.

24. Formally, these visitations were outlawed on June 16th, 1965, by a decree of the Council of Ministers of the Lithuanian SSR. See V. A. Kuroedov et al., eds., *Zakonodatel'stvo o religioznykh kultakh,* 2d ed. (Moscow: Iuridicheskaia literatura, 1971), p. 252. This collection was printed for official use only.

25. "O meropriatiakh po usileniiu ateisticheskogo vospitaniia naseleniia," *O religii i tserkvi: sbornik dokumentov,* 1965, pp. 85–92.

26. Kolarz, op. cit., p. 198.

27. A. Barkauskas, *Komunistas* (Vilnius), No. 11, 1964, pp. 6ff.

28. In the Lithuanian SSR, this provision is a part of Art. 143 of the republic's criminal code. See *Baudžiamasis kodeksas* (Vilnius: Mintis, 1970), pp. 143–44; 281–82.

29. Mailleux in Marshall, op. cit., p. 378.

30. *Baudžiamasis kodeksas,* pp. 382–83.
31. Raišupis, op. cit., p. 295.
32. Rimaitis, op. cit., p. 21.
33. See an article about this translation in *Zhurnal Moskovskoi Patriarkhii,* No. 4, 1974, pp. 72–76.

CHAPTER VII
THE CONSTITUTION, THE LAW AND THE CHURCH

1. English text of Soviet translation of the 1936 document in *Constitution (Fundamental Law) of the Union of Soviet Socialist Republics* (Moscow: Foreign Languages Publishing House, 1956). Text of the new (1977) Soviet Constitution in *Moscow News Supplement* to issue No. 42 (2770), 1977.
2. J. Rimaitis, *Religion in Lithuania* (Vilnius: Gintaras, 1971), p. 30.
3. "I Cattolici In Lituania," *La Ragione* (Italy), December, 1975.
4. *Moscow News,* June 19–26, 1976, p. 10.
5. V. M. Chkhikvadze, ed., *The Soviet Form of Popular Government* (Moscow: Progress Publishers, 1972), p. 20.
6. Ibid.
7. Transcript of the trial; for the text see *The New York Times,* October 15, 1968; see also speech by Vladimir K. Bukovsky at his trial in Pavel Litvinov, *The Demonstration in Pushkin Square* (Boston: Gambit, 1969), pp. 123–27.
8. Cited in *Draugas* (Chicago), February 21, 1975, p. 1.
9. "Ob oshibkakh v provedenii nauchno-ateisticheskoi propagandi sredi naseleniia," Postanovlenie TsK KPSS, November 10, 1954, *O religii i tserkvi: sbornik dokumentov* (Moscow: Izdatel'stvo politicheskoi literatury, 1977), p. 75.
10. Statute of the Communist party of the Soviet Union, Kommunisticheskaia partiia Sovetskogo Soiuza. *XXII Sezd Kommunisticheskoi Partii Sovetskogo Soiuza,* 17–31 Oktiabria 1961 goda. Stenograficheskii otchet. Vol. III (Moscow: Gosudarstvennoe izdatel'stvo politicheskoi literatury, 1962), pp. 238–355. Quoted text in I. 2. g.), p. 338.
11. Program of the Communist party of the Soviet Union, ibid., pp. 229–335. Quoted text in V. l. e), p. 319.
12. Aksamitas, ed., *Religijos ir ateizmo klausimai* (Vilnius: Valstybinė politinės ir mokslinės literatūros leidykla, 1963), p. 333. The author cited is E. Juškys.
13. Ibid., p. 363.
14. Dietrich A. Loeber, "The Legal Position of the Church in the Soviet Union," *Studies on the Soviet Union,* Vol. 9, No. 2, 1969, p. 17.
15. *Polnoe sobranie sochinenii,* 5th ed., Vol. VII, 1959, p. 173.
16. Translation of Šeškevičius' defense speech in *The Violations of Human Rights in Soviet Occupied Lithuania: A Report for 1971* (Delran: Lithuanian American Community, Inc., 1972), pp. 42ff; *AS* 882.
17. Loeber, loc. cit., p. 17.
18. A. Veščikovas, *Tarybiniai įstatymai apie religinius kultus* (Vilnius: Valstybinė politinės ir mokslinės literatūros leidykla, 1963), p. 7; *Instructions of 1969,* Art. 11, p. 5; *Zakonodatel'stvo,* Art. 8, p. 152. For these entries see ft.

21 and 23; G. R. Gol'st, *Religiia i zakon* (Moscow: Iuridicheskaia literatura, 1975), pp. 40–43, 60.

19. English texts of the decree of 1918 and the law of 1929 in the Appendix, pp. 233–44. The amended law of 1929 was published in *Vedomosti Verkhovnogo Soveta RSFSR*, No. 27, item 572 (July 3, 1975). Its English translation in *Review of Socialist Law*, Vol. I, No. 3 (September 1975), pp. 223–234, and *Radio Liberty Research* 155/76 (March 31, 1976). For interpretation, especially as it applies to the Orthodox church, see the report prepared by Eugen Voss, editor of *Glaube in der 2. Welt*, and his staff, and transl. by Michael Bourdeau and Walter Sawatsky; further see the letter by Lev Regelson and Rev. Gleb Yakunin to Dr. Philip Potter of the World Council of Churches. Both in U.S. Cong., House of Representatives, 95th Cong., 1st Sess., *Hearings Before the Commission on Security and Cooperation in Europe*, Vol. II (Washington, 1977), pp. 221–248. See also Gerhard Simon, "Das neue sowjetische Religionsgesetz," *Osteuropa*, No. 1, 1977, pp. 3–19.

20. *LKBK*, No. 26 (1977), pp. 20, 23; *Laikas ir įvykiai*, No. 5, 1977, p. 13; text in *LTSR Aukščiausios Tarybos ir Vyriausybės žinios*, No. 22 (August, 1976), item 191–93. Russian text in *AS* No. 2841v.

21. Ibid., No. 1, Vol. I, p. 68; No. 26, p. 22; I. P. Shafarevich, *Zakonodatel'stvo o religii v SSSR* (Paris: YMCA Press, 1973), pp. 9ff, 77. Changes in the statute that governed the Russian Orthodox church are found in Robert Stupperich, ed., *Kirche und Staat in der Sowjetunion* (Witten: Luther Verlag), pp. 41–5; these changes reflected new instructions of the Council of Religious Affairs.

22. V. A. Kuroedov, A. S. Pankratov, G. R. Gol'st, D. M. Nochvin, eds., *Zakonodatel'stvo o religioznykh kul'takh*, 2nd ed. (Moscow: Iuridicheskaia literatura, 1971). Hereafter cited as *Zakonodatel'stvo*.

23. Religijų Reikalų Tarybos prie TSRS Ministrų Tarybos Įgaliotinis Lietuvos Respublikai. *Del kultų įstatymų taikymo tvarkos* (Vilnius: rotoprint at the National State Library of the Lithuanian SSR, 1969). Hereafter cited as *Instructions* of 1969.

24. "Instruktsiia po primeneniiu zakonodatel'stva o kul'takh," *Zakonodatel'stvo*, pp. 150–160.

25. English translation of this summary in Vytautas Vaitiekūnas, *A Survey of Developments in Captive Lithuania in 1965–1968* (New York: Committee for a Free Lithuania, n.d.), pp. 149–50.

26. For example, on Nov. 30, 1973, the Communist party's daily *Tiesa* published a translation of "The Law and Religious Cults" that originally had appeared in the Nov., 1977, issue of Moscow's Russian language journal *Agitator*. In 1970, "Mintis," a Vilnius publishing house, printed an authoritative 80 page pamphlet on the same topic entitled *Tarybiniai įstatymai apie religinius kultus ir sąžinės laisvė* by J. Aničas and J. Rimaitis.

27. *Lietuvos Tarybų Socialistinės Respublikos Baudžiamasis Kodeksas* (Vilnius: Mintis, 1970), pp. 85–87; 281–83. Cited as *Kodeksas*.

In a book, *Bor'ba s narusheniiami zakonodatel'stva o religioznykh kul'takh* (Moscow: Iuridicheskaia literatura, 1967), written by V. V. Klochkov "for official use," the author explains how the Criminal code should be used to organize and to adjudicate cases of alleged violations of religious laws. This volume is not available for public information but was published as a manual for the perusal of "the prosecutor's office, the courts, officers of public order enforcement, the KGB, councils on religious affairs, and divisions of local government committees that have corresponding responsibilities" (second page of the inside title page).

28. *Zakonodatel'stvo,* pp. 78–83; cf. Otto Luchterhandt, "Die Rechtsgrundlagen der sowjetischen Staatskirchenbehörden," *WGO. Monatshefte für osteuropäisches Recht,* Vol. 18 (1976), pp. 315–330.

29. Ibid.

30. Ibid., pp. 168–69.

31. Changes in the law are examined by Walter Sawatsky, "The New Soviet Law on Religion," *Religion in Communist Lands,* Vol. 4, No. 2 (Summer, 1976), pp. 4–11. He also traces the very interesting history of revisions of the law of 1929.

32. A. I. Ivanov, P. K. Lobazov, *Politika sovetskogo gosudarstva po voprosam religii i tserkvi* (Moscow: Znanie, 1973), p. 58.

33. Oxana Antic, "Assistant Chairman of Council on Religious Affairs Comments on Churches in the USSR," *Radio Liberty Research* 91/77 (April 20, 1977). The article relates Vasilii Furov's speech as reported by the *Khronika tekushchikh sobytii.*

34. One documented diaspora case stems from 1959. It involved a parish of largely Lithuanian deportees in Krasnoyarsk where Father Ciszek replaced a mysteriously expired Lithuanian priest who had served the unregistered parish. Later, it was discovered that this priest was Father Jonas Gustas, a Salezian father, and former professor of theology in Vilnius. See Walter J. Ciszek, S.J., with Daniel L. Flaherty, S.J., *With God in Russia* (New York: McGraw-Hill Book Company, 1966), pp. 252–53.

Believers have current difficulties with registration in Lithuania as well. In 1976, the *Chronicle* reported cases of attempted recovery or reconstruction of church buildings that had been gutted by fire or closed down and a concomitant refusal to register religious associations. In one instance, as soon as the believers organized to apply for registration, a local collective farm took over the vacant church building and remodeled it into a mill. In another case, believers were ordered to join a neighboring association. See, for example, *LKBK,* No. 21, Vol. III, p. 320; No. 22, Vol. III, p. 370.

35. Ivanov, Labozov, op. cit., p. 52.

36. Ibid., p. 54.

37. *Zakonodatel'stvo,* p. 151. This provision has not been expressly or implicitly overridden by the new law of 1975–76; Gol'st, op. cit., pp. 29, 60–61.

38. Cf. *LKBK,* No. 26 (1977), pp. 44–45; *Zakonodatel'stvo,* pp. 161, 168.

39. See *Zakonodatel'stvo,* pp. 106–120; Gol'st, op. cit., pp. 62–64.

40. J. Aničas, J. Rimaitis, *Tarybiniai įstatymai apie religinius kultus ir sąžinės laisvė* (Vilnius: Mintis, 1970), p. 38; Gol'st, op. cit., pp. 26–31.

41. Text in *LKBK,* No. 11, Vol. II, p. 202; cf. Gol'st, op. cit., pp. 32–33.

42. *Zakonodatel'stvo,* p. 151; *Instructions of 1969,* p. 4; the new law granted the right of veto to government agencies only.

43. *Zakonodatel'stvo,* pp. 110–20.

44. *LKBK,* No. 9, Vol. II, p. 102.

45. Ibid., No. 11, Vol. II, pp. 200–201.

46. Ibid., pp. 182–83.

47. Reported in *Draugas* (Chicago). Cf. private information.
48. Cf. *LKBK*, No. 10, Vol. II, p. 119.
49. *Tiesa*, November 22, 1974, p. 2.
50. *LKBK*, No. 10, Vol. II, p. 119.
51. Ibid.
52. *LKBK*, No. 26 (1977)," pp. 41–44.
53. Ibid., p. 42. Text of Stalinist contract, pp. 39–41.
54. *Vedomosti Verkhovnogo Soveta RSFSR*, Vol. 12 (1966), items 219, 220, 221, pp. 219–220.
55. *Kodeksas*, pp. 281–83.
56. V. Kuroedov, "Church and State Separated in the USSR," *Nauka i Religiia*, No. 6, 1968, p. 7.
57. *Izvestiia*, January 31, 1976, p. 5.
58. *Nutarimai ideologiniais klausimais* (Vilnius: LKPCK, 1971), p. 13.
59. *LKBK*, No. 3, Vol. I, pp. 127–39.
60. *Tiesa*, January 23, 1969, p. 4.
61. *Sovetskaia Litva*, February 27, 28, March 1, April 1, 1973; also *A Chronicle of Human Rights in the USSR*, No. 2 (April–May, 1973), pp. 27–28. They were convicted under Art. 144, par. 1 and 2 of the Lithuanian Criminal code, Art. 212 of the Latvian and 227 of the Russian republic's code. Sentences ranged from 3 to 5 years of prison.
62. Rev. L. Povilonis was charged with the violation of Arts. 94, 181 and 164 and a law of December 25th, 1958. He received eight years of prison. His assistant, Rev. B. Burneikis, was charged with identical violations and was sentenced to four years. Mssrs. B. Alsys, A. Paškevičius, J. Mikalauskas, J. Krivickas, and Ms. A. Klovaitė were found guilty of violating Art. 177, 117 and 94 and were sentenced from five years to six months respectively. These civilians were managers of either factories, warehouses, or construction and housing enterprises.
63. *LKBK*, No. 8, Vol. II, p. 56. In 1963, Rev. Šeškevičius received a prison sentence for manufacturing devotionals, crucifixes, etc. *Švyturys*, No. 5, March 15, 1963, pp. 18–19.
64. Ibid., No. 19 (p. 23 of the original).
65. Iuridicheskaia Komissiia pri Sovete Ministrov RSFSR. *Kodeks o brake i sem'e RSFSR* (Moscow: Iuridicheskaia literatura, 1969), pp. 4–5; this is the federal family code of 1969.
66. For example, in 1961, two Lithuanian Adventist parents had their children taken away to be educated by the state because they refused to allow the children to attend school on a Sabbath. See *Tarybinis mokytojas*, May 21, 1961, p. 3. This of course could be done in an earlier day and on different grounds.
67. Testimony by Evgeny Bresenden, a Christian-Pentecostalist emigrant from the USSR, U.S. Congress, House of Representatives, 95th Cong., 1st sess., *Hearings before the Commission on Security and Cooperation in Europe*, Vol. II (Washington, 1977), p. 20. Gol'st, op. cit., p. 102ff, and Klochkov, op. cit., pp. 235–36, stress the importance of the Family code in the "struggle" against violations of laws on religion and indicate its value in proceedings that involve possible loss of parental rights because of such violations.

CHAPTER VIII
ATHEISM: APPARATUS AND METHODS OF PROMOTION

1. Cited in *Voprosy nauchnogo ateizma,* Vol. 4 (1967), p. 34.

2. P. Aksamitas, ed., *Religijos ir ateizmo klausimai* (Vilnius, 1963), p. 363.

3. Reasons for abolishing religion are in detail spelled out in the editorial of *Pravda* of August 21, 1959, which is usually reprinted in collections of party and government statements on religion. See *Kommunisticheskaia partiia i sovetskoe pravitel'stvo o religii i tserkvi* (Moscow: Gosizdat politicheskoi literatury, 1961), pp. 95–99. The editorial explains that religion interferes with the construction of communism, keeps people away from participating in this construction process, hurts the development of the "friendship of nations," helps bourgeois nationalists, damages labor discipline. For a Western interpretation of Soviet hostility to religion, see Bohdan Bociurkiw, "The Shaping of Soviet Religious Policy," *Problems of Communism* (May–June, 1973), p. 38. Religion's "anti-scientific" character and its Western commitment is explained by E. Maiat, "Nekotorye voprosy ateisticheskoi propagandy v sovremennikh usloviakh," *Politicheskoe samoobrazovanie,* No. 6 (1974), esp. pp. 82, 87–88.

4. Aksamitas, op. cit., p. 330.

5. *Nutarimai ideologiniais klausimais* (Vilnius: LKPCK, 1971), p. 13.

6. Antanas Gaidys in J. Aničas, ed., *Ideologinė kova ir jaunimas* (Vilnius: Lietuvos TSR Mokslų Akademija, 1972), p. 100.

7. J. Minkevičius, "Methodological Aspects of the Confrontation of Science and Religion," *Lietuvos TSR Mokslų Akademijos Darbai,* No. 4 (1976), p. 36.

8. Cf. Maiat, loc. cit., p. 84.

9. A. Okulov, "Ateisticheskoe vospitanie," *Pravda,* January 14, 1972, p. 4.

10. *Pravda,* editorial of August 21, 1959.

11. See the Program of the Communist party of the Soviet Union. Text in Herbert Ritvo, ed., *The New Soviet Society* (New York: The New Leader, 1962), esp. pp. 203–207.

12. A. I. Kholmogorov, *International Traits of Soviet Nations,* transl. in *Soviet Sociology* (Winter–Spring, 1972–73), pp. 268–271.

13. M. S. Fazylov, *Religiia i natsional'nye otnosheniia* (Alma-Ata: Khazakstan, 1969), pp. 3–4.

14. This role of atheism is totally overlooked in Western literature on Soviet atheist activities. For example, see the competently researched comprehensive work on atheist propaganda by David E. Powell, *Anti-Religious Propaganda in the Soviet Union: A Study of Mass Persuasion* (Cambridge: The MIT Press, 1975).

15. J. Barzdaitis, *Ateizmas Lietuvoje* (Vilnius: Mintis, 1967), p. 90.

16. "I kiss Žalys," a story by J. Maciukevičius, *Pergalė,* No. 2 (February, 1975).

17. *Tiesa,* March 5, 1960, p. 2.

18. Joan Delany, "Origins of Anti-Religious Organizations," in Richard H. Marshall, Jr., *Aspects of Religion in the Soviet Union: 1917–1967* (Chicago: University of Chicago Press, 1971), pp. 103ff.

19. Donald A. Lowrie and William C. Fletcher, "Khrushchev's Religious Policy, 1959–1964," in Marshall, op. cit., p. 131.
20. K. Surblys, *Lietuvos KP veikla, ugdant socialistinę darbininkų klasę* (Vilnius: Mintis, 1976), p. 81.
21. *Nutarimai* as in ft. 5, pp. 14–15.
22. Ibid.
23. Report of the Ideological Commission of the CPSU CC, *Partiinaia zhizn*, No. 2 (January, 1964), pp. 22–26. Transl. in *Current Digest of the Soviet Press*, March 25, 1964, pp. 3–4; L. Il'ichev, "Formirovanie nauchnogo mirovozzrenia i ateisticheskoe vospitanie," *Kommunist*, No. 1 (1964), pp. 23–46.
24. "Dobro pozhalovat'," *Nauka i religiia*, No. 8 (1967), p. 20; *Mažoji Lietuviškoji Enciklopedija*, Vol. I (Vilnius: Mintis), p. 109.
25. *Mažoji Lietuviškoji Enciklopedija*, Vol. III (Vilnius: Mintis, 1971), p. 922.
26. These and other statistical data about "Žinija" from the following sources: (1) as in ft. 18; (2) V. Pšibilskis in *LKP istorijos klausimai*, No. 16 (1971), pp. 68–75; (3) P. Mišutis in *Nauka i religiia*, No. 3 (1972), p. 30; (4) S. Nekrašius, *Sovetskaia Litva*, January 20, 1973, p. 4; (5) *Laikas ir įvykiai*, No. 23 (1975), p. 17; (6) *Tiesa*, April 2, 1977, p. 3.
27. *Tiesa*, April 2, 1977, p. 3.
28. Surblys, op. cit., pp. 81–82.
29. *Tiesa*, April 3, 1974, p. 2.
30. "In the Central Committee of the LCP: An Important Link in Ideological Work," *Komunistas*, No. 7 (1975), p. 22.
31. V. Baltrūnas, "An Important Stage in the Life of Komsomol," *Komunistas*, No. 1 (1976), p. 22.
32. "To Inculcate Deep Atheist Convictions of the School Youth," *Tarybinis mokytojas*, May 13, 1977, p. 1.
33. A. Barkauskas, "Osushchestvlenie Leninskikh ideii ob ateisticheskom vospitanii v prakticheskoi deiatel'nosti partiinikh organizatsii," *Voprosy nauchnogo ateizma*, Vol. 10 (Moscow: Mysl', 1970), pp. 155–56.
34. N. Liutkevičiūtė, "Concern for Man, His Consciousness," *Komunistas*, No. 10 (1975), p. 35. In detail, the work of the Council to Coordinate Scientific-Atheist Propaganda at the Central Committee of the Communist party of Lithuania is discussed by P. P. Mišutis, "Opyt sozdaniia sistemy ateisticheskogo vospitaniia v Litovskoi SSR," *Voprosy nauchnogo ateizma*, Vol. I (1966), pp. 202ff.
35. *LKBK*, No. 10, Vol. II, p. 117; *LKBK*, No. 11, Vol. II, p. 200.
36. Cf. Liutkevičiūtė in loc. cit., p. 33.
37. MLI, Vol. I, p. 108.
38. *Laikas ir įvykiai*, No. 17 (September 1975), p. 11.
39. Jonas Aničas, *Socialinis politinis katalikų bažnyčios vaidmuo Lietuvoje 1945–1952 metais* (Vilnius: LTSR Mokslų Akademija, 1971), p. 132.
40. Ibid., p. 133.
41. Further see V. Stanley Vardys, "Catholicism in Lithuania" in Marshall, op. cit., p. 391.
42. *Tarybinis mokytojas*, June 9, 1963, p. 2.
43. *LKBK*, No. 19, pp. 27–30.

44. *LKBK,* No. 18, pp. 29–31; the story of Father Ylius in *Dievas ir tėvynė,* No. 2, pp. 8–55; No. 4, pp. 61–70.

45. Dr. J. Savasis, *The War Against God in Lithuania* (New York: Manyland Books, 1966), p. 107.

46. *LKBK,* No. 10, Vol. II, pp. 150–55.

47. P. Mišutis, "Na nauchnoi osnove," *Nauka i religiia,* No. 3 (1972), p. 34.

48. Aničas, op. cit., p. 150.

49. Ibid., p. 151.

50. See, for example, *LKBK,* No. 8, Vol. II, pp. 33–34.

51. *LKBK,* No. 2, Vol. I, pp. 90 ff.

52. *LKBK,* No. 8, Vol. II, pp. 45 ff.

53. Ibid., p. 44.

54. *LKBK,* No. 22, Vol. III, pp. 394–96.

55. *Tarybinis mokytojas,* August 5, 1961, p. 4.

56. P. Pečiūra, *Tradicijos vakar ir šiandien* (Vilnius: Mintis, 1974), pp. 55 ff.

57. V. Boev, A. Ugrinovich, "Obriady v sovetskom obshchestve," *Nauka i religiia,* No. 3 (1975), p. 37.

58. Ibid.

59. Pečiūra, op. cit., pp. 84–87.

60. Ibid., p. 120.

61. No. 12 (December 1968), pp. 19–78.

CHAPTER IX
EMERGENCE OF RELIGIOUS PROTEST MOVEMENT:
THE STRUGGLE FOR LIBERAL SOCIETY

1. Lithuanian text in Daumantas, op. cit., pp. 432–448; German text in *Anima* (Switzerland, 1950).

2. English edition (with photostatic copies of the original), *Mary Save Us: Prayers Written by Lithuanian Prisoners in Northern Siberia,* transl. by Kęstutis A. Trimakas (New York: Paulist Press, 1960). The prayerbook was secured from behind the then Iron Curtain in 1959 by Father L. Jankus (1912–1968), executive director of United American Lithuanian Relief Fund, Inc., that has sent food and clothing packages to Lithuania's needy, among them former opponents of the Soviet regime in Lithuania. Rev. Jankus also took care of the prayerbook's translations and publication. There possibly exists a causal relationship between these activities and charges of "killing hundreds of Jews" that the Soviets made against the priest in a Soviet Lithuanian court in 1964. Tried *in absentia,* Rev. Jankus was given a 15 year prison sentence. Jankus was tried with five other defendants, some of whom already had served sentences on similar charges. The priest declared to *The New York Times* that in 1941, he was a local Red Cross director [in Skuodas, Lithuania] and in this role was "permitted to deliver [to the arrested Jews] clothing and food donated by the townspeople." See *The New York Times,* March 9, 1964, p. 7; March 16, 1964, p. 3. The regime has continued propagandizing against the United American Lithuanian Relief Fund in the press. See A. Miniotas, *Atsargiai, Balfas!* (Vilnius: Mintis, 1973). For further information on the prayerbook and Rev. Jankus, see *LE,* Vol. XXXVI, pp. 263–64, 371–72.

3. See *Tiesa,* December 22, 1960; *Literatūra ir menas,* No. 52 (1960); *Tarybinis mokytojas,* No. 19 (1960).

4. Abraham Brumberg, ed., *In Quest of Justice* (New York: Praeger Publishers, 1970), pp. 5ff. It contains texts of petitions and statements by early Soviet dissenters. Foreign relations aspects of dissent are examined by Frederick C. Barghoorn, *Detente and the Democratic Movement in the USSR* (New York-London: The Free Press, 1976).

5. Text in Brumberg, op. cit., pp. 232–240.

6. Text in *A Cry of Despair from Moscow Churchmen* (New York: Synod of Bishops of the Russian Orthodox Church Outside of Russia, 1966), pp. 5ff.

7. *Vedomosti Verkhovnogo Soveta Sovetskikh Sotsialisticheskikh Respublik,* No. 17 (1415), April 24, 1968, pp. 243–48.

8. *LKBK,* No. 9, Vol. II, p. 105.

9. See Russian gubernatorial correspondence reprinted in A. Alekna, *Žemaičių vyskupas Motiejus Valančius,* 2nd ed. with introduction by V. Trumpa and appended texts (Chicago: Lituanistikos institutas, 1975).

10. *LKBK,* No. 9, Vol. II, pp. 103–105.

11. Ibid.

12. Ibid.

13. Text in *Draugas,* April 2, 1970, p. 3.

14. Ibid.

15. *AS* 692.

16. *AS* 7661 highlights in VHR 71, pp. 34–35.

17. *LKBK,* No. 1, Vol. I, pp. 65–69.

18. *The Situation of the Church in Lithuania, 1975,* p. 9 (Mimeographed by Lithuanian Religious Aid, Inc.).

19. *LKBK,* No. 1, Vol. I, p. 64.

CHAPTER X
CONFRONTATION WITH THE GOVERNMENT AND
MOBILIZATION OF OPINION

1. J. Savasis, *Kova už Dievą Lietuvoje* (Putnam: Immaculate Press, 1963), p. 71; other personal information about Father Šeškevičius from Raišupis, op. cit., pp. 222ff; *Švyturys* (Vilnius), March 15, 1963, pp. 18–19; *AS* 652, p. 5.

2. *LKBK,* No. 17, p. 2.

3. Description of his trial from *AS* 652; his defense speech in *AS* 882.

4. It never was. It was the secret instruction of the Council on Religious Affairs, reprinted in *Zakonodatel'stvo,* pp. 150ff; also the *Lithuanian Instructions of 1969.* Further see chapter on the law.

5. *AS* 652, p. 8.

6. *AS* 653, pp. 6–7.

7. Information about Zdebskis trial in *LKBK,* No. 1, Vol. I, pp. 27ff.

8. Full text in *LKBK,* No. 1, Vol. I, p. 31.

9. Text in ibid., pp. 32–33. See also *The New York Times,* September 27, 1971.

10. Information about the trial in ibid., pp. 33ff; *Khronika tekushchikh sobytii,* No. 21, p. 17, reported the arrest, No. 23, pp. 23–25, reported the trial; also *The New York Times,* Sept. 27, 1971, p. 5; Nov. 27, 1971, p. 10.

11. For the text of Zdebskis' defense speech see *LKBK,* No. 1, Vol. I, pp. 41–50; also *AS* 1067.

12. Text of defense speech in *LKBK,* No. 1, Vol. I, pp. 51–54; also *AS* 1203.

13. *LKBK,* No. 1, Vol. I, p. 70.

14. *LKBK,* No. 1, Vol. I, pp. 51 ff; *KTS,* No. 23, p. 25.

15. Excerpt from an interview conducted by the British Broadcasting Corporation, repr. in *Congressional Record,* June 3, 1976, p. E 3096.

16. Details for each listed case in *LKBK,* No. 7, Vol. I, pp. 307–13; No. 8, Vol. II, p. 54; No. 1, Vol. I, pp. 57–58; No. 3, Vol. I, pp. 148–51; No. 1, Vol. I, pp. 62–63. The government's attitude toward such activities by the clergy has not changed in at least more than a decade. *Tarybinis mokytojas* of June 25, 1961, p. 3, reported the following actions termed "illegal": organizing "a community of Jesus Heart"; organization of children's church choir; urging prayers for atheists.

17. On October 22, 1975, Ms. Eugenija Žukauskaitė of Kaunas was fined 40 roubles for teaching catechism to children. The fine was imposed by the "administrative commission" of Požėla district in the city of Kaunas. *LKBK,* No. 20, Vol. III, pp. 244–246. On November 16, 1976, Rev. A. Svarinskas of Viduklė was fined 50 roubles for obstruction of traffic that allegedly resulted from a religious procession he led, *LKBK,* No. 26, pp. 22–23. Rev. L. Jagminas of Šventybrastis on September 9, 1976, was warned for preparing children for their first communion, *LKBK,* No. 24, p. 34. Similarly warned was Rev. A. Jakūbauskas of Pociūnėliai, ibid.,pp. 36–39. On July 5, 1975, Rev. A. Petrauskas of Raguva was fined 30 roubles for catechisation of children, ibid., p. 42. On June 14, 1974, Rev. P. Baltuška of Daugailiai was fined 30 roubles for inviting ten priests from other districts to perform religious services in his parish. *LKBK,* No. 12, Vol. II, p. 232. Rev. P. Adomonis of Obeliai was fined 50 roubles for preparing young people for confirmation, ibid., p. 233. Rev. J. Kazlauskas of Stakliškės on June 28, 1974, was fined 50 roubles for teaching religion, ibid., p. 241. *LKBK* has reported many more than the cases listed here.

18. Text in *LKBK,* No. 2, Vol. I, pp. 76–80; *The New York Times,* May 22, 1972, p. 5.

19. *The New York Times,* July 23, 1972, p. 9.

20. March 28, 1972, p. 1.

21. Texts in *LKBK,* No. 6, Vol. I, pp. 246 ff and No. 7, Vol. I, p. 297.

22. Text in *LKBK,* No. 4, Vol. I, pp. 189–192.

23. *LKBK,* No. 8, Vol. II, pp. 22–25.

24. *LKBK,* No. 5, Vol. I, pp. 228–230.

25. *LKBK,* No. 3, Vol. I, pp. 141–42.

26. *LKBK,* No. 2, Vol. I, pp. 101–103.

27. *LKBK,* No. 2, Vol. I, pp. 105–107.

28. *LKBK,* No. 7, Vol. I, pp. 293–97.

29. *LKBK,* No. 2, Vol. I, pp. 87–88; No. 3, Vol. I, p. 143.

30. Excerpts in *LKBK,* No. 2, Vol. I, pp. 81 ff; full text in *AS* 1109.

31. *LKBK,* No. 2, Vol. I, p. 82; text in *AS* 1204.

CHAPTER XI
THE CHRONICLE OF THE CATHOLIC CHURCH OF LITHUANIA:
THE VOICE OF THE MOVEMENT

1. *LKBK,* No. 13, Vol. II, p. 254.
2. *LKBK,* No. 11, Vol. II, p. 45.
3. *LKBK,* No. 22, Vol. III, p. 389; No. 9, Vol. II, p. 84. After his release from prison, Father Zdebskis was continuously harassed by the authorities. In 1976, he was accused of drunken driving, refused a blood test after demanding it, arbitrarily charged with driving under the influence of alcohol, and deprived of a driver's license. He protested the charge, insisting that "in 24 years of my work no one has ever seen me drinking." *LKBK,* No. 22, Vol. III, pp. 374–76. However, this charge was repeated in the official press. On April 24, 1977, p. 4, the Communist party daily *Tiesa* carried an article written by the newest ex-priest (one of the 20 who quit in 30 years) in which he asserted that Zdebskis liked "to sip cognac" and that the suspension of Zdebskis' driver's license did not indicate any persecution of believers or violation of civil rights. See also *LKBK,* No. 23, pp. 39–43. Zdebskis' license was suspended for 18 months.
4. *LKBK,* No. 17, Vol. III, p. 62.
5. Petitioning did not cease entirely, but continued in the form of individual or small group letters. One of the latest collective petitions was the letter by 66 clergymen, or two-thirds of the Vilnius diocese clergy, written to the Commissioner for Religious Affairs in Lithuania on August 25, 1975. It asked for the return of Bishop Steponavičius to Vilnius. See *LKBK,* No. 21, Vol. III, pp. 284–86. On April 8, 1976, several hundred believers of Simnas asked the Commissioner for Religious Affairs for a free admissions policy to the theological seminary and for the publication of a catechism and other religious books. *LKBK,* No. 23, pp. 38–39. Further see Appendix B.
6. *LKBK,* No. 12, Vol. II, p. 222.
7. The first mention of a Lithuanian prisoner is found in No. 8, p. 22 (AS). Balys Gajauskas, the prisoner, was reported to have signed a letter to the General Prosecutor of the USSR explaining why Aleksander Ginzburg, the dissident writer who was confined in the same camp, began his hunger strike.
8. Antanas Terleckas, *Respect My Rights,* from the original Lithuanian appeal by the author to KGB chief Y. V. Andropov, transl. and publ. by the Lithuanian World Community, Chicago, 1976; Lithuanian text in *LKBK,* No. 21, Vol. III, pp. 291–313; on Yakir's arrest and trial see *The New York Times,* June 22, 1972, p. 2; August 28, 1973, p. 1; August 30, 1973, p. 8; September 2, 1973, p. 12.
9. *LKBK,* No. 14, Vol. II, pp. 362–63; No. 21, pp. 261–71. *The New York Times,* December 10, 1975, p. 14; December 11, p. 11; December 13, p. 7.
10. See *A Chronicle of Human Rights in the USSR,* No. 14 (April–May, 1975), pp. 20–21.
11. *Khronika tekushchikh sobytii,* No. 22, p. 15 *(AS).*
12. *A Chronicle of Human Rights in the USSR,* No. 11–12 (September–December, 1974), pp. 30–31; *LKBK,* No. 13, Vol. II, pp. 249–250. Also see *Delo Kovalëva* (New York: Khronika, 1976).
13. *Khronika tekushchikh sobytii,* No. 22, p. 16 *(AS).*

14. *Samizdat* text of interrogation in *Index* (London), No. 3 (Autumn, 1975), pp. 56–61, passim; see *Delo Tverdokhlebova* (New York: Khronika, 1976).

15. Text in *Religiia i ateizm v SSSR* (August–September, 1976), pp. 8–16. The letter to the Presidium of the Supreme Soviet of the USSR (with a copy for the World Council of Churches) was signed by representatives of Pentecostals, Adventists, Baptists, Church of Christ, Catholic church of Lithuania, Russian Orthodox church. The Lithuanian signers were: Rev. K. Pukėnas of Nemenčinė, Rev. S. Valiukėnas of Vilnius, E. Volončuvičius, V. Petkus (also a member of the Lithuanian Helsinki Committee for whom the KGB is preparing a criminal case), J. Petkevičienė, J. Petkevičius, J. Šilaitis, M. Jurevičius. News about Petkus comes from L. Alekseeva, a member of the Helsinki group in Moscow, who was forced to emigrate. See "Liudi stali men'she boiatsia, chem prezhde," *Posev,* March, 1977, pp. 5ff. Petkus was arrested.

16. *Aušra,* No. 5 (45), p. 44; see also Reuter's release from Moscow, VHR 76, p. 25; *AS* 2841a. Further see RL 12/77 (January 19, 1977) which characterizes the group and RL 242/77 (October 19, 1977) which summarizes its statements. The group's initial documents in full have been published in *LKBK,* No. 29 (1977) (statement on religious persecution) and *Draugas,* Sept. 7–22, 1977. See also testimony by Tomas Venclova and Liudmila Alekseeva in *Hearings Before the Commission on Security,* op. cit., Vol. I, pp. 53–62; and Vol. IV, pp. 34–35. A photostatic copy of a letter by Soviet Consul A. Ermakov in San Francisco that informed Tomas Venclova of the order of the Presidium of the Supreme Soviet of the Soviet Union to strip the poet of Soviet citizenship as of June 14, 1977, has been published by *Draugas,* Sept. 8, 1977, p. 1; *LKBK,* No. 29, p. 31.

17. *LKBK,* No. 19, Vol. II, pp. 179–80.

18. *LKBK,* No. 15, Vol. II, p. 357.

19. *Khronika tekushchikh sobytii,* No. 5, p. 27 *(AS).*

20. *LKBK,* No. 9, Vol. II, p. 109.

21. *LKBK,* No. 18, Vol. III, p. 121.

22. *LKBK,* No. 24, pp. 22, 49.

23. *LKBK,* No. 10, Vol. II, p. 122.

24. *LKBK,* No. 4, Vol. I, pp. 166–67.

25. Ibid.

26. Ibid.

27. *LKBK,* No. 8, Vol. II, p. 10.

28. *LKBK,* No. 10, Vol. II, p. 113.

29. *LKBK,* No. 15, Vol. II, p. 359.

30. *LKBK,* No. 10, Vol. II, p. 123.

31. *LKBK,* No. 2, Vol. I, p. 117.

32. *LKBK,* No. 5, Vol. I, p. 242.

33. *LKBK,* No. 7, Vol. I, p. 321.

34. *LKBK,* No. 6, Vol. I, p. 280.

35. *LKBK,* No. 7, Vol. I, p. 329.

36. *LKBK,* No. 16, p. 45.

37. *Soviet Analyst,* Vol. 4, No. 14 (July 3, 1975), p. 6.

38. *LKBK,* No. 10, Vol. II, pp. 116–17.

39. *LKBK,* No. 20, Vol. III, p. 241.

40. Venclova's letter in *LKBK*, No. 19, Vol. III, pp. 180–82; Žilius' letter in No. 22, pp. 403–404. Žilius' letter to party Secretary Griškevičius was published after he left.

41. *LKBK*, No. 19, Vol. III, pp. 183–87.

42. See, for example, *LKBK*, No. 19, Vol. III, pp. 195–198; No. 16, Vol. III, pp. 33–35; No. 18, Vol. III, pp. 151–53; No. 10, Vol. II, pp. 150–55.

43. *LKBK*, No. 19, Vol. III, pp. 207–208; No. 21, Vol. III, pp. 330–31. *Aušra* has reported the closing of Lithuanian schools in Belorussia. The *Chronicle* has reported petitions by Rodunė district Lithuanians of the Belorussian SSR to transfer their ethnographically Lithuanian district to the Lithuanian SSR. *LKBK*, No. 19, Vol. III, p. 208.

44. *LKBK*, No. 8, Vol. II, p. 36. Further destruction of crosses reported in, among others, *LKBK*, No. 12, Vol. II, pp. 242–44; No. 18, Vol. III, pp. 142–145; No. 23, pp. 57–58; No. 23, p. 25; No. 18, Vol. III, pp. 142–46, 148.

45. *LKBK*, No. 17, Vol. III, pp. 112–13.

46. *LKBK*, No. 10, Vol. II, p. 116.

47. *LKBK*, No. 20, Vol. III, pp. 241–42; No. 22, Vol. III, pp. 401–02. The first case reported a strike by auto transport workers, the second, a strike on a collective farm.

48. *LKBK*, No. 8, Vol. II, pp. 46–47.

49. Ibid., p. 47.

50. *LKBK*, No. 20, Vol. III, pp. 228–30, reported the publication of its first issue.

51. *LKBK*, No. 24, p. 50.

52. *LKBK*, No. 4, Vol. I, p. 177.

53. English text in *A Chronicle of Human Rights in the USSR*, No. 11 (September–December, 1974), pp. 30–31; see also *LKBK*, No. 13, Vol. II, pp. 249–250.

54. *LKBK*, No. 9, Vol. II, pp. 103–104.

55. *LKBK*, No. 17, Vol. III, p. 98.

56. See, for example, *LKBK*, No. 21, Vol. III, pp. 316–17; 372, 389, 323; No. 11, Vol. II, p. 189; No. 9, Vol. II, p. 95; No. 8, Vol. II, pp. 33–34.

57. Especially *LKBK*, No. 26, pp. 2–5.

58. For example, *LKBK*, No. 21, Vol. III, pp. 372–373; No. 26, pp. 18, 25–26, 30–31, 50.

59. Appeal to Cardinals A. Samoré and J. Slipyi on episcopal appointments, No. 23, pp. 1–5.

60. *LKBK*, No. 15, Vol. II, p. 359.

61. *LKBK*, No. 4, Vol. I, p. 173.

62. *LKBK*, No. 19, p. 1. The visit of Cardinal Bengsch has been in some detail reported in the German Catholic press. See, for example, *Klerusblatt* (Munich), October 15, 1975, p. 239ff; also *Katholische Korrespondenz*, No. 15–16 (April 13, 1976), pp. 7–8.

63. *LKBK*, No. 4, Vol. I, p. 166.

64. Ibid., p. 172.

65. *LKBK*, No. 9, Vol. II, p. 78.

66. *LKBK*, No. 10, Vol. II, p. 115.

67. "S.O.S.," *LKBK*, No. 26, p. 1.

68. *LKBK*, No. 19, Vol. III, pp. 177–78. The *Chronicle* kept repeating this

warning during the entire year of 1977. In issue No. 28 which reached the West in November, the editors of the journal wrote that "We have an impression that in order not to spoil relations with Moscow's atheists, [world] Catholics have chosen the tactics of silence. The Holy Father is supposed to have said 'It is necessary to pray and to wait quietly and with patience.' We are used to being misled and do not believe that the Holy Father would have given us such counsel." The duty of the Church, the editorial further pointed out, is to evangelize. How can this duty be reconciled with silence? "How can we keep silent and wait when the atheists neither stay silent nor wait?" (p. 13).

69. Ibid.

70. Ibid., p. 8.

71. *LKBK*, No. 28, p. 7. The *Chronicle* further wrote: "They [these Protestant sects] discovered the best methods [of apostolate] for the Soviet Union. They are spiritually and materially supported by their brothers living abroad. They have developed a spirit of apostolate that is afraid neither of suffering nor death; they are provided with the most recent press; they have created a disciplined organization with diversely prepared leaders for groups, villages, urban communities, provinces, Republics, etc." (pp. 13–14).

72. Ibid.

73. Ibid., p. 8.

74. Ibid., p. 21.

75. Ibid., pp. 21–22.

76. Ibid., p. 4.

77. Ibid., p. 22.

CHAPTER XII
CATHOLICISM AND NATIONALISM IN THE 1970s

1. Cf. V. Stanley Vardys, ed., *Lithuania under the Soviets* (New York: F. A. Praeger, 1965), esp. pp. 237–59; V. Stanley Vardys, "The Baltic Peoples," *Problems of Communism* (September–October 1967), pp. 55–64; V. Stanley Vardys, "Recent Soviet Policy Toward Lithuanian Nationalism," *Journal of Central European Affairs*, No. 3 (October 1963), pp. 313–331.

2. Further see V. Stanley Vardys, "The Role of the Baltic Republics in the Soviet Union," in Roman Szporluk, ed., *The Influence of East Europe and the Soviet West on the USSR* (New York: Praeger Publishers, 1976), pp. 147–149.

3. For a more extensive discussion see V. Stanley Vardys, "Modernization and Baltic Nationalism," *Problems of Communism* (September–October 1975), esp. pp. 44–47.

4. *Tiesa*, March 4, 1971, p. 7.

5. *Pravda*, January 24, 1969, p. 3. Lithuanian Communists of this stripe very likely are similar to Slovene Communists in 1944–45, who objected to the Serbian manned tanks shooting at Catholic crossroad chapels, on grounds that these chapels represented "part of their national culture." See Dusko Doder *(The Washington Post)*, "Slovenes Communist Mystery." *The Norman Transcript*, August 1, 1976, p. 44.

6. *The New York Times*, November 29, 1970, p. 1; December 1, 1970, p. 1. For the story of Kudirka's attempted defection see Algis Rukšėnas, *Day of Shame* (New York: David McKay Co., 1973); U.S. Congress, House of

Representatives, 91st Cong., 1st sess. *Attempted Defection by Lithuanian Seaman Simas Kudirka.* Hearings before the Subcommittee on State Department Organization and Foreign Operations of the Committee on Foreign Affairs; also *Report* of the same. Kudirka served about four of the ten years, mostly in the notorious Vladimir prison east of Moscow, but in August of 1974, he was released and in November of the same year, was allowed to leave for the United States together with his mother and his family. The happy ending of this dramatic story was the result of work of Kudirka's sympathizers in New York with the cooperation of the U.S. Government. The committee of sympathizers discovered that Kudirka's mother had been born in Brooklyn, New York. The United States acknowledged citizenship for his mother and for him, and the Soviets released him at American request. In the Soviet Union, however, Moscow prevented Kudirka's mother from communicating with the American Embassy, but with the help of Sergei Kovalëv and other Russian dissidents, these obstacles were overcome. In December of 1975, Kovalëv was tried and sentenced in Vilnius. The story of Kudirka's return to the United States in *The New York Times,* November 6, 1974, p. 1 ff. Kudirka's plan to defect may have been influenced by other, then publicized attempts to escape the Soviet Union. On June 15, 1970, Edward Kuznetsov and a group of Jews had planned to seize a plane; on October 15, two Lithuanians, the father and son Pranas and Algirdas Brazinskas, succeeded in capturing a plane and forcing it to land in Turkey; on November 9, just two weeks before Kudirka's own try, a young couple, Vytautas and Aldona Simokaitis, failed in their attempt to hijack a plane to fly to Sweden, the land that Kuznetsov had intended to reach. Kuznetsov's story in Edward Kuznetsov, *Prison Diaries* (New York: Stein and Day, 1975); on Simokaitis see *The New York Times,* January 20 and February 1, 1971; *KTS,* No. 17, pp. 40, 68; No. 18, p. 29; No. 19, p. 34; No. 22, p. 9. Story of the Brazinskas in *The New York Times,* October 18, 1970; October 21, 1970; see also *Pravda,* October 16, 1970, p. 6.

7. Text of this speech in *International Herald Tribune,* August 7–8, 1971, pp. 1–2.

8. *Pravda,* January 24, 1969, p. 3.

9. *Tiesa,* December 4, 1970, p. 4; *Literatūra ir menas,* November 21, 1970; *Kultura* (Paris), September 1972, p. 103. Two other linguists died shortly afterward. *Kultura* suggested that one of them died because he was an inconvenient witness to Kazlauskas' case. Ibid. See also *Aušra,* No. 2, p. 24.

10. *Tiesa,* April 26, 1972, p. 4.

11. Greeting to the Lithuanian Komsomol conference by the Central Committee on the Lithuanian Communist Party, *Tiesa,* March 16, 1972, p. 1.

12. *KTS,* No. 8, pp. 15–16.

13. *KTS,* No. 7, p. 27; No. 8, p. 17; *AS* 110.

14. Lots were drawn, according to one reliable source, on May 1, at the same park where the self-immolation occurred. According to this source, the lot specified the time and place for the action.

15. This account is based on sources as in ft. 26; *KTS,* No. 26, pp. 22–24; *KTS,* No. 27, pp. 17–20; "O kaunasskikh sobytiiahk (rasskaz ochevidtsa)," *Posev,* No. 2 (February 1973), 18; *The New York Times,* May 22, p. 5; May 25, p. 4; May 28, IV, p. 2; June 14, p. 1 ff, 1972; *Draugas* (Chicago), June 7, p. 3.

16. Text of this report in *The Violation of Human Rights in Soviet Occu-*

pied Lithuania: A Report for 1975 (Glenside: The Lithuanian American Community, 1976), pp. 10–24; the item cited is on p. 23.

17. Eyewitness report, from a European source reprinted in *Draugas* (Chicago), June 7, 1973, p. 3.

18. *LKBK*, No. 3, Vol. I, p. 159.

19. *Tiesa*, June 3, 1972, p. 1.

20. For a report on these three, see *KTS*, No. 26, p. 24; *The New York Times* of July 6, 1972, p. 3, reported the self-immolation of still another Lithuanian worker A. Kukavičius. Private communication revealed the name of the fifth as Vaclovas Čarneckis, born in 1942. His suicide occurred in Pažėrai.

21. Jurašas, op. cit., p. 23.

22. *Literatūra ir menas*, July 18, 1972, p. 3; *KTS*, No. 26, p. 25.

23. *Tiesa*, May 21, 1972, p. 4.

24. TASS International Service, May 26, 1972, as reported by Foreign Broadcast Information Service, Vol. III, No. 103, 1972, p. J13; on May 27, Vilnius radio in its English broadcasts to Europe and North America repeated the same in a longer and more detailed story. See *FBIS*, Vol. III, No. 105 (1972), pp. J3–4.

25. *LKBK*, No. 3, Vol. I, p. 159.

26. "Nashe interview" in *Sovetskaia Litva*, May 27, 1972, p. 4. The same interview appeared in *Tiesa* of the same date.

27. *Sovetskaia Litva*, June 3, 1972, p. 1.

28. *Tiesa*, May 27, 1972, p. 2.

29. Ibid.

30. *Tiesa*, June 20, 1972, p. 2.

31. Ibid.

32. *Tiesa*, August 26, 1972, p. 4.

33. Jonas Bielinis, *Tiesa*, July 15, 1972, p. 4.

34. *Literatūra ir menas*, July 8, 1972, p. 3.

35. Ibid.

36. Ibid. Six months later he made another almost identical statement. See *Literatūra ir menas*, January 27, 1973, p. 3.

37. See Česlovas Kantauskas in *Tiesa*, March 10, 1973, p. 2; *LKBK*, No. 17, Vol. III, pp. 113–14.

38. *Komunistas*, October, 1975, pp. 76–79.

39. *Tiesa*, October 5, 1972, p. 4. The other sentenced defendants were: A. Kačinskas, 24; R. Baužys, 18; V. Žmuida, 24; J. Prapuolenis, 21; J. Macijauskas, 19; V. Urbonavičiūtė (under age; younger than 18);V. Truškauskas (age not given) was separately charged in another case that allegedly involved group rape. The Soviets never explained how this was related to the May events.

40. *LKBK*, No. 10, Vol. II, p. 128.

41. Armenian groups appear to be somewhat more politically oriented. See *KTS*, No. 16, p. 10.

42. *LKBK*, No. 10, Vol. II, pp. 128 ff.

43. *Tiesa*, March 17, 1974, p. 4.

44. *LKBK*, No. 9, Vol. I, pp. 85–88.

45. Terleckas' letter to Jurii Andropov, chief of KGB, op. cit., p. 17; text also in *LKBK*, No. 21, Vol. III, pp. 291–313.

46. *LKBK*, No. 21, Vol. III, pp. 273–84.

47. Tomas Venclova, Kęstutis Jokubynas in *Draugas,* Sept. 7, 1977, p. 1; resp. Sept. 10, p. 4; also *LKBK,* No. 29, p. 31.

CHAPTER XIII
THE KREMLIN vs THE *CHRONICLE:*
PERSONALITIES OF THE PROTEST MOVEMENT

1. "Tserkovniki prisposablivaiutsia," *Sovetskaia Litva,* August 12, 1972, p. 3; *The New York Times,* August 15, 1972, p. 5.
2. *LKBK,* No. 5, Vol. I, p. 207ff.
3. *Laikas ir įvykiai,* No. 8 (April 1976), pp. 18–19.
4. *LKBK,* No. 6, Vol. I, p. 261.
5. Peter Wohl, *Christian Science Monitor,* July 21, 1973, p. 6.
6. Michael Parks, *Baltimore Sun,* May 17, 1973.
7. *LKBK,* No. 26, p. 18.
8. Ibid.
9. *Tarbinis mokytojas,* May 13, 1977, p. 1.
10. *LKBK,* No. 10, Vol. II, p. 222; No. 26, p. 18.
11. *LKBK,* No. 7, Vol. I, p. 298.
12. *LKBK,* No. 12, Vol. II, p. 209.
13. *Tiesa,* November 22, 1974, p. 2. Text of such letters in *LKBK,* No. 12, Vol. II, pp. 210–13; No. 15, Vol. III, pp. 366–69.
14. *LKBK,* No. 13, Vol. II, pp. 258–297.
15. Ibid., p. 257.
16. *LKBK,* No. 16, pp. 7–8; *Tarybinis mokytojas,* January 24, 1975.
17. *Laikas ir įvykiai,* No. 23 (December, 1975), p. 18.
18. *LKBK,* No. 23, pp. 10, 12, 56.
19. *Ibid., pp. 40–45;* No. 25, p. 8, 35–38, 50.
20. *LKBK,* No. 3, Vol. I, p. 158.
21. *LKBK,* No. 6, Vol. I, pp. 258–59.
22. "In Whose Voice? From the Courtroom," *Tiesa,* March 17, 1974, p. 4.
23. *LKBK,* No. 13, Vol. II, p. 304.
24. *LKBK,* No. 8, Vol. II, pp. 9–22; No. 9, Vol. II, pp. 78–84.
25. *LKBK,* No. 13, Vol. II, p. 304.
26. *Tiesa,* December 3, 1973, p. 4; also *Sovetskaia Litva,* December 23, 1973, p. 4.
27. *LKBK,* No. 13, Vol. II, p. 249.
28. *LKBK,* No. 14, Vol. II, pp. 326–63; *The New York Times,* December 24, p. 3; December 28, p. 4; December 30, p. 6, 1974.
29. *LKBK,* No. 13, Vol. II, p. 304.
30. The trial is recorded in No. 13 of *LKBK,* Vol. II, pp. 249–304; definitions of crimes taken from the Lithuanian SSR penal code, ed. of 1970.
31. *LKBK,* No. 13, Vol. II, p. 266.
32. *Tiesa,* December 29, 1974, p. 4. The article, entitled "The Slanderers Punished," lists the charges, briefly tells about the trial, but does not mention the *Chronicle,* merely publication of "slanderous fabrications," etc.
33. *LKBK,* No. 16, pp. 1–2.
34. *LKBK,* No. 17, pp. 1–14.
35. *LKBK,* No. 13, Vol. II, p. 303.

36. Ibid., p. 294.
37. *LKBK,* No. 17, Vol. III, p. 72.
38. Samuel K. Padover, ed., *A Jefferson Profile as Revealed in His Letters* (New York: John Day, 1956), p. 120.
39. *LKBK,* No. 21, Vol. III, pp. 261–284; *The New York Times,* December 10, 1975, pp. 9, 14; December 11, pp. 10, 11, 44; December 12, p. 14; December 13, p. 7. *Delo Kovalëva* (New York: Khronika, 1976) gives the speech of the prosecutor at the scientist's trial, charges, testimony of witnesses, Kovalëv's statement, sentence. In Lithuania, party journal *Komunistas* published an interview with Judge M. Ignotas who presided over the dissident's trial. In this interview, Ignotas summarized the Soviet point of view. See "The Slanderer Sentenced," *Komunistas,* No. 4 (1976), pp. 74–76.
40. Ibid., p. 284.
41. Ibid.
42. *LKBK,* No. 25, pp. 1–9.
43. *LKBK,* No. 26, p. 7.
44. *LKBK,* No. 29, p. 10; *Tiesa,* Aug. 21, 1977.
45. See his story in *LKBK,* No. 10, Vol. II. pp. 137–39; No. 20, Vol. III, pp. 213–221; *Aušra,* No. 2, pp. 19–22.

CHAPTER XIV
EFFECTS OF SOVIET RELIGIOUS POLICY ON THE CHURCH:
AN INSTITUTIONAL BALANCE SHEET

1. Statistics on Lithuanian churches from Lithuanian Religious Information in Rome; cf. Soviet figures in J. Rimaitis, *Religion in Lithuania* (Vilnius: Gintaras, 1971), p. 18; *Elenchus omnium ecclesiarum et universi cleri provinciae ecclesiasticae Lituanae pro anno Domini 1940* and *Catalogus ecclesiarum et cleri archidioecesis Vilnensis pro anno Domini 1939.*
2. *LKBK,* No. 18, Vol. III, p. 123.
3. See *L'Osservatore Romano,* March 19, p. 1. The *Chronicle* wrote that until 1950, the government closed down approximately 50 Catholic churches in Vilnius and Kaunas and forbade the use of chapels. No. 18, Vol. VI, p. 123.
4. *LKBK,* No. 12, Vol. II, p. 211.
5. *LKBK,* No. 23, p. 38.
6. *LKBK,* No. 18, Vol. III, p. 127.
7. *LKBK,* No. 18, pp. 2–7; *Laikas ir įvykiai,* No. 16 (1975), p. 15; *Tiesa,* Aug. 13, 1975, p. 4.
8. Account by artist V. Žilys, a recent emigrant from the Soviet Union, entitled "Centers of Russification in Lithuania," *Draugas,* May 15, 1974, p. 4.
9. See V. Stanley Vardys, "Recent Soviet Policy toward Lithuanian Nationalism," *Journal of Central European Affairs,* Vol. XXIII, No. 3 (Oct., 1963), p. 319ff.
10. *LKBK,* No. 4, II, p. 173ff.
11. Cit. by J. Savasis, *Kova už Dievą Lietuvoje* (Putnam: Immaculate Press, 1963), p. 61.
12. J. Aničas, "Realizatsiia reshenii II Vatikanskogo sobora v katolicheskoi tserkvi v Litve," *Katolitsizm v SSSR i sovremennost'* (Vilnius: Akademiia nauk Litovskoi SSR, 1971), p. 91.

13. *LKBK,* No. 5, Vol. I, p. 237.

14. *LKBK,* No. 4, Vol. I, p. 197; No. 7, Vol. I, p. 306.

15. Ibid.

16. Sources of statistical information on the clergy as in ft. 1.

17. Casimir Pugevičius (ed.), *World Lithuanian Roman Catholic Directory* (Putnam, Conn: Lithuanian Roman Catholic Priests' League of America, 1975), p. 102. The total number of priests given in this Directory for 1974 is 773. The discrepancy results from the fact that the Directory's figures are from September of 1974.

18. Ibid.

19. Data from Lithuanian Religious Information in Rome. Recent data, 1968–72, also given by the *Chronicle;* see *LKBK,* No. 7, Vol. I, p. 268; No. 22, Vol. III, p. 389. Details of pre-1968 enrollment in J. Raišupis, op. cit., p. 295.

20. *LKBK,* No. 26, p. 2. The *Chronicle* complained, however, that of the 30 candidates for admission, the authorities passed only the worst young men. On prospects for candidates, see Raišupis, op. cit., p. 295ff.

21. *Sovetskaia Litva,* Aug. 12, 1972, p. 2. This is a general Soviet phenomenon. In the past, hostile government policies and frequently brutal administrative behavior have driven believers of various churches into underground worship despite the existence of officially approved services. A good example of this is the Russian Orthodox Church. The emergence of the Russian Orthodox underground, according to William C. Fletcher, was due largely to such government policies and pressures. See his *The Russian Orthodox Church Underground* (London: Oxford University Press, 1971), pp. 1, 99.

22. *LKBK,* No. 2, Vol. I, p. 112. The journal openly spoke about the work of the underground church in No. 28, p. 18ff.

23. *LKBK,* No. 12, Vol. II, pp. 216–17; No. 19, Vol. III, p. 175.

24. V. Privalskii and A. Uzlian, "Sviataia rumba," *Ogonek,* No. 39 (Sept., 1960), p. 20ff.

25. *Kalba Vilnius,* No. 5 (1974) cit. in *LKBK,* No. 9, Vol. II, p. 65.

26. *LKBK,* No. 22, Vol. III, p. 389.

27. "The Knights of the Swamp," *Tiesa,* Jan. 18, 1974, p. 2; K. Urbonas in *Tiesa,* May 7, 1976, p. 2, cont. on May 8, p. 2; S. Laurinaitis, "Truth about Monasteries," *Komjaunimo tiesa,* April 1, 1971, p. 2, cont. on April 2, p. 2.

28. Document, typewritten in Lithuania, that explains the duties and prayer intentions of "friends of the Eucharist." In private possession.

29. *LKBK,* No. 28, p. 18.

30. For the *Chronicle's* opposition, see *LKBK,* No. 24, p. 10; for Butkus's warning to theology students see ibid., p. 27. The Rector's concern with his personal standing in the Papal Curia came to light in the summer of 1977, when Rome received a copy of a letter Butkus had written to Commissioner Tumėnas. In this letter, dated June 13, 1977, Butkus protested that he had never given the interview which Moscow's foreign language weeklies *Moscow News* and *Nouvelle de Moscou* had published in June of 1976. (See Chapt. VII, ft. 4). In this interview, Butkus was quoted as praising freedom of religion and availability of religious publications in Lithuania. This letter represented the Rector's apparent reaction to the *Chronicle's* translation and criticism of the *Moscow News* interview (No. 24 of October 1, 1976, pp. 1–11). After Butkus's protest became known in the West, the *Chronicle* responded by publishing it

together with a statement that it was "impossible to believe" the letter was not a result of conspiracy between the Rector and the government, because usually protests of similar nature resulted in the punishment of their authors. Butkus, however, continued in the position of Rector unassailed (*LKBK*, No. 29, p. 23, fall of 1977). Some Lithuanians in the West have considered this letter a genuine expression of protest against Soviet abuse (see the letter and story in *Draugas*, the daily of Catholic American Lithuanians, of July 20, 1977, p. 1) that throws favorable light on the Rector's personality; however, Lithuania's *Chronicle* disagrees. The interests of Msgr. Butkus and the Soviet government may coincide. The Rector's unusual, even daring protest against the government newspapers' alleged behavior should probably be read against the background of the impending selection of new bishops to fill the vacant Lithuanian diocesan seats. The letter was probably intended to strengthen in the Vatican the otherwise very controversial Butkus candidacy to one of those seats; this objective would make the collusion between Msgr. Butkus and Commissioner Tuménas very likely because both, apparently, sought a bishop's miter for the Monsignor.

31. *LKBK*, No. 19, Vol. III, p. 170.

32. Jonas Aničas, *Socialinis politinis katalikų bažnyčios vaidmuo Lietuvoje 1945-1952 metais* (Vilnius: LTSR Mokslų Akademija, 1971), p. 160.

33. Jonas Aničas, *Laikas ir įvykiai*, No. 23 (December, 1975), p. 18; *Tiesos kelias*, No. 1, p. 32.

34. Ibid., p. 5ff.

35. Text in *LKBK*, No. 12, Vol. II, pp. 211-212.

36. *Tiesa*, Nov. 22, 1974, p. 2.

37. *Bažnyčia ir LKB Kronika*, p. 2.

38. It is also possible that he had far reaching influence on the ill and dejected Bishop Paltarokas in the latter's last years as administrator, encouraging Paltarokas' accommodating posture. Krivaitis also functions as the chairman of the Lithuanian Commission on Liturgy and as secretary of the Lithuanian Episcopal Council. He is regarded by some as a "resourceful and diplomatic leader in church affairs" and takes credit for the recent Soviet permission to publish several volumes of documents as well as the new translation of the New Testament. See Rev. K. Balčys, "Welcome to the Administrator of Vilnius Archdiocese," *Vienybė*, March 7, 1975.

39. Cf. "Priests of Occupied Lithuania in Rome," *Tėviškės žiburiai*, June 2, 1965, p. 6.

40. A. Rudzinskas, "Moshenniki v gernykh sumanakh," *Pravda*, Jan. 14, 1962, p. 6.

41. Rimaitis, op. cit., p. 21.

42. *LKBK*, No. 4, Vol. I, p. 167.

43. *LKBK*, No. 19, Vol. III, p. 173.

44. Ibid., p. 172.

45. *LKBK*, No. 4, Vol. I, p. 168.

46. Ibid., p. 167.

47. Ibid., p. 169.

48. Ibid., p. 168.

49. *L'Osservatore Romano*, May 7, 1976.

50. *LKBK*, No. 12, Vol. II, p. 209.

51. *LKBK,* No. 19, Vol. III, p. 173.

52. Segretaria de Stato, Ufficio Centrale di Statistica della Chiesa, *Raccolta di Tavole Statistiche 1969* (The Vatican: Tipografia Poliglotta Vaticana, 1971), p. 113. The number of Lithuanian Catholics listed in the summary table was 420,000. When the author asked about this unusually low figure, Secretary of State Archbishop Benelli replied in a letter that this was a "typographical error." For all Vatican figures, see: *Annuario Pontificio per l'anno 1975* (Citta del Vaticano: Tipografia Poliglotta Vaticana, 1975), entry for the Telšiai diocese.

53. Reported by the Lithuanian Human Rights Commission chaired by Dr. Domas Krivickas, U.S. Congress, House of Representatives, 95th Cong., 1st sess., *Hearings Before the Committee on Security and Cooperation in Europe,* Vol. II, pp. 52–53. The Commission's data is based on Bishop Vincent Brizgys, *Religious Conditions in Lithuania under Soviet Russian Occupation,* 2nd ed. (Chicago: Lithuanian Catholic Press, 1975).

54. Professor Bociurkiw compiled these figures for a paper entitled "Catholics in the Soviet Union Today" that has been published in *A Symposium: Religion in the USSR* (Munich, 1975).

55. *Financial Times,* April 5, 1977.

56. Aničas' statement reported in *LKBK,* No. 15, Vol. II, p. 325.

57. Hubertus Guske, "Die katholische Kirche in der Litauischen SSR," *Begegnung,* No. 1 (1969), p. 12.

58. V. Pomerantsev, "Vchera i segodnia," *Nauka i religiia,* No. 4 (April, 1966), pp. 5ff.

59. Pečiūra, op. cit., p. 119.

60. Mišutis in *Mokslas ir gyvenimas,* No. 3 (1967), p. 5.

61. In Kaišiadorys diocese the number was 1,972; Kaunas — 5,282; Klaipėda's prelature — 1,290; Panevėžys — 3,489; Telšiai — 4,174; Vilkaviškis — 4,981.

62. Centrinė statistikos valdyba, *Lietuvos TSR ekonomika ir kultūra 1970 metais* (Vilnius: Statistika, 1971), p. 22.

63. P. Mišutis in *Kalba Vilnius,* No. 5 (1974), cit. by *LKBK,* No. 9, Vol. II, pp. 65ff.

64. *LKBK,* No. 9, Vol. II, pp. 69ff.

65. Ibid.

66. Antanas Gaidys in J. Aničas (ed.), *Ideologinė kova ir jaunimas* (Vilnius: Lietuvos TSR Mokslų Akademija, 1972), p. 96.

67. Ibid., p. 97.

68. *LKBK,* No. 5, Vol. II, p. 70.

69. Gaidys in Aničas (ed.), op. cit., 95–96. The total percentage given in the source is 120, not 100, as it should be. This probably means that percentages are taken from different question categories.

70. Ibid., p. 97.

71. Cit. in *LKBK,* No. 5, Vol. II, p. 77; ibid., No. 28, p. 15.

72. Jonas Jurašas, *Į Laisvę,* No. 63–64 (Aug., 1975), p. 65.

73. *Tiesos kelias,* No. 1, p. 9.

74. See V. Stanley Vardys, "Soviet Social Engineering in Lithuania," *Lithuania under the Soviets* (New York: F. A. Praeger, 1965), p. 255.

75. See V. Stanley Vardys, "Catholicism in Lithuania," in Marshall, op. cit., p. 502.

76. *Baltimore Sun,* May 17, 1973.

CHAPTER XV
COMMUNISM AND CATHOLICISM IN THE SOVIET STATE:
IS CO-EXISTENCE POSSIBLE?

1. Jonas Aničas, "Soviet Laws on Religious Cults and the Policy toward Religion and the Church by the Communist Party of the Soviet Union and by the Soviet State," *Laikas ir įvykiai,* No. 5 (March, 1977), p. 13.

2. From the draft published in *Pravda,* June 4, 1977, pp. 1–4.

3. M. Rutkevich, "The Socialist Way of Life and Its Development," *Voprosy filosofii,* No. 11, 1975, p. 52. Transl. from Radio Liberty Research 227/76 of April 29, 1976.

4. "In the Central Committee of the Lithuanian Communist Party: To Promote Deep Atheist Convictions of Students," *Tarybinis mokytojas,* May 13, 1977, p. 1.

5. Ibid.

6. Ibid.

7. Ibid., p. 2.

8. *LKBK,* No. 27 (1977), p. 2.

9. Vladas Balkevičius, "The Causes of the Existence of Religion under the Conditions of Socialism," *Laikas ir įvykiai,* No. 3 (February, 1977), pp. 13–16.

10. J. Minkevičius, "Methodological Aspects of the Confrontation of Science and Religion," *Lietuvos TSR Mokslų Akademijos Darbai/Trudy Akademii Nauk Litovskoi SSR,* seriia A, No. 4 (57), p. 36.

11. Cf. Peter Reddaway, "The Development of Dissent and Opposition," in Archie Brown and Michael Kaser, eds., *The Soviet Union Since the Fall of Khrushchev* (New York: The Free Press, 1975), p. 135; also cf. Ludmilla Alekseeva, a member of the Russian Helsinki Committee forced to emigrate, in *Suchastnist'* (New York) as reported by *Elta* (New York), May, 1977, p. 4.

12. Barbara Jancar, "Religious Dissent in the Soviet Union," in Rudolf Tőkes, ed., *Dissent in the USSR* (Baltimore: The Johns Hopkins University Press, 1975), p. 223. See also my paper "Modernization and Latin Rite Catholics in the Soviet Union," delivered at the Southwest Texas State University, San Marcos, March 21–23, 1976, and later published in a symposium ed. by Dennis J. Dunn, *Religion and Modernization in the Soviet Union* (Boulder: Westview Press, 1977).

13. Jonas Aničas in *Nauka i religiia,* No. 8 (1975), p. 12; Balkevičius, as in ft. 9; Jonas Mačiulis, "The Socio-Political Evolution of the Catholic Church under the Conditions of Socialism," *Laikas ir įvykiai,* No. 3 (1976), p. 14ff; "Convictions and Loyalty to Principles," loc. cit., No. 8 (1976), p. 18; Jonas Aničas, "Realizatsiia reshenii II Vatikanskogo sobora v katolicheskoi tserkvi v Litve," in Akademiia nauk Litovskoi SSR. Otdel filosofii, prava i sotsiologii pri institute istorii, *Katolitsizm v SSSR i sovremmenost'* (Vilnius, 1971), p. 90ff.

14. Anatole Shub, "The Escalation of Soviet Dissent and of Soviet Repression," *The New York Times Magazine,* Sept. 10, 1972, p. 94.

15. A. Bal'sis [Balsys], "Klerikalizm i natsionalizm na sluzhbe antikommunizma," *Nauka i religia*, No. 7 (1976), p. 81.

16. Ibid.; see also I. A. Matsiavichius [Matsevičius], "Katolitsizm i sovremennaia ideologicheskaia bor'ba," *Voprosy filosofii*, No. 8 (August, 1976), p. 162; also Genrikas Zimanas, "Stil' iubileinogo goda," *Zhurnalist*, No. 7 (1972), esp. p. 7; A. Iu. Snechkus [Sniečkus], "Vechno zhivaia sila," *Zhurnalist*, No. 12 (1972), p. 12.

17. *LKBK,* No. 28, p. 12.

18. The objectives and motivation of the Vatican's *Ostpolitik* are beyond the subject matter of this volume. For analysis, see the following: Hansjakob Stehle, *Die Ostpolitik des Vatikans* (München: R. Piper, 1975); Wilfried Daim, *The Vatican and Eastern Europe* (New York: Frederick Ungar, 1970); Knut Walf, "The Vatican's Eastern Policy," *Aussenpolitik,* No. 4 (1973), pp. 416–426; Reinhard Raffalt, *Wohin steuert der Vatikan?* (München: R. Piper, 1973); Dennis J. Dunn, "Papal-Communist Detente: Motivation," *Survey,* Spring, 1972, pp. 140–154.

19. Johannes S. Brehm, "Litauische Realitäten (II)," *Katholische Korrespondenz,* No. 15/16 (April 13, 1976), p. 8. The author writes: "Durch eine kluge vatikanische Politik kann ihre Lage sogar verbessert werden."

20. Professor Fletcher suggested this thesis in the paper he read and discussion that was held at the conference on modernization and religion in the Soviet Union that was sponsored by the Research and Development Committee of the American Association for the Advancement of Slavic Studies and took place at Southwest Texas State University, San Marcos, Texas, March 21–23, 1976. The study has since been published in the cited symposium ed. by Dennis Dunn.

APPENDIX

1. Russian text of the 1977 Constitution in *Vedomosti Verkhovnogo Sovieta SSSR,* No. 41 (Oct. 12, 1977), item 617 (pp. 671–707). Transl. from *Moscow News* supplement to issue No. 42 (October, 1977). Text of 1936 Constitution from *Constitution (Fundamental Law) of the Union of Soviet Socialist Republics, as amended and Added to at the First, Second and Fourth Sessions of the Supreme Soviet of the USSR, Fourth Convocation.* Moscow, 1956.

2. Russian text in *Konstitutsiia (osnovnoi zakon) Litovskoi Sovetskoi Sotsialisticheskoi Respubliki c izmeneniiami i dopolneniiami, priniatymi Verkhovnym Sovietom Litovskoi SSR do VIII sessii vos'mogo sozyva vkliuchitel'no.* Vilnius, 1975. Translated by Catherine V. Ewing.

3. Russian text in *Sobranie uzakonenii i rasporiazhenii rabochekrestiianskogo pravitel'stva RSFSR,* No. 18 (1918), item 263. Translation from U.S. Congress. Senate. 88th Cong., 2nd sess. Committee on the Judiciary. *The Church and State under Communism.* Part I (Washington, 1964), p. 11.

4. Russian text in *Sobranie uzakonenii i rasporiazhenii raboche-krestiianskogo pravitel'stva RSFSR,* No. 35, 1929, item 353. Amendments in ibid., No. 8 (1932), item 41, II, 6. Translation from U.S. Congress. Senate. 88th Cong., 2nd sess. Committee on the Judiciary. *The Church and State Under Communism.* Part I (Washington, 1964), pp. 12–17.

5. Decree No. IX-748 of July 28, 1976. Translated by V. Stanley Vardys from Russian text, publ. in *AS* 2841v. Source: *Lietuvos Tarybų Socialistinės Respublikos Aukščiausios Tarybos ir Vyriausybės žinios,* Aug. 10, 1976, items 191-93.

6. Juridine komisija prie Lietuvos TSR Ministru Tarybos. *Lietuvos Tarybų Socialistinės Respublikos baudžiamasis kodeksas.* Vilnius, 1970. Transl. by V. Stanley Vardys.

7. Ibid.

8. *LKBK,* No. 30, pp. 6-7. Transl. by V. Stanley Vardys.

9. *LKBK,* No. 2, pp. 76-80 (Vol. I of the Chicago edition). Transl. by *RLR.*

10. *LKBK,* No. 28, pp. 1-22 (June 29, 1977). Transl. by Rev. Casimir Pugevičius. Subtitles added by the author of the present volume.

Abbreviations

AS — Arkhiv samizdata
Baltic States — see U.S. Congress, House of Representatives, *Third Interim Report of the Select Committee to Investigate Communist Aggression and Forced Incorporation of the Baltic States into the USSR*
Chronologinis rinkinys — Lietuvos TSR įstatymų, Aukščiausios Tarybos Prezidiumo įsakų ir vyriausybės nutarimų chronologinis rinkinys
EL — Encyclopedia Lituanica
FBIS — Foreign Broadcast Information Service
LE — Lietuvių Enciklopedija
Le Saint Siège — see volumes of documents edited by Pierre Blet et al.
KTS — Khronika tekushchikh sobytii (Chronicle of Current Events)
LKBK — Lietuvos Katalikų Bažnyčios Kronika (Chronicle of the Catholic Church of Lithuania)
MLTE — Mažoji Lietuviškoji Tarybinė Enciklopedija
Nazi-Soviet Relations — see U.S. documents edited by Raymond J. Sontag and James S. Beddie
Nutarimai — see *Nutarimai ideologiniais klausimais*
Protocol — Protocols of Conferences of Lithuania's Bishops
RLR — Radio Liberty Research [bulletins]
Soviet Documents — documents edited by Jane Degras
VHR — Violations of Human Rights in Soviet Occupied Lithuania
VPMP Leidykla — State Publishing House for Political and Scientific Literature
Zakonodatel'stvo — see documents edited by Kuroedov, V. A., et al.

Bibliography

This bibliography lists only those used documents and publications that have been cited in this volume. To describe the current religious situation in Lithuania and, generally, in the Soviet Union I drew primarily from published and unpublished *samizdat* manuscripts and from Soviet documents, including periodicals. Western reports, too, were occasionally helpful. Reconstruction of the Stalinist years would not have been possible without *samizdat* sources and reports by survivors in the West. Analysis of church-state relations during the period of independence and the first year of Soviet rule, 1940–41, gained from the use of some yet unpublished archival documents, as for example, the protocols of the conferences of Lithuania's bishops. Periodicals and newspapers of this period, too, were very helpful though, unfortunately, only a very limited number of such periodicals with large chronological gaps was available in the United States. Similarly incomplete is the list of Lithuanian periodicals covering the crucial summer of 1940 and the first year of Soviet rule, 1940–41.

Samizdat materials, generally, are available in *Arkhiv Samizdata* that has been published largely for researchers' use. The *Arkhiv,* however, does not yet include all Lithuanian language documents. At the time of writing, many Lithuanian *samizdat* sources used for this book, including underground journals, were not yet published in any form.

Russian language *samizdat* documents, generally, are not frequently translated. Of the Lithuanian sources, the most often translated publication has been the basic source of information on the religious situation, namely, the *Chronicle of the Catholic Church of Lithuania.* In English, the *Chronicle* is serially published by the Lithuanian Roman Catholic Priests' League of America (351 Highland Boulevard, Brooklyn, N.Y. 11207). Translations of long excerpts from the *Chronicle* have appeared in *VHR* and in *Elta* (both in the United States). English summaries of individual issues of the journal are found in *RLR* (Munich, Germany). Occasional pieces have been translated in *Religion in Communist Lands* (England) and *Religion in Communist Dominated Areas* (U.S.A.). A complete German translation of individual issues of the *Chronicle* is published by the quarterly, *Acta Baltica* (Konigstein, i. T., Germany). Frequent German translations of long excerpts and summaries appear in *Glaube in der 2 Welt* (Switzerland). Occasional Italian translations have been published in *Russia christiana* (Milan, Italy); complete texts are found in the Italian language *Elta-Press* (Rome). In 1976, La Casa di Matrona, a publishing house in Milan, published Vol. 1 of the full text of *LKBK* entitled *Cronaca della Chiesa Cattolica in Lituania.* In French, some texts have appeared in *Cahiers du samizdat* (Belgium).

In Lithuanian, the first twenty-two issues have been published in three volumes entitled *Lietuvos Katalikų Bažnyčios Kronika* (Chicago: Lithuanian

Catholic Religious Aid Auxiliary Society, Inc., 1974–76). Citations of these first twenty-two issues of the *Chronicle* in this book refer to this Chicago edition. I translated and cited the later issues from individual copies of the typewritten original.

Of other Lithuanian *samizdat* documents, generous excerpts are published by *VHR* and *Elta*. In Lithuanian, the Academic Scouts' Movement has published six issues of *Aušra,* 1975.x–1977.11.16 (Chicago, 1977). A *samizdat* biography of Archbishop Reinys, used for this volume, has since been published as a book, entitled *Arkivyskupas Mečislovas Reinys* (Chicago: Association of Lithuanian Christian Democrats, 1977). Similarly, some of the documents pertaining to 1940–41 have since been published by Bishop Brizgys in his memoirs (1977; see listing below).

Samizdat *and Other Original Documents*

Arkhiv samizdata (Archive of Samizdat, Munich).
Aušra (The Dawn), 1975– . *Samizdat.*
Dievas ir tėvynė (God and Fatherland), 1976– . *Samizdat* journal.
Iš vyskupo Plataroko užrašų. (From the Notes of Bishop Paltarokas). *Samizdat.*
Khronika tekushchikh sobytii (Chronicle of Current Events), 1968–1972; 1973– . *Samizdat.*
La Chiesa in Lituania, a pro-memoria submitted by Bishop Vincentas Brizgys to the Second Vatican Council.
Lietuvos bažnytinės provincijos vyskupų konferencijų protokolai (Protocols of Episcopal Conferences of Lithuania's Church Province), 1926–1944. Unpublished.
Lietuvos Katalikų Bažnyčios kronika (The Chronicle of the Catholic Church of Lithuania), 1972– . *Samizdat.*
Memuarai apie arkivyskupą Matulionį (Memoirs about Archbishop T. Matulionis). *Samizdat.*
Memuarai apie arkivyskupą M. Reinį (Memoirs about Archbishop M. Reinys). *Samizdat.*
Pro Memoria by Bishop T. Matulionis and other documents from 1940–41 and after 1944. *Samizdat.*
Tiesos kelias (The Way of Truth), 1976– . *Samizdat* journal.
Unpublished notes (with documents) on Church conditions in 1940–41 by Bishop Vincentas Brizgys.
Unpublished archival materials and individual *samizdat* documents on Church conditions since the 1960s (mainly from Lithuanian Religious Information, Rome).
Varpas (The Bell), 1977– . *Samizdat* journal.
The Violations of Human Rights in Soviet Occupied Lithuania. Annual report, published since 1971 by the American Lithuanian Community, Inc., with translations of many *samizdat* texts.

Government Documents, Statistical Yearbooks, Directories

Annuario Pontificio. 1965–75. The Vatican.

Blet, Pierre et al., eds. Le Saint Siège et la Situation Religieuse en Pologne et dans les Pays Baltes, 1939–1945. The Vatican, 1967.

Degras, Jane, ed. Soviet Documents on Foreign Policy. London, 1953.

Catalogus ecclesiarum et cleri archidiocesis Vilnensis pro anno Domini 1939.

Elenchus ecclesiarum et cleri Archidioecesis Vilnensis cum additamento catelogorum cleri aliarumque notitiarum nonnullarum dioecesium Provinciae Ecclesiasticae Lituaniae. Vilnius: Curia Archdioecesis Vilnensis, 1971.

Elenchus omnium ecclesiarum. 1920.

Elenchus omnium ecclesiarum et universi cleri Provinciae Ecclesiasticae Lituan'ae. Pro Anno 1939.

Elenchus omnium ecclesiarum et universi cleri provinciae ecclesiasticae Lituanae. Pro anno Domini 1940.

Iuridicheskaia Komissiia pri Sovete Ministrov RSFSR. Kodeks o brake i sem'e RSFSR (Marriage and Family Code of the Russian SFSR). Moscow, 1969.

Juridinė komisija prie Lietuvos TSR Ministrų Tarybos. Lietuvos Tarybų Socialistinės Respublikos baudžiamasis kodeksas (The Criminal Code of the Lithuanian SSR). Vilnius, 1970.

Kommunistichestiaia partiia Sovetskogo Soiuza. XXII s'ezd Kommunisticheskoi Partii Sovetskoga Soiuza (17–31 oktiabria 1961 goda). Stenograficheskii otchet. Vol. III. Moscow, 1962.

Kuroedov, V. A. et al., eds. Zakonodatel'stvo o religioznykh kultakh (Legislation on Religious Cults), 2nd ed., Moscow, 1971.

Lietuvos statistikos metraštis (The Annals of Lithuania's Statistics). Vol. XII. Vilnius, 1940.

Lietuvos TSR CSV. Lietuvos TSR ekonomika ir kultūra 1970 metais (Economy and Culture of the Lithuanian SSR in 1970). Vilnius, 1971.

Lietuvos TSR CSV. Lietuvos TSR ekonomika ir kultūra 1972 metais (Economy and Culture of the Lithuanian SSR in 1972). Vilnius, 1973.

Lietuvos TSR Teisingumo Ministerija. Lietuvos TSR įstatymų, Aukščiausios Tarybos Prezidiumo įsakų ir vyriausybės nutarimų chronologinis rinkinys (Chronological Collection of the Laws of the Lithuanian SSR, the Decrees of the Presidium of the Supreme Soviet and the Decisions of the Government). Vol. I. Vilnius, 1956.

Ministerių kabineto priimtasai Lietuvos valstybės 1925 metams biudžeto projektas (Draft of the Lithuanian State Budget for 1925 adopted by the Council of Ministers), Kaunas, 1925.

Raccolta di Tavole Statistiche 1969. The Vatican, 1971.

Receipts and Expenditures of the Republic of Lithuania for the Year 1938. Kaunas, 1938.

Religijų Reikalų Tarybos prie TSRS Ministrų Tarybos Įgaliotinis Lietuvos

Respublikai. *Dėl kultų įstatymų taikymo tvarkos* (On the Question of Applying the Laws on Religious Cults). Vilnius, 1969.

Sontag, Raymond J., and Beddie, James S., eds. *Nazi-Soviet Relations, 1939–1941.* Washington, 1948.

U.S. Congress, House of Representatives, Commission on Security and Cooperation in Europe. 95th Cong., 1st sess. *Hearings before the Commission on Security and Cooperation in Europe.* 4 vols. Washington. 1977.

————, Committee on Foreign Affairs, 91st Cong., 1st sess. *Attempted Defection of Lithuanian Seaman Simas Kudirka. Hearings before the Subcommittee on State Department Organization and Foreign Operations of the Committee on Foreign Affairs.*

————, Select Committee on Communist Aggression. 83d Cong., 1st sess. *Hearings before the Select Committee to Investigate the Incorporation of the Baltic States into the USSR.* Washington, 1954.

————, Select Committee on Communist Aggression. 83d Cong., 2d sess. *Third Interim Report of the Select Committee to Investigate Communist Aggression and Forced Incorporation of the Baltic States into the USSR.*

U.S. Department of State. *Documents on German Foreign Policy, 1918–1945.* Series D (1937–1945). Vol. VIII. Washington, 1954.

World Lithuanian Roman Catholic Directory, ed. by Casimir Pugevicius. Putnam, 1975.

Encyclopedias

Bol'shaia sovetskaia entsiklopediia (The Great Soviet Encyclopedia). Moscow.

Encyclopedia Lituanica. 5 vols. Boston, 1970–75.

Entsiklopedicheskii slovar' (Encyclopedic Dictionary). 82 vols. St. Petersburg, 1890–1907.

Lietuvių Enciklopedija (Lithuanian Encyclopedia). 39 vols. Boston, 1953–1969.

Mažoji Lietuviškoji Tarybinė Enciklopedija (The Small Soviet Lithuanian Encyclopedia). 3 vols. Vilnius, 1966–75.

Books

Akademiia nauk Litovskoi SSR. *Katolitsizm v SSSR i sovremennost'* (Catholicism in the USSR and Contemporary Times). Vilnius, 1971.

Alekna, Antanas. *Katalikų Bažnyčia Lietuvoje* (The Catholic Church in Lithuania). Kaunas, 1936.

————. *Žemaičių vyskupas Motiejus Valančius* (Samogitian Bishop M. Valančius), 1st ed. Kaunas, 1922; 2d ed., Chicago, 1975.

Aliev, A. K. *Narodnye traditsii, obychai i ikh rol' v formirovanii novogo cheloveka* (National Traditions, Customs and Their Role in the Formation of the New Man). Makhachkala, 1968.

Aksamitas, P., ed. *Religijos ir ateizmo klausimai* (Questions of Religion and Atheism). Vilnius, 1963.

Aničas, J. *Antiliaudiniu keliu* (On the Anti-People Way). Vilnius, 1976.

———. *The Establishment of Socialism in Lithuania and the Catholic Church.* Vilnius, 1975.

———. *Katalikiškasis klerikalizmas Lietuvoje 1940-1944 metais* (Catholic Clericalism in Lithuania, 1940-1944). Vilnius, 1972.

———. *Socialinis politinis katalikų bažnyčios vaidmuo Lietuvoje 1945-1952 metais* (Sociopolitical Role of the Catholic Church in Lithuania, 1945-1952). Vilnius, 1971.

Aničas, J. et al., eds. *Ideologinė kova ir jaunimas* (Ideological Struggle and the Youth). Vilnius, 1972.

Aničas, J., and Rimaitis, J. *Tarybiniai įstatymai apie religinius kultus ir sąžinės laisvė* (Soviet Laws on Religious Cults and Freedom of Conscience). Vilnius, 1970.

The Annual Reporter for the Year 1894. London, 1895.

[no author] *Arkivyskupas Mečislovas Reinys* (Archbishop M. Reinys). Chicago: Lietuvių Krikščionių Demokratų Sąjunga, 1977.

Armstrong, John A. *The Politics of Totalitarianism.* New York, 1961.

Bagdanavičius, V. et al., eds., *Kovos metai dėl savosios spaudos* (The Years of Struggle for the Native Language Press). Chicago, 1957.

Baltinis, Andrius. *Vyskupo Vincento Borisevičiaus gyvenimas ir darbai* (Life and Works of Bishop Vincentas Borisevičius). Rome, 1975.

Baranauskas, B. et al., eds. *Archyviniai dokumentai apie antiliaudinę veiklą* (Archival Documents on Anti-People Activity). Vol. 1-8. Vilnius, 1960-66.

Baranauskas, B., and Erslavaitė, G. *Žudikai bažnyčios prieglobstyje* (Murderers in the Refuge of the Church). Vilnius, 1960.

Barghoorn, Frederick C. *Detente and the Democratic Movement in the USSR.* New York and London, 1976.

Barzdaitis, J. *Ateizmas Lietuvoje* (Atheism in Lithuania). Vilnius, 1967.

Beeson, Trevor. *Discretion and Valour.* London, 1974.

Bogdanov, I. M. *Gramotnost' i obrazovanie v dorevoliutsionnoi Rossii i v SSSR* (Literacy and Education in Pre-Revolutionary Russia and the USSR). Moscow, 1964.

Brizgys, Vincentas. *Katalikų Bažnyčia Lietuvoje 1940-1944 metais* (The Catholic Church in Lithuania, 1940-1944). Chicago: publ. not indicated, 1977.

———. *Religious Conditions in Lithuania under Soviet Russian Occupation.* Chicago, 1968.

Brumberg, Abraham, ed. *In Quest of Justice.* New York, 1970.

Čepas, R., and Vasiliauskas, Z., eds. *Archyviniai dokumentai* (Archival Documents). Vol. IX. Vilnius, 1968.

Ciszek, Walter J., with Flaherty, Daniel L. *With God in Russia.* New York, 1966.

Chkhikvadze, V. M., ed. *The Soviet Form of Popular Government.* Moscow, 1972.

Churchill, Winston. *The Gathering Storm.* Boston, 1948.

Conference in Defense of Peace of all Churches and Religious Associations in the USSR. Zagorsk, 1952.

Crankshaw, Edward. *The Shadow of the Winter Palace.* New York, 1976.

Daim, Wilfried. *The Vatican and Eastern Europe.* New York, 1970.

Dallin, Alexander. *German Rule in Russia, 1941–45.* New York, 1970.

Daugirdaitė-Sruogienė, V. *Lietuvos steigiamasis seimas* (The Constituent Assembly of Lithuania). New York, 1975.

Daulius, J. *Komunizmas Lietuvoje* (Communism in Lithuania). Kaunas, 1938.

Daumantas, J. *Partizanai* (The Guerillas). Chicago, 1962.

[no author] *Delo Kovalëva* (The Case of Kovalëv). New York: Khronika, 1976.

[no author] *Delo Tvërdokhlebova* (The Case of Tvëerdokhlebov). New York, 1976.

DeGeorge, Richard T., and Scanlan, James. *Marxism and Religion in Eastern Europe.* Dordrecht, 1976.

Dičius, Pranas. *Santuoka ir šeima Tarybų Lietuvoje* (Marriage and Family in Soviet Lithuania). Vilnius, 1974.

Domaševičius, K. *Tarybinio valstybingumo vystymasis Lietuvoje* (The Evolution of Soviet Statehood in Lithuania). Vilnius, 1966.

Dunn, Dennis, ed. *Religion and Modernization in the Soviet Union.* Boulder, 1977.

Fazylov, M. S. *Religiia i natsional'nye otnosheniia* (Religion and National Relations). Alma-Ata, 1969.

Fletcher, William C. *The Russian Orthodox Church Underground, 1917–1970.* London, 1971.

Friedman, Philip. *Their Brothers Keepers.* New York, 1957.

Gaigalaitė, Aldona. *Klerikalizmas Lietuvoje, 1917–1940* (Clericalism in Lithuania, 1917–1940). Vilnius, 1970.

Gečys, K. *Katalikiškoji Lietuva* (Catholic Lithuania). Chicago, 1946.

Gedvilas, Mečislovas. *Lemiamas posūkis, 1940–1945 metai* (The Fateful Turn, 1940–1945). Vilnius, 1975.

Giannini, Amedeo. *Il Concordato con la Lituania.* Rome, 1928.

Girnius, Juozas. *Pranas Dovydaitis* [a biography of P.P.]. Chicago, 1975.

Gol'st, Georgii Robertovich. *Religiia i zakon* (Religion and the Law). Moscow, 1975.

Graham, Malbone W. *New Governments of Eastern Europe.* New York, 1927.

Gregorauskas, M. *Tarybų Lietuvos žemės ūkis* (Agriculture of Soviet Lithuania). Vilnius, 1960.

Halicz, E.; Kieniewicz, S.; and Miller, J. *Dokumenty Komitetu Narodowego i Rzadu Narodowego, 1862–1864* (Documents of the National Committee and National Council, 1862–1864). Wroclaw-Warszawa-Krakow, 1968.

Hermanovičius, Joseph. *Raudonųjų stovyklose* (In the Camps of the Reds). London, 1969.

Iablokov, I. N. *Krizis religii v sotsialisticheskom obshchestve* (Crisis of Religion in Socialist Society). Moscow, 1974.

Ivanov, A. I., and Lobazov, P. K. *Politika sovetskogo gosudarstva po voprosam religii i tserkvi* (Policy of Soviet Government on Questions of Religion and Church). Moscow, 1973.

Jurgėla, K. R. *Lietuvos sukilimas 1862–1864 metais* (Lithuania's Insurrection, 1862–1864). Boston, 1970.

Kancevičius, V. *1940 metų birželis Lietuvoje* (June of 1940 in Lithuania). Vilnius, 1973.

Kasulaitis, Algirdas. *Lithuanian Christian Democracy.* Chicago, 1976.

Kenevich, S. et al., eds. *Vostanie v Litve i Belorussii 1863–1864 gg.* (Insurrection in Lithuania and Belorussia, 1863–1864). Moscow, 1965.

Kholmogorov, A. I. *International Traits of Soviet Nations.* Transl. in *Soviet Sociology,* 1972–73.

Khrushchev Remembers. Boston, 1970.

Klochkov, Valentin Veniaminovich. *Bor'ba c narusheniiami zakonodatel'stva o religioznykh kul'takh* (The Struggle Against Violations of Legislation on Religious Cults; for government use). Moscow, 1967.

Kolarz, Walter. *Religion in the Soviet Union.* London, 1961.

Kommunisticheskaia partiia i sovetskoe pravitel'stvo o religii i tserkvi (The Communist Party and Soviet Government on Religion and Church). Moscow, 1961.

Krikščionybė Lietuvoje (Christianity in Lithuania) [ed. by P. Mantvydas or K. Barauskas]. Kaunas, 1938.

Kushner, P. I. *Etnicheskie territorii i etnicheskie granitsy* (Ethnic Territories and Ethnic Boundaries). Moscow, 1951.

Kuznetsov, Edward. *Prison Diaries.* New York, 1975.

Laurinaitis, S., and Bistrickas, S. *Jų Dievas* (Their God). Vilnius, 1962.

Lenin, V. I. *Polnoe sobranie sochinenii* (Full Collection of Works), 5th ed. Vol. VII. Moscow, 1959.

Leonhard, Wolfgang. *Kreml ohne Stalin.* Cologne, 1959.

Lietuvos valstybės konstitucijos (Constitutions of the Lithuanian State). Toronto, 1952.

Litvinov, Pavel. *The Demonstration in Pushkin Square.* Boston, 1969.

Loeber, Dietrich A. *Diktierte Option.* Neumünster, 1972.

Lossowski, Piotr. *Kraje baltyckie na drodze od demokracji parlamentarnej do dyktatury: 1918–1934* (Baltic Countries on the Road from Parliamentary Democracy to Dictatorship, 1918–1934). Wroclaw, 1972.

Maldeikis, Petras. *Mykolas Krupavičius* [A biography of M.K.]. Chicago, 1975.

Marshall, Richard H., Jr. et al., eds. *Aspects of Religion in the Soviet Union: 1917–1967.* Chicago, 1971.

Miniotas, A. *Atsargiai Balfas!* (Be Careful! Balfas!) Vilnius, 1973.

Minkiavichius [Minkevičius], Ia. V. *Katolitsizm i natsiia* (Catholicism and the Nation). Moscow, 1971.

———. *Sovremënnyi katolitsizm i ego filosofiia* (Contemporary Catholicism and its Philosophy). Vilnius, 1965.

Myllyniemi, Seppo. *Die Neuordnung der baltischen Länder, 1941–44.* Helsinki, 1973.

Niunka, V. *Nuo Vatikano Pirmojo iki Vatikano Antrojo* (From Vatican I to Vatican II). Kaunas, 1963.

———. *Vatikanas ir antikomunizmas* (The Vatican and Anti-Communism). Vilnius, 1970.

Nutarimai ideologiniais klausimais (Decisions on Ideological Questions by the Central Committee of the Lithuanian Communist Party). Vilnius, 1971.

Ochmanski, Jerzy. *Historia Litwy* (History of Lithuania). Wroclaw-Warsaw-Cracow, 1967.

———. *Litewski ruch narodowo-kulturalny w XIX wieku* (Lithuanian National-Cultural Movement in the XIX Century). Bialystock, 1965.

O religii i tserkvi: sbornik dokumentov (On Religion and the Church: Collection of Documents). Moscow, 1965. New ed. 1977.

Padover, Samuel K., ed. *A Jefferson Profile as Revealed in His Letters*. New York, 1956.

Pakarklis, P. *Ekonominė ir teisinė Katalikų Bažnyčios padėtis Lietuvoje (XV-XIXa)* (Economic and Legal Situation of the Catholic Church in XV-XIXc). Vilnius, 1956.

Pečiūra, P. *Tradicijos vakar ir šiandien* (Traditions Yesterday and Today). Vilnius, 1974.

Powell, David E. *Anti-Religious Propaganda in the Soviet Union: A Study of Mass Persuasion*. Cambridge, 1975.

Private Kelley by Himself. London, 1954.

Propolanis, C. *L'Eglise Polonaise en Lithuanie*. Paris, n.d.

Rabikauskas, Paulius, ed. *Relationes status dioecesium in Magno Ducato Lituaniae*. Vol. I. Rome, 1971.

Raišupis, M. *Dabarties kankiniai* (The Martyrs of the Present Time). Chicago, 1972.

Rimaitis, J. *Religion in Lithuania*. Vilnius, 1971.

Ritvo, Herbert, ed. *The New Soviet Society*. New York, 1962.

Royal Institute of International Affairs. *The Baltic States*. Cambridge, 1938.

Rukšėnas, Algis. *Day of Shame*. New York, 1973.

Sabaliūnas, Leonas. *Lithuania in Crisis*. Bloomington, 1972.

Šadžius, H. et al., eds. *Lietuvos TSR istorija* (History of the Lithuanian SSR). Vol. IV. Vilnius, 1975.

Savasis, J. *Kova už Dievą Lietuvoje* (The Struggle for God in Lithuania). Putnam, 1963.

_____. *The War Against God in Lithuania*. New York, 1966.

Scholmer, Joseph. *Vorkuta*. London, 1954.

Senn, Alfred E. *The Emergence of Modern Lithuania*. New York, 1959.

_____. *The Great Powers, Lithuania and the Vilna Question*. Leiden, 1966.

Shafarevich, I. P. *Zakonodatel'stvo o religii v SSSR* (Legislation on Religion in the USSR). Paris, 1973.

Sheinman, M. M. *Vatikan vo vtoroi mirovoi voine* (The Vatican During the Second World War). Moscow, 1951.

_____. *Religiia v period imperializma* (Religion in the Period of Imperialism). Moscow, 1955.

Sholkovich, S., ed. *Pol'skoe delo po otnosheniiu k Zapadnoi Rossii* (The Polish Question in Relation to Western Russia). 2 vols. Vilna, 1885, 1887.

Šimkus, Morkus, ed. *Profesorius Augustinas Voldemaras: Raštai* (The Works of Professor A. Voldemaras). Chicago, 1973.

Simon, Gerhard. *Church, State and Opposition in the USSR*. Berkeley, 1974.

Stehle, Hansjakob. *Die Ostpolitik des Vatikans*. München, 1975.

Stupperich, Robert, ed. *Kirche und Staat in der Sowjetunion*. Witten, 1962.

Surblys, K. *Lietuvos KP veikla, ugdant socialistinę darbininkų klasę* (The Activities of the Lithuanian CP in Educating Socialist Working Class). Vilnius, 1976.

Terleckas, Antanas. *Respect My Rights*. Chicago, 1976.

Tőkes, Rudolf, ed., *Dissent in the USSR*. Baltimore, 1975.

Vaitkus, Mykolas. *Keturi ganytojai* (Four Pastors; memoirs). Chicago, 1960.

————. *Nepriklausomybės saulėj, 1918–1940* (In the Sun of Independence, 1918–1940; memoirs). Atsiminamai. 2 vols. London, 1968.

Vaitkus, E., ed. *Vatikano Antrasis ir po jo* (The Second Vatican Council and Its Aftermath). Vilnius, 1971.

Vardys, V. Stanley, ed. *Lithuania under the Soviets*. New York, 1965.

Vėbra, R. *Lietuvos katalikų dvasininkija ir visuomeninis judėjimas* (Lithuania's Catholic Clergymen and Socio-political Movement). Vilnius, 1968.

Venclova, Antanas. *Vidurdienio vėtra* (The Storm at Noon; memoirs). Vilnius, 1969.

Veščikovas, A. *Tarybiniai įstatymai apie religinius kultus* (Soviet Laws on Religious Cults). Vilnius, 1963.

X. Y. [Mykolas Roemeris]. *Lietuvos sovietizacija* (Sovietization of Lithuania). Augsburgas, 1949.

Yla, Stasys. *Nerami dabartis ir ateitis perspektyvos* (The Restless Present and the Perspectives of the Future). Marijampolė, 1940.

Žiugžda, J. et al., eds. *Lietuvos TSR istorijos šaltiniai* (Sources of History of the Lithuanian SSR). Vol. II. Vilnius, 1965.

Articles in Scholarly Journals and Books
(Newspaper and popular journal articles are cited only in references)

Aničas, J. "Ateistinis darbo žmonių auklėjimas Tarybų Lietuvoje (1940–1941m)" (Atheist Education of the Working People in Soviet Lithuania (1940–1941)), *LKP istorijos klausimai*, Vol. VIII, 1969, pp. 33–46.

————. "Lenininio sąžinės laisves dekreto idėjų įgyvendinimas Lietuvoje 1940–1941 metais" (The Realization of the Ideas of the Leninist Decree of Freedom of Conscience in Lithuania in 1940–41), *LKP istorijos klausimai*, No. 9, 1970, pp. 31–50.

Barkauskas, A. "Osushchestvlenie Leninskikh ideii ob ateisticheskom vospitanii v prakticheskoi deiatel'nosti partiinikh organizatsii" (The Realization of Leninist Ideas on Atheist Education in the Practical Work of Party Organization), *Voprosy nauchnogo ateizma*, Vol. 10, 1970, pp. 51–61.

Baužys, J. "Religinių prietarų egzistavimo kolūkiečių sąmonėje priežasčių klausimu" (On the Question of Causes for the Existence of Religious Superstitions Among Members of Collective Farms), *Lietuvos TSR Mokslų Akademijos Darbai*, Series A, Vol. 2 (1965), pp. 253–74.

Bociurkiw, Bohdan. "Catholics in the Soviet Union Today," in *A Symposium: Religion in the USSR, 1975*. Munich, 1975, pp. 36–76.

————. "The Shaping of Soviet Religious Policy," *Problems of Communism*, May–June, 1973, pp. 37–51.

————. "Religious Dissent in the USSR: Lithuanian Catholics," paper delivered at the International Slavic Conference at Banff, September 5, 1974.

Brizgys, Vincentas. "Mano santykiai su NKVD" (My Relations with the NKVD), *Lietuvių archyvas*, Vol. II, 1942, pp. 249–60.

————. "Kunigų seminarija Kaune bolševizmo metais" (The Theological Seminary of Kaunas During the Year of Bolshevism), *Lietuvių archyvas*, Vol. I, 1942, pp. 56–65.

Gidžiūnas, Viktoras. "Didžiojoje Lietuvos Kunigaikštijoje" (Catholic Church in the Grand Duchy of Lithuania), *Lietuvių enciklopedija,* Vol. XV, pp. 131–41.

Jancar, Barbara. "Religious Dissent in the Soviet Union," in Rudolf Tőkes, ed., *Dissent in the USSR* (Baltimore: The Johns Hopkins University Press, 1975).

Jarmalavičius, J. "LKP kova prieš klerikalizmo įtaką respublikoje socializmo kūrimo laikotarpiu (1944–1951m)" (The Struggle of the LCP Against the Influence of Clericalism in the Republic During the Period of Construction of Socialism), *LKP istorijos klausimai,* No. 17, 1975, pp. 101–15.

Jatulis, Paulius. "Motiejus Valančius-idealus vyskupas" (Motiejus Valančius — Ideal Bishop), *Aidai,* No. 5, 1975, pp. 193–207.

Kašauskienė, V. "Lietuvos KP veikimas, pertvarkant mokymo-auklėjimo darbą respublikos mokyklose" (Activities of the Lithuanian Communist Party in Reorganizing Educational-Teaching Work in the Republic (1940–1941)), *LKP istorijos klausimai,* No. 11, 1971, pp. 29–43.

Kaslas, Bronis J. "The Lithuanian Strip in Soviet-German Diplomacy, 1939–1941," *Journal of Baltic Studies,* No. 3, 1973, pp. 211–25.

Kemėšis, F. "Religija ir tautybė mūsų gyvenime" (Religion and Nationality in Our Life), *Naujoji Romuva,* December 3, 1933, pp. 964–66.

Krasauskas, Rapolas. "II. Carinės okupacijos laikais" (The Church During the Tsarist Occupation), *Lietuvių Encyclopedija,* Vol. XV, pp. 141–46.

———, Gulbinas, K. "Die Lage der katholischen Kirche in Litauen," *Acta Baltica,* Vol. XII, 1972, pp. 9–44.

Luchterhandt, Otto. "Die Rechtsgrundlagen der sowjetischen Staatskirchenbehörden," *WGO. Monatshefte für osteuropäisches Recht,* Vol. 18, 1976, pp. 315–330.

Loeber, Dietrich A. "The Legal Position of the Church in the Soviet Union," *Studies on the Soviet Union,* No. 2, 1969, pp. 16–34.

Maceina, A. "Tauta ir valstybė" (The Nation and the State), *Naujoji Romuva,* March 19, 1939, pp. 227–30.

Matulis, Steponas. "Lietuva ir Apaštalų sostas, 1795–1940" (Lithuania and the Holy See), in Lietuvių Katalikų Mokslo Akademija, *Suvažiavimo darbai,* Vol. IV, 1961, pp. 151–74.

Merkelis, A. "Masinis lietuvių išvežimas į SSSR" (Massive Deportations of Lithuanians into the USSR), *Lietuvių archyvas,* Vol. II, 1942, pp. 15–50.

Minkevičius, J. "Metodologiniai mokslo ir religijos konfrontacijos aspektai" (Methodological Aspects of the Confrontation of Science and Religion), *Lietuvos TSR Mokslų Akademijos darbai,* Series A, No. 4, 1976, pp. 27–37.

Mishutis [Mišutis], P. P. "Opyt sozdaniia sistemy ateisticheskogo vospitaniia v Litovskoi SSR" (Experience of the Formation of System of Atheist Education in the Lithuanian SSR), *Vosprosy nauchnogo ateizma,* Vol. I, 1966, pp. 200–20.

Muravëv, M. N. "Vsepoddanskii otchet grafa Muravëva po upravleniiu severozapadnym kraem (c 1 maia 1863 g. do 17 aprelia 1865 g.)" (Report to the Tsar by Count Muravëv on the Administration of the Northwest Territory), *Russkaia starina,* June, 1902, pp. 487–510.

Pavalkis, Viktoras. "Arkivyskupas Mečislovas Reinys Vilniuje (1940–1947)" (Archbishop M. Reinys in Vilnius), *Aidai,* No. 2, 1974, pp. 56–63.

Pšibilskis, V. "Miestų partinių organizacijų vadovavimas politinių ir mokslinių žinių skleidimo draugijai 1947–1958 metais" (The Leadership of City Party Organizations over the Association for the Propagation of Political and Scientific Information, 1947–1958), *LKP istorijos klausimai*, No. 16, 1974, pp. 63–76.

Reddaway, Peter. "The Development of Dissent and Opposition," in Archie Brown and Michael Kaser, eds., *The Soviet Union Since the Fall of Khrushchev*. New York, 1975, pp. 121–56.

Rimšelis, Viktoras. "Archbishop Jurgis Matulaitis and the Lithuanian Church." *Draugas* literary supplement, December 18, 1976.

Sawatsky, Walter. "The New Soviet Law on Religion," *Religion in Communist Lands*, No. 2, 1976, pp. 4–10.

Šležas, Paulius. "Bažnyčios ir valstybės santykiai Žemaičių vyskupystėje Valančiaus laikais (1850–1875)" (The Relations Between Church and State in the Samogitian Diocese During the Times of Valančius (1850–1875)), *Židinys*, Vol. XXVII, No. 7, 1938, pp. 47–59.

Vaišnora, Juozas. "Jurgio Matulaičio kelias į Vilniaus vyskupo sostą" (J. Matulaitis' Road to the Vilnius See), *Aidai*, No. 3, 4, 5, 6, 7, 1977, pp. 97–104; 166–70; 218–22; 271–75; 321–25.

———. "III. Nepriklausomaisiais ir okupaciniais laikais" (The Church During Independence and in Times of Foreign Occupation), *Lietuvių Enciklopedija*, Vol. XV, pp. 146–51.

Vardys, V. Stanley. "Catholicism in Lithuania," in Richard H. Marshall, Jr. et al., eds., *Aspects of Religion in the Soviet Union*. Chicago: 1971, pp. 379–404.

———. "Modernization and Baltic Nationalism," *Problems of Communism*, September–October 1975, pp. 32–48.

———. "The Role of the Baltic Republics in Soviet Society," in Roman Szporluk, ed., *The Influence of East Europe and the Soviet West on the USSR*. New York, 1977, pp. 147–79.

———. "Latin Catholicism and Modernization," a paper delivered at a conference on religion and modernization in the Soviet Union, held at San Marcos Texas Southwest University, March, 1975.

Vėbra, R. "Lietuvių nacionalinis judėjimas 1865–1883 m." (Lithuanian National Movement in 1865–1883). *Lietuvos TSR Mokslų Akademijos Darbai*, Ser. A., Vol. 2 (59), 1977, pp. 49–59.

Walf, Knut. "The Vatican's Eastern Policy," *Aussenpolitik* (English ed.), No. 4, 1973, pp. 416–26.

Journals and Newspapers

A. Soviet

Agitator (Agitator, Moscow, Russ.).
Darbininkų žodis (The Word of the Workers, Kaunas, Lith., Summer, 1940).
Darbo Lietuva (Labor Lithuania, Kaunas, Lith., Summer, 1940).
Izvestiia (Truth, Russ., Moscow).
Komjaunimo tiesa (Truth of the Communist Youth, Lith., Vilnius).
Kommunist (Communist, Russ., Moscow).

Komunistas (Communist, Lith., Vilnius).
Kultūros barai (Fields of Culture, Lith., Kaunas).
Laikas ir įvykiai (Time and Events, Lith., Vilnius).
Lietuvos TSR Mokslų Akademijos darbai (The Works of the Academy of Sciences of the Lithuanian SSR), series A, Lith. and Russ., Vilnius).
Literatūra ir menas (Literature and Art, Lith., Vilnius).
LKP istorijos klausimai (Questions on Lithuanian CP History, Lith., Vilnius).
LTSR Aukščiausios Tarybos ir Vyriausybes žinios (News of the Lithuanian SSR Supreme Soviet and Government, Lith. and Russ., Vilnius).
Mokslas ir gyvenimas (Science and Life, Lith., Vilnius).
Moscow News
Nauka i religiia (Science and Religion, Russ., Moscow).
Nemunas (youth liter. journ., Lith., Kaunas).
Ogonёk (Light, Russ., Moscow).
Partiinaia zhiz'n (Party Life, Russ., Moscow).
Pergalė (Victory, Lith., liter. journ., Vilnius).
Politicheskoe samoobrazovanie (Political Self-education, Russ., Moscow).
Pravda (Truth, Russ., Moscow).
Sovetskaia Litva (Soviet Lithuania, Russ., Vilnius).
Švyturys (Light Tower, Lith., Vilnius).
Tarybinis mokytojas (Soviet Teacher, Lith., Vilnius).
Tarybų Lietuva (Soviet Lithuania, Lith., 1940).
Tiesa (Truth, Lith., Vilnius).
Valstiečių laikraštis (Peasant Newspaper, Lith., Vilnius).
Vedomosti Verkhovnogo Soveta RSFSR (News of the Supreme Soviet of the SFSR, Russ., Moscow).
Vedomosti Verkhovnogo Soveta Sovetskikh Sotsialisticheskikh Respublik (News of the Supreme Soviet of the USSR, Russ., Moscow).
Voprosy filosofii (Questions of Philosophy, Russ., Moscow).
Zhurnal Moskovskoi Patriarkhii (Journal of Moscow Patriarchate, Russ., Moscow).
Zhurnalist (Journalist, Russ., Moscow).

B. Lithuanian
(Publ. in independent Lithuania)

Lietuvos aidas (Echo of Lithuania, Lith. daily, Kaunas, 1940).
Naujoji Romuva (The New Romuva, Lith. weekly, Kaunas, 1930–1940).
Tiesos kelias (Way of Truth, Lith. monthly, up to 1940).
XX Amžius (XX Century, Lith. daily, 1940).
Židinys (The Hearth, Lith. cult. monthly, up to 1940).

C. Western

A Chronicle of Human Rights in the USSR
Acta Apostolicae Sedis (The Vatican)
Acta Baltica (Germany)
Aidai (Echoes, Lith., USA).
Baltimore Sun

Chicago Daily News
Christian Science Monitor
Current Digest of the Soviet Press
Department of State Bulletin
Draugas (The Friend, Lith. daily, USA).
Elta (Lith., Eng., Italian, bull., USA, Italy).
Financial Times (England)
Foreign Broadcast Information Service
Į Laisvę (Toward Freedom, Lith. journal, USA).
Index (England)
Journal of Baltic Studies
Journal of Central European Affairs
Katholische Korrespondenz (Germany)
Klerusblatt (Germany)
Kultura (Culture, Polish, France).
La Ragione (Italy)
Lituanus
Los Angeles Times
L'Osservatore Romano (The Vatican)
L'Unita (Italy)
Lux Christi (Lith. journal, USA).
The New York Times
Norman Transcript
Osteuropa (Germany)
Posev (Sowing, Russ. magazine, W. Germany).
Problems of Communism
Radio Liberty Research (Germany)
Religiia i ateizm v SSSR (Religion and Atheism in the USSR, Russ., W. Germany).
Religion in Communist Lands (England)
Review of Socialist Law (Holland)
Studies on tne Soviet Union (Germany)
Tėviškės žiburiai (Lights of Homeland, Lith. weekly, Canada)
Times (England)
Vienybė (Unity, Lith. weekly, New York)
WGO. Monatshefte für osteuropäisches Recht (Germany)

D. Other

Begegnung (E. Berlin, German Democratic Republic).
Lietuvių archyvas (Lithuanian Archive, Lith., Kaunas, 1942).
Russkaia starina (Russian Past, Russ., St. Petersburg).

Index

EAST EUROPEAN MONOGRAPHS

The *East European Monographs* comprise scholarly books on the history and civilization of Eastern Europe. They are published by the *East European Quarterly* in the belief that these studies contribute substantially to the knowledge of the area and serve to stimulate scholarship and research.

1. *Political Ideas and the Enlightenment in the Romanian Principalities, 1750-1831.* By Vlad Georgescu. 1971.
2. *America, Italy and the Birth of Yugoslavia, 1917-1919.* By Dragan R. Zivojinovic. 1972.
3. *Jewish Nobles and Geniuses in Modern Hungary.* By William O. McCagg, Jr. 1972.
4. *Mixail Soloxov in Yugoslavia: Reception and Literary Impact.* By Robert F. Price. 1973.
5. *The Historical and National Thought of Nicolae Iorga.* By William O. Oldson. 1973.
6. *Guide to Polish Libraries and Archives.* By Richard C. Lewanski. 1974.
7. *Vienna Broadcasts to Slovakia, 1938-1939: A Case Study in Subversion.* By Henry Delfiner. 1974.
8. *The 1917 Revolution in Latvia.* By Andrew Ezergailis. 1974.
9. *The Ukraine in the United Nations Organization: A Study in Soviet Foreign Policy. 1944-1950.* By Konstantin Sawczuk. 1975.
10. *The Bosnian Church: A New Interpretation.* By John V. A. Fine, Jr., 1975.
11. *Intellectual and Social Developments in the Habsburg Empire from Maria Theresa to World War I.* Edited by Stanley B. Winters and Joseph Held. 1975.
12. *Ljudevit Gaj and the Illyrian Movement.* By Elinor Murray Despalatovic. 1975.
13. *Tolerance and Movements of Religious Dissent in Eastern Europe.* Edited by Bela K. Kiraly. 1975.
14. *The Parish Republic: Hlinka's Slovak People's Party, 1939-1945.* By Yeshayahu Jelinek. 1976.
15. *The Russian Annexation of Bessarabia, 1774-1828.* By George F. Jewsbury. 1976.
16. *Modern Hungarian Historiography.* By Steven Bela Vardy. 1976.
17. *Values and Community in Multi-National Yugoslavia.* By Gary K. Bertsch. 1976.
18. *The Greek Socialist Movement and the First World War: the Road to Unity.* By George B. Leon. 1976.
19. *The Radical Left in the Hungarian Revolution of 1848.* By Laszlo Deme. 1976.

20. *Hungary between Wilson and Lenin: The Hungarian Revolution of 1918–1919 and the Big Three.* By Peter Pastor. 1976.
21. *The Crises of France's East-Central European Diplomacy, 1933–1938.* By Anthony J. Komjathy. 1976.
22. *Polish Politics and National Reform, 1775–1788.* By Daniel Stone. 1976.
23. *The Habsburg Empire in World War I.* Robert A. Kann, Bela K. Kiraly, and Paula S. Fichtner, eds. 1977.
24. *The Slovenes and Yugoslavism, 1890–1914.* By Carole Rogel. 1977.
25. *German-Hungarian Relations and the Swabian Problem.* By Thomas Spira. 1977.
26. *The Metamorphosis of a Social Class in Hungary During the Reign of Young Franz Joseph.* By Peter I. Hidas. 1977.
27. *Tax Reform in Eighteenth Century Lombardy.* By Daniel M. Klang. 1977.
28. *Tradition versus Revolution: Russia and the Balkans in 1917.* By Robert H. Johnston. 1977.
29. *Winter into Spring: The Czechoslovak Press and the Reform Movement 1963–1968.* By Frank L. Kaplan. 1977.
30. *The Catholic Church and the Soviet Government, 1939–1949.* By Dennis J. Dunn. 1977.
31. *The Hungarian Labor Service System, 1939–1945.* By Randolph L. Braham. 1977.
32. *Consciousness and History: Nationalist Critics of Greek Society 1897–1914.* By Gerasimos Augustinos. 1977.
33. *Emigration in Polish Social and Political Thought, 1870–1914.* By Benjamin P. Murdzek. 1977.
34. *Serbian Poetry and Milutin Bojic.* By Mihailo Dordevic. 1977.
35. *The Baranya Dispute: Diplomacy in the Vortex of Ideologies, 1918–1921.* By Leslie C. Tihany. 1978.
36. *The United States in Prague, 1945–1948.* By Walter Ullmann. 1978.
37. *Rush to the Alps: The Evolution of Vacationing in Switzerland.* By Paul P. Bernard. 1978.
38. *Transportation in Eastern Europe: Empirical Findings.* By Bogdan Mieczkowski. 1978.
39. *The Polish Underground State: A Guide to the Underground, 1939–1945.* By Stefan Korbonski. 1978.
40. *The Hungarian Revolution of 1956 in Retrospect.* Edited by Bela K. Kiraly and Paul Jonas. 1978.
41. *Boleslaw Limanowski (1835–1935): A Study in Socialism and Nationalism.* By Kazimiera Janina Cottam. 1978.
42. *The Lingering Shadow of Nazism: The Austrian Independent Party Movement Since 1945.* By Max E. Riedlsperger. 1978.
43. *The Catholic Church, Dissent and Nationality in Soviet Lithuania.* By V. Stanley Vardys. 1978.